Christianity and revolutionary Europe, 1750–1830

Christianity and revolutionary Europe, 1750–1830 provides a comprehensive and accessible summary of the role of the Churches during this turbulent period in European history. How did the Churches survive the political and intellectual challenges posed by the French Revolution, despite institutional upheaval and the widespread questioning of dogma and tradition? Nigel Aston answers this question by drawing on three decades of research, and argues that pre-revolutionary Christianity had a vitality and resilience that should not be underestimated. Aston takes the story forward to 1830, dealing with both the immediate aftermath of the Revolution and its longer-term impact, and offering comprehensive guidance to the complicated strands of change and continuity. The text is supported by illuminating illustrations, and a glossary of unfamiliar terms gives further help to the student reader. It will be of key interest to all those following courses on religious history and the French Revolution.

NIGEL ASTON is a Lecturer in Early Modern History at the University of Leicester. His most recent book is *Religion and Revolution in France, 1780–1804* (2000).

NEW APPROACHES TO EUROPEAN HISTORY

Series editors
WILLIAM BEIK *Emory University*
T. C. W. BLANNING *Sidney Sussex College, Cambridge*

New Approaches to European History is an important textbook series, which provides concise but authoritative surveys of major themes and problems in European history since the Renaissance. Written at a level and length accessible to advanced school students and undergraduates, each book in the series addresses topics or themes that students of European history encounter daily: the series embraces both some of the more 'traditional' subjects of study, and those cultural and social issues to which increasing numbers of school and college courses are devoted. A particular effort is made to consider the wider international implications of the subject under scrutiny.

To aid the student reader, scholarly apparatus and annotation is light, but each work has full supplementary bibliographies and notes for further reading: where appropriate, chronologies, maps, diagrams and other illustrative material are also provided.

For a list of titles published in the series, please see end of book.

Christianity and revolutionary Europe, 1750–1830

Nigel Aston

University of Leicester

CAMBRIDGE
UNIVERSITY PRESS

PUBLISHED BY THE PRESS SYNDICATE OF THE UNIVERSITY OF CAMBRIDGE
The Pitt Building, Trumpington Street, Cambridge, United Kingdom

CAMBRIDGE UNIVERSITY PRESS
The Edinburgh Building, Cambridge, CB2 2RU, UK
40 West 20th Street, New York, NY 10011-4211, USA
477 Williamstown Road, Port Melbourne, VIC 3207, Australia
Ruiz de Alarcón 13, 28014 Madrid, Spain
Dock House, The Waterfront, Cape Town 8001, South Africa

http://www.cambridge.org

First published 2002

Printed in the United Kingdom at the University Press, Cambridge

Typeface Plantin 10/12 pt.   *System* LaTeX 2$_\varepsilon$ [TB]

A catalogue record for this book is available from the British Library

Library of Congress cataloguing in publication data

Aston, Nigel.
Christianity and revolutionary Europe, 1750–1830 / Nigel Aston.
    p.   cm. – (New approaches to European history; 25)
Includes bibliographical references and index.
ISBN 0 521 46027 1 – ISBN 0 521 46592 3 (pbk.)
1. Europe – Church history – 18th century.   2. Church
and state – History – 18th century.   3. Europe – Church history –
19th century.   4. Church and state – History – 19th century.
5. France – History – Revolution, 1789–1799 – Religious
aspects – Christianity.   I. Title.   II. Series.
BR735 .A77   2002   274′.07 – dc21   2002067618

ISBN 0 521 46027 1 hardback
ISBN 0 521 46592 3 paperback

For
Ian Beckett and Larry Butler:
resilient in adversity

Contents

List of illustrations

Preface

Writing this book has forced me to think out the convergences and cleavages of the religious world on either side of the French Revolution in a way which I might not otherwise have done. So I am very grateful to Professor Tim Blanning for giving me the opportunity to do so by asking me to contribute to this series and trust that he feels his confidence has not been misplaced. Without question, this final version of the text has benefited appreciably from his constructive comments on the chapters as they have been written. The co-founder of the *New Approaches to European History* series, Professor Bob Scribner, was also encouraging in the first stages of writing and read over the first chapter. His tragically early death prevented me, like other historians, from having the benefits of his insight thereafter. I also much indebted to Sheridan Gilley and John McManners, who have unflinchingly read over the entire text and made innumerable suggestions for improvement. I hope that they, too, consider that the final version indicates that I have been listening beneficially to their good counsel. Jeremy Black and Brendan Simms have also commented helpfully on several sections of the book, while, among historian friends, Matthew Cragoe and Peter Nockles have provided particular support as the enterprise has proceeded. Above all, I am grateful to the innumerable historians, living and dead, whose scholarship is the indispensable foundation of this book. If it succeeds in distilling the fruits of their labours to a wider audience then I shall count myself richly repaid.

At Cambridge University Press I am unreservedly obliged to Richard Fisher, Elizabeth Howard and Sophie Read. Their patience in waiting for the manuscript to reach the Edinburgh Building appeared to have no limits. The British Academy, the University of Luton and the Open University all made available financial assistance that offset research costs and other expenses involved in the writing and the completion of the book. Archivists and librarians, especially at the British Library and Bibliothèque Nationale de France, were unfailingly courteous. Katy Cooper was my alert and patient copy editor. My thanks to them, and to my wife, Caroline Aston, who, once again, tolerated the absence of the author with forbearance, good humour, advice and encouragement. The book was completed against a background of the impending closure of the History Department at Luton and the dispersal of a fine team of six colleagues. It is wholly appropriate that it should be dedicated to two of the most doughty of them.

Date list

1750	Upper Consistory established in Prussia
1753	Concordat signed between Spain and Benedict XIV
1753	Paris *parlement* issues a long remonstrance against clerical power in France
1755	Silence imposed by the Crown in dispute between the Gallican Church and the Paris *parlement*
	Lisbon earthquake
1761	Mary of the Immaculate Conception officially declared patronness of Spain
	Hontheim publishes *On the Condition of the Church and the Legitimate Power of the Roman Pontiff*
1768	Campomanes coauthored one of the great Spanish regalist tracts of the century, the *Juicio Imparcial*
1772	Feathers Tavern petition rejected in Parliament
1773	*Dominus ac redemptor* issued
1774	Quebec Act privileges Roman Catholicism in British Canada
1778	Catholic Relief Act passed for England
	Gottfried Lessing's writings censored in Brunswick
1780	Gordon Riots in London
1782	Catholics allowed right to worship in Ireland
1783	Joseph II reorganises diocesan boundaries in the Habsburg Empire
1784	Samuel Seabury consecrated as first Anglican bishop in the United States by (nonjuring) Scottish bishops
1786	'Mutinous' Riksdag in Sweden
	Cardinal Rohan disgraced in the Diamond Necklace affair
	Synod of Pistoia in Tuscany
	'Punctuation' of Ems
	Don gratuit increased in France
1787	First Anglican bishop for Canada (Nova Scotia) consecrated by Archbishop Moore of Canterbury
	Edict on non-Catholics passed in France

Archbishop Loménie de Brienne named principal minister
of France

Bishop Richard Woodward of Cloyne initiated a pamphlet
controversy over the security of the 'Protestant Ascendancy'
in Ireland

1788   Declaration of Potsdam published by Frederick William II
of Prussia

Revolt of the *curés* in France

1789   Estates-General and junction of the 3 Orders

Abolition of annates and suspension of the tithe in France

Sephardic Jews granted toleration by the National Assembly

1790   Failure of Dom Gerle's motion to have Catholicism declared
France's national religion

Civil Constitution of the Clergy passed

Regular clergy largely disbanded in France

Bagarre at Nîmes

1791   Oath imposed to the Civil Constitution of the Clergy

First bishops of the Constitutional Church consecrated

Civil Constitution of the Clergy condemned by Pius VI

Ashkenazim Jews granted toleration by the National
Assembly

Roman Catholic Relief Act passed in England

1792   Roman Catholic Relief Act passed in Ireland

Toleration for former nonjuring Scottish Episcopalians
sanctioned

September Massacres in France include scores of clergymen

1793   Second Roman Catholic Relief Act passed in Ireland

Outbreak of the Vendée

Dechristianisation begins in France

1794   Papal Bull *Auctorem fidei* condemns *Richerism*

Robespierre sponsors the cult of the Supreme Being

First meeting of Grégoire's 'United Bishops'

1795   Law of 3 *Ventôse* in France restores freedom of worship

Maynooth College opened in Ireland

1796   Kilhamite secession in English Methodism

Papal Brief *Pastoralis Sollicitudo*

1797   First national council of the Constitutional Church in France

1798   Irish Rebellion

Second 'Reign of Terror' in France

Proscription of the Belgian Catholic clergy after the failure of
the peasant uprising

French troops under Bertier occupy Rome – Pius VI exiled

1799	Death of Pius VI
	Sanfedisti led by Cardinal Ruffo in the kingdom of Naples
	Schleiermacher's lectures on religion (*Reden über die Religion*) were first published
1800	Election of Pius VII
1801	Act of Union unites Britain and Ireland and creates the United Churches of England and Ireland
	Concord between France and the Vatican
1802	Gallican Articles unilaterally imposed by First Consul Bonaparte on the Church
	Chateaubriand publishes the *Génie du Christianisme*
1803	Abolition of all the German ecclesiastical electorates
1804	Coronation of Napoleon in Notre-Dame Cathedral
	F. J. W. von Schelling publishes his *Philosophy and Religion*
1806	Dissolution of the Holy Roman Empire
	G. W. F. Hegel publishes *The Phenomenology of the Spirit*
1807	Occupation of the papal states by a French army
1808	Napoleon invades Spain
1809	Pius VII removed from Rome
1811	Formation of the Primitive Methodists
1812	Concordat 'of Fontainbleau'
1813	Unitarians given formal right to freedom of worship in England
1813–14	German 'War of Liberation'
1814	Pius VII released from imprisonment
	Jesuits were universally restored by the Bull *Sollicitudo omnium ecclesiarum*
1817	New Concordat in France
	Frederick William III creates a united Protestant state Church for Prussia
1821	Greek War of Independence begins
1825	Jubilee Year in Rome
1828	Test and Corporation Acts repealed in Britain
1829	Catholic emancipation finally conceded in Britain and Ireland
	Election of Pius VIII

Introduction

This book makes no apology for taking an unusual slant on its subject. Most historians, whatever their topic, either stop before the French Revolution, or make that major event their primary concern, or commence after it. Here the trajectory is quite different: this book's primary purpose is to see how much of Europe's religious culture was changed immediately before and during the period c.1790–1815 and what stayed the same. The high-quality scholarly work produced over the last thirty years on the different Churches of Europe makes a synthesis and an overview considerably overdue, especially one straddling both sides of the revolutionary 'divide'. By going forward to c.1830, I can deal more satisfactorily with the effects of the Revolution, both in the limited term and by noting the indicators for the long-term impact. What, apart from the name of Christian, linked the Churches and the churchgoers of 1750 with their great-grandchildren three generations on in 1830? This is the question at the heart of *Christianity and Revolutionary Europe*. The book's organisation reflects my Janus-faced approach to Christianity in a revolutionary era: surveying it before and after the deluge and trying to establish what survived of pre-1789 structures and practices – and what did not. The period c.1750–90 is not covered chronologically. Instead there are four chapters introducing the reader to the ordained ministry of the Churches and the structures within which they worked; the nature and variety of Christian beliefs and forms of worship; religion and the intellectual concerns of the Europe *des lumières*; and the perennially unpredictable relationship of Confessions to states and to each other.

The political and intellectual challenges to Christianity between 1750 and 1830 were as acute as any since its adoption as the principal religion of the Roman Empire in the fourth century, and yet the Churches were able to regroup and reclaim an organisational and credal strength that endured well into the twentieth century. At the heart of this book is an attempt to understand how this survival was achieved despite institutional upheaval and the widespread questioning of dogma and tradition. One of my central claims will be that eighteenth-century religion

1

generally had a vitality and a resilience which historians have underestimated; these qualities played a key role in enabling the Churches to withstand the often traumatic experience of revolution. It is time to insist on the underlying religiosity of eighteenth-century Europe, the deep roots of a culturally dominant Christianity that revolutionaries and republicans found impossibly hard to dislodge, and the unwillingness of the average man and woman across the continent to relinquish a belief system which conferred meaning on their lives in this world and conditionally assured them of a better one in the next. The inherent attractiveness of an active religious life was hard to deny. Catholicism had moved away from the high spiritual demands of the seventeenth century in favour of re-emphasising the simple evangelical message of the Gospels. Elites and masses welcomed the trend, and found much in it to sustain their different understanding of faith. Eighteenth-century Protestants, on the other hand, could take pride in the 'reasonableness' of their religion or, if that seemed spiritually insufficient as it did to many of them, find emotionally liberating the inward conversion that evangelists taught was essential to salvation.

At this distance in time there is no excuse for teleological distortions or the covert partisanship which has so often reduced the value of studies in the religious culture of the era. Scholars no longer have any uses for the extreme historiographical traditions that on one side emphasise a martyrology and a triumphant early-nineteenth-century religious renewal and, on the other, the irresistibility of a Paris-based secularising enlightenment. And, while it is generally admitted that state Churches were under pressure from within the establishment in the later eighteenth century – the limited toleration of minority communions, diminution of other privileges such as mortmain, reduced elite interest in a life of active piety – these gestures need to be seen as in some sense just the latest manifestation of incessant Church–state tensions over one-and-a-half millennia and set against the corresponding strengths of the major confessions: a restraining moral influence on their flocks, the primary uses of the parish as an organisational unit in Europe, and the unique legitimacy Christian sanction conferred on government. As recent studies by Adrian Hastings and others have pointed out, the Churches and their followers helped form national identities and provided structures wherein they could be articulated to a degree that historians of nationhood have been slow to admit.

The high point of orthodoxy came late in the western Churches, approximately 1720–50, immediately before this book commences, so if, as is often alleged, it was harder for the Churches to make headway after the Seven Years' War, that should hardly be surprising. The work of the Churches had become less to extend the faith than to confirm it, and there could only be a falling away from the heights of good Christian practice and grasp of the faith that had been reached by 1750. Away from the Ottoman enclaves in the east, Europe contained a thoroughly Christianised people, and that remained fairly much the case in 1830 as it had been eighty years earlier. The eighteenth century was the great age of missions into rural Europe, and the missioners – whether Jesuits or Passionists, Methodists or Pietists – did their work well. They set out to win the attention of entire populations and all age groups and they largely achieved their objectives. In as much as it can be gauged, public opinion was broadly, though not uncritically, content with the work of the clergy (at least the *lower* clergy) on the eve of the French Revolution and was far from losing faith with them. Certainly, when the Revolution came to the countryside in the 1790s neither its propagandists nor its armed agents could readily persuade or intimidate villagers into abandoning either churchgoing or loyalty to their priests and ministers. After 1792–3 any hope that Christianity could be the ally or the midwife of the Revolution became implausible, but in turning the majority of practising Christians into the opponents of Revolution, the Jacobins turned Christianity into the motor of the counter-revolution, for the most part stronger and more popular than Revolution. Even Napoleon saw the sense of coming to terms with an international organisation that could reinforce rather than undermine French hegemony on the continent. Despite the range of alternatives on offer, Christianity displayed a remarkable capacity for survival in the half century from 1780 to 1830: the religious life may have been less unanimously followed in 1830 compared with 1789, but it was more authentic and profound.

The Christianity on offer in the later eighteenth century was projected towards men as much as women. If that appeal was gradually diminishing over time, one must be cautious about talking in terms of the feminisation of any confession at any point in the span covered by this volume. The principal vehicle of dechristianisation for the average French male was the army; yet elsewhere the armies of the militarised Europe of 1792–1815 were well stocked with chaplains as a deliberate counterpoint to the French example of faithlessness. In sum, the relationship between militarisation and dechristianisation is a complex one that has yet to be convincingly unravelled, and the presumption that large-scale enlistment in the armed forces unstitched allegiance to the Churches after 1815 remains doubtful. Much the same may be said of the Enlightenment. What might be called the Gay/Aries/Vovelle model of enlightenment predicated on overt hostility to institutional Christianity has fallen out of favour as historians of Britain, France, Italy and Poland have come across many examples of Churches and congregations endorsing or facilitating 'enlightenment' aims of educating, eradicating superstition and increasing toleration.

Away from France, the Churches and the clergy could be called broadly progressive forces. Protestant clergy and laity were happy to fit into that bracket. An earlier book in this series by Professor W. R. Ward insisted that Protestants remained alert to the possibility that Catholicism was still bent on extirpating the Reformation communions and that there was some basis for these apprehensions well into the eighteenth century. But one of the emphases of this volume is on the marked growth and recovery of Protestantism between 1760 and 1830 aided by the weakening of its historic enemies: the papacy and the Jesuits. The Jansenist reformist impulse – which ruined the Jesuits – was at the heart of the Catholic contribution to the Enlightenment, but was also deeply divisive within Catholicism and prevented the Church from concentrating its energies on irreligious enemies outside its gates.

One sees a remarkable continuity of Jansenist impulses in a variety of forms throughout this period, persistently attractive to regimes through to Napoleon's. Why did they matter to officials? Why to so many educated clergy? The book tries to answer both questions, and in doing so queries the extent to which one should see the period of 1773 to 1791 between the abolition of the Jesuits as an order and the Civil Constitution of the Clergy as two precarious decades. If Catholicism was reverting to a conciliar or monarchical model, that was as likely to produce consolidation rather than disintegration. Emollient, undogmatic Protestants such as the United Irishmen leader, Wolfe Tone, spread the word that Catholicism had been 'depapalised', but the extent to which the experience of Catholicism in countries such as Gallican France had ever been 'papalist' made his glad tidings something of a half-truth. For papal power nowhere in Catholic Europe rode roughshod over monarchical wishes either before 1789 or after 1815, which is why both Pius VII and the restored monarchies of post-Napoleonic Europe were so anxious to clarify their mutual rights in the form of negotiated concordats.

One last warning and serious caveat. The religious geography of most countries varied appreciably in a manner which any general survey can only inadequately register, for instance the tremendous devotion of northern Spain and northern Italy which persisted into the modern era compared with the much less-practising southern parts of those countries. This book, trying to draw attention to general trends, is embarrassingly aware of the exceptions to them. Attempts to shoehorn materials into convenient moulds have been resisted: the reader will gauge how successfully.

Part 1

Later eighteenth-century religion

1 Church structures and ministry

The Christian culture of Europe

From Ireland to Russia and from Sweden to Sicily, the peoples and states of Europe in the mid-eighteenth century predominantly professed Christianity. Even Europeans living within the Ottoman Turkish Empire – in the Balkans, Greece and the eastern Mediterranean littoral – had largely held on to the faith and not adopted the rival Islamic monotheism of their overlords. Its roots went deep. Since the Arab conquests in the Middle East and North Africa, Europe had been confirmed as the heartland of Christianity, with its main spiritual leaders in 1750 resident in Rome, Constantinople, Moscow, Canterbury and Geneva. For most men and women Christianity was not one option among competing alternatives; it was part of one's inheritance. To be born a Frenchman or a Dane, a Scot or a Hungarian, or into any other European nation or empire, was by definition to be born a Christian unless one belonged to one of the numerically insignificant minority religions, principally Judaism. Christianity had to be actually disclaimed; otherwise the assumption was universally made that, to whatever extent, the individual subscribed to the Christian view of the world and the scheme of salvation it offered to man.

Even the deists respected the figure of Jesus Christ while rejecting his claims to divinity. They tended to present him as someone who, like themselves, had been misrepresented by the authorities of the day as a threat to their power. Unbelievers had to be exceptionally courageous to avow their infidelity. Deists and Christians alike saw the profession of atheism as a threat to social cohesion. Voltaire, the most famous *philosophe* of them all, was apprehensive that moral anarchy would inevitably follow on from a denial of God: it was not until the 1760s that he felt safe to publish extracts from the so-called *Testament* of the French country priest Jean Meslier (d. 1729), by which date some Parisian salons, notably the Baron d'Holbach's, had flung aside concealment and were openly fostering atheist publications and values. D'Holbach had few imitators. Irreligious sentiments articulated with conviction remained a rarity, largely confined to the upper reaches of society and seldom heard in public utterance. They belonged to a well-established libertine tradition. Clerical concern that these views were on the increase and spreading among the population at large could not just be dismissed as alarmist by the later eighteenth century when public, written challenges to the faith were appearing, especially in the western European states, designed for a wide readership and combining the old slogans against 'priestcraft' with the latest enlightenment materialism. There is a limited sense in which such writings were sapping the prevailing Christian culture, but equally the influence of these 'Men of Letters' (except for the greatest among them, like Voltaire) was minimal in comparison with the omnipresence of the Church on the ground through its ministry to the mass of people.

That ministry, in all its diversity, gave some lingering credibility to the notion of Christendom as commensurate with the frontiers of Europe, although not in the shape of a seamless medieval web (in as much as there had ever been one), for the Reformation had led to the 'confessionalisation' of a unitary Christendom, fragmented into at least three main confessional Churches. With the last public reference to Christendom in the Treaty of Utrecht 1713, it 'slowly entered the limbo of archaic words'.[1] Nevertheless, there survived a general Christian polity characterised by denominational tensions among Catholic, Protestant and Orthodox believers coexisting with an underlying commitment to the same historic faith differently perceived; the litany used in the Church of England still included prayers for Catholic Christians threatened by the Turks. Religion was formative in the maturing of national identities: Gallican Catholicism took pride in having a longer pedigree than the French monarchy and members of the Church of England were taught to look on its providential survival as a sign of God's favour towards the nation. These were relatively settled states where national identity was not much contested. Other ethnic communities struggled to secure recognition. In the Ottoman Empire the Greeks made the most of the Hellenisation policy favoured by the Porte, regardless of its effects on other Christian national groups trying to survive in a multinational and multiconfessional polity. More and more national Churches were allotted to the oversight of the (Greek) patriarch in the Ottoman capital, Constantinople. In 1766 the Serbian patriarchate of Péc was suppressed, and the following year the Bulgarian Church came under the aegis of the patriarch with the forced retirement of Arsennis, archbishop of Ochrid. Catholics in

---

[1] Denys Hay, *Europe: The Emergence of an Idea* (rev. edn, Edinburgh, 1968), 116.

Ireland and Poland found external influences in the shape of Britain and Russia hard to contain. Polish Catholics were increasingly coming under Prussian, Russian and Austrian control after the Partitions of 1772, 1793 and 1795. By and large, toleration was extended to Polish Catholics by their new Russian overlord. Indeed in 1798, the very year that French troops occupied Rome, Paul I created six new sees for Roman Catholics and twelve for Uniates, an orthodox tsar as protector of the papacy.

The Czech educational pioneer, Jan Amos Comenius, had hoped in the late seventeenth century that European unity could be founded on religious federation and toleration. It was visionary but impractical. Religious schism had given Christians an overriding loyalty to their own preferred allegiance, but there were always a few, such as Archbishop William Wake of Canterbury early in the century, who had a wider vision of what united the Churches. He had entered into conversations with several French churchmen after the contentious passing of the Bull *Unigenitus* directed at Jansenists in 1713 to see if a basis could be found for a working union of the Anglican and Gallican communions. Though the scheme had lapsed by the late 1720s, it played its part in diminishing tensions between the two Churches down to the French Revolution and beyond. Within a British context, well-connected Irish Catholics in the 1780s with the Franciscan friar Fr Arthur O'Leary as their spokesman urged Anglicans to look favourably on the Irish version of 'Gallicanism' – shorn of Jacobitism and papalism – as a far more suitable ally than Protestant sects of dubious credal orthodoxy. Other Anglicans reactivated the links between the Church of England and Orthodoxy dating from Archbishop Laud's primacy in the 1630s. Charles Daubeny (1745–1827), later archdeacon of Salisbury, was in Russia between 1771 and 1772 and made a study of Orthodox theology and ecclesiology, which was of importance in the formation of his own influential brand of high churchmanship.

In Germany, there was a more generous attitude to inter-confessional relations evident at elite level towards the end of the century. More than one scheme for Church reunion was mooted, that winning support at the Congress of Ems in 1786 attracting most notice, though less than it deserved, overlaid as it was by the Congress' extreme anti-papalism. In Hungary, the distance between the Catholics and the Calvinists was narrowing even in Maria Theresa's reign (1740–80). The abilities of József Batthyány, primate of Hungary at Joseph II's accession, could not be denied by Protestants. Their spokesmen could find little worse to say about him than that he was inordinately fond of his skills as a chess player. When famine broke out he provided for his Calvinist serfs just as for the others.

Between 1750 and 1790 the Protestant sense of solidarity gradually diluted as Catholicism became less of a threat. When one of Archbishop Herring's clients, Ferdinando Warner, spoke in 1752 of 'those amiable qualities in your grace [which] are acknowledged by protestants of all denominations, not only in our three kingdoms, but in the most distant countries'.[2] Anglican interest in their co-religionists beyond the British Isles had already passed its peak. In the Seven Years' War (1756–63), another archbishop of Canterbury, Thomas Secker, tried to foster links between the Church of England and continental congregations looking to Britain's ally, Frederick II of Prussia, for protection, but the return of peace in 1763 made the increasing number of non-latitudinarian Anglicans less inclined to speak sympathetically of non-Episcopalian Churches where heterodoxy appeared to flourish. Ministers still made gestures of solidarity. Henry Seymour Conway, when British secretary of state for the Northern Department between 1765 and 1768, urged British diplomats to agitate for full civil liberties for Protestants in Poland and to co-ordinate their efforts with those of the Russians. But this was one of the last such requests.

Attitudes to other faiths

The vast majority of Christians were suspicious, sometimes overtly hostile to other faiths. Anti-Semitism was rife at every level of eighteenth-century society, with Ashkenazim stereotypes impossible to displace from both the popular and elite consciousness. These images were decisive in the public agitation in England surrounding the Jew Bill of 1753 and pushed the Pelham administration into repeal and an embarrassing volte-face; in France, some limited concessions were offered to the monied Sephardim traders of the Bordelais in return for additional tax burdens, while their Ashkenazim cousins in Alsace and Lorraine were left to pay the poll tax and suffer other social indignities, perhaps because of their usefulness as money-lenders to the gentiles. Enlightenment thinkers did little to dilute popular resentments, seeing Hebraism as a conservative, marginal and backward-looking culture which resisted integration, and progressive politicians fought shy of alleviating the Jews' uncertain legal status precisely because nothing raised the temperature in eighteenth-century public culture more than changes to the religious status quo. Muslims were, if anything, less indulged and their faith was presented in every sort of Christian apologetic as a sham, a travesty and

---

[2] Ferdinando Warner, *A Rational Defence of the English Reformation and Protestant Religion* (London, 1752), v–vi.

a blasphemy with Muhammad traditionally condemned as an imposter. Positive acknowledgement of his extraordinary qualities as a leader and law giver were only gradually given in the late Enlightenment.

The infidel and the exotic enticed as well as repelled the European gaze. This slant is well seen in a stock character like Osmin, overseer of Pasha Selim's harem in Mozart's *Seraglio*, who combined a hatred of Christianity and a cruel nature with the repression of women. This venomous perspective partly reflected the fact that Islam had been pushed to the margins of Europe only within living memory and its containment could not be assumed. The Barbary corsairs, pirates from North African states dependent on Ottoman Turkey, still preyed on western trade and rumours regularly circulated in the Mediterranean ports of forced conversions. In the east, the Austrian Empire had been steadily extended at Ottoman expense after the successful campaigns of the 1690s and 1716–18, but there was no room for complacency. The Ottoman Turks revealed their military resilience in the war of 1737–9 when they recaptured Belgrade from the Habsburgs, and down to the mid-century there was no shortage of interest in proposing (on paper at least) joint offensives of the European states against the infidel. The Order of Malta, a Catholic crusading Order that ruled Malta, had branches throughout Europe, especially in France, and still took its historic role seriously. Increased commercial contact and a growing number of western travellers in Islamic areas of Europe only slowly altered perceptions of the Turks and their holy book. The stereotype might equate Turkish rule with tyranny, but on the other hand, Orthodox Christians living in Ottoman territories often found the sultan's yoke remarkably light, and the patriarch of Jerusalem can be found in 1798 warning his flock off liberty, that foreign invention, to render tribute to Caesar (in this case the sultan) and be glad 'that this our Orthodox faith flourishes in this powerful empire'.[3] Challenged on the fringes of Europe by Islam, the Christian reaction to the discovery of the New World had been to win it over to Christ, backed by the support of sponsoring states. By the mid-eighteenth century, the Roman Catholic Church had a massive institutional presence in Spanish South and Central America, the Philippines and French Canada; in the British thirteen colonies of North America, a variety of Protestant faiths jostled for supremacy, fearful of the popish threat until that was neutralised by British success in the Seven Years' War. By that date, Christianity was as much part of the dominant American culture as it was of the European.

---

[3] Quoted in Richard Clogg (ed.), *The Movement for Greek Independence 1770–1821* (Basingstoke, 1976), 56–62, at 59.

Roman Catholicism

While religious allegiances could assist in the construction of national identity, the varieties of confessional Christianity in the eighteenth century were rarely coterminous with state boundaries. That was especially true of the Roman Catholic Church, with its own independent head in Rome directly descended, as it was claimed, from St Peter. The Catholic Church, as its apologists were not slow to point out, was an institution which predated every contemporary European state, whose hierarchy existed alongside the secular bureaucracies of nation states, and declared itself uniquely to possess the hallmarks of divine inauguration. In numerical terms alone, Roman Catholicism was the dominant Christian communion as much in the 1750s as it had been a century previously, instructing men and women in their sacramental and social duties in this world and preparing them for eternity in the next. It was a Church that had already displayed its capacity for adaptation and survival when confronted with the Protestant challenge of the Reformation, and the steady implementation of Tridentine initiatives first formulated in the mid-sixteenth century was reaching a successful conclusion in the mid-eighteenth. Ireland was the most recent region to display what has been called a 'Tridentine surge' and, though dated as late as the 1770s, bore fruit in the form of tighter clerical organisation, regular episcopal visitations, more diocesan conferences and the moral improvement of the laity. At the other end of Europe, the Church had since 1699 benefited numerically from the advances made into former Ottoman lands and the active patronage of the empress Maria Theresa. Islamic expansionism had been checked and so, it seemed, had Protestantism, which had made no significant European conquests since about 1600, though the problem of clandestine Protestantism (*Geheimprotestantismus*) among minorities caused much restlessness to over-anxious officials in the Habsburg monarchy. Despite the reconquest of Hungary, the majority of its nobility remained stubbornly attached to their Calvinist faith as a means of safeguarding their legal freedoms from imperial encroachment. Meanwhile, beyond Europe, missionaries of the different denominations looked to win new followers from among indigenous peoples and swell their ranks that way.

Even where governments were hostile to Roman Catholicism and its representatives (and thus had no envoy resident at the Vatican), there was frequently a Catholic minority in a state's population – as in Prussia or Britain – that was increasingly left unmolested whatever the strict letter of the law. Elsewhere, in the majority of European states – Ireland, France, the kingdoms of Spain, Portugal, the Italian principalities, about

one-third of the Holy Roman Empire, most of the Habsburg hereditary lands, Bavaria, Poland – Catholics composed the vast bulk of the
Christian population. In Germany there were even several ecclesiastical
states (there were thirty-seven voting members of the spiritual bench of
the *Reichsfüstenrat* in 1792) where one ruler combined the role of prince
and prelate, notably the three electoral Rhineland states of Cologne,
Mainz and Trier, whose possession had until recently been a subject
of intense diplomatic competition. Whatever the local usages in worship and observances (and they were not inconsiderable), people of all
backgrounds heard the offices in the same Latin tongue, and respected
the ecclesiastical hierarchy at the same time as they grumbled about it.
Church membership and responsibility as citizens and subjects were still
inextricably linked.

Protestant denominations

The pretensions to universalism implicit in the word Catholic remained
despite the reality of religious division on the continent. Certainly, Protestantism continued to see the Roman communion as much intent on its
destruction as it had been at the height of the Counter-Reformation
in the previous century, never mind the legal provisions upholding
the confessional status quo for Germany contained in the Treaty of
Westphalia (1648). These apprehensions reflected the inherent vulnerability of Protestantism on account of its own divisions and a gradual
diminution of vitality within most denominations since the later years
of the Reformation. But, as will be discussed later, renewal was already
under way in Britain and Germany by the 1750s and the Protestant denominations would slowly recapture their sense of initiative, fuelled by
an enlightenment perception that Protestantism was, uniquely among the
Churches, on the side of moral and cultural progress. Such confidence
was apparent in the influential writing of Friedrich Karl von Moser,
a Pietist and hater of princely absolutism. His pamphleteering in the
Osnabrück succession crisis – especially *Concerning the Government of the
Ecclesiastical States in Germany* (1787) – classically linked Protestant pride
in its reasonable faith with progressivist hopes. By contrast, in the words
of one Scottish critic of 1781, the Roman Catholic faith 'hath ever evinced
itself to be most inimical to the Civil and Religious rights of mankind'.[4]

The various Protestant Churches had one key advantage over their Catholic counterparts: they were used to working with secular governments

---

[4] Joseph Callender to Lord Hailes, 2 January 1781, National Library of Scotland, New
Hailes MS. 25303, f. 106.

(indeed their legal subordination to state power went back to the Reformation) and were mostly adaptable enough not to be constrained thereby. The times of defensiveness and sometimes persecution were almost over, and the years between 1750 and 1790 brought recovery as well as theological liberalism on one hand and evangelism on the other, as some Protestants opted to dilute orthodoxy just when their brothers and sisters were taking a stand on it. The mainstream Reformed Churches still belonged either to the Lutheran or Calvinist traditions, although the dividing line between them became increasingly blurred. Lutheranism's principal bastions remained centred on a Baltic zone: Sweden, Denmark and Prussia with the majority of other German states. Calvinists looked, as they had always done, to Geneva as their mother Church, but outside Switzerland had substantial numbers in eastern Europe (Poland and Transylvania), as well as Scotland, the United Provinces and a minority of German states.

In the course of the eighteenth century both Lutheran and Calvinist Churches became characterised by a formalism (especially visible in forms of worship) that bore witness to a blunted evangelical impulse. That was left more and more to minority Protestant groups such as the Baptists, whose numbers rose steadily. For many Protestants the message of Christian salvation, while still at the heart of their faith, had became somehow less urgent, not least since the legacy of the Thirty Years' War had been to make men doubt the value of conversion at any price, including the life of anyone unresponsive. Those, as in Germany, who rejected arid theological disputation in favour of Pietism, with its fostering of practicality and benevolence, downgraded interest in the niceties of doctrine concerning Christ's redemptive work; but Pietism had a deeply spiritual dimension as well, which satisfied the inner aspirations of thousands of Germans and helped to turn it into such a formidable presence within contemporary Protestantism. Initially distrusted by the Lutheran hierarchy, from the mid-century Pietism became the new German Protestant orthodoxy in Prussia thanks to powerful support from the Hohenzollern monarchy, and it made significant inroads in Holland, Scandinavia and Switzerland.

Its spiritual emphases much influenced John Wesley, co-founder with his brother, Charles, of the Methodist revival within the Church of England. Like the vast majority of eighteenth-century Anglicans, the Wesleys saw their Church as unflinchingly Protestant despite pre-Reformation survivals such as the division of the ministry into bishops, priests and deacons, and an influential strand of teaching on the Eucharist which went well beyond the merely commemorative. Anglicans were to be found wherever English was spoken, and in some parts of the

British kingdoms where it was not: despite establishment, Anglicanism was slowly giving ground to dissent in Wales, it was professed by no more than 20 per cent of the population in Ireland, and it was technically illegal in Scotland from 1689 to 1792 unless clergy and their congregations renounced Jacobitism to take advantage of the 1712 Act of Toleration. Membership of the Church of England functioned as a token of good citizenship and this contributed to its distinctive mid-century stress on benevolism rather than personal piety. Nevertheless, from the 1750s, the growth of Methodism and the high church revival between them rekindled an interest in the Church's spiritual heritage hitherto submerged: Wesley's insistence that every penitent sinner had access to Christ's saving grace recalled the Arminian theology of 1630s Laudianism and was just one aspect of the Caroline inheritance of the Church of England and its apologists – Henry Hammond, Jeremy Taylor and Peter Heylyn – which young Oxford-educated clerics such as George Berkeley, Samuel Glasse, George Horne and William Jones found an inspiration in their own ministry.

The Orthodox Churches and the Uniates

The Orthodox Church in Russia was, like the Church of England, seen as the appropriate focus of allegiance in the tsar's domains for all his loyal subjects, and attempts at non-Orthodox proselytisation had been prohibited in 1702 and 1735. Yet alone of the principal European denominations, the Russian Orthodox Church was afflicted by schism. Perhaps one-fifth of the population was made up of the so-called Old Believers. This minority (themselves divided into sub-sects) had broken away in the late seventeenth century primarily on theological grounds from the main body of the Church protected by the tsars, and their existence was tolerated after the accession of Peter III in 1762. But Orthodoxy flourished beyond the Russian frontiers. Historically, its centre was not Moscow but Constantinople, the New Rome and the old capital of Byzantium, and its head – taking precedence over the patriarch of Moscow – was the ecumenical patriarch, resident in a city that had been controlled by the Ottoman Turks since 1453. In practice, the ecumenical patriarchate was controlled by the prosperous and influential Greek families of Constantinople, the Phanariots, and they made narrowly Greek concerns uppermost in Orthodox politics across the Balkan region. In Serbia and Bulgaria, birth into a Slavic culture brought with it membership of the Orthodox Church, and a sense of being on the front line against Islam. Its Slavic character, distinctive rituals and rejection of the universal claims of Rome had largely isolated it from the post-Reformation conflicts of the western Churches, and this left it less exposed to enlightenment challenges. Meanwhile, the historic schism with the western Church was reignited in 1755 when, for the first time, doubt was cast upon the validity of baptism administered by Latin Catholics in the patriarchal decree, the *Oros* of that year, issued by Kyrillos V.

With confessional divisions exacerbated, Orthodoxy felt particularly exposed to Catholic intimidation on its western frontier, despite Benedict XIV's sensitive letter *Allatae sunt* of 1755, issued to Latin missionaries and advising them against unseemly zeal in trying to make proselytes among eastern Christians. Rome's main ally in these parts was the Uniate (or Greek Catholic) Church, whose rivalry with Orthdoxy went back centuries. The Uniates recognised papal supremacy; the Orthodox, of course, did not. In line with the respective imperial interests, the two emp-resses adopted predictably contrasting policies. Maria Theresa always tried hard to guarantee Uniate independence, whereas Catherine saw it as a threat to Romanov sovereignty, and she readily approved an intensi-fication of the Orthodox Church's longstanding proselytising of Uniates. In 1773, the very year the Russian empress proclaimed religious liberty, forcible conversion to Orthodoxy began in the former Polish provinces of Volhynia and Podolia. With Cossacks billeted on villagers, resistance brought torture or death. Many 'conversions' were merely nominal and by Catherine's death in 1796 at least one-fifth of Uniate populations re-mained true to their ancestral faith and were accorded a limited degree of respite and recognition by her son and successor, Paul I (1796–1801). Orthodoxy received fewer favours from the Russian crown in Poland. The single Orthodox prelate, the bishop of Mohilow, was forced to look for protection from the Protestant nobility in the face of a Catholic confes-sional predominance. After the first partition, Catherine in 1773 created a Latin see at Moghilev in White Russia and attached all Catholics to it as a means of both extending her control and winning over Polish Catholics to their new ruler.

The growth of toleration

No single theme united eighteenth-century critics of the European reli-gious heritage more than the deprecation of intolerance. Partly as a result of pressure from such gifted spokesmen for this cause as John Locke and Pierre Bayle in the early Enlightenment (1680–1720), governments pres-surised the leading denominations to move towards abandoning the active persecution of religious dissidents. The trend has a massive significance. Since the Reformation it had been a commonplace of statecraft that a plu-rality of faiths resulted in political instability, and the underlying principle of the Treaty of Augsburg (1555) – 'cuius regio, eius religio' – had recognised as much. Religious toleration was for weak states; strong ones, like Louis XIV's France as recently as 1685, threw out their minorities. Yet even those countries that had not participated in the Thirty Years' War could see that the Treaty of Westphalia, with its guarantees for the established position of Calvinism, Lutheranism and Catholicism in particular territories in the empire, pointed to the bankruptcy of any policy aimed at compulsorily imposing religious uniformity. This was a commitment to toleration in a highly legalistic format via religious checks and balances in the constitution of the German *Reich*. These ensured that the Catholic majorities in the *Reichstag* were not converted into a voting bloc which could always have the whip hand over the Protestant deputies making up the Corpus Evangelicorum in the Council of Princes (*Fürstenrat*) and the Council of Cities (*Städterat*). It also justified many hardheaded local arrangements. At Frankfurt-am-Main, the main city church belonged to the Catholics but, with Lutheranism as the dominant confession locally, Catholic clergy were forbidden from holding public processions. In some towns iron gates and partitions in church marked out the space to which each was entitled.

Individual princes might convert from one faith to another; the post-1648 Church order in Germany stood unchanged. It was, in any case, rare for confessional allegiances to take primacy over state ones, as the alliance of Catholic spiritual princes and Protestant territorial states in the *Fürstenbund* of 1785 suggested in the face of Joseph's aggressive imperial policies. Neither side lightly contemplated giving up the benefits of Westphalia, though it could not constrain the Habsburgs in Maria Theresa's time from trying to impose Catholicism on Protestant communities in eastern Europe (converts were lured by government 'pensions'), or provoking a rising in 1760 among Orthodox Transylvanians who had no wish to be forced into the Uniate Church. Still more notoriously, a Church-dominated statelet, Salzburg, under its archbishop, Firmian, expelled 18,000 Protestants in 1731–2. Such a use of coercive power was unusual by that date. Churchmen might still talk in the early eighteenth century of 'religion' in the sense of the one *true* religion, but they were also facing up to the fact that neither Protestantism nor popery were broken forces, and that some sort of contingent recognition of the cultural persistence of the other was unavoidable. Religious tensions slowly decreased as it became apparent that no great power alliance was interested in trying to extirpate a particular confession. Even so, ordinary subjects still tended, however misguidedly, to see wars as confessional conflicts casting Frederick II of Prussia as a (very unlikely) Protestant champion, for the Seven Years' War looked like a confessional conflict due to the Diplomatic Revolution of 1756 which had aligned the Habsburg and Bourbon dynasties.

It was the sheer persistence of religious minorities that defied assimilation that made toleration (however partial and restricted) a *de facto* reality quite as much as the outraged writings of the *philosophes*. The rights of Catholics in the United Provinces were deliberately limited but that did nothing to reduce their numbers, relying as they did on the long-established tradition of tolerance in the Dutch Netherlands. Elsewhere, such civilised restraint could still not be relied on, and religious homogeneity remained the norm outside Britain, France (a Huguenot presence made a nonsense of the legal pretence that they had lapsed in 1685, and Lutherans in Alsace had legal guarantees) and Prussia where the head of state was Calvinist (since 1613), the majority of his subjects were Lutheran and where there was a strong Catholic minority in Silesia, annexed to Prussia by Frederick II in 1740. Otherwise, in Catholic Iberia and Italy, Protestant Scandinavia, Orthodox central Russia, and the Holy Roman Empire (mainly solidly Catholic or Protestant principalities), uniformity persisted.

But while religious identities could act as a means of group definition they could equally provoke a sense of insecurity among those on the outside. Whatever the development of tolerance within elites, crowds were ready to use religion as a banner around which to focus discontent against minorities, especially during war or an economic downturn, as in Scotland against Catholics in 1778–9, and rational dissenters in Birmingham during the Priestley Riots of 1791. In France, the Seven Years' War rekindled the last campaigns against the Huguenots, popularly perceived as likely British allies in the event of an invasion. Even before war erupted in 1756 there were signs of persecution: at Toulon in 1754 Grand Tourists Henry Lyte and Lord Brudenell saw nine Calvinists brought in from Nîmes to be confined to the galleys for having assembled contrary to law.[5] There as elsewhere, toleration was a precarious growth until very late in the century. Religious leaders only reluctantly conceded a place to opponents in their scheme of things, and in rural parishes the discountenancing of other faiths remained in the last quarter of the century a far stronger emotion than toleration.

The ordained ministry of the Churches

At least most men and women had the proximity to a clergyman that made sacerdotal influence a possibility in forming their reaction to other

---

[5] Henry Lyte to Lord Dartmouth, 9 December 1754, *HMC, 20th Report (1887), MSS of the Earl of Dartmouth*, 331.

denominations and faiths. A sense of the black-coated presence was a background feature to most people's daily lives and underlined the continuing high ratio of clergy to laymen. Only in Catholic France was there anything approaching a 'general crisis of vocations' in the second half of the eighteenth century, and that varied considerably between dioceses. Otherwise, judged by the number of priests and ministers, the eighteenth-century Churches were in a fairly healthy state. Up to 2 per cent of the population of the states of continental Europe described themselves as clerics. Indeed, in the Iberian peninsula there was a surplus of priests (a total of about 170,000, nearly one-third more than in France) for the available benefices. Protestant ministers were generally fewer in number: about 14,000 in Lutheran Sweden, and approximately the same number in England. Among Catholic clergy, the vast majority of priests headed for the parishes rather than the religious houses. Spain was an exception. By 1768, 15,639 parish priests were confronted by 55,453 regulars in Spain, and friars frequently assisted the curate even in places where the number of parishes was adequate. Only in Poland and the Franciscan Order in Spain and Portugal were there exceptions to the international trend of declining numbers entering the religious Orders. Indeed, soon after her accession to the Portuguese throne in 1777, the pious Maria I forbade the institution of new Orders by royal decree. Between 1768 and 1782 in Milan the 5,609 individuals registered in 290 monasteries had been reduced to less than 4,000 in 141 establishments. By contrast, female vocations held up fairly well, if only because the cloister remained the standard alternative to marriage or a lonely spinsterhood, especially for women from better-off families.

The social background of the ordained ministry varied, with younger sons of the nobility dominating the upper reaches of the hierarchy in most states; these formed part of wider patronage networks where kinship and familiarity with court life were crucial to promotion. Lesser nobles predominated among the Spanish and Portuguese bishops, as well as the states of Naples, Venice and Piedmont. The French episcopate in 1789 came to number just two commoners; in the German Empire the imperial knights dominated bishoprics and canonries, and held the Electorates of Mainz and Trier; in Cologne the archbishop had to be at least an imperial count (the Wittelsbach family dominated the see for much of the century). Every Rhineland cathedral chapter and most collegiate foundations had stringent genealogical tests to exclude even nobles with an inadequate number of quarterings or the wrong kind of nobility. In Hungary the leading aristocratic families shared out the archbishoprics among themselves and so formed an exclusive clerical club. Italy went against this trend, with only about 30 per cent of dioceses in the possession of noblemen, though the number of Venetian patricians entering the Church doubled between 1620 and 1760.

Upper-class bishops were by no means inadequate to their task, with colourful as well as able personalities among them: Talleyrand (bishop of Autun from 1788) was a gifted agent-general for the French Church (1780–5), Loménie de Brienne, archbishop of Toulouse, the archetypal *prélat administrateur*, and Frederick Hervey, earl-bishop of Derry (Church of Ireland), a pioneer of harmonious Anglican–Catholic relations. But scholarly or administrative gifts, though prized, were unlikely in themselves to ensure the highest Church offices, with important exceptions, such as Hontheim (a.k.a. Febronius) who rose to be suffragan bishop of Trier, and others in Spain and England. There, prelates such as Joseph Butler, Thomas Herring and Thomas Secker came from humble backgrounds but were as able as any in Europe. Another exception were the imperial monasteries where many of the abbots were also commoners. In Russia an episcopal elite of another sort was emerging, originating increasingly from talented members of the clerical estate or the aristocracy for whom a career in the impoverished monasteries was not enticing.

Few bishops served as parish priests, and the chances of the latter gaining promotion to a mitre were comparably remote. Thus Emmanuel Joseph Sieyes, author of the most influential pamphlet of 1789, *Qu'est-ce que le Tiers etat?*, was advanced to membership of the cathedral chapter at Chartres and became secretary to the bishop but advanced no further. Most beneficed Catholic clergy in the eighteenth century were educated men from lower-middle-class backgrounds, with friends and family living close by, enjoying a high enough standard of living (particularly where they had tithing rights) to employ servants. They had little contact with their diocesan head except during visitations, confirmation tours or political occasions. Only in the Anglican Church were rectors and vicars from gentry backgrounds to be found in any significant number. Social barriers between higher and lower clergy generated limited resentment before the 1790s, reflecting as they did the kind of obstacles to preferment that had their equivalents in the secular world; it was more the poverty of so many benefices and the social disdain of the episcopate which led to the growth of Richerist sentiments in Brittany and the Dauphiné regions of France, with appreciable political consequences in the late 1780s. The bishop/parish priest divide had its counterpart in the gap between beneficed clergy and the clerical proletariat composed of those priests who had no living and were obliged to exist as best they could on the fringes of parish life. In Protestant states where clerical marriage was popular, the resulting indigency affected whole families.

There were immense variations in conceptualising the nature of ministerial vocations. Minority Protestant denominations, which emphasised the personal nature of religious commitment, looked for signs of an inward experience from their would-be pastors. In the mainstream Churches, 'enthusiasm' was frowned upon and motives could be less dramatically compelling. Younger sons from elite backgrounds with political ambitions might find the Church the right vehicle to give them the prominence that birth had denied them, as the growing number of bishops from peers' families packing the upper reaches of the Churches of England and Ireland between 1770 and 1830 testified. At a broader social level among Lutheran and Anglican ordinands, a dynastic tradition could impel young men to the cloth, and every generation would have at least one of its representatives take holy orders. A career in the Church was an appropriate and respectable occupation, especially if there were well-placed relatives to offer the newly priested a helping hand on the high road to preferment. The persuasion and example of the family also played its part in inducing young non-aristocratic Roman Catholics to seek ordination, though the vitality of religious life locally also affected the numbers coming forward. Here, as in all principal confessions, the status conferred by holy orders remained a strong inducement for men considering a ministerial vocation.

Church finances

Another one was the desire to benefit personally from the privileges enjoyed by the Churches. These survived in some number alongside their temporal counterparts and were vigorously defended throughout the eighteenth century. Indeed, as will be considered later, it was customary at coronation ceremonies for new monarchs to swear to uphold existing clerical privileges. These could include tax exemptions, legal immunities, land in mortmain from the bequests of the faithful, and guaranteed seats in local Estates. In countries such as England where minority denominations enjoyed limited toleration, dissenters were quick to defend their statutory concessions and expect to see them upheld by the courts, as in 1767 when Lord Chief Justice Mansfield ruled that the City of London was not entitled to raise funds from dissenters to pay for its new Mansion House. Privilege was not seen as anomalous in eighteenth-century Europe but as the basis of liberty, strong enough to resist the desire of monarchs to bring about a degree of institutional levelling and centralisation in the interests of their own power. Privilege and corporate status thus went together, and ecclesiastical rights should be seen as part of a much wider and often confused jurisdictional framework that stretched across society.

Clerical privileges were bound up with the maintenance of Church wealth. That in turn necessitated limited outgoings in the form of taxation towards the costs of running the state (whatever the risk of compromising a developing public profile for 'patriotism' in its various guises), though it was increasingly difficult for the clergy to avoid shouldering their fair share of costs. Direct tax immunities were most marked in Catholic territories, and where an offering was made, the clergy were keen to emphasise that it should be seen as recognition of a moral obligation rather than a legal requirement. In France the General Assembly of the Clergy was ready to make a voluntary contribution or *don gratuit* to ministers every five years (more in wartime), a device which formally kept the Church outside the taxation system, a preference it successfully defended against attempts to force the First Estate of the kingdom to pay the *vingtième* along with the rest of the population in 1749. Spain's war effort in the 1790s was possible thanks to the generosity of the Church. Protestant Churches, including the established religions in England and Scotland, enjoyed no such exemptions because their lesser property stakes decreased their bargaining power, and the Church of England's Canterbury and York Convocations (which anyway had no tax-raising powers) were prorogued permanently between 1717 and the 1850s.

Whatever the local custom, governments were not disposed to let the clergy escape their share of the tax burden. They were well aware that established Churches, especially Catholic ones, derived the bulk of their income from land and their complete exemption was impracticable. Thus in Austria the Church was subjected to the heavier Contribution (direct tax) introduced by Haugwitz in 1749 on the same basis as other landowners. It has been estimated that in most Catholic states the Church owned between 7 and 20 per cent of the land, rising to 40 per cent in Austria and 56 per cent in Bavaria in 1764. Even in Protestant areas of Germany, where so much had passed to rulers during the Reformation, Church estates still generated considerable income. The Churches depended on land for the maintenance of their status in societies where power was a concomitant of property ownership. Churchmen were constantly watchful of lay and royal encroachment on their estates and their seigneurial rights (where they survived), and litigation on the subject was frequent. But they could not stop the prevention of future mortmain extensions in France in 1749, the Austrian Netherlands in 1753, Venice and Austria in 1767, Naples between 1769 and 1772, Bavaria in 1764, and a statutory tightening of the regulations on that subject for the Church of England in 1736. Such continuing lay generosity and the governmental concern it provoked is one of the interesting indicators that suggests indifference to institutional religion should not be exaggerated.

1. The consecration by Scottish non-juring bishops in Aberdeen on 14 November 1784 of Samuel Seabury (1729–96) as first Anglican bishop to serve in the newly independent United States.

In Russia the restrictions went much further: all ecclesiastical revenues were secularised in 1764. The Russian parish clergy saw little or no material improvements for themselves and still had to rely on collections in kind from their parishioners and the products of the harvest from the land they tilled personally.

Like any other landlord, clergy wanted to maximise income from their holdings, and the Churches were keen to encourage agricultural proficiency on their estates in the second half of the century. In England, parsons farming their own glebe had every incentive to pioneer improvements, and throughout Europe there was appreciable profit to be derived from ecclesiastical property leased out to lay tenants. However, the mainstay of Church wealth were tithes. They were payable by parishioners to the established faith of the state in which they were domiciled, irrespective of their own confessional allegiance. Payment was traditionally in kind or, increasingly after 1750, made in cash. Tithes were levied throughout Europe, except in Russia. They corresponded to approximately one-tenth of gross production, but the variations across Catholic Europe were innumerable. It was on average slightly less than 10 per cent in France, the Austrian Netherlands and Poland, only 4 per cent in Italy, and often as high as 12 per cent in Spain and Portugal. Tithe was intended to support the ordinary parish clergy but this was not always possible where it had been alienated to a lay impropriator (in Protestant states such as England or Prussia), or to another religious body like a monastery or cathedral chapter. They drew the profit, allowing the incumbent only a percentage for his own use. In France this was the *portion congrue*, which kept a high proportion of parish *curés* on or below the poverty line and it was correspondingly resented, despite substantial increases in 1768 and 1786. Tithe was much disliked by unbeneficed clergy who were not eligible for it, and by those who held benefices but were not entitled to the profits. Though the main representative of the Church on the ground, they could be left to struggle along on small fees levied for services of baptism, burial and masses for the dead, fees on which they subsisted, but whose insensitive imposition could easily sour relations with their flocks. These were the neglected foot soldiers of the Church whose services could too easily be taken for granted by the clerical elites.

So while tithe was essential to the Church's financial good health, enabling it to fund education and social welfare and act as a token of its institutional independence from the state, it was a burden rather than a benefit to the tithe payers. It was a heavy load on the laity who paid it at harvest time, and was crucial in fomenting rural anticlericalism. As one clerical poet put it in the early 1760s:

> Too well, alas! too fatally I know –
> From whence these complicated evils flow;
> From tythes, from tythes, the clergy's woes arise
> They mar religion, nay, they rob the skies:[6]

It was especially resented where parishioners were not members of the denomination they were supporting. Thus in Ireland the vast majority of Catholics and Presbyterians were legally required to maintain the Anglican Church, whose clergy relied on professional agents or 'proctors' to collect their dues. It was against their crippling demands that the 'Whiteboys' directed their agrarian attacks in the 1760s. They were the self-appointed spokesmen for a majority Catholic community whose own priests also looked to them for a stipend. These varied with an average income of £65 at the start of the nineteenth century, the equivalent of that enjoyed by large Catholic farmers. This double burden of payments for dissenting congregations supporting their own ministers *and*

---

[6] Rev. William Dodd, LL.D., *Moral Pastorals, and other Poems* (Edinburgh, 1824), 'The Parsons, An Eclogue', 106.

the established Church was a familiar story that crossed confessional boundaries. The financial sacrifices made in adhering to a cult that might be only precariously tolerated should not be underestimated.

The papacy

The government of the Churches was based on hierarchical gradations that had their counterparts in the secular sphere. The keystone of the Roman Catholic Church was the papal office, the spiritual head of the Church holding the powers bequeathed to his descendants as bishop of Rome by St Peter himself. That, at least, was how the pope's co-religionists justified his authority, one that had been rejected by the Greek Church in the eleventh century (except as first bishop among equals) and subsequently by the Protestant reformers. Even within the Roman communion, papal power continued to slip away to lay rulers and the higher clergy within their realms. Catholic monarchs were willing to subscribe to the pope's *de jure* headship of the Church, and his scope for definitive rulings in the spiritual domain, but otherwise the independent operation of his power in the day-to-day government of the Church was unwelcome. Acceptance of royal patronage inside Churches with their own distinctive national traditions had been the price paid by the papacy for continued princely allegiance at the Reformation; in return, governments had discarded the risky device of summoning general councils of the Church (a feature of European high politics in the fifteenth and sixteenth centuries) to impose their preferred policy on the pope. There were signs that their return might be imminent. Indeed, in 1786 the Punctuation of Ems subscribed by the archbishops of Mainz, Cologne, Trier and Salzburg – the most powerful prince-prelates in Germany – pronounced that only a general council of the Church could wield supreme power, and denounced alleged extensions of papal authority.

Conciliarism was actually an irrelevancy when pope and cardinals were willing to endorse national policies, seen, most spectacularly, in the reluctant dissolution of the Jesuits decreed by Clement XIV in the brief *Dominus ac redemptor noster* (Our Lord and Redeemer) of 1773. That still left Catholic states with a requirement to obtain papal approval for episcopal nominations and other senior appointments (governed by the Concordat of Bologna (1516) in the case of France), but experienced members of the foreign diplomatic corps resident in Rome (themselves often holding a cardinalate) were usually on hand to guard against any rupture in relations with the Holy See. Devout Catholics expected the state to uphold their Church. When monarchs wavered, it was enough to encourage renewed interest in the uses of papal authority, as in France during the 1750s and 1760s when the Crown failed to buttress Church authority against Jansenism in its judicial guise. But if ultramontanism was not, after all, a nineteenth-century innovation, neither was it a serious policy option for Catholic states before 1789. Only when the French government and its satellite states turned decisively against the Church at the revolutionary end to the century was there a fundamental conflict of loyalties for laymen between Church and state, and the need to reinvent the interventionist potential of the Vatican. Even then, as will be seen, conservative monarchs were reluctant to admit the necessity.

Scholars have presented the eighteenth century as the nadir of the papacy's international power and prestige, but caution is advisable: despite limitations in power politics, the later eighteenth-century papacy remained the symbolic hub of the Catholic world, with a prestige inseparable from a continuous existence co-terminal with the Christian era. Indeed, the very fact that the Catholic powers sought a papal decree dissolving the Jesuits rather than relying on the sufficiency of national expulsion was an unwitting recognition of the unique standing of papal decrees. In intelligent hands, the office still counted for much, and a continuing prominence in Italian politics was some compensation for a reduced impact elsewhere in Catholic Europe. The pre-revolutionary popes generally made the most of their opportunities to influence policy and patronage in the arts as well as official appointments, drawing on the resources of the extensive Vatican bureaucracy and guidance from their secretary of state who, like Cardinal Pallavicini in Clement XIV's reign, was often a former diplomat himself (he had been nuncio to Madrid). Clement XIII (1758–69) tried hard to make the papacy a dominant force within Italian politics and fought a long rear-guard action throughout his pontificate to block the all-out offensive against the Jesuits that originated in Portugal, including a defence of the Society with the constitution *Apostolicum pascendi* of 1765. He declared the Jesuits to be a fit instrument in every way for the Church's mission, a cradle of saints, and a powerful influence for good on the laity; any attack on the Society was in error against the Church. The Order had still not been dissolved at his death.

He was succeeded as supreme pontiff by Lorenzo Ganganelli, a man of gentleness, benevolence and lively conscience whose virtues were obscured in his lifetime by the unrelenting clamour directed at the Jesuits. Taking the name Clement XIV (1769–74), this Franciscan friar and physician's son prevaricated on this overriding issue for a further four years to within fourteen months of his death, a stance ridiculed in the cynical comedies performed on the Roman stage. He finally had to give ground when the condé de Floridablanca arrived in Rome in 1772 and insisted that there would be an unbridled Gallican-style Church in Spain unless the pope sacrificed the Jesuits. Floridablanca prepared the first Latin draft for his Holiness and Clement eventually signed the brief *Dominus ac redemptor* 'for the peace of the Church'. The next in line, the aristocratic Giovanni Angelo Braschi, Pius VI (1775–99), was elected after a 134-day conclave but initially elicited the renewal of good will from the monarchies of France, Spain and Portugal. His problems came in Germany and the Austrian Empire: his long trip to Vienna in 1782 to persuade Joseph II to rethink the suppression of some religious Orders and transfer of jurisdiction over monastic houses from pope to bishops brought a resounding rebuff that was noted across Europe. Little wonder that Prince Wenzel Anton von Kaunitz, the worldly Austrian chancellor, who had earlier shocked Pius by shaking rather than kissing his hand, remarked that the pope had been given a black eye. Protestants expressed surprise, even sympathy, at the papal plight that forced many to reconsider the enduring post-Reformation demonological identification of the papacy with the Antichrist mentioned in the First and Second Epistles of St John and further treated in the Book of Revelation. In fact, the two Clements and Pius VI had led the way in diminishing historic confessional tensions within the European elite. Grand Tourists were no strangers in the precincts of the Holy See, but they went further: Clement XIII encouraged Cardinal Alessandro Albani to persuade George III's brother, Edward Augustus, duke of York, to visit Rome in Holy Week 1764, and loaded the dissolute young prince with souvenir prints, mosaics and tapestries when he came. It was the prelude to the Holy See refusing to recognise the Catholic Young Pretender as king of England on his 'succession' in 1766. Clement XIV had a 'general kind affectionate manner of receiving the English',[7] followed his predecessor's example and hospitably welcomed Anglican members of the British Hanoverian royal family in 1772–4. Pius VI, a considerable patron of the arts, received the Lutheran Gustavus III (1745–92) of Sweden to the Vatican in 1783–4 and personally showed him around the new Museo Pio-Clementino (started under Clement XIV as a Vatican museum of classical art) on New Year's Day, after the king had attended the papal Christmas Mass in St Peter's. Such cordiality with 'heretic' princes was in instructive contrast to the problems these pontiffs had encountered with royal members of their own communion.

---

[7] Steddy Greenfield to James Harris, 4 January 1775, Hants. RO, Malmesbury MS. 9M73/155/171. This correspondent even subscribed to rumours that the pope had been poisoned.

There was a sense in which the pope found in culture and hospitality an escape from his undoubted lack of influence within the Catholic world beyond the papal states. But while papal power appeared undeniably weak by comparison with his predecessors, Pius was arguably more capable of repositioning the institution than scholars have usually conceded and, in admitting its reduced status in temporal matters, his tactical retreat earned him the cordial respect of monarchs elsewhere who had no intention of questioning his spiritual supremacy. In the last years of his pontificate, that supremacy would turn out to have a value that could not be guessed at before 1789.

The episcopate

Most Protestants grudgingly accepted the pope's title as bishop of Rome (or 'pretended' bishop), while Gallican and Febronian canonists denied that his office made him anything more than 'first among equals' within the episcopate. Bishops were the main leadership cadre of most eighteenth-century confessions. The eight archbishops and fifty-two bishops who governed the Spanish Church were aptly decribed by Cardinal Lorenzana of Toledo (primate after 1772 and a model of the enlightened bishop) as 'prelates placed upon a high lookout point' who combined the duties of 'shepherd, citizen, good vassal of the king and good neighbour'.[8] They, like colleagues elsewhere, possessed an authority founded – with appropriate differences of emphasis – on scripture and tradition alike, which, at least as far as Catholics, Orthodox and a minority of Anglicans were concerned, connected the contemporary episcopate in unbroken succession with the Apostles themselves. When the first Anglican bishop for North America, Samuel Seabury, was consecrated in late 1784 by the leaders of the nonjuring Church in Scotland, John Skinner's sermon was quite unambiguous: the Anglican Church drew its authority from Christ through the apostolic succession of its minstry. If bishops were free to concentrate on whatever aspects of their office most interested them, pastoral responsibility was primary to the job. Bishops were 'Fathers-in-God' just as the pope was 'servant of the servants of God', and there were numerous post-Reformation role models for inspiration, such as St Charles Borromeo for Catholics and Lancelot Andrewes for Anglicans, men of ability, austerity and concern for the well-being of their flocks.

Few prelates of the 1760s and 1770s could meet these exacting specifications, but every Church had its heroic, often unsung, mitred labourers

---

[8] Quoted in William J. Callahan, *Church, Politics and Society in Spain, 1750–1874* (Harvard, 1984) 10.

who travelled across their dioceses to confirm and preach, held regular visitations enquiring into the state of their clergy, and stayed at their post until illness or old age prevented them from carrying out their duties (eighteenth-century bishops did not 'retire', they died in office). In large or upland dioceses, these could be onerous tasks indeed, but prelates known for their administrative talent could often turn it to good effect pastorally, not least by relieving dearth and distress at times of harvest failure or epidemic, as did Archbishop Rajey of Santiago de Compostela in Spain who provided food for 1,300 people daily during the crisis of 1768–9. In pastoral matters, much depended on the size and social composition of the see – and the temperament and personal preferences of the bishop. The variations were immense and cut across the Catholic–Protestant divide. The leading reformer on the Anglican bench, Bishop Richard Watson of Llandaff (1782–1816), poured his energies into preaching and polemical literature and when not in London or Cambridge was more likely to be found at his residence in the Lake District than in his impoverished South Wales diocese. Watson was an academic rather than a pastor, but every Church included bishops like Urbain de Hercé, bishop of Dol from 1767 until killed in the counter-revolutionary defeat at Quiberon Bay in Brittany in 1795. He was forever on the road, putting himself at the head of missions in his diocese, and attracting ordinands from outside the area to receive holy orders at his hands. Then there was another Gallican prelate, de Conen Saint-Luc of Quimper, also in Brittany, who travelled the highways and byways of his remote see in a litter pulled by a hired horse.

Quimper was a modestly endowed diocese, and not all its holders had been satisfied living there in provincial isolation. Ambitious bishops in France expected to start their episcopate in a small, unlucrative diocese, then move on up the ladder of promotion as soon as vacancies occurred. News travelled when a bishop was known to be dying, and ministers could receive letters soliciting a post even before the existing holder was buried or, in some cases, actually dead! Such was, nevertheless, the typical career pattern across Catholic and Anglican Europe. Most ambitious prelates were alert to further promotion possibilities after they had gained their first mitre. The wealthiest dioceses – Sens, Strasbourg, Cambrai and Metz in France, Winchester, Durham and London in England, Derry and Armagh in Ireland – were every junior prelate's hope. No diocese could be accurately described as poor in any of these countries, though the cluster of sees in Languedoc created in the fourteenth century generated little wealth, and the dioceses of Bristol, Oxford and Rochester were not those in which bishops hoped to stay long before translation. Thus the French diocese of Apt was worth about 20,000 *livres* (the most profitable generated more than ten times that income), low enough for Bishop Eon de Cély to top it up with a pension of 12,000 *livres* and the titular headship of the rich priory of La Valette in the Toulouse archdiocese. In England, the see of Rochester often went with the prestigious deanery of Westminster, while Thomas Newton, bishop of Bristol from 1764 to 1782, boosted his status – and his income – by also being dean of St Paul's Cathedral. Such arrangements were increasingly viewed by Church reformers as unacceptable anomalies incompatible with a bishop's primary pastoral duties. But while debate intensified about the shape and objectives of reform in the several national Churches, such pluralism persisted, a reminder that material impoverishment was held by a wide swathe of public opinion to be an insult to those exercising office at the apex of the ecclesiastical hierarchy.

As seen earlier, across Europe the episcopate was becoming a preserve of the nobility and landed elite. In France, Hungary, the Austrian Netherlands and the Catholic principalities of the empire in Germany, it was almost impossible for commoners to aspire to a bishopric. In France nine commoners became bishops between 1700 and 1740, but only one, the abbé de Beauvais, between 1740 and 1788. The nobility were also in the ascendant in the Portuguese Church. It was typical of the hierarchy that that the archbishop of Braga from 1758 to 1789 should be a bastard son of John V, noted for his grand manners and charity. Elsewhere in Europe, convention and prescription were only slightly less rigorous. Spain, like England, recruited prelates from outside the nobility and gentry, but in the former country the leading offices, including the wealthy archbishopric of Toledo, were customarily inaccessible for anyone holding rank below *hidalgo*. Everywhere kinship, friendship and college associations made all the difference in the competitive preferment stakes where the patron–client relationship remained the norm. Every Church, including the Protestant ones, had its clerical dynasties where fathers and uncles would help the next generation into places of power and profit. In France, young elite clerics were prepared for the day when they would have their own diocese by assisting a kinsman or a patron in the running of his diocese with the title of *Grand vicaire*. Such practices were deprecated by nineteenth-century historians, but formed part of legitimate familial duties a century earlier, an era when merit was only a minor criterion for office-holding in either Church or state. It was the blood relationship that induced Talleyrand-Périgord, archbishop of Reims from 1777, to turn a blind eye to the dissipated high-living of his nephew, the future bishop and Napoleonic foreign minister, simply because he wanted his younger kinsman to hold high office in the Church comparable with his own.

Such beneficiaries of nepotism were nurtured within a network that anticipated financial reward from ecclesiastical office (enough at least to support the appropriate dignity of a cadet member of a landed family) but were also aware of the onerous responsibilities implicit in episcopal office and were prepared to shoulder them. The Hon. Brownlow North would probably never have ascended through three bishoprics in three years (he was only thirty when first promoted) if his brother had not been prime minister in the 1770s, but his occupation of Winchester from 1781 to 1820 was not undistinguished. Like others, North grew into his post, exhibiting a pastoral diligence and concern that was not uncommon among these well-connected nominees and, in his case, a Latinity that impressed the learned friends of the warden-elect of Winchester College, George Isaac Huntingford, in 1789. A financially lucrative see was no sinecure that dispensed the holder from looking after his clergy and people – at the same time as possession and patronage would help secure the material prosperity of his own family for the next generation.

In a world where kinship and connection were the means to high office in politics, it was appropriate that consanguinity counted for so much in the Churches. Bishops belonged to the ruling elite, and wherever one looks the younger sons, brothers and nephews of politicians major and minor received plum episcopal appointments. In the Church of Ireland, Synges, Agars and Beresfords, in the Church of England, Drummonds and Norths, in France, La Luzernes and Briennes, in Portugal the brother of the ruthlessly vindictive Pombal, could all be found at the top of the hierarchy. Bishops embodied the tight Church–state bond that existed across the continent, as chapter 4 will detail; those occupying large or lucrative sees (the two aspects usually went together) had a political importance in the late eighteenth-century which no government could possibly ignore. Each vacancy in the three electoral principalities of Cologne, Mainz and Trier generated great power lobbying to secure a favourable candidate. In the Balkan principality of Montenegro (technically independent, but claimed by the Turks), secular authority was in the hands of the Orthodox prelate, an office which had been held since 1697 by the same family. In larger states, many bishops presided over their own judicial structures and exercised an administrative oversight that could make all the difference in ensuring whether government policies worked in the localities. The increased number of visitations in the dioceses of western Poland led to prelates summarising information about local conditions and needs in statistical form. At least as importantly, prelates were indispensable agents within the complicated patronage networks that oiled the workings of every state. Some even hankered after holding Cabinet office themselves, though there was no equivalent of Richelieu or Mazarin in the period between 1760 and 1790.

Non-episcopal Church leadership

Though the Anglican and Lutheran communions retained the pre-Reformation Church ministerial order of bishop, priest and deacon, Protestant Churches that belonged to the Reformed or Calvinist tradition regarded such an arrangement as unscriptural and 'popish'. No matter what an individual minister's responsibility within these Churches, he could never rise in formal status beyond the ministerial rank conferred on him at ordination. In practice, the opportunities for leadership and the exercise of power were there to be exercised by the gifted and the well connected, such as Jacob Vernet in Geneva. Clerical and civic elites had long been mutually entwined and supportive in great urban centres including Glasgow and Amsterdam, Geneva and Basel, the historic heartlands of Calvinism. By the late eighteenth century, an enlightened, undogmatic Protestantism was characteristic of the ministers preaching, teaching and writing in all these cities and, in Geneva at least, verged sufficiently on open espousal of the Socinian heresy (a forerunner of Unitarianism) to win the controversial endorsement of d'Alembert in the *Encyclopédie*, Voltaire and other *philosophes*. It was symptomatic of the breakdown in a common clerical culture other Reformed Churches were experiencing. In Scotland, the Kirk was dominated by the 'Moderate' party in the 1760s and 1770s under the benevolent and sensitive leadership of William Robertson, the principal of Edinburgh University and an esteemed historian. Robertson's allies were decent, intelligent Christians such as the Reverend Thomas Somerville (1741–1830), who found the persecuting tendencies of his predecessors in the Kirk most unfortunate and rejoiced that the spirit of toleration was softening all forms of religion. 'Moderates' like Somerville were increasingly unrepresentative of the 'Evangelical' ministers in the majority of parishes who retained their suspicion of Catholics (as the riots against the Relief Bill of 1779 vividly demonstrated) and sceptics such as David Hume, protected by his 'Moderate' friends in Edinburgh. Reformed Churches in Switzerland, Scotland and the United Provinces operated with synodal rather than episcopal structures; individual congregations held considerable influence in appointments and policies which they were reluctant to concede to the centralisers and the power-brokers, especially when they detected any softening of doctrinal rigour and evangelical purpose. Where Calvinist minorities were still technically subject to penal laws, as in Ireland, France and Hungary, synods either functioned irregularly or not at all, but there was no serious danger of a return to repression in most European states: minorities had attracted the protective notice of too many enlightenment polemicists and progressive monarchs for that to be the case. In both England and Ireland, Presbyterian Protestants received some limited monetary support from the Hanoverian monarchy in the form of a grant called the *regium donum*. Beleaguered Reformed communities could also draw on their own strengths of congregational determination, an organisation attuned over time for survival, and outstanding individual ministers like Paul Rabaut and his son, Rabaut Saint-Etienne, in France, who saw them through to the confirmation of toleration in the 1780s.

Cathedrals and canons

The Scottish Kirk was proud of its established status and its several cathedrals, including the 'high Kirk', St Giles' cathedral in Edinburgh. For a Presbyterian body to use such exalted premises was, on the face of it, anomalous since a cathedral was the mother church of a diocese administered by a chapter of canons. But the Kirk made the most of the endowments it had received at the Reformation (St Giles' was divided into a number of churches, as was Glasgow cathedral), and the Calvinist Churches in Switzerland and the United Provinces did no less. Their cathedrals might be spartan buildings with their whitewashed walls and plain glass windows, but ministerial appointments conferred prestige as well as a large stipend on the fortunate beneficiaries and the posts were much sought after. Those on the staff of these Protestant centres retained a pastoral function that did not belong to Roman Catholic and Anglican canons. Its absence was a mixed blessing. Chapter membership had a social status universally admitted (in Lyon they were 'canon-counts', a sign of their temporal jurisdiction) but the preoccupation with internal business and the absence of duties towards the wider world afforded hostages to fortune in a late eighteenth-century world where 'usefulness' was increasingly the principal criterion by which institutions were assessed. For the most part, they had ceased to be seats of learning in their own right. There remained close connections between cathedrals and universities in isolated cases (Oxford and Salamanca), and the ideal had not ceased to inspire the clergy – one Leicestershire clergyman, William Hanbury (d. 1778) actually proposed such a foundation in his own village – although enlightenment critics were unimpressed. As for the urban laity, the presence of well-fed cathedral clergy ensured that an acerbic anticlericalism was transmitted down the generations. Tempering the

The Curate.

—————— *And first,—the Curate,*
Humming and hawing to his drowsy herd

2. Robert Dighton, 'The Curate'. This image well captures the threadbare status of unbeneficed clergy in the Anglican and Roman Catholic Churches in the later eighteenth century.

disdain was the hard-edged reality that they were major employers hiring servants and estate workers, and paying as well as their lay counterparts.

Cathedrals and collegiate churches were to be found across Europe, proud corporate bodies, protective of their historic rights and well placed to defend them. Frequently, bishops had very limited powers of intervention in capitular affairs; in French cities such as Toulouse or Poitiers, there could be several chapters coexisting, ensuring ample work for lawyers in every generation, less from institutional rivalry than the on-going litigation associated with the land owned by chapters and the disputes over leases and rentals. The value of cathedral and capitular posts varied with each stall. All generated a variable income from the prebendal land attached to them. Some, like the so-called 'golden stall' at Durham, were worth much more than the average English bishopric; others might belong to more recent foundations, for instance abbeys converted to cathedrals at the Reformation or some of the poorer Irish sees. There were far more canonries than bishoprics for which to compete – 2,300 in Spain – but not enough to satisfy the number of applicants. Appointment was usually in the gift of the Crown, so a well-placed patron was vital. His presence did not guarantee success, but the result could sometimes be spectacular, as for John Fountaine, named dean of York aged thirty-two in 1747, thanks to the intervention both of his uncle, Thomas Sherlock, bishop of Salisbury, and of the duke of Newcastle, 'the ecclesiastical-minister'. The family connection was, as usual, a decisive factor in the patronage stakes and in some foundations there was no possibility of entry unless a candidate was nobly born: in the *Reichskirche*, chapters were dominated by the lesser Roman Catholic nobility, affording them a system of outdoor relief. Once admitted, the job was for life unless convention dictated otherwise or promotion to a bishopric was obtained, and could be held in plurality with other posts. Fountaine, for instance, held office until his death in 1802 and was, by contemporary standards, diligent in managing the chapter and active in his own duties. Holders of cathedral canonries or prebendal stalls drew their incomes and were 'in residence' for a stipulated number of weeks (unless they could find a substitute to do their duty) in rotation before handing over to a colleague to take the services. Also on the payrolls of most cathedral foundations were innumerable minor canons, lay clerks, vergers, organists, sacristans and sextons, who sang the services, cleaned the vestments, prepared the communion vessels, patrolled the premises and generally ensured the functioning of the cathedral and collegiate churches which they served. They did the work for little material reward, and were scarcely noticed even by authors who dismissed their masters – deans, canons and prebends – as little better than drones.

The religious Orders

At least Protestant Churches were immune from similar criticism about the regular clergy, having abolished their own monastic foundations for both men and women at the Reformation. Even in Orthodox states, the eighteenth century was not an easy period in which to pursue an ascetic vocation – Catherine II of Russia dissolved many monasteries in the 1760s, and by the end of her reign in 1796 just 161 of the 572 existing at the start were still functional. It was hard to find Orthodox spirituality lived out in its fullness in any of them, and it was only subsequently that the sainted monk Tikhon of Zadonsk (1724–82) was acknowledged as initiating a revival in miniature. Nevertheless, the empress's adviser, Platon, believed in a rejuvenated monastic ideal, the creation of a new humanity reared behind monastery walls, ready to counter the corrupting influences of society in a manner that had overtones of the views of Jean-Jacques Rousseau.

The Polish–Lithuania commonwealth uniquely went against the contractional pattern. More than 200 new monasteries were founded in eighteenth-century Poland, 158 of them in the comparatively under-Christianised areas of Lithuania and the Ukraine. Despite the involvement of many monks and nuns in education, charity and hospitals, contemporary anticlericals found them the same easy targets for criticism as their Erasmian precursors had done two centuries previously: the ideal of an enclosed religious community cut off from society offended the cardinal enlightenment principle of usefulness in *this* world, while the practice of monasticism never failed to disclose instances of scandal or unnatural practices for which the reading public had an insatiable appetite: one of the hits of 1770 in Parisian salon society was a three-act drama by La Harpe, *Mélanie*, looking again at convents, forced vows and the fate of unwanted daughters. The self-interest of of the monastic Orders sometimes fitted the detractors' image all too comfortably in matters financial and sexual. Thus the richest endowments and benefices of the Uniate Church were monopolised by the Basilian Order from whom all the Uniate prelates were drawn. Fearing the diminution of their incomes and authority, the Basilians blocked attempts at reform. Policing celibacy was an insistent problem for the Spanish Church, with the regulars playing a major role in its confessional life; the several cases in which female penitents found themselves propositioned or blackmailed damaged the Church's image persistently and stoked up anticlericalism.

The Church hierarchies were only too aware of their vulnerability to criticism in this area, but had limited scope for action. Hierarchies dominated by aristocrats expected to be able to supplement the meagre incomes of smaller bishoprics by appointments as titular abbots and priors without ever going near the houses themselves; relaxed discipline appealed to others who saw no reason why the vows of poverty, chastity and obedience should prevent them enjoying creature comforts, especially when high incomes permitted it. Thus at Cassan in Languedoc the seven or eight Augustinian canons still on the premises in the 1750s commissioned Jean-Antoine Giral, the Montpellier architect, to build the most impressive classical frontage in the province; their one concession to asceticism in the dining-room was the absence of a fireplace.

Such an emphatic assertion of wealth and privilege was exceptional, but it was among the motives inducing Church and state authorities across Europe to rationalise structures, test vocations more rigorously and bring the religious Orders unambiguously within the limits of episcopal jurisdiction. It satisfied both reforming clergy inspired by what they took to be the ideals of the early Church and government ministers anxious to deploy state power even in the cloister, divert the appreciable wealth of these spiritual corporations to more general use, and curtail anomalous ecclesiastical peculiars in the empire. Powerful figures such as the duc de Choiseul and Kaunitz wanted the independent scope of the regular clergy kept to a minimum; so did rulers of smaller states, even when they were clergy themselves as were successive archbishop electors of Mainz, Emmerich Joseph von Breidbach (1743–74) and Friedrich Karl von Erthal (1774–1802), the latter putting money from dissolved foundations into endowing the University of Mainz. They had all concurred in the dissolution of the Jesuits in 1773 and meanwhile kept up the pressure on Church leaders to undertake and monitor wholesale reform of the remaining Orders. The result in France was the establishment of the *Commission des réguliers* in 1766. It decreed that vows could not be taken before the age of twenty-one (eighteen for women), abolished several Orders outright, closed smaller monasteries and redistributed their assets among those left. The *Commission*, at least, was chaired by an archbishop, Loménie de Brienne of Toulouse, working hand in hand with the Crown; in the Habsburg Empire, the impatient and frantically energetic Emperor Joseph II in the early 1780s accelerated his mother's more cautious campaign against the privileges of the religious Orders and unilaterally imposed his own blueprint for change on them, while ignoring the protests of the hierarchy. In addition to placing them under episcopal jurisdiction (1781), monasteries were declared released from control by the heads of their Orders resident in Rome. That was not in itself unusual – in 1776 Tanucci had tried to separate the Neapolitan Carthusians from their French superior. But it was the scale of Joseph's changes that staggered commentators: 700 monasteries were shut, and 38,000 religious out of 65,000 pensioned off, though many found alternative employment as secular clergy in the Church.

Paradoxically, such changes improved the vitality of the religious Orders in the medium term in both the empire, Italy and France. Many pursued vigorous evangelising missions, most famously the Passionists and the Redemptorists, founded by St Alphonsus Liguori (1696–1787) in 1732. Generally, novices were older and more committed, discipline was re-emphasised, and numbers declined at a slightly slower rate. The Brienne *Commission* certainly seems to have stemmed the net decline in numbers and strengthened the academic life of the French religious Orders: Benedictine and Oratorian schools remained popular with parents. The Maurist congregation of Benedictines continued to produce high-calibre scholar-monks and teachers, convent libraries stocked up on enlightenment publications and, with many proud to consider themselves 'réguliers-citoyens', the male orders enjoyed a final Indian summer that showed the limits of their detachment from contemporary society. By contrast with Austria and Bohemia, where numbers of nuns decreased by half over the next fifteen years from 3,250 in 1768, in the French female Orders, one can even talk of a religious revival in the later decades of the century, especially within congregations dating from the Counter-Reformation who were not living in abbeys, monasteries and convents – in other words *congréganistes* rather than *religieuses*. Among them were the Orders of the Visitandines, the Ursulines and the very recent Daughters of Charity; the latter recruited well down to the Revolution, when they numbered fewer than 15 per cent of the total of nuns. More than any others, these bore the burden of caring for the sick and the old in hospitals and other charitable foundations, brought supplementary poor relief to the most needy, and were involved in running schools. By the 1790s, when persecution rather than just dissolution was on the horizon, both male and female communities had already been toughened and tested by exposure to wide-ranging government-sponsored reforms. They were in a much stronger position than in earlier decades to lead popular resistance to the anti-Catholicising practices of the revolutionary armies.

The secular clergy

The funds and land-holdings of regular clergy in Habsburg territories were redirected towards paying for more parish clergy, the most highly esteemed cadre of churchmen in the view of governments and the laity generally after 1750. There were many reasons for this trend. First, the spread of Jansenism from France into Italy and the Austrian Netherlands fostered an *esprit de corps* among lower clergy; when combined with Richerist sentiments (see chapter 5), the result could be militancy and confrontation with local prelates. This was particularly apparent in the Dauphiné area of south-east France from the 1770s onwards, where the *curé* Henri Reymond emerged as the leader of the cause and attempted to win over the new power of public opinion in France. Secondly, perhaps uniquely within the Church, the parochial clergy were obviously useful to society, as they went about their ministry among the poor and the disadvantaged. They were not idle, they had limited worldly privileges, and they were not too obviously involved in the defence of obscure dogmatics. To be a priest was almost by definition to be a virtuous man, an exemplar of practical Christianity who for contemporaries called to mind the high standards of the primitive Church. In Florence, conscientious curates like Giovan Battista Landeshi, the 'rustic Socrates' of San Miniato, could be learned by any standard but lived for their people. Another translated the *Imitatio Christi* into language that would make sense to the barely literate.

Catholic clergy were by education and training better equipped to carry out pastoral work in the parishes than at any time since the Counter-Reformation, with the exception of much of Spain, Portugal and southern Italy. Recent research has discovered that some Spanish clergy based well away from the Castilian heartlands owned small libraries, suggesting that even in remote areas, the situation may not have been as backward as was often alleged. Virtually every diocese had set up its own seminary – as the Tridentine decrees had stipulated two centuries earlier – producing clergy who could offer a ministry of word and sacraments to all their flock and set an impressive example of personal rectitude in their own lives. It was a novel development in some places: Poland had a system of diocesan seminaries only from the beginning of the century (the figure had climbed to thirty-five by 1772), and Charles III of Spain founded new ones and improved existing ones as late as 1766, obviating the need for poorer men to complete their education in one of the numerous monastic colleges. Important dioceses such as Salamanca, Seville, Toledo and Santiago de Compostela were sees where the bishops had relied on education in a university college for scholarship students and were happy with the results. A better-educated clergy could lead to tensions and resentments among their flock as chapter 2 will consider, but sensitive leadership and pastoral involvement kept these to a minimum, and conscientious clergy could agonise about how far to extract tithes from hard-pressed parishioners in times of poor harvest and dearth.

Russian Orthodox seminarians were also undergoing more rigorous training. Catherine advanced the career of her protégé Platon Levshin (1737–1812), who became metropolitan of Moscow in 1775 and did much to improve the education of the higher clergy. Seminaries worked hard to raise educational standards. Despite the stand-off between Rome and Moscow, Latin was the language of instruction, with staff drawn mainly from the Ukraine, and the emphasis was on scholastic and German philosophical thought. Few of the parish clergy gained access to these institutions, and their lack of educational attainments could be embarrassing. The Greek clergy were, if anything, still more ignorant. Many could barely read. One said the Trojan War was waged against Troy by the Greek and Roman emperors, the king of France and the seven German electors – and he was reputed to be a great scholar! They had resisted an attempt by the patriarch in 1753 to open an academy on Mount Athos where they would be lectured on German metaphysics. These intellectual deficiencies were in part a reaction against the sophistication of the patriarchal court.

European towns were full of clergymen. In Bayeux, Norman centre of a large and important bishopric, there was a clerical population of 500 to 600 crammed into a town of 10,000 souls. These smaller centres were particularly dependent on them to keep the local economy profitable and to staff schools and hospitals as well as the churches. Any overall downturn in numbers – as in some parts of France from the 1750s onwards – may have been partly due to the uncertain material prospects of the cloth, as when tithing rights belonged not to the beneficed priest but to a great monastery or even a layman (a process known as impropriation); the best they could hope for in those circumstances was a meagre allowance. In the Toledo archdiocese it was estimated that 55 per cent of the parishes lacked the minimum income judged necessary for basic sustenance of a priest. Even obtaining a living was an unattainable prospect for thousands of clergy, who would pass their entire ministry as assistants in a parish, threadbare curates scraping a living on expenses from burial fees and taking marriage services. These made up the huge priestly proletariat of late *ancien régime* Europe, forgotten by governments and bishops alike, but generally esteemed by the people whom they served. So while the Churches were producing higher-quality clergy than before, there were plenty of frustrated careerists of lowly social origins (petit bourgeois, rather than rural, backgrounds tended to be the norm) who felt hedged in by parochial duties and wanted to display their talents to better advantage – and be better paid for doing so. These men were increasingly inclined not to question the existence of the hierarchy, but the opportunities for promotion inside it.

Protestant Churches were subject to much the same pressures. It was, on the whole, easier for well-educated parish clergy to aspire to higher office, a canonry or an archdeaconry at least. Even then, having the right patron or marrying a well-connected wife was highly advisable. Any education for the parochial ministry was either minimal or non-existent, though there were signs of incipient change. Edward Bentham, regius professor of divinity at Oxford from 1763 to 1776, introduced annual academic lectures for intending Anglican clergymen, attempting to give his pupils a fair impression of the Bible as a whole and introducing them to the New Testament in Greek. This was a bid to provide for the first time some form of professional training before they had taken their MA degree. Encouraged by Archbishop Secker, his labours were continued by his successors Benjamin Wheeler and Thomas Randolph. In May 1792 the latter brought out a five-volume *Manual for the Use of Divinity Students*. At Brasenose College, Oxford, by 1789 there were four-year exhibitions for young men to study divinity before taking holy orders.

Otherwise, future clergymen attended university with the rest of their contemporaries (apart from those affiliated to the German Lutherans, seminaries scarcely existed in Protestant countries) and if they sought ordination after taking their degree it was often granted by the bishop with few questions asked. Too often the end result was a highly educated parson stuck in rural isolation and having little idea of how to win the sympathies of his flock; the problem could be particularly acute for a newly married former college don moving out of the university for the first time. Clergy wives were not always staunch helpmates, or demure figures in the background. The Reverend Charles Powlett, grandson of the 3rd duke of Bolton, a Hampshire incumbent and chaplain to the Prince of Wales, married an extravagant wife in the late 1790s, who spent so much on clothes – often revealing ones that bedazzled local society, including the young Jane Austen – that eventually the couple had to flee abroad to escape their creditors.

Every rural clergyman needed outside interests, and many opted for agricultural improvements. In eastern Europe, pastors joined agricultural societies and tried to instruct the peasantry in the benefits of the new practices. In Scandinavia, their efforts gained them the title of 'potato priests'. J. G. Mayer (1719–98) was a country pastor in Württemberg for fifty-seven years who possessed a missionary fervour for the cultivation of clover and its fertilisation with gypsum; Samuel Tessedik, the Lutheran pastor of Szarvas in Hungary, founded an agricultural school in his parish, which trained boys in farming, artisanry and trade. He inspired the planting in his lifetime of 100,000 acacias on the dry Hungarian plains. Anglican clergy tended slightly more to the sporting than the agrarian (except where it concerned their own glebe land). With no concept of clerical retirement, it was hardly surprising that many incumbents found recreation more to their taste than pastoralia, and enjoyed the hunting, shooting and other outdoor sports the countryside offered. That was all very well if not done excessively, argued George Horne. Otherwise, it 'metamorphoses a divine into a gamekeeper, or a huntsman'.[9] Laurence Sterne turned author because of his tardy advancement in the York archdiocese – '[For] ought [sic] I know I may not be preferr'd till the resurrection of the Just'.[10] These diversions contributed to a growing public perception of self-interest, even careerism, within the Church of England, and this was not confined to a rural setting.

Many Anglican clergy fretted over the worldliness they detected in their colleagues. The curate of Hunslet, present at a meeting of clergy at the Angel Inn in Leeds in the 1750s, regretted that there was 'not one word of spiritual things among us'.[11] Some English parishes seldom glimpsed a resident parson at all, except when it was time to descend on them for tithe gathering. Absenteeism, however, was often unavoidable when parishes were poorly endowed in material terms and creating new ones or even reorganising boundaries was a long and complicated legal process: clergymen looking to support their family therefore had little choice except to hold two benefices. Few parishes could be described as pastorally neglected; impoverished curates had to be prepared to ride out in all weathers to cover Sunday duties over a considerable radius for ample thanks but slight remuneration. In Lutheran countries such as Sweden, Denmark and much of Germany, a tradition of direct state involvement in Church organisation (Erastianism) ensured greater equality of income for parish ministers. The Reformed or Calvinist Churches also functioned on that basis. In Geneva ministers were members of *La Venerable Compagnie*, which appointed to all vacant pastoral offices subject to approval by the Council of 25. They enjoyed a fixed public salary of £60, about twice as much as those outside the city. One English visitor in 1761 tellingly favourably compared the diligent pastoral work in evidence in Geneva on a small salary to an English parish where pluralist clergy might leave it 'to the mercy of some indigent curate'.[12]

The arts in the service of faith

The physical presence of the Churches across Europe was a constant visual reminder of their importance. All the main Christian denominations at the Reformation inherited a multitude of cathedrals, great abbeys

[9] Cambridge University Library, Add. MSS. 8134, B(7), f. 3, commonplace book, vol. II, 1787.
[10] Lewis P. Curtis (ed.), *Letters of Laurence Sterne* (Oxford, 1955), 76.
[11] Quoted by R. G. Wilson, 'Georgian Leeds', in D. Fraser (ed.), *A History of Modern Leeds* (Manchester, 1980), 34.
[12] George Keate, *A Short Account of the Ancient History, Present Government, and Laws of the Republic of Geneva* (London, 1761), 117.

and convents. Protestant denominations had no obvious use for this bequest. Where religious houses did not become new cathedrals or parish churches, as at Woburn Abbey and Anglesey Abbey in England, they had been granted to great secular landlords who used them as stone-quarries for the new houses constructed on their sites. In Catholic realms, despite the destruction inflicted during the Wars of Religion in France, the Thirty Years' War in Germany, and the on-going warfare against the Turks on Europe's eastern frontier, they remained mostly in good order, despite the unfashionability of the Gothic style for much of the eighteenth century. The glorious Baroque constructions of Italy, Austria and other parts of central Europe had all been erected by the 1750s, reaching a final splendour in the libraries in the abbeys of Altenburg (1740) and Admont (c. 1745) in Austria and Zimmermann's Wies church in Bavaria (1745–55). More recent ecclesiastical designs found inspiration in classical ideals, as in George Dance's All Hallows, London Wall or, in Paris, Soufflot's masterpiece of Sainte-Genèvieve, which the Revolution would turn into the Panthéon, the final resting-place of national worthies including Voltaire, Rousseau and Mirabeau. Austerity and the primitive became still more the watchwords as the Greek revival got under way around 1780, as can be clearly seen in the stumpy Tuscan columns in the cloister of the Capuchins (Lycée Condorcet, rue du Havre), by Alexandre-Théodore Brongniart. Classical rebuilding also occurred in innumerable European cathedrals, with much whitewashing of the walls and the replacement of coloured glass with plain, irrespective of whether they belonged to Catholic or Protestant authorities.

These churches were being filled with classical monuments by Pigalle and Houdon, Roubilliac and Flaxman and other sculptors. The scale of eighteenth-century monumental commemorations of the dead varied appreciably, as any visit to Westminster Abbey will confirm. In smaller churches this sculptural *théatre de mort* could dominate the complete building, as one finds in Strasbourg (the Maréchal de Saxe), Nancy (Louis XV's father, the last duke of Lorraine) or Boughton in Northamptonshire (the dukes of Montagu). Churches such as Bath Abbey still contain plaques and memorials and portrait busts to the new rich who had flocked to the pump room without finding the waters a cure for their illnesses and debilities; at least in death they would be sure of a place alongside established gentry families. Surviving village graveyards of the period still show that provincial stonemasons were in strong demand from those who could not afford burial indoors. Whatever their reservations about ritual and the place of art in services, all denominations played their part in fostering the remarkable flowering of sculptural design in the eighteenth-century tomb and memorial down to Canova and beyond.

The constant patronage of the Roman Catholic Church ensured that religious painting remained at the apex of painterly values. Artists from Tiepolo to David (his 'Saint Roch' of 1780 for the chapel of the Plague Hospital at Marseille established his independent career) produced masterpieces in that genre for palaces and the salons, and their lead was imitated by a host of minor artists sending religious paintings direct from their studios to cathedrals and collegiate churches. They were usually installed above the new neo-classical altar-pieces, a means of underlining the centrality of the Eucharist in Christian devotion. The second half of the eighteenth-century is one of the forgotten epochs of great religious art. In central Europe, fresco painting in the late-Baroque style produced artists hardly less gifted than those responsible for the original outpouring of creativity half a century earlier. Matthäus Günther (1705–88), director of the Augsburg Academy, working in Tyrol and Bavaria, was responsible for frescos in Würzburg and Wilten (Innsbruck) that had a marvellous plasticity and drama offset by colours of a delicate, almost pastel quality. Johann Jakob Zeiller, Christian Wenzinger, and Franz Anton Maulbertsch were contemporaries who attracted little less critical acclaim for frescos on the grand scale, like Zeiller's dome at Ettal (Bavaria), with its seventy-foot span and 400 figures arranged on heavenly clouds. Martin Knoller (1725–1804) worked later on the choir at Ettal, and the ever-stronger classical influences in his painting – reflecting the major impact of Johann Joachim Winckelmann and Anton Raphael Mengs from the 1750s onwards – can be found in so much religious art of this era. Many Protestants remained suspicious. As the curmudgeonly traveller and novelist Tobias Smollett remarked in Rome: 'The altar of St Peter's choir [Rome], notwithstanding all the ornaments which have been lavished upon it, is no more than a heap of puerile finery, better adapted to an Indian pagoda, than to a temple built upon the principles of the Greek architecture.'[13]

The Orthodox Church, of course, had icons at the heart of its worship and this period saw some of the loveliest and most refined examples of these sanctified images. Even Protestant Churches were overcoming their suspicions of art in church as an aid to idolatry rather than devotion. Thornhill, Hogarth, Reynolds and Constable all produced altar-pieces in this period; so did the American Benjamin West, Reynolds' successor as president of the Royal Academy in 1792. His plans to fill St George's Chapel, Windsor, with religious paintings commissioned by George III were, regrettably, no more realised than Reynolds' scheme of 1773 to do much the same in St Paul's cathedral.

---

[13] Tobias Smollett, *Travels through France and Italy*, ed. Frank Felsenstein (Oxford, 1981), 256.

Musically, the Church was still more important, offering talented musicians posts as organists and choirmasters, and setting the highest standards of musical excellence in settings for the liturgy. The works of Mozart and Haydn in Germany, Stanley and Boyce in England and Mondonville in France may have varied in quality, but all in their different ways provided appropriate musical settings for the Missal and the Book of Common Prayer, which have permanently enriched the repertoire. In Spain Francisco Fajer, *maestro di capilla* of La Seo in Saragossa from 1756 to 1809, persuaded many cathedrals to return to an entirely Latin liturgy and to ban the singing of recitatives and arias in the style of Italian opera. Only in the German-speaking Lutheran Church did standards in choral music wane after 1750. Powerful patrons were partly to blame. In the statelet of Schaumburg-Lippe, the court *Concert-meister*, Johann Christoph Friedrich Bach (1732–95), found the ruling prince's indifference to sacred music and Lutheran worship (he was a Calvinist fascinated by every aspect of the *Aufklärung*) as offensive as the miserable sum paid to his musicians. Lutheran choir schools were less frequently supported by town councils, and congregations were left without musical leadership to struggle with the few tunes they knew. Precentors sometimes led the singing, and embellished vocally the pauses at the end of lines. Lutheran Church music at parish level thus closely resembled English congregational singing, where Tate and Brady's *New Version of the Psalms* (1696) complemented Sternhold and Hopkins' Psalter of 1562. Though the standard of musical attainment in English parish churches was overall probably higher than was once admitted, great hymn writers including Isaac Watts, Philip Doddridge and Charles Wesley were producing inspired new verses to satisy public demand (especially among Protestant nonconformists) and the growing number of Methodists found their sense of salvation inspired and confirmed by the 600 hymns of Charles Wesley, which so appealingly combined lyricism, emotion and an impeccable Christological emphasis. In the Orthodox liturgy, too, hymns were composed in huge numbers to supplement elaborate chants. This outburst of creativity in art and music helped ensure that across Europe the services taking place in cathedrals and large city churches in the eighteenth century had a ceremony and dignity that has never been surpassed and would not survive the Revolution.

Conclusion

From Galway Bay to the Danube delta, from Greenland to Gibraltar, Europe in the later eighteenth century can be considered a diversified Christian culture, but emphatically a Christian one. In any Catholic state the traveller would find crucifixes every few miles on the highways, clergy both secular and regular on the streets, genuflexions and doffed hats as the host was carried by, with small cathedral cities like Sées and Comminges in France dependent for their economic well-being on the presence of the canons, and with only the remotest countryside far from the sound of bells. Protestants, too, with their preaching houses, their presence in the schools and universities and political life, were at the centre of public affairs in states such as Britain, Sweden and many of the smaller German principalities, more confident than they had been at the turn of the century that they had weathered the Counter-Reformation storm. In all denominations clergy were numerous and better equipped for a pastoral role than they had ever been. On the whole, they were more willing to try to get on with those of other traditions than at any time since the Reformation as the civic virtues of toleration became hard to resist. It gave all non-established denominations new scope and they prospered in these last decades of the old order.

The Churches tried not to be fearful of change. They saw it as a dynamic process of renewal within an identifiable Christian heritage and so readily endorsed evangelism, whether in the form of the religious Orders leaving an indelible imprint on the religiosity of rural Catholic Europe or a John Wesley covering more than 100,000 miles on horseback. These very different forms of itinerancy were superimposed on the centuries-old machinery of Church government, which could creak quite noisily. But while archaic parish structures in Spain, England and Italy worked against the effective use of clerical resources, in other states diocesan reorganisation was readily undertaken when anachronistic boundaries became unmanageable or populations shifted. Thus sees in Bohemia and Moravia were increased in 1754, and in Hungary in 1776–81; five new bishoprics were founded in Portugal in the 1770s. Similarly, motivated Anglican bishops were beginning to reactivate the office of rural dean to ensure good government of their, very often, scattered dioceses. Bishop Bagot of St Asaph required them to undertake repairs and decent fitting-up of the churches he had found in a poor state when translated from Norwich in 1790. This was not a heroic standard of leadership but it was an effective one, at its best in diocese, parish and convent when combining administrative tidiness with pastoral sensitivity. From a lay angle, whether educated or otherwise, it could, however, appear obtrusive and either too much in love with change or not sufficiently so. For if this was a Christianised laity it was also a critical one, increasingly enlightened as well as evangelised and less prepared to accept clerical *diktats* of any sort without consultation.

2 Beliefs, society and worship: the expression of Christianity in Europe c. 1750–1790

Finding out the faith

All branches of European Christianity were historically committed to a teaching ministry – the *lex docendi* – instructing the laity in the correct beliefs and behaviour required for unselfish, neighbourly conduct in this life and the securing of salvation in the next. This ministry was a priority for them all despite the core Protestant dogma that salvation was a result of inner conversion mediated between God and the individual rather than conferred sacramentally through the Church's offices. Since the Reformation, considerable variations had developed in the content of the instruction offered to the faithful, with dire warnings for those who lapsed or looked elsewhere. Church teaching still tended to equate salvation with adherence to a particular confession, beyond which nothing could be guaranteed for erring mortals except the usual penalty for heretics and schismatics – damnation. That was the classic formulation only just giving way by the mid-century to a more emollient view of those outside one's own communion.

There remained a fundamental division in western Christendom between the Roman Catholic Church with its insistence that good works as well as faith might count towards eternal life, and the Lutheran and Reformed traditions which taught that faith in the risen Saviour exclusively availed fallen mankind. And if the classic Calvinist emphasis on the predestination of individuals either to eternal bliss or torment was rekindled in England, Wales and British North America as part of religious revival, in the Swiss heartlands of the Reformed faith there was an imperceptible move away from this hardline position towards a new liberalism of spirit. Though the traditional suspicions and hostility were not eliminated, the trend can be seen as part of the wider blunting of dogmatic differences in the later eighteenth century as part of the continuing reaction against what was perceived as the 'enthusiastic' zeal of the previous century.

Perceptive foreigners had the sense that the English felt comfortable with their religion, perhaps excessively so. 'It is easy to perceive from the phlegm with which the English perform the duties of their religion, that they are very little impressed by a sense of its awfulness' [*i.e.* awe inspiring].[1]

There had always been more Christian consensus on the ethics of everyday life. The Churches expected men and women of every rank to observe all the Ten Commandments, which, in Protestant churches, were often written out on large boards for all to see and constituted one of the few visual displays permitted. If a German Lutheran or Church of England congregation grew bored with the preacher and his text, they might look up from their pews to see a boldly painted decalogue, often with figures of Moses and Aaron in relief adjacent to it. No less emphasis was placed on Christ's commandment that men should love their neighbour as themselves, not least as a means of preventing local breaches of the peace. Unless all quarrels and bickering were admitted and resolved amicably, Protestant communicants could not take the sacrament of the Lord's Supper, and the Catholic confessional was used to achieve much the same result.

Appropriate Christian behaviour and right belief depended on instruction at an early and impressionable age. All the mainstream Churches had this objective, and progressively worked to eliminate misguided popular versions of belief and observance that passed for Christianity. By 1760 they had achieved a formidable degree of success in achieving their missionary objectives, most recently in the more inaccessible, remote, upland areas of Europe. Whether Catholic or Protestant, Anglican or Orthodox, churchgoers were more likely to be literate and better informed about the redemptive message of the Gospel than at any point since the beginning of Christianity itself. This gave the institutional Churches a position of strength at the popular level that both offset the waning of elite adherence and provided a bedrock of support that contributed to survival during the revolutionary era of 1790 to 1815. Indeed, the revolutionaries would try to imitate but never quite match or displace the fundamental pedagogic weapon of the Churches – the catechism – which had settled on a standard format by 1750 in Catholic countries.

The catechism was the oral instruction by the priest or minister of his younger parishioners in the fundamentals of Christianity as they were defined by the Church of his allegiance. His teaching would be built around the subjects expounded in printed form, which technically constituted the catechism itself, for in time the catechumens would be expected to reply by rote but with understanding to the set questions

---

[1] M. d'Archenholz, *A Picture of England* (trans. from French) (Dublin, 1791), 107.

provided to test their belief. Correct catechising was designed to produce a basic uniformity among Christians, and give believers access to the supplementary works of piety that their instructors were confident would reinforce correct belief. In 1750 60,000 catechisms were distributed in the Hungarian diocese of Györ. Irish Catholic bishops in their pastoral instructions of the 1780s and 1790s laid repeated emphasis upon them as a means of combating lay ignorance and an essential preliminary to confirmation. It was not always a reliable means of teaching: the catechism could only be taught orally to illiterate countryfolk, so the post-Tridentine linking of literacy and solid religious culture could not be made. In Ireland the problem was partly overcome when the bishops established the Confraternity of Christian Devotion to assist in the task.

All except non-Trinitarian groupings would draw on the three historic Creeds – the Apostles', Nicene and Athanasian – to supplement scriptural revelation, but Catholics and Orthodox would, of course, include references to tradition and the intrinsic authority of the Church that had no Protestant counterpart. This was a ministry directed especially towards young people, one that had developed at a tremendous pace since the sixteenth century as the Churches competed to shape and confirm the faith of the next generation of believers. As the 59th Canon of the Church of England observed, using a form of words closely imitated in other communions:

every parson, vicar, or curate, upon every Sunday and Holy-day . . . shall, for half an hour or more, examine and instruct the youth and ignorant persons of his parish in the Ten Commandments, the Articles of the Belief, and in the Lord's Prayer; and shall diligently hear, instruct, and teach them the Catechism set forth in the Book of Common Prayer.

Anglican clergy took this stipulation earnestly and tried to insist on some basic familiarity with the tenets of the faith for all candidates preparing for confirmation. They were not always so active as their Catholic brethren. In Lancashire, a stronghold of Catholic recusancy since the Reformation, catechetical activity was a distinctive hallmark of the minority community. John Barrow, priest at Claughton from 1766 to 1801, gave catechetical instruction every Sunday between 9 and 10 a.m., with a related sermon at the parish Mass. In Sweden under the canon law of 1686 the parish priest was obliged to check the literacy of his congregation annually in parish catechetical meetings, which were interrogations held with all members of the household, and then report the results to his bishop. Across the continent, as boys and girls approached adolescence, they received catechetical instruction, which was, by the 1760s, a conventional preliminary to episcopal confirmation, adult baptism or

3. The pulpit and box pews in Old Dilton church, Wiltshire. This eighteenth-century interior shows the high importance attached to the ministry of the word by the Church of England.

full membership of a Presbyterian denomination. The results could be spectacular: One curate, of Churchill near Bristol, recalled his ministry among 'deplorably ignorant and profane' children, who were gradually won over to regular church attendance where 'to the admiration of the whole parish, [they] publicly said the catechism every Sunday, with intelligent correctness'.[2]

The primacy of the pulpit

With isolated exceptions, such as the Quakers, the principal pastoral resource of the Churches to nourish adult congregations in the faith was the sermon. In eighteenth-century Europe it remained as much a primary mode of communication as it had been since the Reformation, albeit one competing against newer forms of public discourse in an ever-expanding print market. Preaching had always been a hallmark of Protestantism, but a new development was the way Catholic country clergy were making sermons as much a part of their ministry as the confessional. The seminary curriculum also reflected this trend. A reputation as a good preacher was no disadvantage to any clergyman seeking preferment (especially when a monarch or nobleman with many benefices in his gift was in the congregation), and those with pretensions for sparkling or inspiring language had every opportunity of displaying their talents. 'Fr Platon does as he likes with us; if he wishes us to cry, then we cry', was Catherine II's comment on her great metropolitan.[3] Some churches had a particular reputation for pulpit oratory, such as Saint-Nicolas-des-Champs in Paris where the police were instructed to keep order and eject women whose dress was more appropriate for an evening assembly than a church service; in Venice one prelate complained that famous preachers came to his diocese for a fee 'like that of opera-singers'.[4] In most Protestant churches, the pulpit was more conspicuous than the holy table, with innumerable Anglican churches possessing a three-decker pulpit combining pulpit proper, reading-desk and parish clerk's desk. Except on sacrament Sundays, the whole service could be conducted from this point. Wealthy Roman Catholic parishes across Europe erected pulpits in the latest design fashions; after the Gospel

---

[2] Revd Edward Barry, M.D., *Sermons, preached on Public Occasions* (3rd edn, Reading, 1805), sermon xii, 223.

[3] R. L. Nichols and T. G. Stavrou, *Russian Orthodoxy under the Old Regime* (Minneapolis, 1978), 76.

[4] Prospero Lambertini [Benedict XIV], *Raccolta di alcune notificazioni etc.* (2 vols., Naples, 1772), vol. I, 103 ff., quoted in Owen Chadwick, *The Popes and European Revolution* (Oxford, 1980), 166.

reading the priest would ascend the lavishly crafted stairway to perch high above the pews and there expound his text. There was a cultural expectation that homilies would not be brief; a minimum of half an hour was the norm even in Catholic churches, despite the south-German proverb that 'countrymen love short sermons and long sausages'. Hogarth's engraving of 'The Sleeping Congregation' graphically captures the tedium that worshippers risked from a verbose or dull parson, but there was no attempt to introduce shorter addresses and any such move would not have pleased the clergy. Congregations anyway expected an extended discourse at the main Sunday service, as one Anglican bishop reminded his clergy in 1789: 'The people naturally expect to hear something original from their Minister; and those absenters from Church, who plead that they can read a good sermon at home, have a better, though not a full Apology, if their Preacher has no instruction of his own to give them.'[5]

The sermon was such a versatile device. It was an essential medium of social control in an over-regulated but under-policed society where deference to established authorities (including the Churches) could never be assumed. Joseph II's administration in Hungary was frantic to be reassured that the clergy were toeing the official line: an edict of 1783 for monitoring sermons stipulated that a written record should always be made by the priest and, if a book provided his sermon's text, it must be specified and approved in advance. Not surprisingly, sermons drawing on apostolic injunctions such as 'Fear God and honour the king' (1 Peter II.17) were a constant resort of preachers, in Protestant buildings echoing the scriptural extracts often found inscribed on whitewashed walls. Some pastoral priorities complemented public policy: correct belief and Christian conduct were identified from the pulpit and recommended according to the teaching of different denominations. This exposition was pitched at a level appropriate to the congregation. The range varied: the elementary explication of the Gospel expected by a church full of labourers and servants; refined reminders to city sophisticates of what their rank and status required of them in charitable giving; exegesis of scripture or controversial engagement for academics and students. Preachers could see the uses of the pulpit for denouncing unbelief, immorality, anticlericalism – or any other matter at variance with Church teaching – just as their predecessors had done. Indeed, the increasingly anti-Christian character of the late Enlightenment intensified the pressure on them to reply by any means at their disposal.

[5] *The Bishop of Hereford's Charge to the Clergy of his Diocese at his Primary Visitation in June 1789* (Hereford, 1789), 10.

Clergy broaching such subjects would expect to turn their spoken word into print at the first opportunity, to feed the huge demand for printed sermons in most countries. As Reed Browning has well observed, 'The pulpit was as important as the bookstall in the political wars of the eighteenth century.'[6] Indeed, the sermon *was* prominent on the bookstall. There were collections of sermons for every Sunday of the year, the habitual recourse of undertrained or undermotivated clergy, who could bank on their congregations not catching them out. They were a publishers' staple in this period, increasingly aimed at specialist markets such as young women, catered for by such as James Fordyce, Dr Johnson's friend and minister to the Church of Scotland congregation in London, with his best-selling *Sermons to Young Women* (1767). Any excuse would serve to print sermons: a coronation, victory in war, appointment to a bishopric or an important dissenting tabernacle, the death of an eminent divine, or emergency directives from central government at times of dearth or disease. The clergy were expected to rise to the occasion (and there were many complaints that they too often did not) and mould as well as encapsulate the sentiments of the widest cross-section of what was becoming universally recognised as 'public opinion'. Publishing lectures or sermons explaining the faith on catechetical lines was a popular way for the ministry to enhance its reputation with middle-class readers and play up the truth-claims of their own denomination. This thought motivated John Skinner, the ambitious new bishop of Aberdeen, when he brought out a course of Lent lectures in 1786 instructing readers in the faith, practice and worship of 'that pure and primitive part of the Catholic Church, in which he has the honour to serve'. In his case it was the nonjuring Scottish Episcopalians.

The influence of the plain English preaching of John Tillotson (archbishop of Canterbury, 1691–4) set the tone for almost a century after his death, especially in Germany and not just among Protestants. Good works, benevolence, charity and social responsibility were the habitual watchwords of preachers to 'polite' congregations. The dogmas of Christianity were downplayed in favour of exhortations to moral conduct favoured particularly by the Moderate leaders of the Church of Scotland, epitomised by Hugh Blair (1717–1800), the first professor of Rhetoric and Belles Lettres at Edinburgh University from 1762 as well as minister of the High Kirk of St Giles', Edinburgh. 'For what purpose', asked Blair in one of his sermons, 'did God place thee in this world, in the midst of human society, but that as a man among men thou mightest cultivate

---

[6] Reed Browning, *Political and Constitutional Ideas of the Court Whigs* (Baton Rouge, 1982), 90.

humanity; that each in his place might contribute to the general welfare?'[7] Rather less was said about the Trinitarian unity of the Godhead and the mystery of the Incarnation, and the result was frequently a sermon that 'could be preached equally well in Paris, London, or Constantinople'.[8] In a pastoral letter of 1762, Cardinal Trautson of Vienna was scornful of the insubstantial doctrinal trappings of so many sermons. Preachers, he lamented, nowadays do not preach the word of God. The Lutheran minister and luminary of the German Enlightenment, Herder, urged ministers to be first and foremost preachers of God's word, not just pleaders for moral duties and civil virtue. There were strictures against excessive refinement in preachers, of dandified parsons striving for effect – and failing. As one English critic complained of their sermons, 'they may please the fancy and tickle the ear, but they touch not one feeling of the heart'.[9] Such criticism abounded, but it overlooked the willingness of churchmen to speak to the men and women in the language of their own time.

For all churchmen, the sermon was a primary demonstration of the uses of rhetoric in the services of the faith. Florid, orotund phraseology was distrusted and little used, but was the new simplicity and straightforwardness any more effective in pastoral terms? Preaching was central to the teaching ministry of the Churches, but was it inspiring? Perhaps that was most the case in the more traditional country parishes, especially where they were Catholic, and preaching in the vernacular was a recent innovation. Meanwhile, against the current, one could still hear week by week from the pulpits of rural clergy a catechetical emphasis on sin and the need for repentance. Inspiration was not far removed from fear. Spanish parish preachers used theatrical gestures that even the most illiterate in their churches could not fail to recognise, like rattling the chains of the damned on the pulpit: reforming preaching by such as Nicolás Gallo was one of the most dynamic aspects of eighteenth-century Spanish Catholicism. In France, the emphasis on human sinfulness persisted and with it the need to attend church and pray regularly, relying on the intercessionary power of the Virgin and the saints. Such injunctions may have sacrificed politeness, but could still be inspirational if a preacher tapped into the spiritual hunger of his auditors. Simplicity and intelligibility was the first priority of St Alphonsus Liguori (1696–1787) and his followers in the Congregation of the Holy Redeemer he had founded in 1732. The Redemptorists went out into the Italian countryside ready

[7] Hugh Blair, *Sermons*, I (Edinburgh, 1777), 15–16 quoted in David Daiches, 'The Scottish Enlightenment' in David Daiches, Peter Jones and Jean Jones (eds.), *The Scottish Enlightenment 1730–1790: A Hotbed of Genius* (Edinburgh, 1996), 1–41, at 13–14.

[8] See *Tableau de la littérature au XVIIIe siècle* (Paris, 1813), 109; *Journal Ecclésiastique*, July 1774, 69.

[9] *The Fashionable Preacher; or, Modern Pulpit Eloquence displayed* (London, 1792), 7.

for any number of dialect variations, preaching earnestly but charitably before whole communities about the fear of God and the need for repentance to escape the worst on the Day of Judgment. Increasing numbers of Protestants, too, had similar emphases, as the phenomenal rise of Methodism and Pietism in the first half of the century testified, and John Wesley could be no less censorious about worldliness and immorality than St Alphonsus; both men were unashamed about bringing their message of salvation to the lowliest in society. Methodism's appeal broadened rather than diminished from 1750 onwards, leaving mainstream Anglicanism struggling to adapt. Most worryingly for the authorities, a force like Methodism was not susceptible to ready clerical control, as it showed that preaching could be predominantly a lay activity, undertaken as readily in the open air as in a church building. Redemptorists, on the other hand, could only enter a parish with the permission of its priest.

Religion and schooling

Apart from catechising and preaching as a means of instructing the laity, the Churches in most European states also exercised a controlling influence over schools: the grammar schools and charitable foundations predominantly staffed by the clergy to be found in towns and cities. Clergy had been the great advocates of popular instruction since the Council of Trent. Activist bishops still promoted the spread of the 'little schools' in France late in the century and, though the effectiveness of this pattern varied, it was vital in explaining the accomplished Christianisation of the countryside by around 1750. Their efforts were not always appreciated by governments, especially as high numbers of Jesuits were involved in the process. Attempts inspired by Maria Theresa's adviser, Gerhard van Swieten, to reduce their numbers in favour of lay teachers in Austria were hampered by the scarcity of qualified staff, though this did not stop her son, Joseph II, going further in the 1780s and dissolving all teaching Orders in the empire except for the Piarists (at work in the Habsburg lands since the late seventeenth century). The Austrian state thus pushed the Church to the sidelines in a manner hardly encountered elsewhere, though religious precepts were stressed just as before. In Hungary, van Swieten's mixed confessional schools pleased neither Catholics nor Protestants, and were suppressed by the Diet in 1790 along with other educational reforms of the late king-emperor, including a non-denominational handbook for use in primary schools.

Educationalists may have wished to do without ordained teachers but this alternative cadre was, for the most part, non-existent. In Baden, Johann Schlosser sought to break clerical control of education after his appointment in 1774 but the manpower was lacking. Schlosser, too, was no secularising zealot; his *Catechism of the Christian Religion for the Peasantry* (1776) combined a simple deism with a mystical Lutheranism. In the Rhineland, a more practical curriculum resulted in decreased clerical influence. Not so in Protestant Hanover and Brunswick, where the clergy were more successful in retaining control of schooling. The fees charged by grammar schools marked them out as mainly for the sons of the 'middling sort'. The curriculum was still centred on classical texts as well as scriptural study. Nevertheless, modern subjects were increasingly provided, as by the Oratorian Order in France (their old boys included the *philosophes* Montesquieu and d'Alembert) who pioneered post-classical history and mathematics. In England, the dissenting academies at Daventry and Warrington were heavily subscribed for just that reason.

In the rural population, boys were wanted on the land at busy times of the agricultural year so it happened that girls were often more likely to receive some basic teaching than their brothers. In France this was thanks to the *béates*, usually a widow or spinster popularly respected for her piety – and acceptable to the ecclesiastical hierarchy – with just enough education herself to teach lace-making to the village girls while they recited their catechism. They were often the only teachers available, despite a proclamation of 1724 requiring every parish to have a male and a female teacher. In England the problem was partly solved by the existence of more than 1,500 charity schools by 1750 sponsored by the Society for the Propagation of the Gospel. There was additionally the rapid expansion of Sunday Schools from the mid-1780s as a disincentive to crime and idleness, backed by figures as eminent as Beilby Porteus, the bishop of London, and William Wilberforce, the Evangelical MP and friend of Pitt the Younger. Local initiatives sprang up all over the country. In the Colne Methodist circuit in Lancashire, ministers conducted a school at Heptonstall on Saturday nights in the 1780s, and taught reading, writing and arithmetic to young people in a fast-industrialising area; a formal Sunday School was started in 1795 with teachers paid ten shillings monthly. Not everyone approved. A common fear that their advocates had to overcome was that Sunday Schools would keep boys and girls out of church. As one critic put it in 1786:

I have no objections to Sunday Schools in Salford, provided they are properly regulated, and the children are brought duly and constantly to church; otherwise you are teaching the children this false and wicked principle, that for the sake of learning to read and write, or other worldly advantages, it is lawful to neglect the public worship of God.[10]

---

[10] Robert Kenyon to ?, 13 December 1786, *H.M.C. Kenyon MSS., 14th Rpt* (1894), 523.

Promoters of the English Sunday School movement, many of them women like Sarah Trimmer, were usually capable of anticipating these objections. In 1786 she hired three teachers for the 140 girls and two for the eighty boys in Old Brentford, Middlesex, and issued clear directives for the children to receive from the teachers 'the best instructions in their power, respecting their duty to God and men'.[11]

Finance was another recurrent obstacle in expanding educational provision. In Austria it stultified the ambitious blueprint for primary education devised for the empress Maria Theresa by the Augustinian abbot Johann Ignaz Felbiger, as promulgated in the decree of 1774 introducing compulsory school education. In Poland there was more progress. A Commitee of Education worked towards a national system after the Jesuits were abolished in 1773, and achieved some success in the next two decades by following the innovations associated with the Piarist leader, Stanislaw Konarski, and his emphasis on raising the nation's leaders within the moral framework of enlightened Christianity. Much that was distinctively innovative came from individuals working on their own, such as Fr Ferdinand Kindermann, parish priest of Kaplice in southern Bohemia, who introduced locally what would become known as 'industrial schooling' between 1771 and 1774. He aimed to give underprivileged youngsters destined for jobs as labourers or servants access to a range of practical skills that would keep them out of the workhouse throughout life. Fundamental to the process was spending time in a local factory while still registered at the school. After 1774 the empress put Kindermann in charge of primary education in Bohemia, and under his guidance the province set the pace for the rest of the Habsburg Empire. Despite his own tepid deism, Frederick II of Prussia also encouraged the spread of a biblically centred elementary educational system and, in Russia, Catherine placed a similar emphasis on religious instruction. She doubled the number of schools down to 1800 after decreeing a new elementary system in 1786.

In Catholic countries, missionary activity complemented the teaching available in churches and schools. Between 1767 and 1770, despite internal strife and Russian military activity, the Jesuits alone conducted some 3,000 missions into parishes throughout Poland–Lithuania. In Tuscany and the papal states, the Redemptorists had their efforts seconded by the new Passionist Order (recognised by Clement XIV in 1769), comparable to reformed Franciscan friars in their commitment to the well-being of the poor and known for their devotion to the cult of

---

[11] Appendix in Sarah Trimmer, *The Oeconomy of Charity; or, An Address to the Ladies Concerning Sunday Schools & c.* (London, 1787), 167.

the Sacred Heart. In France could be found Lazarists in Anjou, the Fathers of Christian Doctrine in Gascony and the Pyrenees, and completely new companies of priests such as the Mulotins who adopted emotionally charged tactics during their missions across the west. These missioners stayed in their selected parish for three to six weeks, urged local people to follow new paths of piety and renew their practice of Christian observances, propagated Marian devotions, and staged highly dramatic presentations of scenes loosely based on stories from the Gospels. For the most part they were welcomed by the majority of parish priests (except those of a Jansenist persuasion), who were encouraged to carry on the good work after the missioners had left. Their presence in rural backwaters could be a high point in community life, and it seems likely that areas visited by parochial missionaries were less likely to experience 'dechristianisation' from the 1790s onwards. In Spain the Jesuit missionary Pedro de Calatayud spent the half-century prior to 1767 tramping between the remote villages and townships of central and northern Spain preaching the Gospel. Such efforts were by no means confined to the countryside. The Capuchin Fray Diego de Cádiz (1743–1801), the most popular preacher in the kingdom, could hold the engrossed attention of several thousands when he appeared in town. This is a reminder that teaching for the vast majority of ordinary Europeans in 1750 to 1790 still meant Christian teaching and that literacy was only just beginning to be recognised as a good in its own right rather than a means to help the individual achieve salvation as mediated (in most cases) through the good offices of his or her local priest or pastor.

Later eighteenth-century religiosity

The continuing vitality of Catholic missionary work in rural areas and the growth of Protestant lay preaching and its association with the 'enthusiastic' language of religious revival were only two variants within changing patterns of religiosity in the period from 1760 to 1790. These, as ever, were usually manifested on a confessional basis that reflected the cultural inheritance and national tradition of the Churches. Of course, the religious dynamic of a historic religion such as Christianity worked against hasty alterations in outward observances, even in an 'enlightened' age. The Churches encouraged and expected lay men and women to nurture a spiritual life which both satisfied them as individuals as well as conformed to credal orthodoxy. There was nothing new in that. The conventional aids to lay piety were readily available to all literate people, such as lives of the saints and Marian devotions for Catholics, including a masterwork like Alfonso Liguori's *The Glories of Mary* (1750), which Owen Chadwick has called 'one of the most influential books to come out of the eighteenth century'.[12] For Protestants, older edifying tracts and incentives to Godliness in their own vein, such as the *Whole Duty of Man* (translated into most languages, always in print), were supplemented by new handbooks to scripture. The emerging consumer society found that commercialisation and evangelism could, at times, sit comfortably together. The Freemason and Wilkite clergyman, the Revd William Dodd, anthologised the Bible and turned out moral tales for *The Christian's Magazine*, as part of marketing the Gospels – as well as himself. These new productions did nothing to guarantee that readers would pull them off the shelves, as the parson-poet and satirist, Charles Churchill, pointed out when he deplored contemporary ignorance of the Bible:

The Poor think themselves absolved from consulting it because so much of their time is taken up by their necessary labour; and the Rich no doubt must be excused, some because they never read at all, and others because their meditations are turned another way, and they are better employed in perusing and raising trophies to more modern Productions, where indecency passes off for wit, and infidelity for reason.[13]

Churchill was referring to Protestant England, but in continental Catholic states Bible reading in the eighteenth century was probably more intensive, intelligent and ubiquitous than at any point in history. A higher proportion of Catholics than ever had received some form of rudimentary education and had a familiarity with scripture derived from reading it for themselves rather than being offered selected extracts by the clergy. In a Brief of 13 June 1757, Benedict XIV permitted the use of the Bible in the vernacular so long as the consent of the Holy See had been granted, and it facilitated translation in several European languages. The archbishop of Milan from 1781, Antonio Martin, a strong reformer and collaborator of the duke, Peter Leopold, worked on the first official translation of the Bible into Italian. In 1783 the Spanish Inquisition even authorised the reading of the Bible in the vernacular and a complete Castilian translation was available by 1793. French Jansenists had translated and circulated the Bible around parishes from the late seventeenth century, Louis XIV had encouraged 'former' Protestants to continue reading it after 1685 and the revocation of the Edict of Nantes, so that most literate French families read from scripture together by 1750.

Catholic insights into the soul's ascent towards God were drawn on by mystically inclined Protestants such as William Law and John Wesley. They were not alone among their co-religionists in finding inspiration in classics of Catholic spirituality like the writings of Madame Guyon

---

[12] Chadwick, *The Popes and European Revolution*, 27.
[13] Charles Churchill, *Sermons* (London, 1765), no. iv, 87.

and Antoinette Bourignon's *Le Nouveau Ciel* (1699), texts that acted as a dissolvent of denominational suspicions and became part of a common Christian treasury in the second half of the century. The mystical current in French religious writing, though displaced before Louis XIV's death by moralising tendencies, never wholly ceased and was surging up again just at the time the Jesuit Order was dissolved. It could be found in former Jesuits such as Père Grou (1731–1803), one of the most pre-eminent contemplatives of the eighteenth century, who wanted in his meditations to link Plato and the *philosophes*, the soul and the head; and Fr Picot de Clorivière (1735–1820), inspired by the mystical saints of previous centuries and author of *Prière et Oraison*, a guide to the meditative life intended for a wide public.

This was a generation which, inspired by Rousseau, had discovered the power of emotion for itself and wanted to experience it at every level, particularly as an authentic, acceptable expression of Christianity. Both sexes looked to Rousseau's writings for guidance on the values by which their lives should be inspired. Personal feeling was becoming the supreme authority. As one of Rousseau's correspondents in 1764 told him: 'The reading of your works, which I have ceaselessly pondered, has inspired in me the courage to consult nothing but my heart'.[14] Many clergy saw the opportunities presented by the cult of sensibility that swept Europe in the later eighteenth century, but the Churches as a whole were slow to respond to the religious creativity it prompted, usually quite independent of clerical control. In his best-selling *Emile*, Rousseau gave the public his *Savoyard vicaire*, a well-meaning priest who adored God in nature but said little about revelation in Jesus Christ. To the Catholic clergy, this was a deplorable omission which flawed the book while, on the contrary, the public took the *vicaire* and his creator to their hearts: the ecstatic apostrophe of praise to the created order to be found in the *vicaire*'s 'confession' kindled the spiritual life of a generation, but the Church authorities were uncomfortable with it. There was general caution about discarding a homiletic tradition which had abandoned the emotive and the heart-searching in favour of a call to benevolence and social responsibility. Even German Pietism had become somewhat rigid in its original heart-lands, or become a form of pantheism which had, in effect, turned its back on Christianity. The clerical elite, Catholic and Protestant, were largely incapable of offering their people the emotionally charged religion so many of them wanted, and this did much to loosen the regard of the middling sort for clerical leadership in other ways.

---

[14] The *Correspondence complete de Jean-Jacques* Rousseau, ed. R. A. Leigh (44 vols., Geneva and Oxford, 1965–85), has many other items of 'fan mail'.

Public interest in mysterious, invisible forces was as high as ever in the 1780s. The excited response to Mesmer's visits to European capitals, the fascination with Rosicrucianism and the occult knowledge it professed, and perhaps the stream of applications for masonic membership witnessed to that. Yet there was no equivalent outpouring of intensive, mystic Christianity within the Churches, either Catholic or Protestant, and mysticism proper was for a minority, often in exotic format by the 1780s, as the vogue for the Swedish mystic, Emmanual Swedenborg (1688–1772), demonstrated. Swedenborg – 'the Buddha of the North' as Balzac later called him in *Seraphita* – was the prophet of a theosophic system, in which God was Divine Man, from whom the two worlds of nature and spirit emanated, and William Blake was only one of those who found his esoteric biblical exegesis irresistibly compelling. Though the Lutheran Church declared him a heretic in 1769, and proceedings were initiated against Anders Knöss, the dean of Skara (the oldest see in Sweden), for propagating his doctrines, Gustavus III would not give up his interest in the subject.

Yet these manifestations of the occult were increasingly at a remove from Church establishments. The bulk of their clergy were uncomfortable with such cabbalistic spirituality on the fringes of orthodoxy or an excessive proclamation of the religion of the heart. It helps to explain why in the Church of England, a communion that was still hesitant about Methodism, low-church 'enthusiasts' belonging to the Olney circle (they included the ex-slaving captain, the Revd John Newton and his friend, the poet William Cowper) had a restricted impact within the establishment, rather more over the medium term on nonconformists beyond it. Anglican Evangelicalism was only making a beginning in the 1780s through Charles Simeon in Cambridge and, though there were important converts including William Wilberforce, it would not be for another decade at least before its impact was felt, partly because so many in the hierarchy found its emotive emphasis on sin and regeneration tasteless rather than theologically unsound.

Formal and less formal worship

Evangelicals valued extempore prayers, long, emotionally charged sermons and relatively unstructured services, and the growing popularity of this style of worship within European Protestantism showed how much a rational belief system mattered less than a stable one, in a world where disease, warfare and harvest failure were still the everyday lot of millions of people. But one should not exaggerate the decline of more formal patterns of worship. That vision of stability offered by the Churches in liturgically structured services within the Catholic, Orthodox, Anglican and Lutheran traditions was a powerful counterpoint to the disharmony and randomness of so many ordinary lives. They might not always understand the theological niceties, but the vast majority of Europeans were more than content to live and die within Christianity's comforting rhythms, and would strive to retain them when they were threatened by revolutionary upheaval later in the century. Liturgy could help define nationality. Croats alone in the west had retained a vernacular liturgy which set them apart from other Latin Catholics and ensured the retention of a unique identity.

One should not underestimate the extent to which liturgical observances generated their own spiritual intensity in a way that was accessible to many kinds of worshippers, although a sizable section of Protestants had always rejected such forms as primarily unscriptural. Their numbers did not diminish in the later eighteenth century. The psychological comfort of belonging to 'a gathered congregation' and professing a hardline Calvinist creed was the preferred option of many Protestants. It could still find minority expression within Anglicanism and other mainstream formularies – indeed, there was a Calvinist revival within the Church of England from the 1770s pioneered by the Revd Augustus Toplady (d. 1778), author of the famous hymn 'Rock of Ages' – but was mainly expressed by self-sufficient Baptists, Congregationalists and Methodists loyal to George Whitefield and Lady Huntingdon who had no truck with either the predominant Arminian theology of the century or the enlightenment belief in mankind's own independent ameliorative capacity. Other churchgoers within a Calvinist tradition – in Amsterdam, Geneva, London and other centres – were moving towards a non-Trinitarian theology and a commitment to earthly progress that often set them at odds with governments as well as Athanasian Christians. They deployed millenarian language to commend political reform in the present in a manner that many artisans, shopkeepers, clerks and small businessmen found immensely compelling. In this context the language of 'enthusiasm' could be applied to secular purpose to advocate the widening of the political oligarchy running Geneva or the extension of the parliamentary franchise in Britain.

Religious benevolence

Arguments over metaphysical niceties were subordinated to a generally distilled Christian benevolence that emphasised usefulness in society and pleased enlightenment theorists. Alexander Gerard (1728–95), professor of divinity at King's College, Aberdeen, declared that 'The great end of religion, doubtless, is to fit men for eternity; but it likewise fits them for all the duties of the present life', and such remarks were commonplace.[15] Most communions advocated the exercise of unwearying charity towards the outcasts and deprived in society, with the Church of England and the Pietists leading the way in urging their membership to recall that Christians would be known by their 'fruits'. Charitable giving by religious institutions reached new heights in the Spanish Church. In the 1780s the bishop of Málaga put aside half his annual income for poor relief, while in Seville, where Archbishop Delgado y Venegas was in possession from 1776 to 1781, the archdiocese distributed 23,000 bushels of wheat to peasants whose crops had been destroyed by hailstones. The massive expansion in hospitals, charitable institutions and schools across Europe owed much to this practical emphasis. There were charitable bequests to the poor, the endowment of voluntary hospitals for expectant mothers and the infirm (twenty-six in England by 1775, mostly outside the aegis of the established Church), and relief when plague or harvest failed. In Catholic France, evidence from last wills and testaments indicates the growth of an 'enlightened piety' in which testators were less concerned about having Masses said for the repose of their souls than making bequests for the disadvantaged such as destitute children and foundling hospitals. Everywhere the laity were encouraged to help out where they could, with figures such as Jonas Hanway (1712–86) held up as the cynosure of the age in late eighteenth-century England, one of the founders of the Marine Society (1756) for the relief of indigent sailors, and the reformer of the foundling hospital, a role model for all those who nursed a Christian concern for the unfortunate. He had many imitators in the practical expression of Christianity, and not just on the grand scale. The future political radical, Horne Tooke, when an Anglican priest, developed a healing ministry for those who could not afford an apothecary. Having studied the works of Hermann Boerhaave and learnt to compound some rudimentary medicines, he set up a little dispensary at his parsonage house. Benevolent initiatives were clerically encouraged but not coerced, and presupposed that churchgoers could discern for themselves the Gospel basis for it. In the longer term, however, there was a price to be paid by the Churches for encouraging these trends to good works, as religious and charitable impulses began to uncouple by around 1790.

Moralists were quick to condemn the motives of those whose practical Christianity was underpinned by the hope of personal salvation;

---

[15] A. Gerard, 'The Influence of Piety on the Public Good', in *The Scotch Preacher* (1775–89), 311, quoted in Ian D. L. Clark, 'From Protest to Reaction: The Moderate Regime in the Church of Scotland, 1752–1805', in N. T. Phillipson and Rosalind Mitchison (eds.), *Scotland in the Age of Improvement* (Edinburgh, 1970), 200–24, at 207.

enlightenment thinkers argued that fellow-feeling to another in distress was justification enough for charity without the bestower's primary concern being his own redemption. It was part of a critical perception in some quarters, whereby commitment to revealed religion assumed an antisocial dimension; it was held to exhaust personal energies which some critics contended might be more constructively employed to the social good. It nevertheless remained rare for commentators to make a serious distinction between religious commitment and the social good; rather, active Christianity conferred social benefits. Thus many ministers of the Kirk were drawn to serve in the Highland missions of the Society for the Propagation of Christian Knowledge and the socially beneficial projects it encouraged in the aftermath of Jacobitism, among them demographic research and land surveys. It was inspired by contemporary influence of civil humanism and sensibility as well as older roots in a traditional Presbyterian discourse of social regeneration.

Spirituality exhausted and renewed

The benevolent emphasis could lead to dogmatic distrust and spiritual thinness, and the period from 1750 to 1790, like others at all stages of the Christian era, saw some currents of religious expression abate while others gathered momentum. Later Jansenism, for instance, turned into a political reforming movement in Spain and Italy patronised by many higher clergy, and thus adapted itself for secular use with, for instance, a stress on a consensual basis to government. As a strictly religious phenomenon, late Jansenism remains understudied. In its original neo-Augustinian format, it had demanded moral rigour as well as personal piety from Catholics as an edifying alternative to what was disparaged as the casuistry and ethical laxness of its Jesuit opponents. The dissolution of the Society in 1773 may have removed Jansenism's *raison d'être*; it left intact the disciplined spirituality that still looked to the long-dissolved religious community at Port-Royal for inspiration. However, those who could strictly be described as Jansenist were few and far between in late *ancien régime* France. In securing the destruction of the Jesuits, the followers of Arnauld and Quesnel may have had their revenge for the Bull *Unigenitus* (1713), but their devotional preferences had never found wide favour among either clergy or laity. Jansenism's view of fallen mankind was too bleak for later eighteenth-century tastes, its moral precision was exactly the kind of emphasis wherewith the opponents of revealed religion could exploit the discrepancies between precepts and practice, and its emotional containment offered nothing to a generation reared on Rousseau or country dwellers who associated religious renewal with missionary visits combining fervent preaching and dramatic display.

There had been a moment in the early 1730s when French Jansenism had looked like opening up a popular dimension. That was when the tomb of the deacon Pâris in the Saint-Médard cemetery had been associated with convulsionary miracles that had drawn the crowds and worried Cardinal Fleury's government. But the moment had come and gone. Half a century later, Jansenism as a theological expression remained a minority option for lay men and women, to be found in the pattern of religious observance experienced in cities such as Auxerre and Lyon where it had once been patronised heavily by the clergy; as a political phenomenon, it had an extended life, as the mid-century disputes betweeen Louis XV and the *parlements* showed.[16] Outside France, in the hands of reforming monarchs, ministers and bishops Jansenism still possessed some elite appeal, but as an agent of institutional rather than dogmatic change, becoming a device to refashion Church structures so that they better reflected the imagined ideals of primitive Christianity.

The real signs of religious renewal in the three decades before 1790 were to be found among Protestants: Methodists in England and Wales, and Pietists in Germany, Holland and North America, although the two movements had long mutually inspired each other, both linking the salvation of the individual with the transformation of the wider society, an agenda that paralleled more secular enlightenment initiatives. Critics might carp at 'the singular phenomenon of a man who, by the means of fanaticism, would lead us to the simplicity of the primitive church',[17] but a Zinzendorf (the butt of this censure) or a Wesley had struck a deep chord. In the Dutch states of Deventer and Overijessel, Pietism renewed lay spirituality sufficiently for new conventicles to be formed, although, like their Methodist counterparts in England, worshippers retained their membership of their existing (Calvinist) church.

By 1760 Methodism was an established force in British life, its call to inner conversion and spiritual renewal no longer shocking in its novelty. The often unaccountable physical symptoms induced among those caught up in events were becoming much less common. At Everton, Cambridgeshire, there was a mini-revival between 1758 and 1760, which led to converts turning very red or almost black. John Wesley thought it genuine after three visits, but the Everton manifestations gradually ceased, one of the last such phenomena in the Methodist awakening. Their cessation did nothing to reduce the wider popularity of Methodism;

---

[16] See below, pp. 128–9.
[17] [John Mills], *Essays Moral, Philosophical, and Political* (London, 1772), 64.

in fact it had the opposite effect as religious 'enthusiasm' became more socially acceptable, part of a wider process within which sensibility and emotional expressiveness were both permissible and fashionable. John Wesley himself would have seen little resemblance between the rapturous outpourings any newly redeemed sinner might wish to offer to the throne of grace and the emotional self-cultivation of Rousseau's readers as they thrilled to texts such as the *Rêveries du promeneur solitaire* (published posthumously in 1782). Wesley continued to treat the world as his parish, travelling thousands of miles annually within the British Isles, and preaching outdoors less from necessity than the impossibility of accommodating all those who wanted to hear him from assembling in their parish church. His combination of extempore prayers and sermons calling for repentance and renewal brought crowds of working men and women from all backgrounds to listen and to go away both chastened and uplifted. Methodism was extraordinarily popular with women, a reflection perhaps of Wesley's willingness to involve them in the movement. No less than 57.8 per cent of the English membership was female in the 1760s.

Historians are much more cautious about identifying women and artisans as necessarily marginalised and ignored by the established Church of England, an organisation once judged hobbled in its outreach by parochial structures which inadequately corresponded to shifts in population. The paradox was that Wesley, who to his dying day never forgot he was an Anglican priest and insisted that his followers remain loyal communicants *within* the Church of England, willingly authorised operations *outside* its structures, giving early Methodism a flexibility and a simplicity unconstrained by canon law. Its uncompromising evangelical insistence elicited an inner, heartfelt response, which enriched the lives of the scores of thousands who heard Wesley and tried to act on his words. Religious externals they took for granted, but Wesley promised them something new, and so they avidly enrolled as class members (as he organised his 'people called Methodists'). He offered them not liturgy, but watch nights and love feasts, all the paraphernalia of revivalist religion, not to mention the chance to show their talents as lay preachers. In search of the salvation Wesley implored them to seek, converts like James Hall of Boridge near Manchester were ready to endure knowing taunts from other villagers along the lines of, 'Tell us what the Methodists do in their dark meetings, when they put out the candles?'.[18] The joke was wearing thin by the 1780s as Methodism became respectable.

---

[18] *Arminian Magazine* 16 (1793), 68, quoted in G. M. Ditchfield, *The Evangelical Revival* (London, 1998), 75.

4. Pews and east-end arrangements in an eighteenth-century Anglican interior.

By that date, cordiality marked the mutual response of Methodists and Anglicans who, after all, were members of the same church. Wesley was scrupulous about asking permission to preach once he arrived in a parish. It was increasingly accorded, and Wesley's own high church background and antipathy to the rebellious American colonists did him no harm in easing his way as he travelled. Some clergy, such as Henry Venn in Huddersfield and John Fletcher in Madeley, both rapidly industrialising areas, made their churches regional centres for Methodism and kept in close contact with Wesley; he relied increasingly on the efforts of such disciples as the limitations of age crept upon him. By the 1780s, the first signs of Methodist institutionalisation were clear, with its annual conference (formalised since its beginnings in the early 1740s) and network of circuits and chapels. The movement was reaching maturity with a dynamic that was impelling it beyond the Church of England, a process Charles deplored and John regretted but did little to stop. Indeed actions such as his own, non-episcopal consecration of ministers and superintendents for North America in 1784 encouraged the parting of the ways. He died in 1791 still urging Methodists – there were 72,000 affiliated members that year – to stay inside the established Church but, without his controlling hand, they went their own way during the revolutionary decade, just as numbers reached a record highpoint.

Wesley had been influenced early in life by Pietism, which set the dominant tone within Protestantism in central Europe. By the late eighteenth century, it was nearly a century old and had long been domesticated within German Lutheranism, and produced offshoots in Holland, Scandinavia and Switzerland. It had not entirely lost its capacity for spiritual creativity. This could be found in communities such as Herrnhut, founded on the estate of Count Zinzendorf (1700–60), whose members became the Moravian Brethren, and also among the so-called Radical Pietists. They were especially strong in small sovereign territories like Sayn-Wittgenstein and Ysenburg-Büdingen, where princely protection was readily extended. The Moravians were sufficiently organised by the mid-century for their members to disperse into the New World, where their religion of the heart had played a crucial role in the Great Awakening of the 1740s, one which has to be seen as fitting in to a pattern within the faith, witnessed, for instance, in the Pietist movement of the later seventeenth century and, indeed, in earlier pre-Pietist movements. Such revivalism, an undeniable sign of spiritual good health, both inside Lutheranism and among separatists, produced its distinctive fault-lines, though these had largely ceased to cause much dissension, partly because of Pietism's perennial capacity to escape confessional supervision, its endorsement of toleration and the emphasis among its protagonists on salvation as a priority over Church politics. It also possessed a hard-edged intellectual quality that in the first half of the century made the University of Halle an educational model imitated across Germany, and in the second informed the philosophy of Immanuel Kant.

Like Methodism, the Pietist emphasis was on awakening the believer to inner spiritual life. That was to be done within the framework of Christian orthodoxy, but without letting dogma obscure fresh insights into religious truth, as God was believed to disclose them to the individual soul. Hence heresy – especially doubts about Christ's divinity – resurfaced. Not all Pietists accepted such deviations. They were not tolerated in Halle, but in Tübingen in south-west Germany, another Pietist centre, action was rarely taken if heterodoxy was minimally publicised. All Pietists emphasised that conversion and salvation were inward gifts of grace. These found external expression in the *Praxis pietatis*, the Pietistic stress on the substantiation of piety through education, benevolence towards the poor, sobriety and personal morality, values inculcated within family life by prayer and scripture readings. No fewer than than 3 million Bibles had been distributed before 1800 by the Canstein Bible Institute, and their importance in sustaining the good health of German Pietism can hardly be underestimated.

Elite religious interests

Religious renewal in Reformation and Counter-Reformation Europe had depended critically for its prosperity on the active endorsement of the nobility and landed elite but, after 1680, the personal interest of these groups in militant and mystic expressions of faith began to be less noticeable. There were exceptions. The nobility of the Austrian Netherlands remained exceptionally devout. 'Here', it was noted of Brussels in 1791, 'the greatest blend with the meanest in all the services which are called religious, however jealous of rank and superiority in civil and social life.'[19] The same could not be said of France. If younger members of the landed elites (especially women) were readily attracted to the new Rousseauian sensibility, it did little to encourage a more intensive expression of Christianity. Jean Quéniart's studies of the Breton nobility indicate that even in that orthodox province, the declining elite interest in books on Christian apologetics and controversies was forcing French booksellers to diversify their holdings by 1789; it was the same story in other areas, leading Daniel Roche to conclude that 'if it is difficult to conclude that there was a fundamental transformation in religious attitudes, there are important indicators of religious detachment among the nobility as a whole'.[20] These were important changes in religious behaviour, but fell well short of outright abandonment of the faith. Open commitment to unbelief remained rare, and funerals could offer occasions for ostentatious displays of aristocratic wealth and heraldic pride within an obviously Christian context. In Paris and the provincial centres of France, fashionable society was well represented at services. On the outer circle of the royal family, Philippe-Egalité's father-in-law, the duc de Penthièvre, noted his communions in his journal, and great noble families such as the Aguesseau, Aiguillon, and Montyon remained Christian.

There can be no denying the conventional elite attachment to upholding existing Church structures – whose upper reaches were filled with members of noble families – and the teachings associated with them, if only as an agency of patronage and social control. In much of Protestant

---

[19] John Owen, *Travels into Different Parts of Europe in the Years 1791 and 1792* (2 vols., London, 1796), vol. I, 16, letter iv.
[20] D. Roche, *Les Républicains des lettres. Gens de culture et lumières aux XVIIIe siècle* (Paris, 1988), 98.

Europe – England, Scotland and Prussia particularly – Church patronage was largely in the hands of the nobility and had been since the Reformation. In the duchy of Milan, that laboratory of enlightened government, the Lombard patricians controlled most places inside the Church (including the archbishopric itself) in a manner that corresponded to much of Italy and Catholic Europe as a whole. The obligations this control entailed could be exercised diligently and generously, as the many churches constructed or repaired at the personal cost of landlords between 1750 and 1790 reminds us. Voltaire himself endowed the parish church at Ferney on the French–Swiss frontier and encouraged his household to attend services just as his campaign of 'écrasez l'infâme!' against institutional religion reached its peak in the 1760s; Edward Gibbon, the great Roman historian, angered the Anglican clergy by his treatment of the rise of Christianity in volume I of the *Decline and Fall of the Roman Empire*, but his admiration for the late Roman aristocracy – 'enlightened' pagans disinterestedly attending temple worship to set an example to their social inferiors – had many echoes in 1776, the year of publication.

The Christian insistence on the subordination of civic virtue to personal salvation was one which did not endear itself to the landed elite, and they were familiar enough with the countervailing Ciceronian political ideal to make them watchful of attempts by the Churches to intrude spiritual priorities too forcefully into the public arena. Noblemen were better educated than previously, and had often imbibed a casual anticlericalism they were not frightened to display. 'We know as much as the priests do about the attributes of God,' declared the marquis d'Argenson in mid-century.[21] This proclamation of universal access to religious truths went with an unwillingness to permit the Church freedom of political manoeuvre, to ensure that its pretensions to regulate society through, for instance, the Church courts were kept in check. Such a determination inspired the resistance of the Paris *parlement* to Louis XV in the 1760s.

At the close of the eighteenth century, the model of the courtier as devout layman in the best tradition of the Counter-Reformation was hard to find. Most of Louis XVI's ministers, for instance, could not be called pious. The spiritual forms of sociability so attractive to the aristocracy in previous generations, the confraternities for instance, had a reduced appeal immediately before the French Revolution when Christian observance was often reduced to external practice. It may be that the predominantly restrained, ethical content of services diverted spiritual energies into non-Christian outlets, or that the majority of noblemen considered that public

---

[21] Quoted in Maxime Leroy, *Histoire des idées sociales en France* (Paris, 1946–54), vol. I, 84.

expressions of religious intensity detracted from their position at the apex of the social hierarchy. Anglicanism, too, was hard pressed for aristocratic role models in the later eighteenth century, and the novelist Samuel Richardson's Sir Charles Grandison was a fictional paragon who wanted for imitators in the polite world. There were high-society converts such as the 2nd earl of Dartmouth, a member of Lord North's (his half-brother) cabinet, and one famously characterised by the poet William Cowper – himself another Evangelical member of the elite – as 'one that wears a coronet and prays'.[22] But such piety was too close to eccentricity for other peers: Dartmouth's support for field preachers helped earn him the nickname of 'the Psalm-Singer'. There were other pious noblemen. In Scotland, the selection of the earl of Leven and Melville, high commissioner to the General Assembly of the Kirk in 1783, brought to the fore a leading member of the Popular party, one whose father had supported Whitefield in his visits to Scotland, and whose wife was one of Whitefield's converts. An eirenic, undogmatic Protestantism was religion enough for the majority of British peers and gentry, one not calculated to infringe norms of politeness culturally dominant throughout the century in which concern for spiritual good-health could be deemed a manifestation of ill-breeding.

It was among some of the wives and widows of the nobility, ladies on the model of Louis XVI's aunts, Mesdames Adelaide and Sophie, or Georgiana, 1st Countess Spencer (mother of the vivacious Whig beauty, the 5th duchess of Devonshire) and Elizabeth Montagu (society hostess and champion of Shakespeare and the English stage against Voltaire) that the spirit of devotion persisted at the highest levels of society. French noblewomen went on buying books of a devotional nature in a higher proportion than their husbands, fathers and brothers. Some ladies went further still. Viscountess Glenorchy in Scotland, a convert of the Revd Rowland Hill, a leading English Evangelical, admired Wesley and Whitefield to such distraction that she abandoned social life for religion. The formidable Selina, countess of Huntingdon, also converted to Methodism in 1739, and was wealthy enough to set up a college at Trevecca for training evangelical (Calvinist) ministers loosely affiliated to the Church of England. But she was exceptional in her unhesitating occupancy of the public sphere: a single-minded noblewoman dubbed 'Pope Joan' for her pains by a sniggering Horace Walpole.

Aristocratic predilections for gambling, drinking, horse-racing and other forms of dissipation attracted far more public notice in western

---

[22] John D. Baird and Charles Ryskamp (eds.), *The Poems of William Cowper*, vol. I, *1748–1782* (2 vols., Oxford, 1980–95), 290: 'Truth', line 378.

Europe than the fulfilment of their religious duties, leading the pious and well-meaning George III in Britain to issue in 1787 a royal proclamation 'for the encouragement of piety and virtue and for the preventing or punishing of vice, profaneness and immorality'. It was aimed principally, but by no means exclusively, at the nobility. The king led the way in sabbath-keeping by abolishing Sunday court dinners, and made it very clear that he deplored the predilection of the wife of Archbishop Frederick Cornwallis (Canterbury, 1768–83) for card parties and routs. Louis XVI similarly headed a reaction in French high society from the 1770s against the prevalence of vice and libertinism. For scions of the nobility of his generation (he was born in 1754 and ascended the throne aged only twenty), his uxoriousness, personal piety and clean habits made for a powerful role model, especially in conjunction with the fashionable Rousseau-inspired spiritual values. So, by 1790 in both Britain and France, the ready equation of the nobility with dissipation was only half the story. Such departure as there was from a conventional attachment to religious orthodoxy in the top ranks of society between 1750 and 1800 was unusual, a departure from earlier – and later – practice. Most country gentlemen in England, like most *hobereaux* in Brittany or *hidalgos* in Castile, were fiercely attached to the practices and beliefs of their traditional religious culture, ones that underpinned their own high social and political standing. William Pitt the Elder told his undergraduate nephew Thomas in January 1754 to 'hold fast by this sheet-anchor of happiness, religion'.[23] The sentiment may have been conventional but it was no less sincere for that.

The religion of the 'middling sort'

The middle ranks of European society took the lead in inspiring and responding to new forms of religiosity and spirituality characterised by emotional intensity. This diverse group had an inclination to self-audit that the confessional box and scripture reading had variously satisfied since the sixteenth century, and it had not been found incompatible with either wealth creation or social respectability. Those attitudes had not changed in the pre-revolutionary era. Attornies, notaries, *rentiers*, guild members and shop owners remained the backbone of German Pietism in the 1760s and 1770s. They bought religious books, read sermons in profusion and looked for the hand of God at work in the world around them, and their Anglican counterparts did much the same.[24] They were determined to uphold their rights under the law against encroachment

---

[23] British Library [BL], Add. MS. 69288, no. 39.
[24] David Vaisey (ed.), *The Diary of Thomas Turner 1754–1765* (Oxford, 1985).

by either the Church or the nobility. Thus Thomas Turner, the Sussex grocer, enjoyed parish office as churchwarden, and other small townsmen like him across Protestant Europe were, as Church Elders or overseers of the poor, the agents for allocating and distributing poor relief – anything that brought participation in parish management. The Churches were only too happy to enlist the laity at this social level in decision-making.

In Paris the middling sort competed among each other to obtain leadership roles such as churchwardenships, membership of the vestry or of the *compagnies de charité* with responsibility for poor relief shared with the *curé*. Jansenism appealed to such men from its emphasis on collective rather than absolutist authority in most institutional contexts. Whether Jansenist or not, the Catholic bourgeoisie were increasingly the backbone of the faith. Jacques Solé, with reference to France, talks of this social group and their 'simple, unaffected piety, attentive to civic duties of the kingdom, one nourished by holy scripture, concerned for the inner life of the layman' but it has an application across western and central Europe between 1750 and 1790.[25]

In the Austrian Netherlands, the middling sort's patronage of cults of the saints and the Virgin, confraternities and relics helped keep popular religious attendance at seventeenth-century levels in Brussels and other centres until the 1780s; then a combination of political unrest and Jansenism contributed to a sense that devotion must be purged of the ridiculous and the irreverent. In Spain, this constituency formed the core membership of the *cofradías*, pious associations (Seville had more than a thousand) that marked the major feast days with ceremonial splendour. Numbers slowly tailed off in Spain. By the 1780s the Catalan authorities found it hard to persuade the guilds to participate in elaborate liturgical ceremonies, not because of religious indifference but from a readiness to hearken to the Church's criticism of popular religious excesses. However, in Portugal the confraternities (*irmandades*) were still numerous, and social divisions mattered: office holders and artisans tended to meet in different *irmandades*. The picture overall suggests that if the confraternities had slipped somewhat in the affections of urban professionals and traders, these key groups remained committed to Catholicism. In most states, they were the ones who invited the religious Orders to help the renewal of urban congregations by sponsoring particular devotions, supported parochial missions, encouraged good preachers, and helped make the Jubilee of 1775 proclaimed by Pius VI a successful celebration of Catholic culture that historians have too easily ignored.

[25] Jacques Solé, *La Révolution en questions* (Paris, 1988), 23.

Just as aristocratic precedence (and comfort) was recognised by up-holstered private pews in places of worship, so municipal pride was as much in evidence in the seating arrangements of urban parish churches. The mayor and corporations of countless European towns had their own stalls, a testimony to corporate power and inherited tradition. Citizens and clergy socialised on an informal basis within urban networks, and used occasions such as Rogationtide to express more formally their sense of common place, purpose and privilege. Such manifestations could take a particular edge in eighteenth-century Ireland where a confessional state benefited·a minority. Access for non-Catholics to guilds and civic bodies was restricted (because of the Test and Corporation Acts, under which all holders of public office had to take communion according to the An-glican rite once a year to qualify), so that Protestant members sometimes had less wealth and property than their Catholic neighbours, and were prepared to stress confessional identity to emphasise their superiority within the state. Much the same was true in Nîmes, where Catholics used their corporate monopoly to keep at bay the Protestant entrepreneurs of the city and its hinterland. Such defensive actions show the limits of tol-eration in pre-revolutionary society. Thanks to the Occasional Confor-mity Acts in England, Congregationalists, Baptists and Quakers (often merchants and manufacturers) were not precluded from participating in municipal life, and their activities in cities including Bristol, Norwich and Nottingham often alarmed Anglican zealots, especially when many 'rational' dissenters took up parliamentary reform and the cause of the rebellious American colonists in the 1770s. Most traders in Ireland – predominantly Catholic or Presbyterian – were excluded from the polit-ical process, as were the Protestant bourgeois of southern French cities, including Montauban and Montpellier as well as Nîmes. These minori-ties nursed a sense of social and political injustice which confessional faiths were reluctant to acknowledge.

Whatever their religion, the urban elites were unhindered from join-ing Masonic lodges, though it is important not to exaggerate the appeal. The 50,000 French masons in 1789 were a tiny part of the population, still vastly outnumbered by those who belonged to confraternities (of course, many bourgeois belonged to both). The commitment of ma-sons to rational benevolence was entirely compatible with contempo-rary clerical injunctions despite the fact that the moral regeneration of society would be undertaken with reduced reference to organised reli-gion. Another potential cause of unease for Catholic masons – the papal condemnation of their craft in Bulls of 1738 and 1751 – was offset by the considerable number of priests among their fellow members and the patronage of royal families in most states. Their presence is a reminder that the links between Freemasonry and a secularising Enlightenment were far less axiomatic than some historians have assumed.

In Germany, denominational boundaries counted for little, undoubtedly acting as a dissolvent of confessional antagonisms in wider society. Elsewhere, masons took religious allegiances into the lodges with them. In Ireland some lodges passed by-laws specifically excluding Catholics from membership. Others, like that patronised by the outstanding general, Richard, 1st Lord Donoughmore (1756–1825) (in favour of Catholic emancipation), had many wealthy papist members. As the masons formally admitted no social distinctions, the chance for the urban elite to acquaint itself with its social superiors flattered family self-esteem and was of immense value in the patronage stakes. Though some lodges apparently attracted notoriety for a very public commitment to egalitarianism, for most initiates into the craft a combination of social mobility and conviviality was the main incentive for joining a lodge. The *Illuminati*, founded in 1776 by an academic at the University of Ingolstadt, Adam Weishaupt (1748–1830), were more controversial, professedly anticlerical (though not without clergy members) and bent on eliminating ecclesiastical power in Bavaria. But they had few bourgeois sympathisers, and membership of masonic lodges before the early 1790s in the Austrian Empire was not considered politically dangerous. So the Catholic Church had no choice but to go with the current and make what use it could of masonic spirituality, however uncomfortable it was with the deistic undertones of it all.

Christianity and the masses in countryside and town

Masonic social accessibility seldom extended to the mass of the population: the lodges founded in rural areas of Ireland shortly before the 1798 Rebellion numbered servants amongst their members, although this seems exceptional on present knowledge. It was at this social level that it was hardest for the clergy to give fresh Christian purpose to the lives of men and women burdened by agricultural toil and weariness. They were the despair of the *philosophes*, who saw them as an obstacle to secular progress, a passive constituency sunk in superstition, in thrall to the Churches. The clerical angle was actually not dissimilar. They would have admitted the underlying loyalty of the rural population to their parish church, but with attendance undertaken as part of socialisation rather than from a desire to receive the sacrament and hear the Gospel preached. Two centuries on from the Protestant and

Catholic Reformations, Church leaders still fretted at the perceived extent to which countrymen remained 'un-Christianised', mistaking superstition for Christian observance.

'Popular Christianity' was the religion practised – or, rather, lived out – by the majority of the people, smallholders, peasants and landless labourers as opposed to the clericalised version of the faith. Innumerable folk rituals survived, less in competition with Christianity than as a supplement to it. The discrepancies were perhaps less of a problem for Orthodoxy and the Protestant denominations. The Orthodox Churches expected there to be a divide between clergy and a largely illiterate laity that could best be bridged by a priest living among his people. On the opposite side of the spectrum, it was a fundamental premise of Reformation theology that Catholicism was nothing but an elaborate fraud imposed on the population to enrich and empower a corrupt priesthood. That uncompromising assertion had not been watered down among staunch independent congregations in England, Wales, Germany and Switzerland, who preached the need for inner conversion and had no time for hierarchical, episcopal structures. For them Catholicism *was* intrinsically superstitious. Protestants had a vernacular liturgy (if they had one at all), and an emphasis on Bible reading to guard the faithful against error, but those were frail barriers in themselves. For instance, Protestant intellectuals liked to argue that their communions had no truck with the diabolic. In 1766 Ferdinand Sterzinger unleashed the so-called 'Bavarian War of the Witches' in a speech alleging that Catholic monasteries condoned the forces of magic and that the whole Church sponsored belief in witches. In fact, it was the scriptural support for witches that helped sustain popular belief in their existence long after witchcraft ceased to be a statutory crime in Britain after 1736; individuals used their family Bible opened at random quite regularly to decide on conduct, the so-called *sortes Biblicae*. Methodism did not disdain these irrational elements in popular culture. Its belief in diabolical possession and exorcism dovetailed closely with popular perceptions.

Anglican and Lutheran concern about religious ignorance and popular distortions of the faith tended to be focused on remote upland areas such as Snowdonia, the Yorkshire Dales and the English Lake District, where parishes were large and populations used to acting on their own devices with minimal clerical oversight. Thick dialects were impenetrable enough to university-educated Anglican clergy, but were nothing compared to the swathes of the Welsh and Irish countryside where the English language was neither spoken nor written. There folk customs were deeply rooted and seen by critics as inimical to correct belief. One commentator on Welsh life in about 1775 noted how the young people of Bangor spent

Sundays 'in dancing and singing to the harp and in playing tennis against the town hall'; elsewhere people would pass Saturday night in 'Singing Eves' (also involving the harp) and not come to service the next day. Heavily wooded areas in English lowland districts like the Forest of Dean or the New Forest also preserved cultures antipathetic to clerical preferences. Folk customs and the religious calendar were hard to separate even in lowland areas. Oak Apple Day, 29 May, was marked by such jollifications as contending for the oak bough from the church steeple at Finedon, Northamptonshire: it should be abolished as 'very disorderly' noted John English Dolben, the son of the local squire, in 1792.[26] Confronted with such survivals, many historians have found it useful to think in terms of a 'long Reformation'. Certainly Archbishop Secker of Canterbury (1758–68) was ceaselessly aware of how much remained to be done to win the hearts and minds of ordinary rural Anglicans to a true understanding of the faith, to complete the process initiated by the Tudor architects of the break with Rome. It was no coincidence that during his primacy relations between the hierarchy and the Methodists improved.

It was the Roman Catholic Church which was most concerned finally to 'Christianise' the countryside and eliminate 'superstitious' usages – in other words the subterranean culture of ordinary Catholics. In so doing, it would complete the objectives set out by the Tridentine fathers as long ago as the 1560s and, in Olwen Hufton's memorable phrase, 'harden the spirituality of the faithful'[27] by eliminating the riotous celebrations of dubious saints' days and pilgrimages to sites of pagan rather than Christian significance. Such a policy stoked up resentment and made the clergy's teaching ministry no easier. In Ireland, priests in the diocese of Ferns were banned in 1771 from acting 'the fairy doctor in any shape' by reading 'exorcisms or gospels over the already too ignorant'.[28] Bishops were anxious to resist popular pressure for the services of exorcism country people demanded on the slightest occasion, down to the excommunication of insects! In Italy in 1781 the archbishop of Ferrara laid down that he must be consulted in advance and, when he had agreed, the service must be held privately, during the day, and with more than one cleric present. Such injunctions also helped to diminish the Church's exposure to enlightenment ridicule, and fulfil the criteria laid out in the influential

---

[26] Northamptonshire Record Office, Finedon (Dolben) Collection 65/16, 29 May 1792.

[27] Olwen Hufton, 'The Reconstruction of a Church, 1796–1801', in G. Lewis and C. Lucas (eds.), *Beyond the Terror: Essays in French Regional and Social History, 1794–1815* (Cambridge, 1983), 21–52.

[28] Quoted in S. J. Connolly, *Religion, Law and Power: The Making of Protestant Ireland 1660–1760* (Oxford, 1992), 155.

Jansenist Lodovico Antonio Muratori's treatise *On a Well-ordered Devotion*.
By the late eighteenth century, monarchs as well as bishops were sympathetic to the project, and what had started life as a Catholic Reformation initiative had become an aspect of the Catholic Enlightenment, dear to Jansenists and classically embodied in the religious policies of Joseph II in the Austrian Empire and his brother Peter Leopold in Tuscany. It could involve risk to life and limb. The bishop of Pistoia and Prato (near Lucca), Scipione de Ricci, was one of those set on eliminating the cult of the Virgin Mary's girdle, causing the crowds to riot against the ban, burn his palace and force him to retire to Pisa. The abolition of time-honoured feast days meant the removal of holidays for working men from the calendar, so the imposition of this reform agenda was often deeply resented at parochial level, leading to superficial conformity while really loosening ties that bound Catholics to their Church. Such considerations were not enough to stop innumerable Catholic clergy from castigating the old ways, like Fr Matthew Horgan, parish priest of Blarney: 'Irish wakes, I say, are synonymous with everything profligate, wicked, wasteful and disgraceful to a Christian people, and every lover of religion, morality and good order should cooperate to abolish such a foul stain on the Irish character.'[29]

State support was often needed to achieve this end but was no guarantee of success. In 1786 peasant unrest forced the elector of Bavaria to restore ceremonies on feast days and abrogate the decree ordering work as usual on them. Popular aversion to imposed changes often made the parish clergy unwilling to obey to the letter episcopal instructions to enforce penances against parishioners who infringed the more disciplined approach, for instance by retaining a miraculous icon at one of the numerous shrines dedicated to the Virgin in Poland. In Alsace, cults recommended for abolition, like that of St Odile, the patroness of the province, persisted because the clergy were sensitive enough to register popular attachment to the festival.

Such men were well placed to appreciate that only a carefully directed teaching ministry would transform popular *mentalités* over the medium term and that rushing the process would be counter-productive. Local saints were as real as their neighbours to unsophisticated rustics, their help sought after in the trials and tribulations of everyday life. In France, it could be a woman washing in a local spring associated with an appearance of the Virgin, or invoking the aid of St John the Baptist in pregnancy on the basis that the executed saint would ensure the baby would be born head first. Small wax phalluses were carried by women as votive offerings

---

[29] Royal Irish Academy, MS. 12/M/11, p. 395, quoted in Kevin Whelan, '*The Tree of Liberty': Radicalism, Catholicism and the Construction of Irish Identity* (Cork, 1996), 27.

to the shrine of the Saints Cosmas and Damian in Isernia (in the Molise region of southern Italy) in the hope of ending their, or their husbands', sterility. The 'cure' involved spending the night near the altar. English antiquarians like Sir William Hamilton and Richard Payne Knight were fascinated by this Priapic survival, but it was only the most bizarre of a vast range of practices. As one historian, Hanns Gross, has said, 'Saints filled the role nowadays played by doctors, psychiatrists, priests, counsellors and insurance agents.' So, in areas such as southern Italy, when the clergy ordered them to cease offering prayers and *ex votos* to dubious saints, they were seen as interfering annoyingly in the domestic lives of their people. For there, 'everyone hath his favourite Saint on whom he places his sole reliance; dates all his good Fortune from him, and lays his ill Luck to the rest; whom, at every unfortunate Rub, he curses most heartily'.[30]

The lower class of Neapolitans decried saints who let them down. For them and for foreign vistors the annual liquefaction of St Januarius' blood was one of the sights of the city. Great things were expected from it. In 1765 Samuel Sharp 'overheard a woman declare that it must be owing to some Protestants in the church, that the miracle went on so slowly'.[31] Everywhere, clergy remained happy to bless bells as a protection against storms. In Catalonia, it was the custom for a man and woman from the village to stand as godparents when the blessing took place.

A higher proportion of Catholics than ever were familiar with the doctrines and teaching of the Church, yet were intent on retaining at least some of their familiar observances, of the sort likely to attract a *philosophe*'s sneers. At the great shrine of St Nicholas in Bari, the priest in 1777 still let down a silver bucket into the hole under the altar, where bones floated, and gave the water as a cure for sore eyes and stomach ailments. Such practices – and this was only one of the best known – afforded the faithful a comfort not to be lightly underestimated. Their persistence should not disguise the fact that an unprecedented level of 'Christianisation' had been achieved across most regions of Europe (by definition, predominantly rural) by 1750, as recent studies such as that by Philip Hoffman on Lyon have shown. The cessation of these practices reflected no diminution of clerical energies, or 'post-Tridentine syndrome', an entropy and lack of spirit shown from the late seventeenth century onwards of which Hanns Gross talks.[32] Episcopal visitations continued much as before in

---

[30] [Sir William Young], *A Journal of a Summer's Excursion, by the Road of Montecassino to Naples, and from thence over all the Southern Parts of Italy, Sicily, and Malta; in the Year MDCCLXXII* (London, 1774?), 26.

[31] Samuel Sharp, *Letters from Italy, Describing the Customs and Manners of that Country, in the Years 1765, and 1766* (London, 1766), letter xxix, December 1765.

[32] Hanns Gross, *Rome in the Age of the Enlightenment: The Post-Tridentine Syndrome* (Cambridge, 1990).

the period down to the Revolution, but there was less work either for bishops or archdeacons to order on their return home. Pastoral energy was mainly directed to maintaining demanding standards, especially in the highly 'clericalised' dioceses of western France. These would, in the 1790s, refuse to give up their Tridentine Catholicism when challenged by regicidal republicans to do so.

Ministry among the urban masses had its own distinct problems, which the varied range of services in most town parishes did not always address. A survey of more than 600 Yorkshire parishes in the primary visitation of 1764 showed that in most centres of population there were two Sunday services and monthly communion, a practice reinforced by the growing numbers of Evangelical clergy; at St Mary's, Hull, there were two daily services, and three at Leeds parish church. But the churches in England and on the continent were vying with a range of competing attractions for attendance at Sunday services, especially among young men. And when they did appear, as Louis-Sébastien Mercier, author of the gossipy twelve-volume *Tableau de Paris* (1782–8), complained of youthful Parisian churchgoers, they were frequently restless, noisy and easily distracted. Festival days – with something more on offer than worship – were popular enough, but on Sunday the temptation to head for the tavern could become irresistible. The social pressure to do otherwise was so much weaker inside the towns for artisans and seasonal labourers in, for instance, the silk industry of Lyon; likewise, in the town of Clermont-de-Lodève, textile workers before the Revolution were notorious for their impiety and irregular Sunday attendance. Itinerants – pedlars, hawkers, postillions and the like – were widely suspected of impiety. The coachmen of Madrid (*calesineros*) were prohibited in 1768 from hanging around in groups near some churches because of their profanities and failure to respect the viaticum when it was taken through the streets. Seasonal migrants also came to town when harvest yields were low and bread prices soared, and were hard for the clergy to categorise as genuine parishioners. These were the anonymous faces in the urban crowds, haunting the unsavoury backstreets, often getting caught up in petty crime. There were few friends to established religion to be found in this milieu where anticlericalism thrived. A few brave spirits took up the challenge. Wesley's peripatetic evangelism brought hope and a clear Gospel message to the colliers of South Wales, Bristol and north-east England, while Catholic missions to towns on the continent could intensify the devotional life of the parish for generations to come. In both cases, they worked to stir up the heart, to match the revelation of the Gospel with an inner revelation that would lead to new spiritual life – as some compensation for an impoverished material one.

Varieties of worship on offer

At the heart of Church life in eighteenth-century Europe was public worship. Its rituals were immensely varied, a reflection not just of confessional divergence but the wider customs and cultures of the continent. The great cathedrals, amply staffed, offered a dignified and sometimes a lavish ceremonial in which liturgy and music combined to reflect the dignity of an institution carrying out its primary function of praising God; similar but simpler services could be found in parish churches from Ireland to Russia, from Sweden to Sicily. The spread of religious toleration in England had encouraged the construction of innumerable chapels – there were 356 for Methodists alone by 1784 – where dissenters (usually Protestant) from the established Churches could gather to sing hymns, pray and listen to long sermons or, in the case of the Quakers, wait in silence on the Spirit. In some English cities long established as nonconformist centres, contemporary buildings such as John Ivory's superb Octagon chapel (1754–6) in Norwich – 'the most elegant Meeting House in Europe', John Wesley called it – provide vivid testimony to the increasing social status of its users while, by the 1780s, even Catholics were confident enough to commission their own chapels for the first time since the Reformation. The result could be surprisingly opulent, such as Lulworth chapel in Dorset built for the Weld family or the neo-classical one at Wardour Castle designed by John Soane for the 8th Lord Arundell in 1788. Where churches continued to be unavailable, worshippers such as Methodists spilled over into barns and fields to praise the Lord, or took to the high peaks of the Cévennes like the Huguenots of the 'désert' in Languedoc.

Amid the variety of worship on offer, one salient point must be stressed: going to religious services was not an option. In Sweden the laity were legally obliged to attend Lutheran services, with the civil magistrates enforcing the rule rather than the clergy themselves. Church attendance was a basic foundation of asserting community identity, a duty of neighbourliness which, in rural districts at least, had no competition on a Sunday. Husbands frequently attended services as the leading representative of their household and, naturally, they would bring their wife, children and servants with them. It was very much a family occasion. In towns, fashionable congregations included Sunday morning worship as part of the social round. If they tired of the preacher they could look around to see who was present – and who was not – and enjoy the company of their friends after the service. Non-attendance on a Sunday without good cause was a dereliction of civic obligation and marked off an individual as irresponsible, a man (absentees were invariably male) on the margins, a likely troublemaker in other areas of local life and a probable drain on scarce poor law resources. In France, Easter communion was almost universally observed, an unprecedented phenomenon before the eighteenth century – or afterwards; performance of the rituals of baptism, confession, confirmation and extreme unction became more regular than ever before. Seasonal variations could play a large part in the overall pattern. As the *curé* of La Madeleine at Cambrai noted in 1781, 'almost everyone neglects instruction and catechism during the harvest'.[33] The picture elsewhere was less reassuring. In Ireland, probably less than half the total number of Catholics attended Sunday Mass regularly by the turn of the century. This was not due to penal laws discriminating in favour of the Church of Ireland; they were either disused or repealed. It was rather that a rising population was not matched by additional priests and the extra services they could offer.

Absenteeism was comparatively rare where a majority of the population belonged to an established Church: if devotion could be measured in terms of church attendance then the 1750–90 generation would score highly. Of course, external conformity assessed on the basis of how many people attended the main Sunday services was not a very accurate gauge of success or failure in guaranteeing that individual lives were conducted according to Gospel precepts. Throughout Europe, public worship for most men and women was prized because it allowed access to the sacraments, the authenticating mark of Christian profession and, as in baptism, an indispensable rite of passage for family members. The possibility of a baby dying without admission into the Church, which marking an infant with holy water in the triune name conferred, terrified parents in an age of high childhood mortality. The Churches registered these fears and permitted lay baptism *in extremis*, usually by a midwife. The future George III of England (1738–1820) had received it on 4 June 1738 in the first hours of life. For Catholics, extreme unction as death approached was a security towards salvation few would willingly deny themselves. It was no accident that the insistence of Archbishop Beaumont of Paris that this sacrament would be denied unless an individual possessed a *billet de confession* (in effect showing he or she was not a Jansenist) provoked a profoundly destabilising clash between Church and state in France in the 1750s. But this was an in-house dispute: the Churches had wearied of sacramental theology as a topic of inter-confessional controversy. Catholics and Orthodox were committed to seven, Protestants (including Anglicans) to two, holy communion and baptism.

[33] Archives départmentales du Nord, 3 G 2838, Enquête sur l'etat des paroisses, 1781, quoted in Gilles Deregnaucourt, *De Fenelon à la Révolution. Le clergé paroissial de l'Archevêché de Cambrai* (Lille, 1991), 153.

This was not a period in which the well-trodden battleground of eucharistic teaching was one any party felt inclined to fight over again. Instead, Catholics had gone on the defensive against *philosophe* criticism that sacraments such as the Mass were a form of magic foisted by priests on a gullible public to confirm their own authority. The insinuation was present at several points in the great *Encyclopédie* (and played its part in delaying its completion) and filtered out into more populist literature and from France spread into Spain and Italy. By comparison Protestant apologists, tending to accentuate the representational character of communion and baptism, were less vulnerable to enlightenment critiques. More striking than inter-confessional polemic was the emphasis placed on the individual making proper preparation for receiving communion, of making his confession (if he was a Catholic), of being charitably disposed to his neighbours, and cultivating the proper spirit of devotion. All the Churches encouraged this approach, and it was classically embodied in Samuel Johnson, the most important lay Anglican of the century, and in another high church sympathiser with strong sacramentalist views, the Revd John Wesley. Persuading ordinary parishoners, whether Catholic or Protestant, to receive the bread and, if non-Catholic, wine was not easily achieved. As one Norfolk cleric told a colleague in 1762: 'As to your intention of having a monthly Communion, I fear it is impracticable in a Place, where the Inhabitants are with difficulty persuaded to communicate, even at the great Festivals. But the little hopes I have of succeeding shall not discourage me from the attempt.'[34] Genevans seem to have had more success than Anglicans: the quarterly celebration of the sacrament in the city's two largest parishes were always crowded occasions.

There was no common ground between Catholics and Orthodox on one hand and Protestants on the other hand when it came to recognition of the intercessory role of the saints and the Virgin Mary in worship. Saints and national identities were bound up in ways that remain unexplored. In Hungary, the return of St Stephen's hand from Dubrovnik (Ragusa) in 1771 confirmed that the Ottoman threat was over and declaring 20 August a major national holiday gave new impetus to his cult. Mariology was fundamental to the Tridentine programme: it was no less the case in the later eighteenth century as the Catholic authorities pressed on with banishing minor local saints from the main altars in the parish churches in favour of approved subjects for veneration, notably the Virgin (and Holy Child) or the Holy Sacrament itself. Clergy encouraged observances that would reinforce the new emphasis, with some success. This helped to keep the membership of confraternities at a respectable level despite

---

[34] Revd John Hatch to Revd Charles Poyntz, 6 March 1762, BL Althorpe Papers, E.18.

new and competing forms of sociability. In Rhineland towns like Mainz, Coblenz and Cologne, processions and confraternities remained the core of popular religious life until the French invasion of the 1790s brought dechristianisation in its wake. In France, many confraternities survived until the Revolution, with at least a dozen in mid-eighteenth century Paris dedicated to the Eucharist; with their own chapels, their special services and – sometimes – uniforms they gave their members a strong sense of identity within the parish that went naturally with leadership roles. The suppression of the Jesuit Order did not hamper the appeal of joining the Marian congregations of laymen in much of Alsace, significantly an area where Lutheranism was strong. In Molsheim there were 400 members and rising in the 1780s. Across the Rhine in Bavaria, it has been estimated that at around 1790 one in two Munich families were involved with the congregations.

In the Catholic archdiocese of Cashel (Ireland) the rosary was said in most churches before Sunday Mass; it had an overwhelming popularity across Catholic Europe by 1800, and proved quite impossible for the French revolutionary armies and administrators to extirpate. Similarly, observation of the Stations of the Cross, which dated back to the fifteenth century, became widespread after Benedict XIV authorised its use in all parish churches. The cult of the Sacred Heart of Jesus also grew in appeal, with its own feast day authorised by the papacy in 1765. Targeted particularly at the uneducated, it caught on rapidly, a Tyrolian mission reporting: 'Already, the most Sacred Heart of the Redeemer is worshipped everywhere in the most intimate fashion; during the missions, the Heart draws forward its countless worshippers as if it were a throne full of grace and charity.'[35] It was temporarily banned during the 1780s in the Austrian Tyrol when the campaign against practices associated with the suppressed Jesuit Order was at its height, but sceptical authorities could not halt the Sacred Heart's spread through the Mediterranean world by the priests of the Lazarist mission. Bishop Tavira of Salamanca tried to do so in the 1780s without making any serious impact. It serves to reinforce Olwen Hufton's point that: 'everything we know about popular religion in the eighteenth century, everywhere in Europe, underscores its total revulsion for anything savouring of the Jansenist ethic'.[36]

Popular liking for the cult of the Sacred Heart meant it came to rival other longer-established religious celebrations and made festivals associated with it bustling occasions. In Spain crowds also flocked to the rites of flagellation associated with Lent – despite discouragement by the

---

[35] Quoted in Laurence Cole, 'Nation, Anti-Enlightenment, and Religious Revival in Austria: Tyrol in the 1790s', *Historical Journal* 43 (2000), 475–97, at 485.
[36] Olwen Hufton, *Privilege and Protest 1730–1789* (London, 1980), 187.

Spanish government under Charles III – that climaxed in the great processions of Holy Week. Such huge gatherings were a constant feature of continental Catholicism between 1750 and the French Revolution. As one British visitor in Toulouse noted at the end of 1788, 'you do not walk ten yards in the street but you are stopt by some Procession or other'.[37] Processions like that of the Black Virgin of the church of the Daraude, who was besought to act as an intercessor against fire, drought or sickness, were the means whereby the Church 'conquered' urban space in Toulouse and affirmed its presence in most other regional centres. Across Catholic Europe, the major festival of Corpus Christi in June brought every section of the population on to the streets. The procession at Barcelona in 1770 began with an eagle cavorting before the holy sacrament, then two giants who danced and leapt, then successively a mule, an ox, a dragon escorted by little devils, then a lion and flag, followed by other animals, then twenty-four kings in historic costume – apostles – and angels with musical instruments. Catholics were permitted to take to the streets even in Galata, a suburb of Ottoman Constantinople (the king of France was Protector of Catholics in the Turkish Empire), where the Holy Saturday procession with banners, candles, trumpets and stringed instruments attracted foreign ambassadors and their retinues.

Such Christian rituals were part of a continuing trend towards increasing the scope for lay participation in religious services, much as might be expected from a well-catechised laity. Extempore prayers were one of the attractions of English dissent, while in Anglican churches across the British Isles congregations had possessed the opportunity to join in the responses since the Reformation. What was new for Catholics was the increasing use of the vernacular in worship, for instance in reading the Old Testament and the Epistle during Mass (especially in France and Spain from the 1770s after the papacy had consented), a duty increasingly delegated by parish clergy to the lay members of the vestry. These opportunities did not lead in themselves to a new reverence and devotional sense among worshippers. Congregations could still be noisy, inattentive, easily distracted in a way that might be expected from an activity like church-going which only a tiny minority questioned let alone gave up. Yet a sense of behaviour appropriate to a sacred space was more widely disseminated than at any point in the Christian past.

Worship was essential to the process of defining identity in eighteenth-century Europe, corporate as well as individual. Ringing the church bells and a spate of civic services marked the Protestant calendar in Britain and Ireland throughout this period, and were given an additional filip

---

[37] 'R.W.C.', *Letters from France* (London, 1788), 8, quoted in John Lough, *France on the Eve of Revolution: British Travellers' Observations 1763–1788* (London, 1987), 153.

by Britain's victories in the long wars against France. Worship was central to those ceremonies and processions that characterised urban life and symbolised social unity under the crook of the Church. St Eloi's feast in Marseille (the patron of farriers) culminated in horse-racing, whose appeal crossed all social boundaries. The day started with coachmen, cabmen and postillions gathering outside the church of the Grands Augustins mounted on their horses, mules and asses with the priest going round sprinkling riders and beasts alike with holy water. The guilds and confraternities gave the impetus for these major urban spectacles combining the sacred and secular. In ordinary rural parishes everywhere (whether Catholic or Protestant), Rogationtide on the days preceding Ascension Day was habitually marked by 'beating the bounds' of the parish. It had value in providing a mental map of the parish for use in boundary disputes where no accurate surveys existed. Enclosure awards in England changed all that and drained the ritual of economic value to ratepayers. It often survived, as in Bath, as something of a tourist spectacle. On Ascension Day 1767:

In the afternoon the Minister and Parish went in Procession from the Church through Abbey Green . . . to Simpson's Rooms, then through Simpson's Walk to the River Avon, preceded by two tip-staves, about twenty Boys with Rods in their hands in pairs, then two French-horns, two Fiddles, two Haut-boys, and followed by a Rabble Rout.[38]

Villagers kept on the ceremony where they could, rather than deny themselves a communal supper; in some places the same ceremony was replicated on 'Holly Thursday' when churchwardens usually put money aside to purchase strong drink, like the 1/- spent on beer at Ellingham, Hampshire, in 1767.

Rural religious practice was ineradicably tied in with the boundaries of the parish and keeping interlopers out of it, especially – in Catholic cases – from those places or objects associated with a saint who provided for them the immediate, physical point of contact with God. Even in Protestant England, the majority of people used saints' or feast days to mark the passage of time rather than the formal calendar of days and months, or for expressions of group solidarity: shoemakers on St Crispin's Day (25 October), lacemakers on St Andrew's Day (30 November), woolcombers on 3 February for Bishop Blaze, their pre-Reformation patron saint, the latter marked at Bury St Edmunds by a procession 2,000–3,000 strong with music provided by workers in the woollen industry. The annual parish feast (or wake) was for everyone. It was usually inaugurated on

---

[38] John Penrose, *Letters from Bath, 1766–1767* (Gloucester, 1983), 102.

the Sunday following the day of the saint to whom the parish church was dedicated and, before descending into merriment, they commonly began with a service that indirectly celebrated that sense of neighbourliness that confirmed loyalties to the Church.

The Christianity of non-elite women

Women were prominent participants on these festive occasions. Their sense of community association was arguably more finely tuned than their husbands' – familial and child-rearing duties were more likely to constrain their movements from parish to parish – and the parish church was a cardinal feature in their sense of place. The church was, in a distinctive sense, their own. Michel Vovelle has talked in terms of the 'feminisation of catholicism' during the eighteenth century and, while it would be an overstatement to claim that by the 1780s women made up the majority of worshippers at Sunday services, they had a loyalty and a prominence in local church life in most of Europe which foreshadowed their importance as lay organisers (and agitators) in the nineteenth century. It was not just a sense of social obligation or pressure from the parson's wife (that important figure neglected by historians) in Protestant countries that ensured they took their seats Sunday by Sunday. They came from a genuine sense of devotion, of what they owed to their families, and because the clergy of all denominations increasingly recognised – albeit privately – that women were a crucial antidote to the easy-going indifference of growing numbers of men to their religious duties. The religious diary was important to many Protestant women as they wrestled to obtain an assurance of salvation without any priestly – and by definition male – intermediary. Mary Langdon of Shropshire's journal, hundreds of pages long, says little about her daily life but looks in unrelenting detail at the state of her soul and her standing with God: 'if I say am I now in a state of salvation I cannot with full assurance of faith say yes but I hope & believe the Lord that has brought me thus far will save me at last'.[39] Swedish middle-class women such as Metta Lillie (1709–88) often asked God or Jesus what plans they had for them, and Christina Hiärne (1722–1804), part of the small community of Moravian Brethren of Stockholm, records her frequent, almost daily, conversations, asking them for advice, exhorting them to punish her enemies, and begging their help for her adventurous only son on his travels.

[39] Shropshire Archives and Research Centre, 5399/2, Diary of Mary Langdon, 1750–85, 11 May 1763.

Women discovered a spiritual satisfaction in orthodox Chrisitianity that had an intensity by and large lacking among men, and there was a new attempt in the second half of the century to increase opportunities for them within Church life. In 1771 the diocesan visitor to the Catalan village of Olesa de Montserrat was shocked to find that four women were carrying candles before the priest and attendants of the Tabernacle or Bed of Our Lady in the Assumption procession. In France, even those women who could not be described as comfortably off were starting to give more to charities and their church than the men and, as ever, they were the staple market for religious tracts. By signing up for membership of the confraternities women were taking full, if belated, advantage of the opportunities for public expression of their faith created by the Catholic Reformation. Confraternities such as those dedicated to the Rosary, the Sacred Heart and St Catherine were a bedrock of female piety before the Revolution. No less important were the new religious Orders for women and parochial missionaries, such as the Sisters of the Christian Doctrine (1694) and the Sisters of Saint-Anne (1709). Three or four sisters would establish unofficial convent houses in villages where they supplemented the efforts of the *curé* in catechising little girls and cared for the sick and dying in what became known in France as 'Houses of Charity'. Little is known about these *filles séculières* in the French provinces. Their importance in stimulating and shaping female religiosity was immense, enough to ensure that the majority of women clung tenaciously to their Catholicism when the Revolution came. They had no exact equivalent in Protestant countries, unless it be some exceptional charity-school mistresses. Thoughtful Protestants were very conscious that their religious culture had been diminished by the abolition of female religious Orders at the Reformation, so that Anglicans like William Law and Sarah Scott were still toying at mid-century with the possibility of unofficially re-establishing them. Nothing came of their hopes until the 1840s, and it was meanwhile left to elite women such as Hannah More to harness the religious instincts of her social inferiors as a means of helping British society survive the threat posed by the French Revolution and Napoleon. More and more Tory Evangelicals were determined to counteract the impact of enlightenment trends to infidelity among the populace at large and she was well aware that other women could prove to be her principal allies in securing her end. With her controversial Blagdon tracts of the early 1800s she embodied the Church militant in a new context, counter-attacking unbelief and using the same methods of popularising her cause as many of her opponents had done for theirs.

Conclusion

Outside some sections of the social elite, lack of religious commitment remained rare in later eighteenth-century Europe, and the continent's public culture was still predominantly a Christian one. Nevertheless, the various confessions found that imposing social discipline through a series of moral codes enforced in the last resort by ecclesiastical courts was breaking down. Thus discipline in the Church of Scotland was faltering from the 1770s onwards as more mobile urban populations became harder for ministers to trace. Dissenting congregations grew in number, irregular marriages increased and enlightened opinion was uncomfortable with lengthy public humiliation as a penalty for extra-marital sex. Only in Dundee and Glasgow was discipline upheld, thanks to an energetic ministerial body. Anglican ecclesiastical courts were fast losing their authority. On the Isle of Man in 1785 churchwardens were complaining to Bishop Claudius Crigan at the practical difficulties involved in having to present offenders to the archdeacon for 'common fame' and for failure to attend church. It was symptomatic of this decreased regard for spiritual penalties that even papal excommunication was not taken seriously, as Clement XIII found when he tried to revive it in 1768.

A less morally regulated society was by no means a non-churchgoing one. Religious practice may have been slightly less extensive than between 1650 and 1750, but participants were better informed about the purpose of worship. Arguably, in the two generations before the French Revolution, Europeans were more familiar with scripture than at any time before or after. Amid the competing varieties of sociability on offer to a wider cross-section of the population (especially those living in or near to towns), churchgoing easily retained its first call on the time of the laity. How can that be explained? One would be rash to underestimate the extent to which the varieties of worship on offer were appreciated by the laity, whether it was the liturgical splendour found in the cathedrals, the simpler comforts offered by a low Mass or matins and the litany from the Anglican Book of Common Prayer, or a long sermon in a plain Protestant meeting house.

Yet, in the last analysis, people went to church because it hallowed the great rites of passage and brought a wide range of society together under one roof. Public worship thus acted as a social and sexual solvent. Men and women often sat apart in pews on separate sides of the church but, crucially, men attended. Of course, the parish clergy were not slow to perceive symptoms of indifference in the general population. It was often difficult to persuade the laity to attend Anglican services, and the problem could be compounded when parson and parishioners were at odds over tithes or service fees. In Catholic states, poor relief and charity could often function as a means of getting the parish into its church. The Church's hold on the general population cannot be gauged without appreciating this point: it was the first point of call for assistance in times of dearth, distress or destitution in a fragile agrarian economy. There are signs of a declining charitable role in the second half of the century, but its impact on relations between Church and people remains to be assessed.

The range of Christian beliefs privately and individually held remains much harder for the historian to measure. It makes some sense to think in terms of a contrast between 'ritual religion' as most people wanted it, collective and communal, and the individualistic piety sought by reformers. The various exponents of religious revival and renewal indefatigably stressed that it was the personal experience of the inner working of the Holy Spirit (as opposed to sacramental regeneration) that marked the true believer. Whether a person subscribed to that theology or not, it was immensely influential because of the wider cultural stress on emotional depth and cultivation of one's spiritual nature. The religiosity of the later eighteenth-century was fundamentally affective, a trait which particularly characterised the female piety of the age, for women played a critical role in replacing the austerities of Reformation and Counter-Reformation spiritualities with this new force. As Rousseau and Wesley taught, in their very different ways, the heart mattered – literally so with the cult of the Sacred Heart of Jesus – and it was a popular emphasis that enlightened opinion would not easily displace.

3 Intellectual challenges and the religious response

Enlightenment and religion: a vigorous interaction

The complex, multiform character of the eighteenth-century Enlightenment is now widely accepted by historians. No longer is France regarded as the European paradigm. As experienced by states, institutions, individuals and Churches, the impact of enlightenment varied extensively and changed over time, so that postulating any necessary conflict between Christianity and the intellectually progressive becomes an unpersuasive exercise, even for France. Indeed, France was the exception to a European pattern in which the Enlightenment originated in reformist-minded Christianity, both Catholic and Protestant, as seen in seventeenth-century Germany, Holland and Scotland. By 1760 virtually no corner of Europe had been left unaffected by the spread and popularisation of mainstream Enlightenment emphases such as those on the rule of law, efficient and non-arbitrary government, religious toleration and freedom of the press. Everyone with a smattering of education and a basic literacy was affected by it, including the clergy – not surprisingly, since their educational attainments had never been higher. The empirical science of Francis Bacon and Isaac Newton had attracted massive public interest (even in France by the 1730s, thanks to Voltaire's championship) and if Cartesian philosophy had been a casualty of their triumph, the rational method associated with it persisted vigorously and had no regard for established doctrine merely on the basis of its survival over time. Arguments which, at the beginning of the century, had been dismissed as dangerously eccentric and destabilising, were the commonplaces of public debate fifty years on and their proponents courted by monarchs and ministers of state. In the 1770s most European regimes were drawing on the professional services of men such as Anne-Robert Jacques Turgot and François Quesnay in France, Kaunitz in Austria, Pedro Pablo, conde de Aranda in Spain, Joseph Banks and William Eden in Britain, even Goethe in Saxe-Weimar, highly competent individuals who, if not committed to upholding ecclesiastical interests, were by no means looking to overthrow them for the sake of other agendas.

The Enlightenment was becoming an unexceptional part of the establishment. Orthodoxy apart, the Churches had for the most part adjusted to the changed situation, if not without discomfort. Protestant regimes perhaps coped better with the challenges posed by the intellectual vibrancy of the altered dispensation. Indeed writers including Bayle and Locke were key figures in shaping the eirenic and non-dogmatic character of the early Enlightenment, building on an emphasis on inclusiveness that was, to some extent, part of the Reformation heritage and, 200 years on, expressed itself in a commitment to religious toleration and modern scholarship. Adaptability came harder for Catholics as members of a Church where authority was entrenched if not always upheld and respected. But, by the 1760s, progressive Catholic clergy and apologists were frequently enlisting the help of the secular powers to implement their reformist programme in Church structures and practices, an experience referred to by modern scholars as 'the Catholic Enlightenment'.

Despite misgivings on a whole range of issues, clergy had up to the 1750s gone along where they could with Enlightenment critiques of the existing order in Church and state, having recourse to the state's repressive apparatus only as a last resort, as with the condemnation of Denis Diderot's *Letters on the Blind* (1749) or the expulsion of Tinkler Ducket from Cambridge University for atheism ten years before. After 1760 there were three significant developments, which tended to increase the defensiveness of established religion and made some churchmen apprehensive that they were losing control of the situation. First, the French Enlightenment took a pronounced, anti-Christian turn. Led by Voltaire, a figure of European celebrity, the object of secular pilgrimages in his own right, the leading *philosophes* scarcely bothered to conceal their hostility to Catholicism and its dogmas. In pamphlet after pamphlet in the 1760s, the tart tracts he dubbed his *petits pâtés*, Voltaire ridiculed the historical claims of Christianity. He might have insisted that his slogan of 'Ecrasez l'infâme' was targeted at superstition, but the clergy had no doubts that texts such as the *Philosophical Dictionary* (1764) with its attacks on the Bible and the Jewish culture from which it emerged, and his tasteless jokes against transubstantiation, demonstrated that Voltaire actually classified Christianity as superstition. His death in 1778 caused a collective sigh of relief among the clergy. As Thomas Balguy, archdeacon of Winchester, told a Scottish friend: 'Voltaire, I suppose, is at last quiet in his grave. It were well if his Books could have been buried with him. Few men, if any, have contributed so much to debauch both the

Principles & the Morals of the age.'[1] Even in the great *Encyclopédie*, a seminal enlightenment text if ever there was, attacks on the Catholic Church by the progressive Swiss Protestant, Louis de Jaucourt, were found in increasing numbers from volume X onwards, all testimony to the cankerous *esprit philosophique* which so aggravated the religious establishment. It is not surprising that the publisher, Louis-François Le Breton (1708–79), censored more of Jaucourt's articles than those of Diderot.

Meanwhile sensationalism became the fashion in France with the abbé de Condillac and then Helvétius giving the epistemology classically associated with John Locke's *Essay on Human Understanding* (1690) an extremist twist that outraged the clergy. *Philosophe* criticism moved rapidly forward from the deism of the 1730s/1740s with Julien de la Mettrie's *L'Homme machine* (1747) setting a trend with its overt materialism that denied man's spiritual qualities or capacities. In the Parisian salons, materialists including Helvétius and d'Holbach received fashionable acclaim, though the latter's *System of Nature* (1770), with its marriage of mechanics and atheism implicitly denying the premises of natural religion, was too much even for Voltaire, as his *Les Cabales* (1772) bore witness. Secondly, there were alarming signs that anti-Christian pamphlets were being popularised for a much wider audience than hitherto, often in the form of lurid pornography. Despite the best efforts of the French authorities, it was possible to seize only a proportion of the manuscripts and pamphlets produced in Amsterdam and other Dutch cities or in the Prussian enclave of Neufchâtel, then smuggled across the frontiers clandestinely. Lastly, countries in southern Europe, notably Spain, previously marginal to the dissemination of enlightenment ideals and influences, had suddenly become receptive to the new thinking and were speedily making up for lost time.

The situation in France had thrown the Gallican establishment on the defensive to an unparalleled degree. To stop the corrosion of belief and respect for religion, the First Estate began to rely more and more on repressive action by the state from the 1750s rather than putting its faith in the deterrent effect of replying to subversive criticisms. But condemnation and ceremonial burning of incendiary texts, whether instigated by the Crown, the Church or the Sorbonne, only increased public notice of the book in question and did nothing to deter other authors like Helvétius with his *De l'Esprit* (1757) from risking their necks if not their reputations. The clergy were concerned at the way immorality at parish level might be fanned by the permissiveness the Enlightenment

---

[1] To Lord Hailes, 21 June 1778, National Library of Scotland, Newhailes MS. 25299, f. 5.

5. Robert Dighton, 'Doctor Phlogiston'. Priestley's work on gases is satirically invoked in the caption along with his notorious reference to igniting a trail of gunpowder underneath the establishment.

appeared to encourage. In 1775, the dean of Mons observed how '*mauvais livres* were freely available at fairs just as the ecclesiastical censor [had] lost a great deal of his power'.[2] Such circumstances scandalised the General Assembly of the Clergy of France. None of its meetings between 1755 and 1788 was without a counter-attack against its detractors. 'Guilty authors', the '*prétendus philsophes*', respected 'neither the purity of morals, the inviolable rights of sovereign power, nor the saintly truths of religion', insisted the clergy assembled in 1755.[3] On 4 June 1780 Cardinal La Rochefoucauld of Rouen, presenting fellow deputies to Louis XVI, reminded the monarch how 'a false and proud philosophy had multiplied its efforts to extinguish the flames of religion in every heart' and warned that 'A few more years of silence and this commotion will become universal, leaving only debris and ruin [in the state].'[4] In fact, the leading French clergy knew well that the monarchy in the 1780s was reluctant to get caught in the polemical crossfire of the Enlightenment: the Church must fight its own battles without relying on government assistance in its cause. Outside France, there were moves to wrest control of censorship entirely from Church hands. It happened in Portugal in 1768, though that did not mean anti-Catholic literature could be circulated freely. In the Austrian Empire, Maria Theresa would only permit the admission of Protestant literature in special circumstances; here, too, the Church was strictly controlled in deciding criteria for publication, and from 1774 censors in the Austrian Netherlands were ordered to refer a decision on any religious work back to the government for final approval.

Elsewhere in Europe, the defensive-mindedness the cause of religion appeared to require meant pessimists abounded, like the English Whig pamphleteer, the Revd Ferdinando Warner, who in 1750 complained of the present times 'When deism, popery, and immorality reign triumphant in our nation'.[5] Matínez Albiach has noted the despondency that affected the Spanish clergy after about 1750, especially monks and friars, and its similar basis. Whether reformers or traditionalists, they were convinced that unbelief and immorality were rife across society. Yet, on the whole, both Catholics and Protestants contained the overt irreligion that in some areas became a feature of the later Enlightenment. They were

---

[2] A. D. Nord, 3 G 2860, Assemblées décanales, Mons, 1753–83, f. 24, quoted in Gilles Deregnaucourt, *De Fenelon à la Révolution: le clergé paroissial de l'Archevêché de Cambrai* (Lille, 1991), 153.

[3] 'Mémoire au roi', from the 'Procès-verbal' of the 1755 Assembly quoted in Darrin M. McMahon, 'The Counter-Enlightenment and the Low-life of Literature in Pre-Revolutionary France', *Past & Present* 159 (1998), 77–112, at 87.

[4] Quoted in John Lough, *The Philosophes and Post-Revolutionary France* (Oxford, 1982), 59, 65. The last extract is from a memorandum of 20 July 1780.

[5] *A System of Divinity and Morality* (5 vols., London, 1750), vol. I, iii.

assisted by the enduring assumption at every level in society that atheism and immorality were inseparable. These twin vices allegedly produced depraved, selfish men and women who had no sense of shame and could contribute nothing to the general good: the notion of a virtuous atheist was a contradiction in terms. If atheists were an eccentric menace to social cohesion, below them could be found innumerable degrees of heterodoxy and infidelity at odds with the Christian creeds. The popularisation of enlightenment critiques and toleration encouraged their proliferation in the pre-revolutionary decades.

Protestant communions were particularly prone to succumbing to heresies, not least in Switzerland and the United Provinces where the reaction against hardline Calvinism was in full flood: Voltaire wanted to settle near Geneva after coming home from Prussia not just because of its excellent doctors but because he believed d'Alembert's account of its clergy as perfect rationalists who had discarded belief in hell. The twin perils of Arianism (which insisted on the supremacy of the Father within the Trinitarian Godhead) and Socinianism (which denied a Triune God altogether) had been reinvigorated by the Reformation break-up of Christendom, and the Enlightenment distrust of Christian dogma further confirmed their appeal. In eastern Europe, Socinianism still had a small foothold among Protestants in the commonwealth of Poland–Lithuania; in England, dissenting groups which earlier in the century had become Arian progressed imperceptibly towards Socinianism. Led by the great chemist and political radical, Joseph Priestley, Socinian groups had an influence out of all proportion to their numbers, and unsettled the Anglican hierarchy. Church of England resistance to amending subscription to the Thirty-nine Articles in 1772–3 and permitting the repeal of the Test and Corporation Acts (1788–90) owed much to a sense that it would be a victory for Priestley and his cohorts, who had talked wildly of lighting a fuse of gunpowder under the religious establishment.

At least blatantly heterodox Anglican bishops were a thing of the past in the late eighteenth century. Bishop Robert Clayton of Clogher in Ireland only escaped expulsion from office for his ultra-Arian *Essay on Spirit* by conveniently dying in 1758, and he had no obvious successors. The more authoritarian structures of Catholicism acted as a defence against heresies disseminated from within. The maintenance of orthodoxy among Catholics was thus not a matter of particular concern to the clergy; they were more vulnerable to attacks coming from outside the fold. More insidious and corrosive over the medium term for Christians of all persuasions was the impact on their faith of living in a world where religious concerns no longer had an unassailable cultural supremacy. Numbers attending services might be holding up well – even among men – but what hold would their Christianity retain in practice once they stepped outside the church door? It was an insistent question in increasingly commercialised societies in which newspapers, journals, pamphlets and pornography competed for readers' notice alongside the devotional materials which until recently had experienced limited competition. The clergy could do little more than instruct and warn about the perils of a ubiquitous print culture, knowing that the inquisitive would take scant notice.

Religion and reason: an alliance under attack

Developments within the Enlightenment from the mid-century grew out of and then outflanked the almost universal insistence of clergy up to that point that Christianity and reason complemented each other, and that it was part of the divine plan that they should do so. Within this scheme, it was the task of philosophy to act as the handmaiden of theology and through critical enquiry disclose those truths about man's nature and his place in the created order that supplemented the scriptural record and its message of salvation. Churchmen took additional comfort, as will be seen, from the manner in which Newtonian physics apparently confirmed and reinforced the partnership between religion and reason. Orthodox divines reminded polite congregations across Europe – especially Protestant ones – that their faith was superior to others on offer as much for its intrinsic reasonableness as the revelation of God in Jesus Christ. From this proceeded the recommendation of a 'rational piety' as one reconcilable with philosophy and politeness alike.

This 'reasonable Christianity' ended in relegating revelation in a way that both undermined personal faith and encouraged the Churches' deist and materialist adversaries. The young people in France who responded so admiringly to Rousseau in the 1770s and 1780s delighted in his unfettered cultivation of the spirit, no less than their counterparts in Germany of the *Sturm und Drang* generation who longed for release from the constraints of rationality and believed they had found it in figures such as Hamann and Klopstock. For all of them, 'Nature' became the supreme test of truthfulness and before it both reason and Christianity might have to give ground. Pressure from this quarter was a formidable challenge to the theological emphasis on 'rational religion' as the most authentic expression of the faith.

Critiques of the assumptions underpinning the marriage of reason and Christianity did not suddenly begin in the 1750s. Versions of deism within the elites flourished in early eighteenth-century Europe, and they all agreed that revelation was not a 'reasonable' position to adopt. In England increased press freedoms from the 1690s had seen the publication of works by gifted polemicists such as Toland and Collins disparaging the historic faith which caused clergy to despair and proclaim the (Anglican) 'Church in Danger'; the English deists had their imitators in France while another strand of opinion, inspired by Spinoza, took a pantheistic view of nature as a single entity identifiable with God. In the face of such assaults, the defenders of orthodox religion still clung to their insistence that Christianity and reason went together, and were never silenced at any point before 1789 by either free-thinking critics or pious conservatives. In France, the future constitutional bishop of the Haute-Vienne, Gay-Vernon, told one gathering of priests and laymen in 1788 that 'Reason alone ought to be our sovereign guide. We ought only to progress in the light of its torch.'[6] It was unexceptionable language, widely echoed in clerical discourses across Roman Catholic Europe in the later eighteenth century, heard in Spain, Italy, much of the empire and Poland; equally, in the Protestant Churches of Germany, most of the hymns sung in church at around 1780 asked God to confer rational knowledge on humanity. A reasonable faith and 'enlightened devotions' were not easily separated anywhere in Protestant Germany.

It was less individual attacks than the inexorable increase in knowledge that gradually made some theologians think the position was unsustainable. Despite earlier hopes, the undeniable complexity of natural phenomena was not easily containable within a biblical framework. For instance, the pioneering work of James Hutton (1726–97) on the Jedburgh Fault in the Scottish lowlands published in his *Theory of the Earth* (1795) threw into doubt the kind of timescale for creation suggested by Genesis, not to mention the Noachian Flood, even if his book retained a benign but impersonal depiction of God. Metaphysics became widely discredited since it was not susceptible to the Lockean orthodoxy that invalidated non-sensory perceptions. The Protestant Churches had been content enough to endorse that position, less so when it was taken further as it was, notoriously, by David Hume in his *Enquiry concerning Human Understanding* (1748), where he argued that reason, correctly understood, could undermine both natural and revealed religion. Hume, like Locke before him in the 1690s, stressed the limitations of human knowledge and man's capacity to establish truth but, unlike Locke, he extended this scepticism much further to encompass what can be known about God, as his posthumously published *Dialogues concerning Natural Religion* (1778) brilliantly suggested. The relations between God and morality remained troubling,

---

[6] Quoted in A. Artaud, 'Gay-Vernon: evêque constitutionnel et député de la Haute-Vienne (1748–1822)', *La Révolution française*, 27 (1894), 314–34, 447–67, 502–31, at 319.

though a naturalist tradition was increasingly making it hard to register a place for divine operation in the world as Hume's work shows supremely. It pointed to Kant's claim that mankind itself legislated the moral law, thus increasing the sense of human autonomy.

Hume undermined orthodoxy in other ways by treating religion as a phenomenon originating and shaped within human society rather than having divine origins. His *Natural History of Religion* (1757) developed this thesis of religion emerging from the natural human tendency to anthropomorphise unknown causes in nature. These insights had their counterpart in France where thinkers like the président des Brosses and Nicolas-Antoine Boulanger (1722–59) were reaching similar conclusions in such works as the latter's *Antiquité dévoilée* (first appeared 1766). Their insistence that religions, Christianity included, were the product of the primitive fears and aspirations of ancient man who needed to cope with the impact of war, famine and disease would later be taken up by Volney and the French *Idéologues* of the 1790s. Awareness of other civilisations and religions in Asia and the Pacific derived initially from the Jesuit missions also chipped away at a sense of a unique, supreme Christian dispensation. Britain's ever-closer involvement in India brought first-hand acquaintance with contemporary Hindus and Zoroastrians, who were found to have some of the same components in their faith inheritance as Judaeo-Christianity, like the story of a great flood. These contacts with non-Christian societies offered plenty of ammunition to critics of the Churches. The Scottish deist, Alexander Dow (d. 1779), author of the *History of Hindustan* (1768, 1772), was anxious to demonstrate the moral superiority of Hinduism to Christianity and was opposed by the great Sanskrit scholar, Sir William Jones, and a former army chaplain, the Revd Thomas Maurice (1754–1824), author of *Indian Antiquities* (1793–1800). In France, the abbé Guillaume Thomas Raynal's *Philosophical and Political History of the Two Indies* (1770) provoked consternation among the clergy, arguing not only that these other civilisations were virtuous, but that contact with Christian intruders had destroyed them. The book sold well, going through seventeen editions between 1772 and 1780. Its condemnation in 1781 was a woefully ineffectual riposte.

Man's view of the past, too, was slowly emerging from a specifically Christian framework. Today the greatest historian of the first half of the century is generally agreed to have been the Neapolitan Giambattista Vico (1668-1744). In his *New Science* (1725), Vico attempted to give an historical demonstration of the existence of divine providence directing the careers of nations, while the actual thrust of his influential book was to direct the reader's notice towards the huge range of variables that had influenced and made up the past and man's capacity for progress inside it. The book inaugurated a trend to divorce history from theology that became the norm from the 1750s. William Robertson, principal of Edinburgh University and himself a minister in the Kirk, showed how explaining the past could be done in purely human terms without reference to any divine purpose or plan. Robertson did that sensitively enough to cause minimal upset for the Church authorities, whereas his English equivalent, Edward Gibbon, was less successful in his monumental *Decline and Fall of the Roman Empire*. In his first volume Gibbon – himself immensely learned in theology – scarcely bothered to conceal his aversion to the excesses of religious zeal as found in the third- and fourth-century monks or the bishops whose careers benefited from persuading the emperor Constantine to convert. What really got Gibbon into trouble was the infamous chapter sixteen of the first book of the *Decline and Fall*, in which he attempted to explain the success of Christianity by omitting any reference to the automatic presumption of the faithful down the ages that it was ascribable to divine providence. Gibbon and Robertson were not writing secularised history, yet they were responding imaginatively and intelligently to a past in which nothing was necessarily foreordained and where reference to God could not be considered as an explanation of anything.

Religion and the progress of mankind

How did the clergy cope as individuals living in a society where the old certainties about their status and beliefs were no longer taken for granted? Predictably, reactions varied according to age, status and temperament. In England, one of the century's most impressive leaders, Archbishop Secker of Canterbury, deplored what he saw as the universal spread of indifference and infidelity, and in his visitation Charges and sermons urged the parochial clergy to do what they could (he was privately pessimistic about the prospects) to guard their people from contamination. A pastoral response to an intellectual attack was crucial according to the archbishop, but it was not his only line of defence. Gifted polemicists among the clergy, George Horne, William Jones (of Nayland) and Beilby Porteus amongst others, were patronised by Secker and ready to fight back against apologists for irreligion. Horne, for instance, furious at Adam Smith's moving description of Hume's calm, un-Christian deathbed, upbraided both of them with wit and ferocity in a pamphlet written 'by one of the people called Christians'.

In France, open hostility to revealed religion was at its height just before Louis XV's death in 1774. As one petition to the General Assembly of the Clergy noted: 'We speak of irreligion, which for some years now has spread in all directions like a torrent, and does the gravest damage among us. This terrible fire consumes everything and if we don't hurry to stop its progress, the malady will be beyond all remedies.'[7] The Gallican clergy and laity tried to help themselves. About 900 replies in defence of the Christian religion were made in France between 1715 and 1789, most after 1750. But it was hard to construct a common Christian front in the 1750s because of the internal wranglings within the Church with supporters and opponents of the Jesuits and Jansenists determined to damage each other no matter how unedifying the average believer found their spats and however much distaste the spectacle gave to the average man. Yet over time the numbers of those enlisting in the anti-*philosophe* cause is not to be underestimated, among them Sabatier de Castres, an expelled seminarian whose grudge was against Voltaire not the Church. He praised clergy defending the Church against an old man who would not stop levelling 'new blows at Christianity and at those who respected and defended it'.[8]

Many French priests who combatted the blatant unbelief of some *philosophes* conceded that the Enlightenment had not been without benefits for Christianity. The abbé Claude Fauchet, a future Girondin and vicar-general of the archbishop of Bourges before 1789, rejoiced that philosophy had recalled mankind to the principles of true religion. For Fauchet and his friends, the desirability of modernising and reforming both attitudes and institutions in their society was a given: the better educated the priest or prelate, the more likely he was to admire the critical insights of a work like Montesquieu's *L'Esprit des lois* (1748) or the great *Encyclopédie* itself. The better-off clergy subscribed to the latter despite its troubled publication history and the Church's official condemnation. Its presence on their shelves alongside sermons, catechisms and devotional literature was not incongruous, for these were discriminating, critical readers. The average *curé* could seldom afford to make his own purchase but was just as interested in reading the great names of modern France as any of his secular counterparts: in the diocese of Verdun in 1789, priests met regularly at each other's houses to study together and, along with the Bible and the history of Church Councils, also pored over Rousseau's *Social Contract*. They were desperately anxious to dispel any doubts that they were *useful* members of contemporary society.

[7] *Requête des fidèles à Nosseigneurs les Evêques de l'Assemblée générale du Clergé de France* (Paris, 1781?), 3, 4.
[8] [Antoine Sabatier], *Tableau philosophique de l'esprit de M. de Voltaire pour servir de suite à ses ouvrages, & de mémoires à l'histoire de sa vie* (Geneva, 1771), vi.

In Scotland the dominant Moderates in the Kirk largely accepted that civic virtue should be inculcated without theological considerations being a dominant part of the educative process. They deferred to purely secular usages, as Roger L. Emerson has noted: 'Religion was still part of the philosophical system, but Christianity and its revelations and grace had been excluded, shunted aside to dogmatic theology.'[9]

When the controversy over compulsory subscription to the Confession of Faith came to a head in the 1770s and 1780s, Moderate clergy boldly argued that all creeds and confessions, even the Westminster one, were necessarily partial and incomplete. They were by training and disposition attracted to a rational Christianity, as were many Pietist ministers in Germany. Leading Prussian theologians like the heterodox Lutheran Johann Joachim Spalding (1714–1804) insisted that a synthesis between faith and enlightened thinking was sociably desirable. Virtue, duty and the 'common good' were, in this dispensation, more esteemed than theological niceties. It was against this background that the Church in Saxe-Weimar in 1786 officially ended penance. Yet this disclaimer of dogma and the failure to establish religious 'proofs' according to exacting intellectual criteria gave a new twist to a sceptical tradition dating back to the Renaissance, looking again into what has been called the 'Pandora's box that Luther had opened at Leipzig'.[10] The exemplar of these benevolent sceptics was Gotthold Ephraim Lessing, whose controversial writings in the years between publishing *Wolfenbüttel Fragments* (1774–8) and his death (1781) proclaimed that sacred subjects should be freely discussed since Christianity's essential truth lay less in scripture or tradition than in meeting the needs of human nature. Lessing's prestige was such that it was hard to silence him, whatever the misgivings of the authorities that his attempt to reconcile Christianity and enlightenment was to the latter's advantage. Lessing's syncretic version of religion was fully displayed in his famous play *Nathan the Wise* (1779), set in the time of the Third Crusade with characters from the late twelfth century displaying attitudes from the eighteenth. His last work, *The Education of Mankind* (1780), summarised the case for a dynamic view of dogmatics, the need to refashion the content of faith in every generation as mankind progressed ever further towards enlightenment.

Many eighteenth-century churchmen combined this vision of unlimited future progress for humanity with an appeal to the past as the blueprint on which the Churches should remodel themselves if they were to recover

---

[9] Roger L. Emerson, 'The Religious, the Secular and the Worldly: Scotland 1680–1800', in James E. Cribbins (ed.), *Religion, Secularization and Political Thought: Thomas Hobbes to John Stuart Mill* (London and New York, 1989), 68–89, at 85.

[10] Richard H. Popkin, *The History of Scepticism from Erasmus to Spinoza* (Berkeley, 1979), 4.

the vision and energy of 'primitive' Christianity. There was nothing pejorative in the contemporary usage of 'primitive'. From the 1750s onwards, it had become the watermark of excellence and authenticity in every area from architecture to the reform of society. So it was in religion. Of course, the case for reconstituting the Church according to an original apostolic model had inspired the exponents of Reformation in both Catholic and Protestant Churches and had never really ceased to do so. The effect of the Enlightenment was to intensify the process again. In England, the cause of primitive renewal in worship, ecclesiology and doctrine inspired the 'Rational dissenters'. They looked forward to the impending time when Church establishments would be cut down to size, bishops denied the political prominence they had enjoyed since the conversion of Constantine, and a purified Christianity would usher in a regenerated world.

A radical ecclesiology had its sting sharpened by a non-Athanasian version of Christianity that rejected the Triune Godhead – another 'corruption' these reformers intended to purge. It was an emphasis that alarmed the majority of dissenters as well as Anglicans, who saw the appeal of a non-Trinitarian creed in some parts of high society. After the failure of the petitioning movement of 1772–3 to change the basis of subscription to the Church of England (the Thirty-nine Articles), a number of influential clergy resigned their posts, including Theophilus Lindsey, the Cambridge don. He promptly opened his own chapel in Essex Street, London, with its own ultra-Arian liturgy. The fashionable and the famous flocked to the services, among them Benjamin Franklin (when visiting London) and the chancellor of Cambridge University, the 3rd duke of Grafton (prime minister, 1768–70). These polite worshippers at the origins of modern English Unitarianism may have been practical politicians but other exponents of a 'rational', unothodox Christianity, such as Price and Priestley, had a millenarian view of the future, the new age that the Enlightenment was already ushering in. They looked eagerly for signs of the new dispensation and, notoriously, thought they saw it when the French Revolution erupted in 1789, providing the occasion for (the Arian) Dr Price's sermon and Burke's magisterial reply in the *Reflections on the Revolution in France*. Similarly, in France, Fauchet found in the Bible the clue to discovering future events. 'We're at the close of decadence [*des excès*]', he wrote on the eve of the Revolution, 'regeneration is approaching.'[11] The sense of participating in a millennial drama was shared by others such as Adrien Lamourette and Pierre Pontard, who would, like Fauchet, become bishops of the Constitutional Church.

---

[11] Claude Fauchet, *De la Religion nationale* (Paris, 1789), 108.

Many such 'enlightened' clergy were more used to hearing these exhortations in their provincial academy or masonic lodge meetings than from the pulpit. That was certainly the case in France, where members of the First Estate saw nothing incompatible between their holy orders and their initiation into the craft. Indeed, the masonic apron distinctly resembled a liturgical garment, a chasuble worn back-to-front. Masonry was fundamental to male socialisation within the broad swathe of the elite in France as elsewhere. In Toulouse, sixty-four priests belonged to the various lodges in the city, approximately 5 per cent of total membership. Many of these were higher clergy with time and leisure to participate fully. In the major cathedral city on the Rhine frontier, Strasbourg, canon-counts of the great chapter belonged to the Candeur lodge, and the prince-bishop himself was sympathetic to this sort of gathering where men called each other 'brother', as in a religious confraternity. Regular clergy also joined, like nine monks at the great abbey of Fécamp in 1778 who founded the lodge of the Triple Unity on their premises. Papal condemnation of masonry made Italian clergy less willing to hazard their careers that way, and their holding back actually intensified the reputation of the Italian lodges for anticlericalism. In the United Provinces, the Austrian Netherlands and much of Germany, there was no such restraint. Clergy signed up in large numbers, including Dalberg, bishop of Constance and the last archbishop-elector of Mainz. German Protestants had the option of joining lodges with strong Pietistic colourings, such as the St Johannisloge in Berlin, where prayers and weeping were all part of the occasion.

The Churches and higher education

Exposure to the culture of Freemasonry could seldom overlay for the clergy the formative academic and socialising experience of higher education. Universities remained, to a considerable degree, inseparably attached to the established Churches: they functioned as training colleges for the clergy, finishing schools for the elite, exposing all undergraduates to an educational experience that privileged theology. As the vice-chancellor of Oxford explained in 1793 to the new chancellor, the 3rd duke of Portland, 'the sole purposes of our academical Institutions' are 'maintenance of Learning, and the furtherance of Religion and morality'.[12] Such bastions were vulnerable to criticism from those excluded by belief (or unbelief), lack of ready money or status, like English dissenters

---

[12] Quoted in V. H. H. Green, 'Religion in the Colleges 1715–1800', in L. S. Sutherland and L. G. Mitchell (eds.), *History of the University of Oxford*, vol. V. *The Eighteenth Century* (Oxford, 1986), 467.

who found the ancient legal requirement of the universities of Oxford and Cambridge that they subscribe to the Test Act and the Thirty-Nine Articles an insuperable obstacle to membership. They frequently took refuge in Scottish or Dutch institutions, where clerical controls were much looser, with a higher proportion of graduates going on to careers in law and medicine.

Likewise, in Germany and Sweden, governments were forcing universities to introduce more vocationally minded degree courses in the sciences to benefit the state. They endowed new professorships – such as those in experimental physics and chemistry at Uppsala University in 1750 – which were not subject to clerical control. Presbyterian Scotland had an impressive range of educational institutions, none more so than its five universities in four cities renowned for their broad curriculum and celebrated teachers, among them James Beattie, John Millar, Thomas Reid, William Robertson and Adam Smith. The Moderate Party of the Church of Scotland dominated all of them except King's and Marischal Colleges in Aberdeen; they kept out their orthodox Evangelical rivals and exerted their grip in the interests of continuing innovation and tolerance. The Evangelicals found it galling to see Moderates in possession of the best university chairs in addition to the important pulpits. In both, one opponent alleged, one could hear them saying 'O Lord, we thank thee for Mr Bayle's Dictionary. Amen.'[13] These charges were explicable but still unfair. The rational moral theology on offer was attractive to many progressive noblemen. A few members of the British elite, such as Lord Shelburne (premier 1782–3), sent their children to Scottish universities precisely because they were indifferent to Anglican hegemony and believed it had a deleterious effect on the education offered at Oxford and Cambridge. Shelburne's son, Lord Henry Petty, was joined in Edinburgh by three other future members of the Whig cabinet of 1830 – Lords Melbourne, Palmerston and John Russell.

No one would deny that universities, then as now, contained their fair share of cautious conservatives, yet evidence of systematic obscurantism is hard to find: as a study of life at Salamanca has revealed, even Spanish universities were not immune from progressive changes during Charles III's reign (1759–88), as the monarchy pushed aside half-hearted clerical resistance to recasting the curriculum, especially in natural philosophy where the last shreds of an antiquated Aristotelianism had lived on. Salamanca's French equivalents still possessed a vigorous institutional life that bore little resemblance to the *philosophes'* squibs about an outdated scholasticism. The Sorbonne, headquarters in the defence of

---

[13] Quotation from J. Witherspoon, *Ecclesiastical Characteristics: or the Arcana of Church Policy . . . the Character of a Moderate Man . . .* (Edinburgh, 1843 [1753]), 37.

theological orthodoxy, was producing outstanding modernising theologians such as Luke Joseph Hooke, who combined reason and natural-law theory in the service of the faith. The Churches were quite able to nurture traditional areas of study alongside newer subjects. In Rome ecclesiastical studies flourished with the Jesuit Francesco Antonio Zaccaria (1714–95), one of the greatest liturgical scholars of the age as his *Bibliotheca ritualis* (1776–81) testified. Further north, in Florence, the scholar-theologian Giovanni Lami (1697–1770) united sacred erudition with a radical politics that made him oppose the Jesuits. He was one of the first clerics in the city to become a mason. Creative Catholic thinkers such as the proto-Romantic Johann Michael Sailer (b. 1751), later bishop of Regensburg, urged theologians to draw on and incorporate the historic sources of Catholic liturgy and spirituality, as expressed in his eclectic *De idea theologi christiani* (1781).

The Eastern Church, of course, went its own way but still bore learned fruit. The monastic reformer, the Ukrainian St Paisy Velichkovsky (1722–94), a monk known for his personal austerity at his community in Moldavia, translated much early ascetic and mystical literature into Slavonic, especially the *Philokalia* (1793), for the spiritual nourishment of a wider audience. He started a spiritual revival which continued the Hesychastic tradition of inner, mystical prayer which was fostered by those among his disciples who became monastic superiors. The community on the Holy Mountain of Athos was the setting for an extraordinary revival associated with St Nikodimos (1749–1809). He urged his followers to communicate frequently and published Greek editions of many Catholic writers including Loyola's *Spiritual Exercises*.

The German Enlightenment centred preponderantly on the universities, among the most vigorous in eighteenth-century Europe and among the most recent. Institutions at Halle (1694) and Göttingen (1737) owed their inception to princely rather than clerical initiatives but, despite the emphasis on medicine and natural sciences, studies were overwhelmingly rooted in a rational piety that only gradually receded in the second half of the century along with what had been the predominant influence of Christian Wolff (1679–1754). Thereafter academic Protestants were defensively protecting orthodoxy, and German universities witnessed many exchanges on the question as scholarship pointed towards a dynamic rather than a static view of the content of faith. It was in this setting that Lessing waged an agonised personal contest to hold on to a shred of Christianity. Secularisation in the curriculum of Catholic universities in western Germany happened fast after 1765, pushed on by the prince-bishops, allowing Protestants and Jews into teaching posts. A university like Würzburg, early in its rejection of scholasticism and adoption of

Wolffian views, became one of the main centres of the Catholic Enlightenment under the protection of its prince-bishops.

As the *Journal von und für Deutschland* proclaimed in 1787:

The Catholic universities in Germany have cast aside almost everywhere their old-fashioned Gothic garb and have been reorganised in a better fashion, more in tune with the taste of our times. The old barbaric tone which used to rule in the lecture halls has been banished from almost all of them.[14]

All the western Churches had by this date largely if reluctantly accepted that social coercion was not enough; debate was unavoidable if Christianity was to be persuasive. Not so further east, where in Russia the first modern university was only established at Moscow in 1755. The Ottomans had their own system of Islamic higher education while the Orthodox Church was determined to prevent enlightenment culture infecting its sphere of influence. Graduates of the new Greek schools were most successful in absorbing enlightenment influences, publishing their work outside Ottoman control, often from Vienna. Life could still be intolerable for controversial teachers like Eugenios Voulgaris. He moved to St Petersburg to become Catherine the Great's librarian from frustration at the Greek Church's repudiation of modern philosophy. The Russian Church was only marginally less hostile than its Greek sister, with traditional antirationalism most entrenched among the hardline Old Believers. Prince Dimitri Cantemir, prince of Moldavia (1673–1723), had been a leading sponsor of Balkan intellectual life in his generation, but his translation of Fontenelle's *Plurality of Worlds* (1686) was blocked for ten years by the Church, which also held up the Russian translation of Pope's *An Essay on Man* (1733–4) until 1757 when changes toning down the Newtonian allusions proved acceptable. The Church authorities were encouraged to show greater openness by Catherine II's reign, and interest in scholarship within Orthodoxy should not be underestimated. Russian learned societies derived much of their strength from the Church. When Princess Dashkova sponsored the creation of the Russian Academy in 1783 its membership included a high proportion of Orthodox priests. Of seventy members from 1783–96, nearly a quarter came from the monastic and parochial clergy.

Reduced recourse to repression

Most Orthodox clerics still wanted active repression. By contrast, the repressive institutions of western Christendom, such as the Inquisition,

---

[14] Quoted in T. C. W. Blanning, *The French Revolution in Germany: Occupation and Resistance in the Rhineland, 1792–1802* (Oxford, 1983), 39.

had become an embarrassment to Catholics of most persuasions. It still existed in the 1760s but with limited power and no assurance that its edicts would be enforced by the secular arm. In Spain, Charles III in 1768 reduced its authority to censor books and in 1770 warned it against imprisoning anyone until his guilt was fully established. This struck directly at traditional procedures, and cases were thereafter pursued half-heartedly by the Holy Office: prosecution rarely commenced even in cases where the evidence indicated a strong prima facie case. In Spain as elsewhere in Europe, thoughtful churchmen knew the good sense of repudiating the stock charges levelled against them by anticlericals. A single instance, well publicised, could at a stroke undo their watchfulness: the Calas affair showed that even in France as late as 1762 it was possible for a Protestant to be tortured and broken on the wheel for the falsely attributed murder of his Catholic-convert son. The resulting furore was orchestrated by Voltaire and did the Gallican Church much damage.

The *Index Librorium Prohibitorum* (List of Prohibited Books) remained as a weapon of regular resort for the papacy, forbidding the faithful to read the titles placed on it. Though Benedict XIV at last removed from it those titles which had supported the heliocentric theories of Copernicus and Galileo, the Index still grew longer annually with modern titles. Clement XIII was busy adding books by Helvétius and Rousseau to it in the 1760s with predictably little effect. Whereas, unlike the Inquisition, the Index was acceptable in principle to Catholic governments, they preferred to impose their own form of censorship, and national Churches had begun to draw up lists of offensive titles independently of Rome. The Gallican Church relied on the learned doctors of the University of Paris to condemn volumes deemed offensive to Christian belief, but their pronouncements tended to increase public interest in proscribed texts and did nothing to diminish a flourishing trade across the frontier in clandestine manuscripts and pirated editions. As the sceptic Friedrich-Melchior Grimm had sardonically observed: 'It's a shame that the thunder of the Sorbonne resembles the thunder of the Opera, which no longer frightens anyone, not even children.'[15] It was not much different further east. In November 1768 the high sheriffs of Hungary were told by the Council of Lieutenancy in Budapest to punish atheists and indifferentists, but the exercise was half-hearted.

In Protestant states, the clergy found it difficult to accept that the battle against what the French authorities called 'mauvais livres' was lost. In Sweden – where Catholicism was prohibited until the nineteenth

---

[15] Quoted in Alan Charles Kors, *D'Holbach's Coterie: An Enlightenment in Paris* (Princeton, 1976), 240.

century – the state Lutheran Church had a range of legal enforcements like the Conventicle Act (1726) in place to reinforce a narrower definition of orthodoxy (still buttressed by Aristotelian scholasticism) than could be found across the Baltic in Germany. This gave the Church considerable powers of censorship in the University of Uppsala that were not finally relinquished until Gustavus III had secured full powers in 1772. In England, the Licensing Act had lapsed in 1695, and the Blasphemy Act of 1697 was, to the Anglican clergy confronted with the torrent of impious literature, more mocked than used in their favour by the Crown's law officers. Nevertheless, orthodox Christianity went virtually unchallenged in Oxford during George III's reign, and the latitudinarian theology of Cambridge was waning fast from the 1770s, upheld almost single-handedly by one or two influential churchmen such as John Hey, Lady Margaret professor of divinity, and Richard Watson, regius professor of chemistry and (non-resident) bishop of Llandaff. Watson's pamphlets in favour of abolition of the Athanasian creed, a revision of the liturgy and a fairer division of funds among the bishops and lower clergy, ensured that he remained unpromoted from his humble see until his death in 1816. Even William Paley, the leading theologian of his generation, discovered that his orthodoxy was not impeccable enough to win him a bishopric from the Crown.

The Catholic Enlightenment

Yet, though in one sense enlightenment rationalism threatened the traditional presentation and articulation of Christian beliefs, in another it impelled the Churches to reposition the faith within a European culture where Christianity could no longer assume a position of unassailable supremacy. While Roman Catholic theologians could be both flexible and formidable in debate, senior clergy looked again at the historic structures they had inherited in the light of the more temperate criticisms directed at them. From this proceeded what David Sorkin has called 'Reform Catholicism'[16] and (particularly after the return of peace in 1763) the more radical and ultimately divisive phenomenon known as the Catholic Enlightenment. The fruits of these movements were visible in France, Italy, the Austrian Netherlands and Austria itself, as well as in the 'regalism' of the Spanish Church under Charles III. The Catholic Enlightenment in one sense continued Counter-Reformation efforts to professionalise the education of the clergy – with impressive results; elsewhere,

---

[16] David H. Sorkin, 'Roman Catholicism and the Religious Enlightenment', *Austrian History Yearbook* (1999), 1–70.

its intolerance of the hybrid religious customs of the lay majority may have pleased secularising intellectuals and Jansenists, but the extirpation of what was presented as error and superstition carried the risk that an enlightened clergy would create not an enlightened laity but a resentful one. Enlightened priests such as the grouping called 'the Great Ones' (*Die Grossen*) in Austria welcomed the final dismantling of Jesuit power over higher education and encouraged well-qualified laymen – not necessarily uncritical of the Church – to take their places as university teachers alongside progressive Orders such as the Oratorians. Jansenists were prominent in their ranks, but the trend had an appeal among educated clergy that transcended party divisions. Well before the last decade of the century, some voices were making it clear they felt the process had gone far enough. Adeodato Turchi, bishop of Parma from 1788, criticised alike toleration, the *philosophes* and the eagerness to read prohibited books.

Turchi and those like him feared the corrosive effect of enlightenment scepticism and unbelief on the attitude of the wider population to religion, and this would intensify once the French Revolutionary wars sent 'armed missionaries' across Europe after 1792 and the *philosophes* were blamed for precipitating the destruction of the old order. It then became imperative to preserve from contamination the lower orders in states hitherto minimally affected. English authors such as John Bowdler would lend their name to the process by which literature was doctored to eliminate anything that could encourage the potentially subversive among the people. Yet, certainly in the countryside, this majority remained relatively untouched by the infidelity fashionable in some elite circles. In this key area, the Enlightenment was not functioning directly as an agency of secularisation.

The decline of deism

One of the most lasting ways in which the Enlightenment had partially unstitched the Christian fabric of Europe was in disposing the educated laity towards some form of deism. As Voltaire declared towards the end of his life in one of his characters in his novella, the *Histoire de Jenni*, 'Let us admit that there is a Being, supreme, necessary, and incomprehensible, who has made us',[17] though his lifelong insistence on the need for a social religion to constrain the masses through 'un Dieu rémunérateur et vengeur' in itself offered the Church little comfort. Deists like him

---

[17] *Histoire de Jenni* (Paris, 1779), chap. 18 – dialogue between Freind (a deist) and Burton (an atheist).

dispensed with Church and scriptures, but the boundary between deism and Christianity was blurred and deism itself was enormously eclectic as well as vague. These two versions of religion tended to meet half-way: deism had its own dogmas and could embrace an ethical version of the traditional faith more or less shorn of its supernatural dimension; correspondingly, many members of the eighteenth-century Churches downplayed revelation as the primary basis of faith in favour of reason and the evidences offered by the created world for a beneficent, divine creator.

Yet the heyday of classic deism was over by the 1750s when it began a slow contraction from its high point of influence earlier in the century. The reasons for this trend are complicated and can only be briefly suggested here. Public boredom with the controversy should not be discounted, while successful counter-attacks by theologians played an important part. Here Bishop Joseph Butler of Durham (1692–1752), the most formidable Anglican theologian of the age, led the way. His acclaimed *Analogy of Religion* (1736) confronted the exclusive deist emphasis on natural religion by pointing out its explanatory limitations: wayward humanity stood in need of a counterbalancing faith in a divine Saviour. Butler's masterpiece held the field for the rest of the century on the continent as well as in England. By contrast with his measured writing, deist literature often sounded an extremist, confrontational note that deterred many readers. Matthew Tindal's *Christianity as old as the Creation; or, the Gospel, a Republication of the Religion of nature* (1730) attracted notice not for making a compelling case but for deist zealotry coupled with a virulent anticlericalism. The destruction of Tindal's reputation dragged down his cause, and he was not the last to suffer that fate. The former Tory minister and adversary of Walpole, Lord Bolingbroke, had as many highly placed friends in France as in England, but his philosophical standing was savaged following publication of his complete works soon after his death in 1751. Bolingbroke's deism was embarrassingly offset by his libertinism, and he was repudiated by Tory high churchmen aghast at the viper their party had unknowingly sheltered.

Deism was both less fashionable and less intellectually compelling by the 1750s, and enlightenment opinion formers went in other directions. Deism had come to seem facile as well as arid, its intellectual underpinnings dependent on a series of premises that would not resist close scrutiny, as Hume's *Dialogues on Natural Religion* (1779) remorsely demonstrated. Nevertheless, a rarefied deistic outlook more than survived in some sections of the elite. It had an enduring influence among some founding fathers of the United States, notably Benjamin Franklin and Thomas Jefferson; they had no time for the supernatural but equally could not detach popular morality from religious observance. The Briton who did so much for the American colonists' cause, Tom Paine, was prepared to go that one further step in his famous *Rights of Man* and *Age of Reason* (1791). Paine almost singlehandly reinvented popular deism as the century ended, much to the consternation of the British establishment in Church and state. In France, too, the writings of the *Idéologues* gave it a new lease of life, albeit at a much more rarefied social level than Paine and his followers.

Science and religion

Whatever the individual's precise religious outlook, he could look to the advance in the natural sciences for its justification. Between 1680 and 1750 this trend had given deism its original impetus, though the clergy had also worked hard to use the findings of empirical science as a buttress for Christianity. The Boyle Lectures, beginning in London in 1691, had inaugurated the trend for Newtonian physics to be deployed by the clergy in defence of the faith, and the alliance remained close into the second half of the century as Newtonianism swept aside the intellectual alternatives in most parts of western Europe: the *Encyclopédie* declared the *Principia* an 'Immortal work, and one of the finest that the human mind has ever produced'.[18] It influenced natural philosophers even on the European periphery. Newtonianism was well established in Russia by the 1750s. The outstanding chemist Mikhail Vasil'evich Lomonosov (1711–65) read Newton's *Principia* while under house arrest for insubordination in 1743–4 and preached its supremacy when professor of chemistry at the St Petersburg Academy. In Greece, too, Copernican–Newtonian cosmology was expounded in Eugenios Voulgaris' (1716–1806) *The System of the Universe* (1805).

But was Newtonianism a prop of orthodoxy or an incentive to abandon it? There were those who worried that Newton's impersonal universe of invisible forces had pushed an active divine agency to the explanatory margins in favour of an all-sufficient nature. That was one concern; two more were the minimal reference to scriptural views of the created world in the published writings of either Newton or the Newtonians, an omission compounded by doubts about where the fall of man and salvation offered by Christ fitted into this scheme of things. These points were forcibly made by John Hutchinson (1674–1737) in his chief work *Moses Principia* (1724), which expounded a system of biblical philosophy, a physico-theology. Hutchinson was influential among Oxford Tories in the

---

[18] Article on 'Newtonianisme'. See generally Henry Guerlac, *Newton on the Continent* (Ithaca, NY, 1981).

1750s, who presented Moses as the first scientist and the Pentateuch as the real guide to scientific knowledge, one containable within an explicitly Trinitarian framework. Other writers were willing to concede Moses' scientific dabblings, but denied they had anything to do with revelation or inspiration. Karl Bahrdt (1741–92) claimed he was just an experimenter in explosives, which could be passed off as divine thunder on Mount Sinai.

Hutchinsonianism won the allegiance of some clergy, particularly those in the Scottish Episcopal Church, right into the next century, but on the whole its impact was limited, even in Oxford: Newton's status as a cultural and national icon was too formidable to be dislodged. Edward Bentham, regius professor of divinity in the university, said in his inaugural lecture in 1764 that theology rejoiced in scientists like Newton, Robert Boyle, John Ray, John Wallis, Stephen Hales and James Bradley, and his was the voice of the majority. Newtonian natural theology and science divided Italian Catholic intellectuals. Ferdinando Galiani, Niccolini and Bartolomeo Intieri used the *Principia* when trying to shift Christianity away from apologetics towards deism and natural theology. Others were less persuaded and acceded to the Boyle Lectures' view of Newtonianism as a bastion of orthodoxy. Newton's contemporary in Germany, Leibniz, had an international reputation almost as great. He influenced the rationalist creed within a Christian framework of Christian Wolff, whose *Theologia naturalis* (1736–7) applied mathematical method to theology and showed how it could be used to reason with unbelievers. His standing among Lutheran academics in Germany and Sweden lasted beyond his death until Kant undermined his moral philosophy.

Wolff insisted that the 'two books' (of nature and scripture) were not contradictory. So did one who was much influenced by him, the Swedish botanist, Carl Linnaeus (1707–88), son of a pastor, renowned throughout the continent for his binomial classification system for living entities based on their reproductive characteristics. He took Genesis very seriously, though by no means uncritically, to the extent that he located the Garden of Eden on a Swedish island and took pleasure in being called 'the second Adam', because he, too, gave plants and animals their names. Such an approach could not prevent theological critics looking suspiciously at Linnaeus' output, with the Jansenist journal, the *Nouvelles Ecclésiatiques*, noting disapprovingly in 1754 how far his classification conflicted with the Bible. Nevertheless, it was one encountered repeatedly as men explored the natural world and found pointers to God. In Russia, Lomonosov described science and religion as 'two kindred sisters, the daughters of one supreme parent' and urged that 'reasonable and good persons must search for means to explain and avert all imagined conflict between them, following the aforementioned wise teacher [Basil the Great] of our Orthodox Church'.[19]

But this comforting presumption was not axiomatic in the second half of the century, when Newtonian science and the natural theology it had supported became less serviceable for Christian apologists. In Britain, the Royal Society, for so long the champion of the working alliance between latitudinarian Anglicanism and Newtonian cosmology, began to waver in its commitment during the decisive presidency of Martin Folkes (1741–53), by which date the Boyle Lectures had ceased to lead the field in up-to-date apologetics. This uncoupling did not take place overnight. It may be seen as part of the wider process of fragmentation and diversification within the Enlightenment, though majority opinion still inclined towards seeing the experimental method as confirming faith. Charles Bonnet (1720–93), the Swiss naturalist, put his innovative work on the parthenogenesis of the aphid and in plant physiology into the service of a Christian natural philosophy, as found in his *Contemplation of Nature* (1764), a perspective still owing much to Leibnizian optimism. For him, bodily resurrection was akin to metamorphoses in the life-cycle. The Cambridge academic, William Paley (1743–1805), produced *Evidences of Christianity* (1794) and *Natural Theology* (1802), texts among the most influential of their generation that still drew on the natural harmony of things as prima facie evidence for the truth of Christianity. It was less a reply to the sceptical caution of Hume's *Dialogues on Natural Religion* than an ignoring of them. Paley also took no cognisance of Kant's *Critique of Pure Reason* (1781), which insisted physics and natural philosophy were by definition incapable of forming the basis for any natural theology and offered merely the logic of illusion. For Kant, natural theologies always collapse because their reach exceeds their grasp, and because they attempt to employ pure concepts incapable of experiential validation. A Kantian emphasis on the moral dimension of human life was nevertheless widely adopted after 1780 among Catholic thinkers, like Benedikt Stattler, a Jesuit down to the Order's suppression and professor of dogmatics at Ingolstadt thereafter. His *De Locis Theologicis* was censored by Rome, which, unlike Stattler, could not see that Kant might be an ally against infidelity in both apologetics and theology.

Kant's influence outside Germany was limited until the next century and had minimal impact on popular theological understanding in Britain

[19] M. V. Lomonosov, *Polnoe Sobranie Sochinenii* (11 vols., Moscow and Leningrad, 1950–83), vol. IV, 373, quoted in Colin Chant, 'Science in Orthodox Europe', in David Goodman and Colin A. Russell (eds.), *The Rise of Scientific Europe 1500–1800* (Sevenoaks, 1991), 333–60, at 357.

and France. Paine's *The Age of Reason*, appearing the same year as Paley's *Evidences*, categorically denied that natural theology and Christianity were linked. Paine's text sold fast, but he could not catch the mood of the educated public as Rousseau had done. For the latter nature spoke of a beneficent Creator though not a distinctively Christian one. And man was to respond to nature with his heart not his mind, as Rousseau made clear in 'Profession of Faith of the Savoyard Vicar', a key part of his *Émile* (1762):

> I perceive the Deity in all his works, I feel him within me, and behold him in every object around me: but, I no sooner endeavour to contemplate what he is in himself: I no sooner enquire where he is, and what is his substance, than he eludes the strongest efforts of my imagination; and my bewildered understanding is convinced of its own weakness.[20]

The Catholic establishment had the book condemned. That did not decrease its sales, or stop even clergy tracking down copies, for Jean-Jacques had a celebrity following that no theologian could equal. He was, as one historian has written, nothing less than 'the inspirational centre of the transformation of the religious consciousness of Western Europe which took place in the eighteenth century'.[21]

The providential and the miraculous

Central to undermining the association of Christianity with a benevolent natural theology was the experience of natural disaster. Deists, too, had no cause for comfort. The optimism commonly associated with it – as in Pope's *Essay on Man* – appeared superficial when set against the woes visited on humanity by an indifferent universe, such as the Lisbon earthquake of 1 November 1755. How could this destructive calamity be ascribed to a benevolent deity? Perhaps as many as 30,000 people died. The additional irony was that many of them had been attending church services when the earthquake struck. The tragedy could not easily be reconciled with the claim that God was working in the universe for good when unmerited misfortune was inflicted on innocent people. At best, He was indifferent to human misery; at worse, He did not exist at all. The earthquake played into the hands of La Mettrie and other militant materialists, and it confirmed the intelligent atheism of Diderot. The writings of Voltaire – his *Poem on the Lisbon Disaster and on Natural Law* (May 1756) followed by *Candide or Optimism* (1759), his supreme short-story masterpiece – ensured that its theological implications were not lost on any reader.

[20] Rousseau, *Emile*, trans. William Kenrick (4 vols., Dublin, 1779), vol. III, 41–2.
[21] J. McManners, *Death and the Enlightenment* (Oxford, 1981), 348.

Yet the Churches drew different lessons and these can be read in the innumerable pastoral letters issued in most European countries. The earthquake gave orthodoxy a new fillip as preachers in most European countries urged their people to turn from sin at this sign of divine displeasure, nourish their inner spiritual lives, and make their religion more than mere outward observance. In the light of Old Testament precedents, it was often said that the hand of God was inflicting punishment for wickedness on the people of Lisbon and that the same fate would be shared by other places unless Christians repented. Bishop Sherlock's providentialist account of the calamity sold no fewer than 100,000 copies. Protestants might once have felt themselves vindicated by the destruction visited on their rival Church, and it says much of the growth of popular toleration that most Protestant sermons on the subject called for prayers of compassion and tried to raise money to help the thousands of families left homeless by the earthquake. The Churches found the unlikely figure of Rousseau crossing swords with other *philosophes* over the Lisbon catastrophe. In his *Letter on Providence* (1756) Rousseau denied that God should be blamed for the death toll: it was the Portuguese not Providence who had created an overcrowded, dilapidated city susceptible to natural disaster.

But if the natural order was an unreliable witness to divine beneficence, Christians found it unprofitable to cite breaches of that order – in other words, the miraculous – as evidence in favour of the truth of the Gospels or the authenticity of Christianity, thereby abandoning this formerly reliable defensive position. The New Testament miracles – including Christ's own resurrection from the dead – were, classically, central to vindications of Protestant Christianity, as Thomas Sherlock's *Trial of the Witnesses of the Resurrection* (1729) had insisted. Miracles coming *after* Apostolic times were more dubious because they had no biblical standing, and although they had their place in Catholic theology, were not readily accepted by the Anglican hierarchy. It was here that Hume chose to attack with his *Essay on Miracles* (1748). He challenged the existence of post-biblical miracles on the basis of unreliable testimony. In his words: 'no testimony is sufficient to establish a miracle, unless the testimony be of such a kind, that its falsehood would be more miraculous, than the fact, which it endeavours to conceal'.[22] It was unacceptable to rely on the uncorroborated 'evidence' of credulous bystanders (up to and including Christ's Apostles) if there were no contemporary analogues for the events they claimed. Hume refrained from directly attacking the

[22] David Hume, *The Philosophical Works*, eds. T. H. Green and T. H. Grose (4 vols., London, 1882), vol. IV, 94.

veracity of New Testament miracles, but the implications of his philosophical critique were gravely damaging for Christian orthodoxy. He was little regarded at the time in England, where more attention was paid to the influential Cambridge academic, Conyers Middleton, who, in his *Free Inquiry* of 1748, while arguing for the high probability of Apostolic miracles (as opposed to those of patristic times) only succeeded in further muddying the waters and prolonging the controversy. The wrangling took a more anticlerical turn in Gallican France. The essay on miracles in the *Encyclopédie* was entrusted to d'Holbach. He needed no encouragement to produce a savage indictment of priestly conjuring tricks which exploited human gullibility for clerical self-interest. Voltaire followed with more temperate and telling points on the subject in his *Questions on the Miracles* of 1765.

Catholic apologists, whose definition of the miraculous encompassed a much longer time-frame, were on the defensive against both Protestants and sceptics; by conceding that miracles had all but ceased after the Apostolic age while continuing to claim validity for those recorded in scripture, Anglican clerics gave themselves more scope for a plausible defence of one of the most vital foundations of the Christian faith. Theirs was a tactical retreat all the same, though one that may have been relatively painless to clergy who felt more comfortable in showing how Newtonian mathematics confirmed God's wisdom via his immutable natural laws. While Butler and Paley satisfied many of their readers, the Church of England could not be said to have won the debate on miracles, while the Gallican Church had definitely lost it. The result was the reduced faith of educated men and women in revelation and the encouragement of the drift towards Socianism among those who were more attracted by Christ's ethical character than his claims to divinity. The debate also afforded further evidence of the incapacity of divines to land a knock-out blow against their detractors. Thus, the tendency of the age to scepticism received a further impetus.

Perspectives on the Bible

Voltaire in the 1760s seized on any aspect of Christianity that looked vulnerable to attack. He was particularly ruthless in presenting the history of the Israelites in the Old Testament as an unwholesome mixture of inconsistent events blended with the morally dubious. It was impossible for any reasonable man to accept all this as factual; if clergy tried to do so then they stood accused of trying to ground Christianity on a most unsavoury Judaic heritage. Voltaire's subversion of scripture conventionally understood as the unimpeachable record of God's dealing with mankind infuriated defenders of orthodoxy who suspected his good faith, but it belonged to a wider interpretative tradition in biblical studies that dated back through the Dutch Arminian Hugo Grotius (1583–1645) to Erasmus (1466–1536). Their work had not discomforted Protestants, far from it. On the other hand, Spinoza and the French Oratorian Richard Simon (1638–1712) had shown that the scriptural text was less stable than members of the Reformed Churches liked to believe. Simon may have considered his criticism a means of confounding Protestants. His superiors, however, thought otherwise. They expelled him from his Order, only to find the great early Enlightenment apologist, Pierre Bayle (1648–1706), popularising Simon's work in his *Dictionary*, a compendium that inspired the numerous deists and sceptics who later plundered it.

By the second half of the century, Germany had become the powerhouse of biblical scholarship and the emerging discipline of hermeneutics. Some radical theologians in Germany were set on undermining most of Christianity's central doctrines. There were early signs of this in a work like H. S. Reimarus' *The Principal Truths of Natural Religion* (1754), an intelligent restatement of deism and a rationalist critique of the Bible. But Reimarus was the exception.

Most German theologians were often ordained ministers, university based, who were inspired by the possibility of recovering a purer form of Christian belief that was compatible with the most rigorous and modern scholarship. This work was seldom undertaken for destructive or polemical purposes. Textual criticism revealed the variants in biblical manuscripts to be more numerous and complicated than previously assumed; authorship according to the name given in the canon was often fancifully implausible. The historical perspective of these scholars could be no less crude, their application of reason to the supernatural and miraculous too reductionist to commend itself either to believers or sceptics. Nevertheless, some fine work was done. Johann S. Semler (1725–91) indicated the degree to which the canon of scripture had been historically determined and altered over time, while Johann Gottfried Eichhorn published introductions between 1780 and 1783 to several books of the Bible which discussed dating, authorship and stylistics as though they were secular texts. Concurrently, the epistemological basis to understanding the past was undergoing a transformation and the Bible was obviously affected by, for instance, the new forms of theological historical criticism pioneered by Church historian Philipp Konrad Henke (1752–1809), who owed much to Kantian rationalism. Lessing was also important in this area, but most famous was Johann Gottlieb Fichte (1762–1814), professor of philosophy at Jena from 1794 to 1799, until he was expelled for alleged atheism and his support of the French Revolution. For Fichte, historical data in the New Testament held no intrinsic ethical meaning nor offered automatic insight into the rational status of the events recorded that would be sufficient to establish its status as revelation.

For German Protestants who followed Luther in seeing the Bible as the ultimate authority in matters of Christian doctrine and moral teaching, the rapid growth of biblical criticism could be quite unsettling. Some Anglican divines were taking an interest in German writing on Protestant doctrine and biblical scholarship as early as the 1770s. Anglicans, for example Bishop John Butler of Oxford, kept up to date thanks to the Revd Alexander Woide, a Reformed cleric, the librarian of the British Museum, with contacts at Helmstad and Wolfenbuttel, the latter possessing one of the most complete biblical collections in Europe. Though an Oxford don, Benjamin Blayney, was in touch with Johann-David Michaelis earlier in the century, it was not really until the 1790s that German methods of research made much impact on British scholarship after Herbert Marsh (1757–1839), a future bishop of Peterborough, had spent several years at Leipzig studying the work of Michaelis and aroused controversy when he published in translation the latter's *Introduction to the New Testament* between 1793 and 1801. Before Marsh, British writers on scripture had taken what could be described as an intelligently literal view of the biblical canon, its contents and absolute authority. Thus Laurence Sterne, the Yorkshire parson and overnight celebrity as author of *Tristram Shandy* (1760), could deploy a wit that was at once subversive and skittish, but not on the Bible. His sermon 'Search the Scriptures'[23] emphasised the 'simplicity' of the Christian message, and his insistence on viewing the Bible as 'that grand charter of our eternal happiness' was one shared by characters like Uncle Toby and Parson Yorick in his novel. Such a position by no means precluded controversy. Priestley and his followers were not slow to stress the absence of explicit references to a Trinitarian Godhead in the Gospels and Epistles; in 1785 Archdeacon Travis deplored the historian Edward Gibbon's slighting references in *The Decline and Fall* to the authenticity of the verses referring to the Trinity (the famous Johannine comma) in the First Epistle of John, usually seen as pivotal to the orthodox case. After the greatest Grecian scholar of his day, Richard Porson, had vindicated Gibbon's learning and shown its Erasmian origins – trouncing Travis in the process – Anglican apologists fell discreetly silent. To adopt a flagrantly 'scientific', deconstructionist approach was politically suspect. It was another Unitarian, the one-time Peterhouse academic, John Jebb, who considered that the 'right

[23] *The Sermons of Laurence Sterne*, ed. Melvyn New (Gainsville, Fl., 1996), sermon 42, 396.

arrangement of political power' and the 'philological knowledge of the Scriptures' were 'combined causes'.[24]

For the most part, English commentators on scripture were content to stress, as their predecessors had done, the importance of typology and allegory. The tendency was seen most unrestrainedly in the writings of the Hutchinsonians. They approached Hebrew as the single language of mankind that existed before Babel, one which, used correctly in interpretation, offered the key to all knowledge, whether secular or religious, and unique insights into God's activities over time. They viewed with misgivings the activities of the Christ Church don, Benjamin Kennicott (1718–83) on the Hebrew text of the Old Testament, as he went about his work of collating biblical manuscripts. Kennicott had the backing of the Anglican establishment for his monumental labours which fell within the Oxford tradition of Hebraic scholarship, and his *Vetus Testamentum Hebraicum, cum variis lectionibus* duly appeared in two volumes in 1776 and 1780. Alongside Kennicott on philology can be placed the work of Robert Lowth (1710–87), later bishop of London, who offered a new insight into Old Testament literary culture in his lectures on Hebrew poetry of 1753 and his translation of Isaiah of 1778. In uncovering the importance of the poetic and the ludic in Old Testament writings, Lowth offered a version of Old Testament times that strove for historical authenticity and would inspire the next generation of critics like Marsh. In France, that tendency was embodied by Jean Astruc (1684–1766). He pioneered the systematic source analysis of the Pentateuch, arguing that the different books had divergent origins but had been combined by Moses himself. Hume and Voltaire, from different approaches, also tried to make the Pentateuch appear ridiculous, a dangerous undertaking in the light of universal belief that it directly prefigured the Christian dispensation. It was a criticism that was exploited by the opponents of the Church in France as they fanned the flames of anticlericalism and tried to persuade the public that the power of the clergy rested on fraudulent foundations.

The war against 'priestcraft': late eighteenth-century anticlericalism

Anticlericalism was often a crude weapon rather than one likely to do incisive intellectual damage to the political power and social prestige of the Churches. Enlightenment critics of clerical power inherited a large

---

[24] Quoted in John Gascoigne, 'Anglican Latitudinarianism and Political Radicalism in the Late Eighteenth Century', *History* 71 (1986), 22–38, at 30.

armoury from the Reformation and Middle Ages, but forged their own more refined weapons. Anticlericalism became an enlightenment commonplace, a ubiquitous critical reflex action to be found, in varying degrees, in texts ranging from Montesquieu's *L'Esprit des lois*, criticising the Church's grasp on society, to the latest pornographic novel featuring lusty monks and lascivious nuns.

It was easy to interest the laity in the subject. Most men and women had mixed feelings about the conduct and character of the clergy they encountered in the classroom, the confessional or the church; as ever, it might take just one individual's display of avarice or arrogance to taint the rest by association. Beyond these personal considerations, the wealth of the established Churches was patently excessive to disgruntled tithe payers forced to hand over hard-earned cash or produce when the parish priest came knocking at their door after the harvest was home. It was this bourgeois audience that anticlerical authors most particularly wanted to win over. Too much invective might be counter-productive, especially if it was the content of Christianity that was impugned rather than its votaries. In the *Encyclopédie*, it tended to be defunct non-Christian priesthoods that an author like d'Holbach ostensibly targeted, well-knowing that his readers would recognise his present-day enemies in the Gallican Church as his real victims.

France was the European focus for anticlericalism in the second half of the century. A recurrent enlightenment criticism of the Church was that its structures and the personnel who manned them defied any rational criteria of usefulness. Taking their lead from the high priests of the Enlightenment – Voltaire, Helvétius, Diderot, d'Holbach – numerous hack pamphleteers played on the discrepancies of income between higher and lower clergy, the drone-like existence of bishops at court scrambling for preferment: Grub Street had a field-day when the news broke in 1785 that Cardinal Rohan, bishop of Strasbourg, had apparently gained the sexual as well as the political favours of Marie-Antoinette in return for a fabulous diamond necklace. Salacious anticlericals of course deliberately overlooked the intelligence and dedication of those inside the Church, those committed to improving its structures and modernising its practices in accordance with the Catholic Enlightenment. Yet, however exaggerated or distorted the charges made against it, the Church was slow to use the talent in its own ranks to produce a convincing defence, with some few exceptions such as the abbé Nicolas-Sylvain Bergier. He emerged in the 1760s at the Collège de Besançon as a formidable controversialist, winning congratulations from both Clement XIII and Clement XIV for his attacks on Voltaire and Rousseau. In 1771 his *Examination of Materialism*, commissioned by the General

Assembly, was a timely riposte to d'Holbach, and its excellences were widely appreciated.

Yet there were not enough talented spokesmen for the Church like Bergier to make a major impact. Respect for established authority corroded away to an extent that remains elusive. Some historians might think in terms of 'desacralisation', but to do so underestimates the pervasive influence of Christianity in French society up to and beyond the Revolution. Prominent religious apologists might not have been asked to join the fashionable salons of society hostesses like Mme Geoffrin, Mme d'Epinay and Mme Necker, but clergy who held on to orthodoxy not uncritically could be found in provincial academies, or the innumerable clubs and coffee houses that informally but effectively spread the Enlightenment. For the most part, the French public was quite capable of appreciating the prevailing anticlerical tone and content of so many *philosophe* texts, but at the same time rejecting merely negative criticism of the First Estate in favour of suggestions for moderate reform of the sort that appear in scores of Third Estate *cahiers* in 1789. The French Enlightenment therefore had the effect less of discrediting Christianity among a large part of the educated bourgeoisie than of fuelling demands for religious renewal in the Gallican Church, of calling it back to first principles.

French critics of the clergy argued that they inculcated principles that were inimical to good citizenship. That was not a charge commonly found in other parts of Europe; quite the opposite. Among German Protestants, the Church was primarily a means of education and reform in society and its ministers were identified as the best means of disseminating the new standards of enlightened sociability among the population at large. There were certainly opponents of priestly influence in Joseph II's entourage. Aloys Blumauer (1755–98), would-be Jesuit and court censor from 1782 to 1793, produced an anticlerical travesty of the *Aeneid*, while Ignaz von Born was well known in Vienna for his satires directed against the clergy. Generally, anticlericalism was rarely articulated by Catholics in the German states. Where it existed at all, it was projected on to the papacy south of the Alps or the easy target of the monastic Orders. It was not, as in France, bound up with a wider campaign to weaken the influence of institutional religion.

In England, anticlericalism had been a formidable force before 1750, closely associated with the political culture of the Whig hegemony established quickly after the Hanoverian accession in 1714. The Anglican lower clergy were overwhelmingly in favour of the Tory high church party, and their side lost heavily in the new scheme of things. It was only after the duke of Newcastle began to supervise religious affairs for the government after Walpole's fall in 1742 that churchmen could loosen their guard as ministers no longer countenanced schemes to diminish the privileges of the established Church, promoted by country Whigs ready to deplore what they called 'priestcraft'. But if serious assaults on clerical power were abandoned, the culture of casual complaint persisted. As one young Oxford don, the future archbishop of York, William Markham, ruefully noted: 'We must know, that, for the sake of jest and raillery only, reports to our disadvantage are favourably heard; and that the imperfections of a single clergyman are not thought to be compensated by the purity of many.'[25]

By George III's accession in 1760, the Church of England could rely on steady government protection, and intellectual forms of anticlericalism fell out of fashion in favour of a cruder material resentment. The parochial clergy on average saw their livings increase markedly in value between the 1750s and the 1830s as the passing of Enclosure Acts transformed large areas of central and eastern England. Agricultural production rose, as did rents and tithes. This new prosperity could open a material gap between the clergy and the average villager that was deleterious to pastoral life; so could the increasing importance of the clergy as magistrates. It is likely that much of the exceptional growth in Protestant dissent in England during the 1790s was fuelled by these trends and was not discouraged by nonconformist ministers, themselves fully capable of playing the anticlerical card against their counterparts in the Church of England. In Ireland, legal rights to the tithe belonged exclusively to the (episcopal) Church of Ireland, and intensified the dislike felt towards it among majority Catholics and the Ulster Presbyterians. During the 1760s this resentment spilled over into the 'Whiteboys' campaign of agrarian violence in parts of Munster and south Leinster directed at clerical property; it increased Anglican insecurities and these remained unabated until the Churches of England and Ireland were legally united at the Act of Union of 1801. Here anticlericalism was no more than part of the confessional divide. In Scotland, it was hardly present at all, for reasons which are still not wholly clear. Minority Episcopalians and Catholics were numerically too small to affect religious life outside their own walls, while the established Kirk was affected by other tensions (there were three secessions in the course of the century) that centred more on patronage rights than on the status and role of the parochial clergy.

The Church of Scotland, like other Protestant denominations, had abolished monasticism at the Reformation. The phenomenon remained

---

[25] William Markham, *A Sermon preached in Lambeth-Chapel, at the Consecration of the Right Reverend Father in God James [Johnson] Lord Bishop of Gloucester on Sunday, December 10, 1752* (2 Tim. I.7) (Oxford, 1753), 29.

present in the Roman Catholic and Orthodox communions, seemingly anomalous in an enlightened Europe, and offering an irresistible focus on which critics of the clergy could concentrate their fire. The comparison between confessions was not lost on the *philosophes*. As Jaucourt wrote in the *Encyclopédie*:

The prodigious numbers of monasteries, which has continued to subsist in the Catholic church, has become a charge on the public, oppressive and manifestly promoting depopulation; it is enough to glance at Protestant and Catholic countries to be convinced of it. Commerce enlivens the one, and monasteries bring death to the other.[26]

There was nothing like a large land-owning monastery in the neighbourhood to guarantee a persistent anticlerical tradition among French tithe payers, especially if their *curé* was diligently going about his duties while living on the breadline.

That was a practical grievance, but there were wider issues of principle to exploit. Here were men and women forced into confinement and 'unnatural' celibacy by prejudice or family vindictiveness – a genuine spiritual vocation was inconceivable – and once confined were subject to the arbitrary government of an abbot or mother superior. Their incarceration also denied them the opportunity to be useful to their fellow creatures, thus infringing a cardinal enlightenment canon. Anticlericals paraded an affected moral concern at this enforced idleness, and dwelt lovingly on the scope offered for sexual indulgence, with a flagrant breach of the vows of chastity in favour of buggery, lesbianism and lascivious enjoyments of every kind. In France the reading public begged, borrowed or stole copies of the latest lubricious novel in a convent setting, like *Thérèse Philosophe*, which featured Father Dirrag and his famous 'cord', one of the century's best-sellers; the *Histoire de Dom B . . . , portier des Chartreux* or the no less lubricious *Nun in a Nightgown*.

Unsurprisingly, these tales of nefarious nuns and lusty friars interested the public more than the continuing vitality of intellectual life within the cloisters, especially in Benedictine communities. In Würzburg, two of that Order, Maternus Reuss and Conrad Stang, drew large audiences to hear their lectures on Kant. Benito Jerónimo, Feijóo (1676–1764), Benedictine monk and professor of theology at the University of Oveido, introduced Newtonian science to the Spanish public. His writings received royal protection from Ferdinand VI in 1750, who forbade further attacks on his prodigious output. Among the leading lights in France

---

[26] From his article on 'Monks', reprinted in John Lough, *The Encyclopedia of Diderot and d'Alembert* (Cambridge, 1954), 175.

were Dom Joseph Pernetty, a Benedictine Maurist and author of a popular course in Newtonian mathematics. He travelled with the explorer Bougainville to the Pacific and saw all learning as part of God's great canvas of universal knowledge. His fellow Benedictine, Dom Pierre Deforis, clashed with Rousseau over some of the educational views contained in *Emile*, while Dom Deschamps, prior of Montreuil-Bellay (diocese of Poitiers), invented a philosophy that anticipated some of the essential ideas of Hegel about the nature of God, and sought to make converts among his colleagues. The great Benedictine scholar, Louis-Mayeul Chaudon, was a learned physicist as well as a philosopher and a formidable opponent of materialism; his *Anti-dictionnaire philosophique* (1775) was, by any measure, a treatise of undeniable quality.

None of these exceptional intellectual achievements inspired anyone to offer an updated defence of the religious Orders on the basis of their adaptability to enlightened times. Monks themselves did not seriously try, an indication perhaps of low morale or, more likely, an intelligent sense among the learned religious that it would offend the progressive-minded in their century. Wider clerical circles also felt disinclined to defend a doubtful cause, and even doubted that it could be defended at all. Monastic immunities and lucrative tithes excited the jealousy of many seculars. The scarce resources they hoarded might be better used elsewhere, entrusted to the state, or given over to the parish clergy. Bishops and higher clergy did not turn into an issue of principle the policies of most secular rulers designed to eradicate glaring anomalies in the religious Orders, confiscate their estates, restrict their numbers and concentrate those who remained. To do so risked losing both political and intellectual influence in government circles. Besides, episcopal power was consolidated when monastic exemptions were curtailed or abolished. So prelates went along with change and made no public utterance of their personal misgivings. And to be involved in the process on the *Commission des réguliers* in France at least gave some degree of control and supervision over the pace of reform. For it must be viewed as monastic reform, not abolition, an attempt to stave off the wholesale disbandment that would come with the revolutionary measures of 1790. But it was not a vindication of the asceticism and contemplative values so unpopular with the eighteenth-century opinion formers; rather, it was a tactical defence which implicitly acknowledged the case of the critics. In the wider interests of their Church, Catholics were obliged to concede the ground, in recognition that the exotic mythology of the cloister was more powerful than the prosaic reality for the majority of the educated laity.

The overthrow of the Jesuits

Reform and reorganisation of the claustral religious Orders was a minor battle front by comparison with the offensive waged elsewhere that led in 1773 to the outright disbandment of the Catholic Church's most prestigious post-Counter-Reformation religious elite: the Society of Jesus. In the century after its formation, the Order was the indispensable ally of Catholic kings and princes, but their mid-eighteenth-century successors wanted it cut down to size. They found willing allies in many higher clergy, jealous of the Jesuits' excessive perceived share of the most lucrative patronage. The Jesuits' special oath of loyalty appeared both subversive and anomalous in an age of state consolidation and national loyalties; their colonial activities in South America brought them into open confrontation with the Spanish and Portuguese Crowns; there were many objections to their views on the theological questions of grace and free will and their moral teachings were ridiculed by their numerous enemies as contorted, self-serving and casuistical.

Of course, these latter charges were not new in the 1760s. They had been a standard commonplace of anti-Jesuit polemic ever since Pascal's satirical masterpiece *The Provincial Letters* had been published in 1655. But when Pascal wrote, the Jesuits had an abundance of friends in high places, which ensured that their standing in court and clerical society was not much damaged, leaving Pascal to speak for a despised Jansenist minority in France that wanted pastoral rigour and a primitive-style Christianity. A century after Pascal's death in 1662, Jansenists strictly defined as such remained a minority but not a despised one. Their austere Augustinian theology may have had diminished doctrinal appeal by that date; the same could not be said for the conciliarist politics they had adopted in their self-defence. These came to maturity in the two generations after Louis XIV had foisted the papal Bull *Unigenitus* on the Paris *parlement* in 1713 condemning 101 propositions attributed to the original Jansenist leadership. Broadly disseminated Jansenist values had much to commend them in post-Baroque Europe and had helped to invigorate a new constitutionalism in both France and parts of the Austrian Empire that had the destruction of the Jesuits as one of its principal aims and that of its concommitant, ultramontanism, as the other.

Monarchs like Louis XV could not endorse an ideology looking to the conciliar practices of the Church for inspiration; equally, he was reluctant to become too associated with defence of the Jesuits once the Paris *parlement* began an investigation into the Order's constitution in 1761 (Jesuit financial shortfalls had given it an opening). Louis hoped it would be enough to cancel their special religious vows and close their colleges.

Other sovereign courts in France shared this more temperate approach believing, like the *parlement* of Pau, that the Order's educational role would not easily be replaced. But the *parlement* of Paris would, in the end, accept no half-measures, and the Jesuits were expelled from France in 1764. That came five years after the marquês de Pombal in Portugal had started the trend. He had laid (trumped-up) charges of an assassination attempt on José I that concealed Pombal's real resentment of the Order's mission in Paraguay and its meddling at home. Fr Malagrida had preached that the Lisbon earthquake was the work of God, divine chastisement for the sins of Pombal's government, and circulated his opinions in print. Pombal reacted ferociously between 1759 and 1761, even having Malagrida garrotted and burnt. By 1767–8 the Jesuits had also been compelled to leave Spain, with the king exclaiming that he felt as if he had 'conquered another new world'. Charles III would not tolerate any hint of a challenge to regalian power and the Order stood accused of involvement in the 'Mutiny of Esquilache' (named after the king's unpopular Italian minister) rioting of March 1766 as well as spreading rumours that Charles was a bastard. The Bourbon states of Italy imitated his example, leaving only the Austrian Empire willing to accommodate the fathers. Even there, the Jesuit domination of educational institutions had been challenged for some time past with the connivance of the imperial family. Count Christoph Migazzi opened clerical training to Jansenist influences after 1757 and broke the Jesuit control of higher education. So Clement XIV's dissolution of the Order was really a response to a *fait accompli*.

The Jesuits' reputation for sophistry originated in pedagogical practices that had been pre-eminent in Europe. Leading *philosophes* had been among the beneficiaries. Diderot received his earliest instruction at the Jesuit school in Langres, Condorcet was another pupil at the Jesuit College of Navarre; the Order's archenemy, Voltaire, was educated by Jesuit fathers, articulated his own consummate talent for ridicule and parody within a tradition they had given him, and then turned these skills against them. As educationalists the Order had few equals; as subtle (and supple) defenders of Catholic Christianity the Jesuits in France were capable of fighting back against deism and unbelief in a way which the *philosophes* and their imitators both feared and respected. For several decades down to the 1760s the *Journal de Trévoux*, written and produced by the Fathers, was the leading organ of the Counter-Enlightenment in western Europe. Month by month, it carried essays and reviews restating the case for orthodoxy and refuting the latest irreligious outpourings of fashionable authors. So the abolition of the Order by papal decree in 1773 could be seen as a major blow to all those fighting to stem the increasingly anti-Christian character of the Enlightenment in France. No wonder that the expulsion of the Jesuits from Portugal, France and Spain was considered by Voltaire to be the greatest event which had distinguished the eighteenth century.

Intellectual failure had harmed the cause of the Fathers. The Jansenist-minded proponents of Catholic Enlightenment within the Habsburg Empire detected a torpor among the Jesuits which was a liability to the whole Church and had not prevented the resurgence of heresies. The Order found it hard to adapt to an era where sacred learning was less valued than half a century earlier. In the late 1750s the head of the Society, General Ricci, had noted the comparative scarcity of Jesuit experts in physics, mathematics and history, though there was a glut of theologians. In 1759 the empress (whose commitment to a Jansenist style of Catholicism has gone unremarked until recently) had Jesuits removed from their positions of control in the philosophical and theological faculties of universities in the empire and in 1763 from the censorship board. Meanwhile, in neighbouring Poland, the dominant Jesuits had presided over a religious culture which, well before 1750, was embarrassingly short of innovative religious content.

Yet, when it came, the removal of the Jesuits sent an educational shockwave across Catholic Europe, with nearly 1,000 colleges and seminaries in Europe shut down, their assets confiscated by the state, their staffs scattered. The Jesuits had been involved in the preparation of the ordained ministry for more than two centuries in the seminaries which most dioceses founded after the Council of Trent. That was a prime reason why so many bishops had fought to retain their services despite royal opposition. The quality of teaching offered to ordinands was, on the whole, adversely affected in the two decades before the outbreak of the French Revolutionary wars intensified the experience of dislocation. In schools and universities generally, the clerical grip was significantly relaxed when the Jesuits were suppressed. It was obviously tempting for governments not to recommit Jesuit endowments for religious or educational purposes; the pious Maria Theresa thus did not hesitate to make large loans to aristocrats from the windfall. Generally, governments at least tried to accelerate the modernisation of the curriculum – with varying results. The problem, as in the Habsburg Empire where Joseph II dissolved all the teaching orders except the Piarists, was always finding enough qualified laymen to take over as teachers. Poland stood out as an exception. The Commission of Education, which received the Jesuits' estates, went some way towards erecting a national system in line with the latest Rousseauian principles.

Part of that Polish Commission was staffed by good Catholics, many of them secular clergy, who took advantage of the Society's demise. The damage that the Bull of 1773 did to the image of a united Catholicism weighed on them but, when set against the new scope for patronage and hopes of access to Jesuit wealth, it was only a secondary consideration. The fact was that influential Catholics considered they had more to gain than lose from closing down the Jesuits, miscalculating the size of the vacuum their demise would create. Not that the Bull eliminated Jesuit influences from the Church as thoroughly as rulers such as Joseph II of Austria and his brother Peter Leopold of Tuscany could have wished. The popularity of cults like the Sacred Heart of Jesus was already well entrenched, while individual former Jesuits proved most adaptable. Some entered alternative religious Orders, others took up a parochial ministry, while watching with pleasure the ability of those who had been educated by them to hold on to a style of piety that was recognisably Jesuit in its form and expression. Many joined the formidable number of those who defended the irreducible core of Catholic theology and dogmatics in the period down to the Revolutionary wars of the 1790s, and a few survived to be readmitted as Jesuits when the Order was reconstituted in 1814. In the bishoprics around Ratisbon and Passau, several former members of the Order were encouraged to resume the low-key catechetical missions (undertaken in co-operation with the parish priest) which had been so successful in the mid-1750s, an initiative that had led to the formation in numerous towns and villages of a Confraternity of Christian Doctrine. A handful hid away in remoter parts of the Habsburg Empire; a more sizable minority fled to Prussia and Russia, Lutheran and Orthodox states, where the papal prohibition had no effect. Pius VI asked Catherine II to expel the refugees, but their educational talents were too valuable for the empress to sacrifice.

Most interested parties rejoiced at the downfall of the Jesuit Order. For Protestants, it amounted to a wish fulfilment that few can have imagined would have happened in their lifetimes. This was the Order which, more than any other, had for two centuries confined and stunted the Reformation achievement. Suddenly, it was gone. What sharper evidence could there be of decadence and decline pointing up the weakness of contemporary Catholicism? For many Protestants, buoyed up by millennial expectations, the way now seemed open to the triumph of the true Gospel and the institutional supremacy of their own Church structures. Only a minority of high church Anglicans were inclined to sympathise with the plight of the disgraced Fathers: they perceived that the real victors by the 1773 Bull were less the Protestant Churches than the loose coalition of Jansenists, deists, sceptics and fellow-travellers who had led the campaign against the Jesuits for upwards of half a century. Without doubt, enlightened opinion across Europe rejoiced in the blow, some, perhaps a majority, from a sense that the Voltairean injunction of 'écrasez l'infâme!'

had scored its biggest victory, others that the way was now clear for a tolerant, undogmatic version of Christianity to commend itself to all.

Paradoxically, the dissolution can also be presented as the Catholic Enlightenment's greatest success. It was opinion *within* the Catholic Church that had identified the Jesuits as a vested interest, a self-serving group and a barrier to the Church modernising its structures and making more of an impact on opinion makers in contemporary society. One can plausibly claim that the destruction of the Jesuits was an attempt by the Roman Catholic Church to re-equip itself to meet the formidable intellectual challenges confronting it. That was certainly the contention of many leading clergy in the Iberian monarchies and across the Austrian Empire. Yet to interested onlookers, the Church's engagement in a bitter internal power struggle was hardly calculated to turn it into to a more effective presence in a world where its intrinsic authority was worth much less than a century previously. And, certainly, the surviving *philosophes* relished its discomfiture and did not see the Church after the Jesuits as likely to prove a stronger adversary.

Conclusion

With or without the Jesuits, the Roman Catholic response overall to the Enlightenment varied appreciably over time according to country and context. There was much in the Enlightenment reconcilable with Christian truths to which progressive churchmen could and did subscribe; the moral and spiritual renewal on offer to believers was part of what Dorinda Outram has aptly called its 'great religious creativity'.[27] On the other hand, the greater prominence of materialism and overt anti-Christian attitudes from the mid-century assisted in the creation of a Counter-Enlightenment mentality. It would flourish from the 1790s as the first attempts were made by the abbé Barruel and others to see the seeds of the destructive events of that decade as being nurtured right down the century.

Within the Anglican Churches, too, there was a sense in George III's reign that an excessive emphasis had been placed on natural religion and that the clergy needed to rediscover the specifically Christian dimension to orthodox belief. The loose alliance of the 1740s in England between Anglicans and dissenters became unstitched as a higher proportion than ever of the latter embraced a 'rational' faith based on Arianism or Socinianism and held fast to enlightenment values such as anti-sacerdotalism and toleration in the face of growing hostility from the establishment.

---

[27] Dorinda Outram, *The Enlightenment* (Cambridge, 1994), 34.

North of the border, Scottish Moderate leaders were ageing fast by the 1780s, and an evangelicalism that had its roots in the parishes was becoming harder to restrain. It had little sympathy with the temperate values emanating from Edinburgh society for more than a generation. In Germany, by the 1780s there was a fascination with the occult and esoteric spirituality which Pietism indirectly encouraged. Outstanding pastors like Herder made afresh the case for viewing societies within a historic context not necessarily invalidated by the universal norms so dear to the *philosophes*. This was among the most brilliant intellectual responses to the Enlightenment. Its wide currency did not prevent two others being equally popular within the Churches: either no response at all or reliance on the state for protection. As the next chapter will suggest, the price in terms of religious autonomy could be high.

4   Church and state

A relationship of equals?

In a European civilisation still denoted by its Christian character, the state was historically required to uphold and protect the faith. That had been the historic position since the emperor Constantine had made Christianity a state religion in 324, and the rulers of eighteenth-century Europe were his cultural legatees. The relationship between Church and state had seldom been stable after Constantine's momentous decision. Instead of coexisting in mutual dependency, the two institutions tended to jostle for the upper hand during the Middle Ages when western Christendom was still undivided; the emperor Henry IV's journey to Canossa in 1085 and the murder of Thomas à Becket in his cathedral at Canterbury by soldiers loyal to Henry II are two well-known examples of how embittered the relationship could become at the top, and it was mirrored by countless squabbles at parochial level over jurisdiction, privileges and money.

The Reformation delivered a decisive advantage to the state. The great natural law jurist, Hugo Grotius, even argued that the state had unlimited competence, making the Churches in Protestant states emphatically subordinate institutions. Few Reformed clergy would have conceded as much. Yet as the price of survival, the new mainstream Protestant Churches – Anglican, Calvinist and Lutheran – expected exclusive protection from the states that professed their faith against both a resurgent Rome and sectarian extremists such as the Anabaptists. In Catholic Europe, powerful monarchies including Philip II's Spain and Henri IV's France would not act as the secular arm of the Counter-Reformation without the papacy (reluctantly) permitting them powers of patronage and jurisdiction over their 'national' Churches that were almost the equal of states no longer in communion with Rome. In Orthodox Russia, the Spiritual Regulations of 1721 had transferred the authority of the patriarch and church councils to the Holy Synod, a government-appointed body, and Catherine II had no plans to return it. It was headed by a chief procurator. One of these, Prince A. S. Kozlovsky, secularised the ecclesiastical lands of the Church, and he was followed by two overt anticlericals, I. I. Melissino and P. B. Chebyshev, the latter of whom was a self-proclaimed atheist. Not that the institutional independence of the Russian Orthodox Church should be underestimated: the chief procurator was a remote figure, usually lacking expertise in canon law or familiarity with how the Church worked in practice.

Nevertheless, the Church–state relationship was increasingly one-sided and, irrespective of confession, grew more so in the course of the eighteenth century. Catherine II's reference to herself 'chef de l'église grécque' in her correspondence with Voltaire was more than just a private joke between friends. She meddled unrepentantly in Catholic as well as Orthodox affairs. First, she imposed Gabriel Podoski as primate of Poland without any reference to Rome in 1766. Then, the following year, Bishops Zaluski and Soltyk were deported to Russia from Poland (this was still five years before the First Partition) and their sees were kept vacant and administered by laymen: the Russian empress would not tolerate public complaints from the Catholic hierarchy and King Stanislas, the protégé of his former lover, could only acquiesce. Notions of an inviolate, visible Church were incompatible with enlightenment monarchism. In Spain regalism found its culmination in the *Junta de Estado* established in 1787 during the ministry of the condé de Floridablanca. It was an institution that initiated regular joint meetings of all the royal ministers, and Church policy usually figured prominently on the agenda.

Such Erastian arrangements did not stop clerical apologists from making the case for the inviolability of the spiritual sphere, insistent that the Church could function as a divinely instituted agency without any validation from the state. It was usually pragmatically articulated in terms of an alliance of Church and state – classically but 'hamfistedly' expounded for the Church of England in William Warburton's *The Alliance between Church and State* (1736)[1] – but deciding where the temporal realm stopped and the spiritual started always rendered this strategy problematic. With Church and state so locked into the mechanisms of government at every level, this was not surprising. The leading high church Anglican layman, George Stevens, was convinced that 'making establishments necessary to the existence of a church, as many are apt to do, is a grievous mistake',[2] but existing structures historically rested on the assumption. Anglicans

---

[1] The phrase is B. W. Young's in *Religion and Enlightenment in Eighteenth-century England: Theological Debate from Locke to Burke* (Oxford, 1998), 41–2.

[2] See his anonymous *Cursory Observations on a Pamphlet entitled, an Address to the clergy of the Church of England, in particular and to all Christians in general* (1773).

found it hard to think of bishops in purely pastoral terms rather than as lords spiritual. It was one of the obstacles that delayed toleration for the Scottish Episcopalians until 1792, and confronted the authorities as new bishoprics were founded in the British Empire. As late as 1793, six years after the first Canadian bishop had been consecrated by Archbishop Moore of Canterbury (Charles Inglis of Nova Scotia), the government designated the first bishop of Quebec a 'Lord bishop' and gave him temporal power commensurate with his English brethren.

In Prussia the co-ordination of royal and ecclesiastical administration assisted the incorporation of the Church into the service of the authoritarian state, with the sovereign possessing a degree of control unsurpassed in Europe, as the Prussian General Code of 1794 made clear. The Code was exercised on his behalf by the Upper Consistory established in 1750, a body staffed by theologians who were all Prussian public servants and whose duties included the close supervision of Lutheran clergy in every province except Silesia and Geldern. That the first president and two other secular councillors were members of the Reformed Church well displays the monarchy's desire to achieve harmonious relations between the denominations. It was an appropriate arrangement in a state where Frederick II laughed at himself for being concurrently the Lutheran pope and the head of the Reformed Church. He allowed the Church to publicise his decrees, but not to impress his orders on his subjects for the purpose of political stabilisation. Meanwhile, his Lutheran subjects sang from a hymn book that reminded them of their obligation to accept life under the Hohenzollen monarchy uncomplainingly or, as the words of hymn number 444 had it: 'Be faithful, hard-working and devoted to those who are above you. May you all be anxious to observe your duties.' The injunction would have been echoed by all heads of state irrespective of denomination.

Whatever the confession, much store was set on administrative tidiness. The Lutheran Gustavus III of Sweden subdivided scores of overgrown parishes and was estimated to have rebuilt or restored as many as 174 churches. Heads of state were no less keen on territorial integrity. In 1783 Joseph II of Austria imposed a policy of diocesan reorganisation so that Church boundaries dovetailed into the Habsburg state. The sees of Salzburg, Konstanz, Augsburg and Passau would no longer hold sway over his subjects; they would be replaced by new dioceses based at Budweis, Leoben, St Pölten and elsewhere. The docile Austrian bishops kept quiet, but those in the *Reich* accused the emperor of violating both his coronation oath and the imperial constitution. Arrangements which permitted the power of foreign diocesans were increasingly seen as anomalous by governments across central Europe. Thus the power of the archbishop of Salzburg over clerical taxation in his diocese ended in 1789. Most Catholic states insisted on taking unprecedented supervisory powers over the monastic Orders. At the least, the latter were expected to respect the power of local rulers rather than look abroad. Thus Charles III of Spain created specifically Spanish congregations, as for the Carthusians in 1783. Monastic wealth and immunities were no longer acceptable in the new climate of opinion, their possession an unpatriotic denial of what was owed to the state; such thinking lay behind Joseph II's suppression of 163 monasteries in the Austrian Netherlands, where 11 per cent of Brabant belonged to them.

Yet, as this chapter will suggest, there were definite limits to what a reforming state could achieve without creating major political instability: antagonising the clergy so much that they allied with the populist opponents of change in Church and state was inadvisable. Moreover, if the power of the Church was curbed excessively then a monarchy stood to lose one of the bedrocks of traditional society; *per contra*, its endorsement of royal powers could facilitate the exercise of the prerogative, a paradox of enlightened government often lost on rulers who, committed to widescale reform, often sacrificed clerical good will by treating the Church as another vested interest in the state to be modernised in a way tailored to suit the monarchy.

The clergy in political life

Monarchical and episcopal authority were historically complementary in eighteenth-century Europe, though it was bishops rather than kings who tended to stress that they held their office according to divine commission. Bishops had usually had to play the courtier to obtain a mitre in the first place; however talented, they needed a politician's favour to win top prizes in the patronage game, like William Warburton and Pitt the Elder or Jérome-Marie Champion de Cicé and Jacques Necker. In Denmark, the temporal authority of the Lutheran bishops was meagre by comparison with their Anglican or Gallican counterparts, but there was still much competition for places at court, with the monarch having exclusive appointment rights.

The best interests of the Church could matter less than satisfying existing political obligations. Thus on becoming premier in 1768, the duke of Grafton appointed his old Peterhouse teacher, Edmund Law, as bishop of Carlisle, unconcerned that Law's latitudinarian views on the nature of the Church were decreasingly shared by his new colleagues. Higher clergy expected that in exercising their office there would be an overlap between pastoral responsibilities and their duties to the state. In

France, bishops were habitually entrusted with the presidency of the prestigious provincial estates in *pays d'états* such as Brittany and Languedoc, while in England and Ireland, the Anglican episcopate all held seats in the Westminster and Dublin parliaments respectively and for the most part could be relied on to vote for government measures and use their pulpits to recommend government policies. In Lutheran Sweden, the clergy made up one of the four orders in the Estates; all bishops and chapters were represented, with one clerical member per ten parishes. In Poland, the seventeen Catholic bishops were members of Senate in the Diets. The archbishop-primate of Gniezno was first senator and held an important role as second dignitary of the Polish Commonwealth during an interregnum in that elective monarchy.

While most bishops aspired to office at court or in the royal household, the long tradition of prelates serving as government ministers was alive and well in most *Länder*. The smaller German states had many uses for the episcopate. In Württemberg, Christoph Friedrich Stockmayer, bishop of Bebenhausen (d. 1782), along with his elder brother Johann Friedrich, was a dominant figure on the executive committee of the *Landtag*; in the Hungarian Chancellery there was always at least one ecclesiastical councillor. Britain had no bishops as Cabinet ministers after 1714 brought the removal of John Robinson, bishop of London, as Lord Privy Seal, in the Whig clean sweep attending the Hanoverian succession. In France, bishops still aspired to the highest offices in the state after Cardinal Fleury's retirement in 1741. Cardinal Bernis, archbishop of Albi, was a lacklustre foreign minister until Choiseul replaced him in 1758, while Brienne, archbishop of Toulouse, received the rare honour of actually being named principal minister in 1787. Since so many bishops came from aristocratic backgrounds, they were not always amenable to taking unpopular roles in the state, especially if deemed incompatible with family honour. The bishop of Metz refused to serve in Archbishop Brienne's controversial Plenary Court of 1788 (it replaced the *parlements*) despite the latter's taunts at ingratitude for royal honours. The bishop tried vainly to tear off his blue sash (*cordon bleu*) saying: 'Don't you know that the Montmorencys come before any cordon, . . . and that every cordon in the world may be damned . . . I will not go.'[3] And where prelates did not hold office, their influence on policy-making could still be considerable. Charles Agar, archbishop of Cashel, attended the Irish Privy Council regularly in the 1790s and played an important part in obstructing the

---

[3] F. A. M. Lescure (ed.), *Correspondence secrete inédite sur Louis XVI, Marie-Antoinette, la cour et la ville* (2 vols., Paris, 1865–6), vol. II, 259.

moves of Pitt's Cabinet towards permitting Roman Catholics to sit in the legislature.

Many prelates were born intriguers, natural courtiers. In Spain, Campomanes encountered formidable opposition at court in the late 1760s and early 1770s from prelates opposed to his modernising projects – especially those affecting the Church – put forward in the Council of Castile where he had held the key office of *fiscal* (finance minister) since 1762. Opposition to regalian interference was led by Isidro de Carvajal y Lancaster, bishop of Cuenca, who, in 1766 after the Esquilache riots in Madrid and the provinces (directed against the minister blamed for high grain prices and Spain's inglorious participation in the Seven Years' War) wrote a letter complaining to the king's confessor to deplore 'the persecution of the Church, despoiled of her goods, outraged in her ministers, and violated in her immunity; but at court nothing is seen because there is no light'. Police examination of the bishop's activities uncovered a nest of discontented aristocrats, clerics and public servants who had been secretly circulating copies of Carvajal's correspondence with the king both inside Spain and abroad. Campomanes also failed to bring in a law of amortisation for the Crown of Castile, one which would have hugely curtailed the acquisition by the Church of real property in mortmain. Clerics, including Carvajal, worked behind the scenes to sabotage the proposal and protect ecclesiastical economic interests. Charles III was not prepared to give his minister unqualified support and listened to the bishops.

Open remonstration was acceptable where conspiracy was not, and there are many instances of prelates risking careers to articulate widely shared anxieties to monarchs in a way that lay politicians might not have dared. Thus in the 1786 'Mutinous' Riksdag in Sweden, Olaf Celsius, bishop of Lund, and Daniel Herweghr, bishop of Carlstad, made a determined bid to insist that Gustavus III address the willingness of his powerful secretary and vicar-general, Elis Schröderheim, to condone the sale of Church preferment as a major source of court revenue. The bishops, whose personal loyalty to the king was never in doubt, secured the backing of influential counsellors, and simonical practices were abruptly halted. Extracting concessions from Joseph II was rather harder, but gestures said much. For all his Jansenism, the prince-bishop of Brixen (1779–91), Count Joseph von Spaur, believed the emperor's ecclesiastical programme was recklessly bold. He declined to publish the Toleration Patent of 1781, and asked Pius VI to call at Brixen the following year on the way home from humiliation at the emperor's hands in Vienna.

The ecclesiology of presbyterianism could hinder royal government of the Church far more than episcopacy. According to this view of the polity, only Christ could hold magisterial power in the Church and monarchs were reduced to the marginal role of nursing father. The leading Popular party theologian in Scotland, John Erskine, was unrepentant about explaining the place of government in theological rather than secular terms. God was in ultimate control of earthly rulers who were 'the ministers of God, and there [sic] services are in kind, degree, and continuance, just what God, whose ministers they are, sees meet'.[4] In Scotland the General Assembly of the Kirk was co-ordinate with the secular power in the state and buttressed on the authority of its own ordained ministers. In practice, it was expected to defer to the preferences of the Hanoverian state. By the 1750s it could not put forward policies that the government in London and its supporters north of the border found unacceptably narrow, and kirkmen stressed instead the complementary nature of the two societies of Church and state, invoking the prototype of Israel where kings and judges ruled the commonwealth, and priests and Levites the Jewish Church.

What made Presbyterian theory academic in the later eighteenth century was the power of the laity in making appointments within the Church of Scotland. It vexed die-hard Presbyterians sorely and periodically caused secessions from the Kirk. The majority stayed on knowing it was the price paid for establishment, just as it was in most European states where appointments to benefices and bishoprics alike belonged predominantly to the lay elite – kings, government ministers and the landed nobility and gentry. It was perhaps the most effective brake on clerical criticism ever devised, for the ambitious man of the cloth knew that the good will of a lay patron (often shown in the form of a chaplaincy) could be crucial in determining a successful career path. Governments were not disposed to see the clergy exercise an independent role in the life of the state. Despite the occasional use of a ballot, clerical representatives elected to the Swedish Riksdag were usually bishops or senior clergy and influence was exerted behind the scenes to keep out more lowly mischief-makers. In England, Whig politicians would not sanction the adoption of policies by the Church hierarchy – the provision of bishops for America, for example – which might engender fears that clerical power was reviving either at home or in the colonies. Gallicans, by comparison, were advantaged. The General Assembly of the Clergy of France was the only central representative body to meet in Paris throughout the century down to 1788, partly because ministers pressed it for cash (the *don gratuit*)

[4] *Prayer for those in Civil and Military Offices* (London, 1779), 18, quoted in John R. McIntosh, *Church and Theology in Enlightenment Scotland: The Popular Party, 1740–1800* (East Linton, 1998), 220.

whenever it met, demanding more and more voluntary offerings from the Church if it was to retain any rights of self-government.

Church, state and religious minorities

During the period 1550–1700 it was a fact of religious life in Europe that minority denominations would not be permitted any legal recognition within a given state's boundaries. This was a principle known as *cuius regio, eius religio*, part of international law since the Treaty of Augsburg of 1555 (further upheld in the treaties of 1648 ending the Thirty Years' War). Then gradually, during the eighteenth century, Church–state relations were further reconfigured by the growth of toleration, that cardinal precept of the Enlightenment. It found favour first in Protestant polities. The regent oligarchs in the urban centres of the United Provinces had long curbed the exclusivist tendencies of fiery Calvinist ministers looking to the princely Orange house for support, while also showing themselves willing to depose ministers who in sermons or pamphlets displayed signs of heterodoxy. In England, a Toleration Act of 1689 finally gave restricted rights to worship for Protestant Trinitarian dissenters from the Church of England (it was supposed to be the prelude to an Anglican comprehensiveness, which was not achieved). Thereafter, Protestant German rulers followed suit (Frederick the Great welcomed everyone to Prussia after 1763, even the Jesuits), while in Catholic Europe there was an uneasy toleration of Protestant minorities, on which the beneficiaries could not rely. A ruler like Maria Theresa found it hard to think of non-Catholics as other than heretics while, in France, Louis XV's long-serving minister of the interior, the comte de Saint-Florentin, was constantly pressing provincial governors and intendants to use the penal laws against the Huguenots.

One abiding reason for government tardiness was pressure from senior Catholic clergy. Any concession of toleration reduced the exclusive rights and privileges enjoyed by one Church over competitors within particular state boundaries. The principle of establishment was not thereby overthrown, but it was amended to admit the limits (even the undesirability) of coercing a kingdom's subjects into one religious groove. Measured toleration *and* confessional privileges became the classic characteristics of the eighteenth-century ecclesiastical polity, since it suited the newly inclusive approach of rulers towards their subjects. Even when a prince converted to another faith it did not, as would have been the case a century earlier, destabilise state life through attempts to impose his choice on unwilling subjects. Thus in Protestant Württemberg the Imperial Aulic Council and the young Emperor Joseph II forced Duke Karl Eugen to reach an accommodation (the *Erbvergleich*) with the Landtag and Privy Council in 1770 after two decades of tension following the duke's adoption of Catholicism, compounded by his taste for lavish, slightly dated Baroque ceremonial.

Imperial needs could make religious toleration an imperative of state survival. With the Jacobite menace fast receding into the past, the British government began to recruit Irish Catholics into its armies fighting the rebellious Americans during the late 1770s, despite the refusal of the Dublin Parliament to grant Catholics freedom of worship until 1782. For Frederick of Prussia and Joseph of Austria, toleration had executive usefulness as a means of keeping minorities loyal to the Hohenzollern and Hapsburg states: the Catholic Silesians, Protestants in Hungary, Moravia and Bohemia, Orthodox in Galicia (up against the Russian frontier). Diversity was an ineradicable part of the confessional pattern. Both monarchs wanted immigrants of high economic quality; in Trieste, Orthodox merchants worshipped in their own church, and in 1778 Lutherans, Calvinists and Anglicans newly arriving in town were granted rights of private worship and schooling.

For monarchs, international rivalries alone justified toleration, but it could be hard for senior clergy to see it that way. Toleration could be deemed a slur on the official religion of the state, a betrayal of trust. It was yet another mutation in Church–state relations where the good of both did not always coincide. During Maria Theresa's long reign, the hierarchy had successfully played on the empress's personal piety to restrict imperial initiatives, but they had no such leverage on Joseph II. All his non-Catholic subjects were accorded religious liberty by the decree of 13 October 1781 (there was further legislation in 1782) and, whereas many Austrian prelates, most famously Charles d'Hebestein, bishop of Laibach, justified the Edict of Toleration on the basis that their usefulness to the state was alone sufficient to justify religious dissidents, the prince-archbishop of Vienna, Cardinal Migazzi, and the primate of the Hungarian church, Count József Batthyány, resisted Joseph's ecclesiastical policies. This was despite the limited nature of the concessions. Only private worship was permitted, spires could not be placed on Protestant churches, and those wishing to be registered officially as Protestants had to submit to six weeks of religious instruction by a Catholic priest whose task was to try to convert them to Catholicism.

It was the clergy of the Austrian Netherlands who were the most zealous against the toleration of 1781–2. *Curés* and Capuchins alike preached openly against the emperor and accused him of Febronianism.[5] The

---

[5] See below, pp. 178–9.

Estates of Hainault registered their hostility and the University of Louvain made its misgivings clear. The reforming legislation on marriage (1784) caused more consternation. It was denounced as a danger in which could be seen the return of Protestant heresy. Joseph, however, stood firm, seeing his policies as a legitimate exercise of prerogative power, which, after fifteen years playing second fiddle to his mother (1765–80), he was keen to deploy. It was a risky strategy, as one visiting Anglican prelate noted: 'the Emperor seems to be ill advised in the manner of bringing about his Reformation, & will certainly add to the disturbances, which seem to prevail in almost every country in Europe, except our own'.[6]

Clerical opponents of extended toleration usually had plenty of followers among the general population. In Scotland, hysterical anti-Catholic feeling obliged North's government to modify its plans for Catholic relief north of the border in the late 1770s, a plan motivated to a large degree by the desperate military requirements of the American War. In 1778 the extension of Catholic relief to England ignited the Gordon Riots in the capital and threatened violence to many bishops. As governments pushed for toleration, churchmen often pushed against it. In France, speakers in the General Assemblies of the Clergy repeatedly urged Louis XV to be more forceful in his defence of the Gallican order by stamping down on illegal Huguenot activities in Languedoc and Poitou. But Choiseul's administration of 1758–70 was most reluctant to return to a policy of persecution of French Calvinists after they had shown themselves such loyal patriots during the disastrous Seven Years' War. Their conduct gave the lie to the habitual Catholic slur that this Protestant minority and their pastors were treacherous, tainted by republicanism. Once France had a new king in 1774, pressure on ministers from prominent laymen like the marquis de Lafayette and the comte de Malesherbes to improve the lot of Huguenots became irresistible, leading to the Edict of Toleration in 1787.

But this narrow enactment did nothing directly to curtail the rights and privileges of the Gallican Church, unless it was to end the legal fiction that had persisted for 102 years that all Frenchmen were by definition Catholics. Public offices remained closed to them and worship could only take place privately. To talk in terms of emancipation for members of the Reformed Church in France would be to exaggerate appreciably, as more progressive members of the hierarchy admitted. The measure found a fluent spokesman during the first Assembly of Notables (February–June 1787) in Bishop La Luzerne of Langres and was actually passed

---

[6] Bishop Brownlow North to Lord Guildford, 28 August 1788, Bodleian Library, Oxford, MS. North d. 26, f. 151.

during the ministry of an archbishop, Loménie de Brienne of Toulouse (May 1787–August 1788). Both prelates thought in terms of adapting the confessional state rather than dissolving it. On the eve of the French Revolution, it remained the predominant European model capable of updating to changing circumstances, surviving the near-universal spread of toleration by the 1780s.

Since many clergy perceived revealed religion to be under attack on more than one front, the protection of the state, however inadequate, was a defence mechanism to be welcomed. Where its withdrawal seemed imminent, the political consequences could be serious, as in a country like Ireland where the established Church numbered no more than 10–15 per cent of the population. Yet the Church of Ireland was no more immune to the spread of state-sponsored toleration (Catholic relief began in the 1770s) than its counterparts elsewhere and, though many clergy put the best face they could on this development, the tensions were only just underneath the surface and broke through openly after Bishop Richard Woodward of Cloyne initiated a pamphlet controversy in 1787 claiming the policy threatened to wreck the Protestant Ascendancy in Ireland on which the Williamite settlement depended. The bishop's efforts won applause in Dublin Castle, but had a negligible effect on deterring Pitt's government from initiating further legislative concessions to Catholics in the early 1790s. As Henry Dundas, the premier's right-hand man in the Cabinet, insisted, it was 'the plainest of all political truths, that a country where a Parliament and a free constitution is allowed to exist, never can submit to the practice of three-fourths of the country being sacrificed to the whims, prejudices or opinions of the other fourth'.[7] But where the majority population was patently attached to the observances of an established Church, there was minimal advantage to even the most reformist-minded monarchs and ministers in changing the status quo, a perception that North's government acted on when legislating to protect the Gallican Church in recently conquered Canada, under the 1774 Quebec Act. A confessional state offered both partners ideological benefits, especially the opportunities for mutual support in ways that legitimated the exercise of power.

The persistence of the confessional state

I take it first for granted, as an incontrovertible proposition, that in every nation there must be some one profession of Religion by Law established.[8]

---

[7] National Library of Ireland, 54/15, 47, 54A/74, quoted in Michael Fry, *The Dundas Despotism* (Edinburgh, 1992), 177.

[8] Cyril Jackson (dean of Christ Church, Oxford) to Lord Leurisham, n.d. (c. 1779?), Staffs. RO, Dartmouth MS, D(W) 1778/V/862.

The term 'the confessional state' has a persisting application to eighteenth-century Europe and retains its usefulness for historians. Used in its classic sense, according to the formula of the Treaty of Augsburg, it denotes a polity that accorded legitimacy to a single Church, such as France after Louis XIV had cancelled the Edict of Nantes in 1685, or the kingdom of Spain and the principalities of Catholic Italy where Protestantism had never gained a foothold, or Sweden where Lutheranism alone was recognised. Yet such religious exclusiveness seldom accorded with the confessional confusion of post-Reformation Europe; even where toleration was officially denied, the resources of the state were usually insufficient to eradicate dissent entirely. Limited recognition of the existence of religious minorities was not tantamount to abolishing the confessional state. One of the most controversial historians of eighteenth-century England, Jonathan Clark, famously argued in his *English Society 1685–1832* and many subsequent publications for the existence of a hegemonic confessional state in Hanoverian England; he would not allow the legal toleration of Trinitarian Protestant dissenters after 1689, or the payment by the government to these non-Anglican Churches of a subsidy known as the *regium donum*, to count against his proposition until the revised version of his book was published in 2000, when he opted instead for the 'near-confessional church'. This amendment properly makes allowance for the range of religious permutations within the Europe of the late *ancien régime* as rulers came to accept that members of minority faiths could be good subjects too. So the confessional state endured, albeit altered (fatally compromised, the opponents of religious toleration would have contended), its exclusive right to demand religious obedience curtailed or abolished, but its other privileges largely left intact, including the right to tithe payments from non-members. The change was not a transformation, and the majority of the masses' experience remained one of conformity.

Nowhere was the concept of state neutrality in religion known to the theory and conduct of public life until 1795 when the Directory in France began to articulate what would later be identified a 'voluntarist' approach to religion. Before the Revolution – and, indeed, well into it – the voluntarist principle was deemed a free-for-all for denominations and was unthinkable to responsible politicians, even radicals: the state would always favour one Church over the rest even when religious toleration was in place. As the dean of Canterbury told a friend in 1787 after the failure of the most recent attempt to repeal the Test Act: 'Accept our congratulations on the defeat of the dissenters, in a question which, stripped of flourishes, is plainly this, whether we shall tolerate them, or accept a toleration from them, if, when in power, they shall be pleased to grant it'.[9]

---

[9] British Library, Althorp Papers, E.18, George Horne to Revd Charles Poyntz, 3 April 1787.

In England, the presumption was that membership of the state Church made one a reliable subject. Rulers were not overly keen on encouraging dissidents; the connexion between religious minorities and political instability remained in place. That was very much the case during the era of constitutional monarchy in the French Revolution (1789–92). A still more fundamental reason for the endurance of the confessional state through the eighteenth century was that it was much too useful to abandon as an essential agency of authority in any state. States both Catholic and Protestant could not easily afford to forego the Churches' involvement in education and social welfare. Even with the bureaucratisation of most European polities, administrative reach and levels of competence remained rudimentary by comparison with the Churches' well-established apparatus extending, parish by parish, into the remotest corners of every state, great and small, a unit which was the basis of local government across Europe. As has been well claimed (and with application well beyond England): 'The ubiquitous agency of the state was the Church, quartering the land not into a few hundred constituencies but into ten thousand parishes.'[10] No wonder that as Catherine II extended her sway into Cossack territories, she was more than ready to finance the building of new churches. Monarchs and ministers intent on enlisting their subjects' co-operation, or even reducing them to obedience, needed the support of the bishops and parochial clergy. It was the latter who kept and updated parish records recording births, marriages and deaths, one of the most reliable sources of information available in the pre-modern state. In return the clergy usually endorsed royal power from the pulpit. Thus sermon evidence of 1775 to 1800 shows nearly all Danish clerics preaching that the national form of government was the best one, though there were many variations on the theme. It was a commonplace that the king reigned to promote the well-being of the people and that moderate social change should not be avoided.

If anything, the civil authorities were keener than ever in the period from 1750 to 1790 to enlist the services of the established Churches. In England, religion enforced the aweful majesty of the law with clergy preaching Assize sermons and acting as chaplains to the judges; municipal corporations held regular services in their local parish church (the City of London had the use of St Paul's cathedral), usually with ornately carved pews set aside for the mayor and aldermen and all their regalia. The arrangement was reproduced on a smaller scale up and down the country, as in St Cuthbert's church, Carlisle, which James Boswell gleefully recalled:

[10] J. C. D. Clark, *English Society 1685–1832* (Cambridge, 1985; 2nd edn, 2000), 277.

'I sat ... in the Corporation seat. I was pleased to have the mayor's crimson velvet cushion before me ... I was wonderfully content.'[11] It was still not uncommon for Acts of Parliament to be proclaimed in English parish churches, especially on matters likely to be relevant to vestry members, while during a time of acute food shortages in the winter of 1800–1, the home secretary, the duke of Portland, circulated a royal proclamation via the bishops, recommending 'Economy in the use of Corn to all Persons during the present scarcity'.

On the continent, the emperor Joseph II relied on parish priests to announce new regulations to their flocks, judging them far more reliable than interested local politicians. The emperor may have closed monasteries and convents; he also established new parishes, 231 in Lower Austria alone, and from the landed estates of dissolved religious houses created the *Religionsfonds* to cover the wages of priests set down in them. He had an almost pathetic faith in the good offices of the parochial clergy. When many Rumanian lower clergy were involved in the Transylvanian peasant rebellion of 1784 against serf impositions, the patriarch tried for appeasement in line with the court's wishes, and Joseph himself urged the clergy to try to pacify the insurgents who had instigated the struggle in his name. The appeal for aid met with mixed success. Neither was co-operation always forthcoming when clergy felt they were being used as the cat's-paws of ministers bent on preserving their careers rather than serving the kingdom. Thus when in April 1787 Alexandre de Calonne, controller-general to Louis XVI, had reached an impasse in his attempts to push tax reforms through the first Assembly of Notables, he attempted a direct appeal to the public (in itself unprecedented in *ancien régime* France) with his *Avertissement*, intended to be read out from the pulpits of every parish church in Paris. Very few of the *curés* complied. Normally, their good will towards the Bourbon monarchy was most apparent. Information about taxation, the militia ballot, the great peace treaties of 1763 (Paris) and 1783 (Versailles), and the death of Louis XV in 1774 was passed on to the populace from the pulpit; in 1774 the baron de Turgot (controller-general, 1774–6) asked the bishop of Saint-Pol-de-Léon in Brittany to involve his *curés* in an investigation concerning beggars, in effect undertaking duties as unofficial government agents. Parish clergy could usually understand and speak a local *patois* when lay officials might not. 'In most of our communities', observed the deputies of the Sélestat district (containing 153 parishes) of Alsace in 1789, 'there are only the *curés* and the councillors [*prévôts*] who know how to read and

---

[11] *Boswell: The English Experiment 1785–1789*, eds. Irma S. Lustig and Frederick A. Pottle, (London, 1986), 10 December 1786, 115.

write, especially the French tongue'.[12] In Britain, such circumstances pertained only in the most remote regions such as North Wales and the Scottish highlands. English beneficed clergy were with increasing frequency given office in local government as justices of the peace, that most essential of all posts in maintaining the peace of the countryside. This combination of clerical and judicial functions could have compromised the pastoral function of the parson, but those who were offered a place on their county's commission of the peace rarely turned it down.

The state in defence of Christianity

The additional lustre conferred on a priest by such leverage on state power was prized; criticism of the role was likely to be dismissed as trouble-making by discontented elements whose loyalty to Church and state was suspect. So clerical authority, appropriately exercised, was generally upheld. In England, Parliament was unsympathetic to the Feathers' Tavern petition of 1772 asking for an alteration to subscription and few MPs were persuaded by the Cambridge academic John Jebb's view that private judgment in religion overrode all public considerations. The average established clergyman, whether Catholic or Protestant, did not want to see the knot between Church and state untied, however unpalatable concessions to religious minorities in the state might be found. The presumption that governments would uphold Christian doctrine and ethics as a concomitant of establishment persisted among churchmen, especially on fundamental questions of dogma. In England in 1777–8 the attorney-general, Thomas Thurlow, helped prosecute the vicar of Tewkesbury, the Revd Edward Evanson, for anti-Trinitarian views. In those circumstances, state power was the ultimate deterrent. At a humbler level, priests and ministers could not always assume that admonition from the pulpit would inculcate the principles of Christian morality in their parishioners; they relied on the worst offenders being handed over to the lay magistrate for punishment, thereby underlining the respect to be accorded to the clergy and their preaching on such moral questions as adultery, bastardy and infanticide. The reduced importance of the Church courts as toleration spread gave this procedure added importance, though, increasingly, the state had other preoccupations than to chastise sinners, and the 'godly magistrate' became harder to find. In Geneva, the power of the consistory was declining sharply over the citizens, and as illegitimate births rose from almost nil, it was hard to hear

---

[12] Quoted in Pierre Pierrard, *Histoire des Curés de Campagne de 1789 à nos jours* (Paris, 1986), 21.

any public articulation of Calvin's sometimes ferocious moral teaching. 'O John Calvin, where art thou now?' exclaimed Boswell in 1764 when he discovered that card playing on a Sunday was widespread. This marked reluctance by the state to enforce an overtly Christian code of ethics based on the Ten Commandments was critical in watering down the link between Christianity and good citizenship.

Nevertheless, with an organised police force still rudimentary in most states, religion remained essential to the legitimation of government. That luminary of the Aberdeen Enlightenment, Alexander Gerard, doubted whether 'a society could at all subsist for any considerable time, if its members were generally destitute of all religious impressions'.[13] Subjects obeyed, in the last analysis, because of biblical injunctions to do so constantly reiterated by the clergy, who insisted that disobedience to the Crown was an offence against God. Admittedly, to set against this was the Calvinist emphasis on the right of magistrates (that is, leading subjects) to throw off the yoke of a tyrannical king, but by the late eighteenth century this tended to be an historical curiosity; thus the leaders of the Genevan revolt of 1782 relied on more recent political theory to vindicate their actions in rising against the dominant city oligarchs. Also, since most other public institutions in a given polity existed under the Crown even when they did not derive their power directly from it, they likewise looked as much to biblical sources for their validation in the same manner as their king. Of course, such a justification for power flew in the face of much enlightenment theory originating with Locke and Montesquieu stressing the rights of subjects, the need for a balanced constitution, and the existence of an original contract between government and governed with penalties for default. Neither was it the presentational angle that appealed to Frederick II of Prussia, the emperor Joseph and other 'enlightened absolutists', who preferred to justify their rule in terms of public usefulness, of acting as the first servant of the state. Louis-Antoine de Caraccioli argued that the first declaration of rights and duties had been made in Sinai; his *Jésus-Christ, par sa tolérance, modèle des législateurs* (Paris, 1784) founded the whole of the Judaeo-Christian heritage on a contract between God and man. Nevertheless, despite these fashionable constitutionalist concepts, the average subject (and this held good down to the end of the century) was far more likely to view his duty towards the king as emanating from the New Testament rather than Locke's *Treatise on Government*.

---

[13] A. Gerard, 'The Influence of Piety on the Public Good', in *The Scotch Preacher* (1775–89), 311, quoted in Ian D. L. Clark, 'From Protest to Reaction: The Moderate Regime in the Church of Scotland, 1752–1805', in N. T. Phillipson and Rosalind Mitchison (eds.), *Scotland in the Age of Improvement* (Edinburgh, 1970), 207.

Even in Britain, where constitutional freedoms were more entrenched under the Revolution settlement of 1688 and the ensuing Hanoverian Succession than in virtually every other European state, there was an almost universal awareness and acceptance throughout the eighteenth century that government was divinely ordained and it followed that subjects owed obedience to 'the powers instituted of God'. Since both Whigs *and* Tories took pride in the accession of George III in 1760 (the first native-born sovereign since Queen Anne) and were equally favoured by him, this rhetoric was cranked up further over the next two decades, especially when the American colonists defaulted on the obedience which most Britons saw as due to them. The sermons of Thomas Nowell before the Commons in 1772 in defence of the 'martyred' Charles I and Archbishop Markham of York to the Society for the Propagation of the Gospel in 1777 on the disobedience of the American colonists both unleashed a considerable backlash. To their dissenting critics, it could sound as if senior members of the Church of England were publicly delivering the kind of high-flying sentiments that belonged to the age of divine right monarchy which had apparently ended with the 'abdication' of James II in 1688.

The fact was that divine right monarchy was a nostalgic nostrum by the time of the American War of Independence, whereas divine right government was not. Even the Vatican had rejected the claims of the Stuarts to their ancestral throne on the death of the *de jure* James III, the Old Pretender, first in 1766, and then more forcefully still when Henry, cardinal duke of York, succeeded his brother, the Young Pretender, twenty-two years later. Hereditary right and legitimacy were becoming separate questions, even for the Supreme Pontiff. Yet the eighteenth century was not an epoch in which dynasties were displaced lightly. The British court Whigs from the time of the 'Junto' in the 1690s, and certainly from Sir Robert Walpole's ascendancy (1721–42), distanced themselves from the rights of resistance which more zealous Whigs asserted as implicit in the events of 1688. For them, there would only be one British Revolution, a point driven home by Edmund Burke in his *Reflections on the French Revolution* in contradistinction to the reformist hopes of 'rational dissenters' including Dr Richard Price and leading members of the Revolution Societies (established to celebrate the centenary of the 1688 Revolution). Inspired anew by events in France, they were willing to contemplate a new settlement of the British state. The high church tradition of *jure divino* government had its uses in a Whig state, and the national day of commemorating King Charles I's execution (30 January) persisted throughout the Hanoverian era with Whig bishops happy to preach before Parliament on the festival of the royal martyr, as some high churchmen insisted on calling him. There was also a 5 November state thanksgiving service commemorating William of Orange's 1688 'deliverance', happily coinciding with the day commemorating the Gunpowder Plot. It meant much to Whigs delighting in their constitution, but the church bells pealing out unsettled old fashioned Tories, intensely devoted to the 'royal martyr' Charles I. The bitter experience of Civil War in the 1640s and 1650s endured for generations afterwards, a reminder of the horrors that could so easily ensue if subjects relinquished the respect they owed to their crowned head and, as the preferred Whig emphasis had it, the status quo in Church and state. Attendance at state services in St Margaret's, Westminster (Commons) and Westminster Abbey (Lords) could be thin, a sign that moderate Whigs found the occasion anomalous and illogical. As the 2nd earl of Radnor expressed it in a speech he prepared for delivery in the Lords, it was a service 'which I think absurd, believe to be hypocritical, & suspect to be profane, a service which requires a sermon whose Doctrines must militate with the Principles of our Constitution'.[14]

Radnor questioned the validity of a commemoration that most British politicians considered, overall, did more good than harm. Preachers tended to use it to recall George III's subjects to their duties under a monarchy whose liberties they extolled as unique in Europe, and the 30 January service would come back into its own again after Britain and France went to war in 1793 and the execution of Louis XVI gave regicide a new contemporary resonance. The feast day of Charles 'King and Martyr' was one of those dates in the Anglican calendar earmarked to highlight the Christian character and origins of the realm, a reminder of the primacy still officially accorded to religio-political justification for the state despite countervailing enlightenment emphases on usefulness, contractual theory and a distrust of the sanction given by tradition to the potential abuse of power. Fast days with special prayers and church services also remained important in both England and Scotland. They were intended to suggest the sense that national repentance in dark times (as during the early months of the Seven Years' War or the latter stages of the American War) was essential in order to acknowledge sinfulness and regain divine favour.

Ceremonial religious, royal and republican

Irrespective of whether a country had a tradition of absolutist or constitutional rule, Christian political theory insisted that royal authority and the state agencies exercising it on the king's behalf depended on

---

[14] Wiltshire and Swindon Record Office, Radnor MSS. 490/1413.

divine rather than popular or aristocratic sanction. When Mary of the Immaculate Conception was officially proclaimed patronness of Spain in 1761, 4,000 candles lit up the Gothic façade of Seville Cathedral and the bells of over 100 churches rang out for several days in celebration. It was correspondingly appropriate that the public ceremonies in which the monarch participated invariably intermingled religious and secular pageantry. The intent was usually to impose the image of power on impressionable subjects, though some occasions called for a display of royal humility – for example, the annual commemoration at Versailles every 15 August by his descendants of Louis XIII's entrusting his kingdom to the protection of the Blessed Virgin Mary. In Venice that medieval protector against the pestilence, St Roch, remained co-patron (junior to St Mark) of the city, his church a place of pilgrimage every 16 August for the doge and the nobility. Royal displays of charity in which princes undertook mock-menial tasks thereby recalling the precedent of the King of kings, Jesus Christ, were not easy to reconcile with contemporary attitudes to politeness. In England, distribution of specially minted money to selected old men on Maundy Thursday was abandoned as long ago as James II's reign (1685–8), though the office of lord high almoner (always a senior bishop) was retained and George III never stinted on private acts of charity. Anyone wanting to see a sovereign sponging the feet of the lucky few would either have to be in Rome on Maundy Thursday to watch the pope perform the rite, or in Poland where Stanislaw Poniatowski, in every other respect the model of an Anglophile enlightened sovereign, washed the feet of twelve old men, gave them new clothes and shoes, and personally served them dinner at the royal castle. A combination of rational theology, constitutional changes and personal dissipation worked against crediting most eighteenth-century monarchs with the healing touch; it may have contravened all the canons of enlightenment, but the masses still hankered for it. Louis XV of France had been obliged to give up the practice in the 1740s under the ban of the Church for keeping a mistress; his morally respectable grandson touched again from 1777 amid general delight. Enough symbolic gestures of charity survived to kindle the ties of loyalty between monarch and subjects and point towards the sacred origins of kingship. Whatever coffee-house politicians might say or write, lesser mortals found it hard to give up the notion that kings were by God appointed.

Coronation ceremonies fed that belief like no other event. The French talked of the *sacre*, not the crowning of their kings, emphasising its primarily religious character. They were spectacular as well as sacred occasions mounted in most states approximately a year after the accession of a new monarch. Protestant as well as Catholic and Orthodox states

6. Bust of Lorenzo Ganganelli, Pope Clement XIV (1705–74), by Christopher Hewetson. A sensitive individual and accomplished scholar, Clement decided that the dissolution of the Jesuits in 1773 was a price worth paying for the normalisation of relations between the papacy and the main Catholic powers.

staged coronations and were happy to employ rituals that were essentially pre-Reformation in character. Thus Anglican and Lutheran clergy wore elaborate vestments and used sacred oils for anointing the king just as their Catholic counterparts did in other parts of Europe. The English king at his coronation became more than a secular person. The wearing of a dalmatic was especially significant since it indicated that, though he was not ordained, he was able to exercise jurisdiction in spiritual matters. No spectator of eighteenth-century coronation ritual and pageantry could doubt the explicit connexion made throughout the service between the sacral status of the state (embodied in the monarch as its head) and hopes for its providential survival under God. At George III's coronation the bishops paid homage before all other peers except royal dukes, touched the crown 'as a sign that they will do all in their power to keep it on the King's head, and kissed him on the left cheek'.[15]

The authorities positively encouraged comparisons with biblical rulers. Thus many pamphlets appeared in 1761 comparing the twenty-three-year-old George III with King David. Coronations were occasions for rejoicing and entertaining hopes of a fresh start, bringing together the diverse peoples of most polities. The 1761 ceremony in Westminster Abbey was only the third in the relatively new British state and the sermon was appropriately preached by a Scotsman, the archbishop of York, Robert Hay Drummond. Britons acclaimed their young ruler, but the rejoicing was more an expression of relief in the Habsburg Empire in 1790 when Leopold II replaced his unpopular brother Joseph II. Habsburg sovereigns were required by precedent to be crowned in more than one of their capitals, but Leopold had only been made king of Bohemia (September 1791) before premature death overtook him in February 1792. His election as emperor prompted an outpouring of sacred music as well as popular relief. A Te Deum, possibly by Salieri, was performed as part of the celebrations in April 1790 surrounding his election, while Mozart's 'Coronation' Mass, written in Salzburg in 1779, was probably performed in Baden, near Vienna, in 1790 or 1791, and may have won its name during the celebrations of Leopold's coronation as king of Bohemia. At Reims in 1775, where the twenty-one-year-old Louis XVI was crowned at the French coronation service, the *sacre*, the hierarchy was not alone in hoping the new king would set a new national tone by repudiating the unedifying libertinism of his grandfather, Louis XV.

Everything about coronations spoke of the indispensability of the Church to the legitimate functioning of the pre-revolutionary state. It was emphatically a Christian occasion with the taking of holy communion,

---

[15] Count Frederick Kielmansegge, *Diary of a Journey to England in the Years 1761–1762* (London, 1902), 34.

and the dedication to God of his people through the mediatory offices of the Church. By the crowning, consecrating and anointing of a ruler with sacred oils, the Church signalled the mystical bonds between a king (or queen) and God; the sovereign for his part swore several oaths to confirm existing legal obligations and corporate privileges including, inevitably, those of the established Church. These oaths were based largely on medieval precedents, though some subtle updating was possible in constitutional regimes. Thus in England monarchs were required to uphold the Bill of Rights and other parts of the 1689 constitutional settlement. All this was done very publicly in the sight of his assembled subjects (or those who could pack into the cathedral) and had important implications for his subsequent political conduct. Gustavus III's *coup d'état* in Sweden of August 1772 took place *after* he had sworn to uphold the aristocratic constitution which had been in place since the 1720s and it compromised his authority with influential sections of the Swedish nobility for the two decades of his rule before his assassination. George III of Britain was much more scrupulous about his coronation oath. When Pitt's government in 1799–1800 moved towards including Catholic emancipation in the Irish Act of Union, the king insisted it would violate his coronation oath to uphold the Protestant religion. The Cabinet resigned in the face of this royal impasse, while the Anglican establishment received a reprieve of three decades.

Not all states staged expensive coronations. In Prussia, for instance, Frederick II's official emphasis stressed enlightened, efficient monarchy. There was no place for expensive 'medieval' flummery in a realm where the king projected a workaday image of himself in a tattered frock coat (distinguished only by the star of a chivalric order) rather than sumptuous coronation robes. Besides, the king had no intention of suggesting his status owed anything to divine sanction conferred by the clergy; in Prussia it was the latter who owed everything to him. Prussia was unusual in foregoing this state spectacular, but it suited Frederick's nature and his wily recognition that the avoidance of oath-taking eased the way to implementing controversial reforms without risking charges of bad faith or violation of his subjects' liberties. Interestingly, an elective monarchy like Poland, which allowed its king little scope for policy initiatives, retained a four-day coronation and staged one on 25 November 1764 for Stanislaw Poniatowski. The king had to be dressed by the archbishop of Lwów and the marshal of the court in a semi-religious garb of a white alb and shirt, a cope and sandals, and permit the primate of the Polish Church to raise the wide sleeves of his shirt to make the sign of the cross in holy oil on his wrists and elbows, then unbutton the back to anoint him between the shoulder blades. In constitutional terms Stanislaw was an elective king; his coronation dress stressed his prelatical status, and his proximity to the Church and to God. Whatever a country's political tradition, that emphasis was central to all coronation ritual in the period from 1750 to 1790.

Stanislaw's latest biographer claims that he was less of a deist than an enthusiast for the values of the Catholic Enlightenment, with a lifelong admiration for the classic Anglicanism he had found in the circle of Bishop William Warburton on his visit to England in 1754. It is certainly striking how seriously the Polish king and most other monarchs of the 1750–90 era took their religious obligations. The personal piety of monarchs like Louis XVI and George III is well known. Gustavus III of Sweden became so obsessed with religion between 1779 and 1782 that courtiers doubted his sanity; he could not hear enough of the Swedenborgian theosophy expounded to him by Johan Gustaf Halldin, a half-crazed mystic rescued from a gaol sentence for high treason. He communicated regularly, fasted on Good Friday, and had a fascination with Lutheran rituals; none of this he judged incompatible with visiting necromancers such as Ulrica Arfvidsson, a man popular with ladies from Gustavus' court and protected by the police. Gustavus was more circumspect in his patronage of the occult and more protective of the Swedish Church after the 1786 Riksdag.

Ferdinand, duke of Parma, attended Mass twice daily, notwithstanding his excommunication by Clement XIII in 1768 after the suppression of the Jesuits. Charles III of Spain dedicated his domains to the Immaculate Conception of the Virgin, and lived a life of frugality appropriate to a member of the Franciscan Third Order. The frenetic, mercurial Peter Leopold of Tuscany had a dancer, Livia Raimondi, as his mistress after 1786 to whom he gave readings in Thomas à Kempis, Fénelon and innumerable Jansenist moral theologians. He came to think of himself as an 'external bishop', and prescribed textbooks for the clergy, banned unorthodox titles from seminaries and convent libraries, and paid the Companies of Charity to carry out the the projects he drew up for them. Joseph II even persuaded Pius VI he was a faithful son of the Church, and quite genuinely told his mother he would give everything he possessed to make all his subjects Catholics. A correspondence between the emperor and the elector of Trier revealed the former's own familiarity with theology, however much he scoffed at papal infallibility, deplored the futility of discussing the Bull *Unigenitus* and defended relaxation of the censorship.

Temporal and spiritual combined: the papacy 1750–1790

Nowhere did Christian political theory have a more central role in determining the character and conduct of a polity than in the papal states. This was, in theory, the archetypal theocratic state, where Church and state were as one, ruled over by the supreme pontiff as Christ's vicar-general on earth. In practice, the state functioned according to practices and precepts operative in most others. As with any principality or kingdom, papal power rested on territorial control, here a swathe of land in central Italy (population 3 million) composed of several provinces with the 'patrimony of St Peter' around Rome at its heart. Like France in the 1780s, the papal states were virtually bankrupt, the product of over-reliance on a series of fiscal expedients and Pius VI's efforts to drain the Pontine marshes. Economic decline was hastened by debasement of the currency, high taxation and fiscal immunities that extended to all the clergy. The holy father governed rather less efficiently than most contemporary rulers through a well-established bureaucracy, the curia. Curial government was dominated by the *prelatura*, well-born young men from the educated Roman nobility who constituted a large part of the pope's *familia* or civil household and had jurisdictional powers but no priestly functions. Their impact on driving forward policy was limited. Reform initiatives of an 'enlightened absolutist' kind were repeatedly obstructed by vested local interests. Thus the last eighteen months of Clement XIV's life were made miserable by the cardinalate, whose revenge for his sacrifice of the Jesuits was to hinder his attempts to reform economic and social abuses within the papal states. Undeterred, his successor, Pius VI, dabbled with further piecemeal reforms. Some reflected the modish prescriptions of political economy, such as instituting free trade in Bologna, the largest and richest city in the papal states, in November 1791, only to find Bologna's dislike of government from Rome obstructing the process. None of these problems deterred the pope from some old-fashioned nepotism. He built the Palazzo Braschi for his two nephews (one a cardinal, the other a duke), and paid other relatives generous allowances.

Apart from their temporal possessions, the popes also claimed a spiritual authority in the religious life of Catholic states, which gave them additional leverage over fellow monarchs and princes, extending in theory to absolving subjects from their allegiance. It could take several forms in the late *ancien régime*. Thus, when the holy father was pronouncing definitively (or *ex cathedra*) on doctrinal matters, his words had an irresistible force. In an age when dogmatic formulae were easily ridiculed and presented as 'enthusiasm', popes were reluctant to pronounce or monarchs and ministers to worry themselves when they did. Then there were a set of well-worn and unexceptionable temporal conventions making up a primacy of honour, including the paying of a token annual sum by Catholic states to the papacy known as Peter's pence or annates, or the ratification in the form of issuing bulls of institution required when appointments were made to bishoprics and abbeys. These usages could not mask the degree to which the papacy had been moving towards a policy of recognising the supremacy of the state since at least the pontificate of Benedict XIV (1740–58), as reflected in the concordats of that era with the Two Sicilies, Spain and Lombardy. There was no question of the popes trying to extend formal powers such as those agreed with France as long ago as the Concordat of Bologna (1516): the nearest equivalent in the years 1750–90 of the stand-off that had existed in the 1680s between Louis XIV and Innocent XI over the French Crown's financial right to *régale* during a vacancy in see came when the king of Naples refused feudal homage to Pius VI by not sending him the white horse that protocol and precedent required. This was more than the stuff of comic opera. Ferdinand IV (1759–1825) was demanding an unfettered right to appoint to bishoprics, causing the pope to respond in time-honoured fashion by refusing canonical investiture to royal candidates. The dispute of the early 1780s with Joseph II never plumbed these depths.

The episode was an indicator that the pressure for change was coming from Catholic monarchs who, while they respected these token relics of papal power, would not tolerate any serious rivalry from the Vatican in controlling their 'national' Churches. There was nothing new in monarchs and ministers ignoring or manipulating papal injunctions and claims to jurisdiction; the Habsburg monarchy's decree of 1767 that all papal instruments had to be seen by the imperial crown before promulgation was in line with this tradition. The diplomatic brinkmanship that might ensue could lead to the threat of seizing isolated papal temporal possessions like the Avignonat in France, as happened in 1790. However, many of these mid-century developments went a step further. The regalian policies of Charles III of Spain building on the powers secured by his predecessors under the Concordats of 1737 and 1753, the ambitious restructuring programme of Joseph II across the Habsburg domains in the 1780s redrawing ecclesiastical boundaries (see above) and requiring clerical oaths to the state and, above all, the nigh-universal insistence from Catholic sovereigns that the Society of Jesus – the strongest international body within the Church, 'curialist' as opposed to 'regalist' – must be abolished, all showed as much. Such behaviour in the sixteenth century might have precipitated further outright ruptures from Rome along the English model; in the eighteenth, the popes knew that resistance within the *curia* to any item of royal policy had little more than nuisance value. They usually contented themselves with a formal diplomatic protest or, when really moved, going in person to complain about the lack of consultation, as Pius VI did when he travelled to Vienna in 1782.

Papal influence in European affairs

Such dramatic reverses have led historians to make negative assessments of that historic *plenitudo potestatis* (fullness of power) claimed by the Holy See. Thus for Olwen Hufton, 'In the history of the papacy, the eighteenth century is emphatically an ebb tide'; for William Doyle, 'Papal authority had received a series of blows which seemed calculated to destroy every vestige of central authority in the Church.'[16] But one should be careful not to overstate the point. Papal Bulls remained usefully authoritative to governments as the unrelenting lobbying of Clement XIV to extract *Dominus ac redemptor* from him in 1773 suggested. A papal death always witnessed complicated manoeuvrings and some sharp rivalries as Paris, Vienna, Madrid and the Italian capitals courted the cardinals to try to secure the election of their preferred choice as successor to St Peter. There was a particularly protracted interregnum in 1758 at the height of the Seven Years' War when France vetoed the first choice of the cardinals as a replacement for Benedict XIV. The judicial importance of Rome was also high, with the *Rota* acting as the supreme ecclesiastic court for civil and criminal appeals from all over Europe against judgments in episcopal courts of law.

Even if it be conceded that papal power was not what it had been a century before, papal influence, exercised astutely, could still bring dividends, as Benedict XIV displayed following the conquest and absorption of the increasingly Catholic-populated province of Silesia into the Prussian state after 1740. The pope's recognition of Frederick II's title as king of Prussia dissuaded that monarch from following up his initial plan of having a Prussian state Church for Catholics under a vicar-general answering to Berlin not Rome. It seems likely that the scope for influence in France of successive popes from Clement XI through to Pius VI has been underestimated. Dale Van Kley's important work shows that the French hierarchy, aghast at the campaign against the Jesuits and angered at the monarchy's inability to contain it, had rediscovered the practical value of papal power by 1770.[17] As pragmatic, non-Jansenist Gallicans in the hierarchy saw it, the holy father might have the French Church's good more at heart than that unreliable roué, Louis XV. The premature death of the French dauphin and his wife in the mid-1760s, the great patrons of the *dévot* party at court, did nothing to discourage this line of thinking. Injured in the contest against judicial Jansenism and feeling itself

[16] Olwen Hufton, *Europe: Privilege and Protest 1730–1789* (London, 1980), 87; William Doyle, *The Old European Order 1660–1800* (2nd edn, Oxford, 1992), 373.
[17] Dale K. Van Kley, *The Religious Origins of the French Revolution: From Calvin to the Civil Constitution, 1560–1791* (New Haven, 1996), 192.

semi-detached from the monarchy from about 1765, the hierachy began to look again to Rome, whatever the 1682 Articles stipulated about
the superiority of an ecumenical council to the papacy. If the point
is accepted, then it requires historians to rethink the character of late
Jansenism with its supposed emphasis on 'national liberties' and to then
re-evaluate the diplomacy attendant on the papal rejection of the Civil
Constitution of the Clergy in 1790–1. As I have suggested elsewhere,[18]
we may well be looking at the strange birth of modern ultramontanism,
unlikely as it may sound, during the pontificates of Clement XIV and
Pius VI.

The exclusive papal prerogative of making cardinals was always a powerful bargaining counter in diplomatic relations between the Holy See
and national monarchies. Senior prelates coveted a cardinal's red hat
as the supreme accolade, more for its intrinsic prestige than the right
it gave of voting in papal elections. There were never enough hats to
go round. Pius received regular requests from Louis XVI via his ambassador in Rome, Cardinal Bernis, to reward leading prelates in the Gallican
Church. Pius was in no hurry. The scandal of Cardinal Rohan's disgrace
in the Diamond Necklace affair of 1786 increased his fears of bringing
the rank of cardinal into disrepute, and it was not until Loménie de
Brienne left his post as first minister in August 1788 that he received a
cardinalate as a consolation prize, one also going to the king's lord high
almoner, Bishop Montmorency-Laval of Metz, in whose family there was
almost an hereditary expectation of such a trophy.

Another key figure nominated by the Vatican was the nuncio or foreign envoy, the equivalent of a royal ambassador, but in this case one
with full legatine powers and spiritual authority. He acted as intermediary between the pope and an individual state, and advised both sides on
patronage. His duties were by no means ceremonial or honorific given
the considerable appointments still in the personal gift of the pope. Some
of these had a seasonable character. In Spain, the Holy See could name
to numerous benefices during eight months of the year, so that the papal
nuncio was flooded with requests from clerics for promotion, particularly those whom the Bourbon monarchy might deem unsuitable; in the
Three Bishoprics, the pope had six months in which he could nominate to
offices, and eight months in Lorraine. Personality and intelligence could
sometimes make an appreciable difference to determining the Holy See's
influence on policy-making. It could not be relied on in this era. Thus
the nunciatures completely failed to prevent the first Partition of Poland

---

[18] Nigel Aston, 'The Golden Autumn of Gallicanism? Religious History and its Place in
Current Writing on Eighteenth-century France', *French History* 13 (1999), 187–222,
at 210.

by Austria, Prussia and Russia in February and August 1772. Their effectiveness was enhanced when the papacy's external relations were the responsibility of a talented secretary of state (appointed for a particular reign, head of the Palatine Secretariats, in effect the pope's prime minister), and there were few of those between 1750 and 1790. That the Holy See came perilously close to a total diplomatic breakdown in the 1760s with Portugal, France and Parma over the Jesuit question owed much to the mild Clement XIII allowing policy to be determined by his imperious pro-Jesuit secretary of state, Luigi Torrigiano.

The latter's defensive stance was only a delaying tactic. With virtually every Catholic power in Europe united on this issue, it was only a matter of time before the papacy capitulated. Meanwhile, the Habsburg monarchy decided to bypass papal non-co-operation in Church reforms by obtaining a series of canon law propositions from Paul Joseph Ritter von Riegger, of Vienna University, based on the numerous anti-curialist precedents since the Habsburgs had first obtained the imperial throne in the fifteenth century. This was the foundation of the Erastian state policies pursued by Chancellor Kaunitz after 1770. Papal non-consent was enough for the majority of bishops not to risk censure from Clement XIV and Pius VI, obliging the empress Maria Theresa and (after 1780) Joseph II to rely more on Jansenist reformers to achieve their objectives. The Habsburg offensive increased the marginalisation of the Holy See as an international power and underscored the point that states would happily see what remained of the papacy's temporal prerogatives fall into disuse. It would be hard to find a contemporary Catholic ruler who could not underwrite these policy objectives, whatever their reservations about Joseph's tactics and timing.

Erastian reformers

Ricci

In fact, it was often reforming clerics who courted royal favour and supplied their would-be patrons with the ideological justification for curtailing ecclesiastical power. In Italy, along the length of the peninsula learned clergy, professors, academicians, seminary tutors, those loosely labelled Jansenists inspired by the historian and theological scholar Lodovico Muratori (1672–1750) and unencumbered by pastoral obligations or hierarchical status, circulated papers that made the case for modernisation that would forge an alliance between the state and the parish priests to accomplish Catholic reform. The term Jansenists was used more loosely than in France to identify a wide spectrum of enlightenment criticism of both Church structures and doctrines. Their main strength lay in the cities (including Rome), as in Genoa where Fr Eustachio Degola used letters and a journal to keep Italian Jansenists in touch with their counterparts north of the Alps. Sometimes, as in Brescia, they found a bishop to take up their cause. The most famous was Scipione de Ricci of Pistoia and Prato in Tuscany who worked in conjunction with Kaunitz and the Grand Duke Peter Leopold, Joseph II's younger brother. Peter Leopold, it must be said, needed little encouragement to act out a Caesaropapal role as a means to revive spiritual life in the duchy. He banned the payment of ecclesiastical imposts outside the country, taxed clerical incomes, introduced a new catechism, abolished the Florentine Holy Office in 1782, reduced the office of nuncio to an ordinary ambassador, and made preaching missions subject to strict controls. As with Joseph II, he aimed to increase the standing of the secular clergy by raising stipends and attacking non-residence.

With theoretical justification for state supremacy over the Church handled by other beneficiaries of imperial patronage in a range of pamphlets, Ricci foisted radical changes on the Tuscan Church – for all his emphasis on the lower clergy as the bedrock of the Church, they were expected not to contradict his authoritarian leadership – that were inspired not just by French and Dutch Jansenism but the scourge of the Medici in the 1490s, the millenarian friar Girolamo Savonarola. Ricci, too, came to see himself as the prophet of the New Jerusalem, now located in Florence. Restrictions on the power of the Church courts and the suppression of numerous monasteries climaxed in 1786 in the Synod of Pistoia, which also adopted the Gallican Articles of 1682. Ricci's hope was that his diocesan synod would be the prelude to one for the whole Grand Duchy, but the Pistoia decisions were too extreme both for his episcopal colleagues and the lay elite, and also for the elector himself, who was unhappy at the poisonous factionalisation of Tuscan politics. An unofficial general assembly of the Tuscan bishops in Florence in 1787 showed that Ricci spoke for few of his episcopal colleagues and, more crucially still, Peter Leopold had deliberately left town: only three of seventeen Tuscan prelates were sympathetic to this Riccian version of Jansenism and riots in Prato showed that the populace was stirring. Unlike his elder brother, the more cautious Peter Leopold knew when it was time to make a tactical withdrawal having, indeed, made it clear to Pius as early as 1780 that there were still many issues which might go to Rome from Florence on appeal. He was aware of the paradox that the more the state sponsored unpopular religious change the more royal power stood to be damaged by the political instability it caused. Disturbances continued in the duchy immediately before and after Peter Leopold handed over power to his son, Ferdinand III, in March 1790, while Ricci resigned his see in 1791.

There were, then, risks for rulers in backing prelates like Ricci for whom an extreme Erastian polity was a tolerable price to pay if it resulted in a new Church settlement along primitive lines. A clerical reaction could often draw on considerable popular sympathies, especially among women, as the reaction to the Civil Constitution in France would later show. But in the generation before Pistoia, reform-minded Catholic higher clergy in central and southern Europe were in no mood to slow the pace of change or listen to majority opinion which could be conveniently, if not always accurately, dismissed as torpid and self-interested: where Church officials and the laity were unco-operative the resources of the state were indispensable if progress was to be achieved. In a real sense, therefore, the ecclesiastical reforms of Joseph II of Austria and lesser rulers were a response to a reform impetus that senior clergy had marked out for them.

Febronius

Denigration of papal authority was a cornerstone of reform schemes. Throughout the *Reichskirche*, the second half of the eighteenth century saw wave after wave of anti-papal diatribe emanating from the ordained ministry on a scale unheard of since the Reformation. Its most famous product was 'Febronius', properly known as Johann Nikolas von Hontheim (1701–90), vicar-general of the archbishop of Trier, as well as professor of law at the university there. His *On the Condition of the Church and the Legitimate Power of the Roman Pontiff* (1763) presented a limited view of the power of Rome (confined to spiritual matters), arguing that in every country the authority of the Church should be exercised by national or provincial synods of bishops leaving the pope as the most senior prelate in the Catholic world. From the papal angle Febronius appeared to be articulating a German form of Jansenism and his book was placed on the Index in 1764, though that could not prevent its translation into most European languages and very wide sales. Papal power was still sufficient to extract a formal retraction from Hontheim in 1779, but his pseudonymous tract acted as a blueprint for the sparkier declamations that followed taking up a 'Febronian' emphasis.

Nowhere was this spirit stronger than in the ecclesiastical electorates where Emmerich Joseph von Breidbach, the elector of Mainz (1763–74) and convert to the Catholic Enlightenment, emerged as leader of the episcopalian party within the *Reichskirche*. A meeting of the three Rhineland electors and other prelates at Coblenz in 1769 revealed the extent of sympathy for the Febronian position: among its articles (or *Gravamina*) were demands to limit the role of nuncios in Germany, abolish dues to Rome and end what remained of monastic immunity to episcopal supervision. They prefigured the Congress (the so-called 'Punctuation') of Ems held in 1786, which attracted a large attendance from across Germany. Here the three German archbishop-electors challenged the authority of the papacy and reasserted the supremacy of general councils in legislative and judicial matters. The idea of a territorial Church geared to the social and economic organisation of distinctive states was one whose time appeared to have come. In fact, the Punctuation of Ems would retrospectively turn out to be the highpoint of a Church reform programme along quasi-Jansenist and national lines in the *Reichskirche* before the French Revolutionary and Napoleonic wars destroyed its material power and, for the most part, removed the monarchs and princes who were to be the agents and protectors of this intended new Catholic order. Significantly, the claims of the German bishops were rejected by Pius VI in 1789.

The rhetoric of Ems (or, come to that, Pistoia) was less incendiary than many contemporaries believed: Hontheim and his allies were only repeating and updating what exponents of 'national' Catholicism had said at intervals since the sixteenth century, including his former professor of canon law at the University of Louvain, Zega-Bernard Van Espen. An insistence on the final authority of a general council was hardly novel; it corresponded to the official position of the papacy since the Counter-Reformation. Indeed, having a council like Ems to overhaul and update the Church was fully within the spirit of the Tridentine decrees, however much the language used in debate might suggest otherwise. Pius VI was hardly threatening a papal counter-offensive against those states which had so vigorously trimmed papal power and influence since the mid-seventeenth century. But senior clergy in the *Reichskirche*, for whom even a papal figurehead was an obstacle to creating a German national Church in the eighteenth century, found it convenient to demonise him. This was the vision that inspired Hontheim, but translating it was problematic. It was not just that the German prelates and the *curia* had incompatible interests; the mutual distrust and divergent agendas of the prelates themselves were never far from the surface, while their creativity stopped with decrees reinforcing episcopal authority at the expense of Rome. They offered no enhanced scope and role to the vast majority of the parish clergy.

The monarchical response to Ems was lukewarm. Led by the emperor himself, states which were Catholic hung back from openly endorsing its deliberations. The princes were suddenly worried that the exaltation of episcopal power at the expense of the papacy would simply replace a distant authority with one likely to offer more effective resistance to the mechanisms of the enlightened state. When Friedrich Karl von Erthal, elector of Mainz (1774–1802), refloated the possibility of a 'German National Church' after the anti-Austrian and Protestant *Fürstenbund* (1785), the proposal significantly attracted no interest from either the emperor Joseph or alarmed Pope Pius. Meanwhile, the German lay rulers were determined there should be no resurgence of the episcopate as territorial princes. Catholic rulers in Bavaria and Austria were aspirants to state Churches but they were to be constructed on a princely not prelatical basis.

Charles III and Jansenism in Spain

Royal power over the Church was already formidable when Charles III made it his purpose to complete the formal subordination of the Church to the throne initiated by the Concordat of 1753. The expulsion of the Jesuits divided the hierarchy, though a majority of the episcopate supported it, forty-two approving, six opposing and eight having no opinion, according to a papal enquiry of 1769. In the universities, the Crown ordered all degree recipients and faculty members to swear not to maintain or teach any ultramontane beliefs conflicting with its regalian rights. Royal censors were established at the universities to ensure this regulation was obeyed. As a counterbalance, satires on the Jesuits were prohibited as early as 1769, the astute Charles knowing he could rely on the Inquisition to support this part of royal policy. The co-operation of the Holy Office could generally never be assumed. The Inquisition investigated charges of Jansenism against the five prelates who had been members of the Royal Commission to try the Jesuits and also against the bishop of Barcelona, suspected of praising the Jansenist Church of Utrecht. Explicit evidence of heresy was wanting and the case was dropped. Charles' long-term policy was to use the prerogative to clip the independent spirit of the Inquisition and entrench it as another part of the royal bureaucracy. Charles felt he had no need to abolish the institution outright, as did his son, the king of the Two Sicilies. 'The Spaniards want it,' he said, 'and it does not bother me.'

Meanwhile, the spread of Febronian ideas among the educated clergy assisted the king's regalian policies over the long term. His minister Campomanes coauthored one of the great regalist tracts of the century, the *Juicio imparcial*, published at government expense in August 1768, a storehouse of historical and legal scholarship on which to rest ultra-regalian, Febronian doctrines. It was so extreme that Charles feared it could work against royal interests, and when five bishops of the *Consejo extraordinario* asked for its condemnation for propositions which the Inquisition found heretical, erroneous and scandalous, the king asked them to rewrite it. The revised *Juicio* that followed, the 1769 edition, defended orthodoxy and papal power while upholding the prerogatives of the Bourbon Crown. Campomanes was damaged; Charles was not. Saragossa University introduced Van Espen's writings on canon law into the syllabus from 1775, and students there and at Valencia and Valladolid were thoroughly familiarised with this line of teaching on the limits of papal authority. By the king's death in 1788, the defenders of an ultramontane or anti-regalist position were few and far between.

The irony was that regalism allowed the king and his allies in Church and state to speed up a Tridentine reform programme. Thus while only eight seminaries had been created in the fifty-six Spanish dioceses before 1753, eighteen more were set up before 1797. High-quality episcopal appointments assisted this drive towards a more streamlined, energetic organisation in which reform and regalism had become synonymous, and Jansenists such as Felip Bertrán and José Climent were made bishops. Campomanes, a brilliant civil and canon lawyer, was happy to enlist their services in creating an exclusively regalist Church. The minister had many enemies but he was essentially orthodox, died a Franciscan tertiary, and respected those ecclesiatics who shared his own passion for improvements. Indeed, the pastoral letters and work of many prelates – by no means all Jansenists – show their zeal in establishing hospitals for foundlings, the old and the ill, creating free schools for boys and girls, and participating in the activities of economic societies and other academies recommended by Campomanes.

Under his aegis in 1761 the Crown took over the administration of the important ecclesiastical tax, the *excusado*, used fraudulently by the clergy to lighten its fiscal burden; in 1765, the government was drawing up plans to limit the further acquisition of landed wealth by the Church. Exclusively clerical concerns ceased to be recognised as Charles fostered a spirit of partnership bringing lay participation even into welfare services as part of a broader government attack on mendicancy from the mid-1770s. Charles told the first meeting of the *Junta de Estado* that 'The first of my obligations and of all my successors is to protect the Catholic religion in all the dominions of this monarchy.' The king meant it, and the clergy, knowing his unimpeachable moral character, could hardly not take him at his word. Unlike Joseph II, Charles III by his tact and timing showed himself one of the most accomplished enlightened monarchs, a careful and capable guardian of the Catholic Church in Spain, working within the reform principles laid down by the Benedictine monk, Feijóo.

He knew that modernisation had to convince the clergy, not just be imposed on them, and welcomed the numerous expressions of support Crown policies elicited from members of the ordained ministry.

Jansenism in France

If Charles III respected and fostered the distinctive forms of Spanish Jansenism, the same cannot be said for his French Bourbon cousins, Louis XV and Louis XVI. In the 1750s and 1760s the former was still enmeshed in political difficulties with the sovereign bodies of France (principally the Paris *parlement*) that owed not a little to magistrates' support for beleagued Jansenists in the Gallican Church and the constitutional principles associated with them. Cardinal Fleury had, with characteristic diplomacy, virtually extinguished Jansenism before his removal from office in 1740 (the Bull *Unigenitus* was declared a law of the state in 1730), but it revived soon after he had quit the scene once the *billet de confession* crisis erupted. The refusal of priests to administer the last rites to those lacking a *billet* was applauded by Christophe de Beaumont, the archbishop of Paris, and condemned by the Paris *parlement*, which declared the clergy's action unlawful and used it as the pretext in 1753 for publishing a compendious remonstrance against clerical power in France. It was a risky strategy, given the Gallican Church's juridical status as the First Estate of the realm: the most powerful organisation inside the kingdom under the monarchy, and the most prestigious branch of the Catholic Church in western Europe. Yet the *parlementaires* had the best of the conflict, since the Crown refused to endorse the Church's uncompromising policy on Jansenism. A law of silence was imposed on both churchmen and magistrates in 1755, followed the next year by a ministerial request to the pope to discourage the refusal of sacraments by publishing an encyclical on the matter. Before his death in 1758, Benedict XIV was ready to endorse a policy of pacification.

As the controversy intensified, so Jansenism became ever more complicated, developing new strands of meaning. The original theological issues became concealed by the blazing antagonism of so many educated Frenchmen (whether inspired by *philosophe* writings or not) to the Jesuits as well as the political dimensions of the dispute. Outside the Paris *parlement*, the so-called *parti janséniste* was the loosest of coalitions. The resort to Rome by both the Crown and the First Estate alarmed those of implacable Gallican principles who regarded such a move as incompatible with the letter of the Articles of 1682. These clergy and laity had never had much sympathy with the austere religiosity of Jansenism. Its politics, however, appeared much sounder than those adopted by the protagonists of orthodoxy. They were shocked (as their parents and grandparents had been in 1713) to find the king having recourse to the holy father for an authoritative pronouncement on Jansenism, thereby flying in the face of Gallican tradition to the point of betraying it. Jansenists and un-compromising Gallicans thus developed a working alliance from the 1750s onwards that ended by making then indistinguishable. The vociferous and effective minority of Jansenist lawyers in the Paris *parlement* such as Louis-Adrien Le Paige become synonomous with what is usually called 'judicial Jansenism'. They quickly adopted for their own uses a polit-ical theory based broadly on the final supremacy of General Councils of the Church over the papacy to justify their own intransigence in the face of royal absolutism. The crisis also brought home to the senior clergy of the Church of France how little they could rely on the French monarchy resolutely upholding the First Estate in its hour of need, espe-cially with a minister like the duc de Choiseul so prominent during the 1760s.

Jansenism and the origins of the French Revolution

The accession of Louis XVI in 1774, the year after the Bull *Dominus ac redemptor*, at last gave the chance for a fresh start in Church-state relations in France; and, for the next decade at least, the opportunity was grasped as churchmen rejoiced at the character of their young monarch. The *parti dévot*, who had supported his father the dauphin, gladly transferred their allegiance to the son, but so did the vast majority of those who had participated in the vexatious quarrels of the last reign. What is most striking about French ecclesiastical politics between the mid-1770s and mid-1780s is its relative stability rather than any predominant contest between the *parti janséniste* and the *parti dévot*. There were the usual areas of tension between Church and state on the perennial issues of clerical taxation, censoring 'mauvais livres' and toleration for Huguenots; otherwise, relative calmness descended as ministers and bishops turned away to pursue new policy initiatives in institutional reform.

Was there a link between the Jansenist dispute and the rhetoric and conduct of reformist politics in France on the eve of the Revolution? If one accepts the highly persuasive claims of Dale Van Kley[19] that con-ciliarist theory was transmitted to lay politicians and enabled them to develop a constitutionalism suited to the secular sphere, then its explana-tory importance is undeniable. And if there is no question that the narrow

---

[19] Dale K. Van Kley, 'The Estates-General as Ecumenical Council: The Constitutionalism of Corporate Consensus and the *Parlement's* Ruling of September 25, 1788', *Journal of Modern History* 61 (1989), 1–52.

majority of clergy which signed up to the Civil Constitution were often much influenced by Jansenist ideas as they had evolved over time, still more numerous were parish clergy in the 1770s and 1780s who were less interested in Jansenism proper than in the Richerist emphasis on their inherent rights that it encouraged.

Another, rather neglected, consequence of the mid-century Jansenist jurisdictional wrangling in France was for higher clergy of all persuasions to take the Church's independent political role more seriously. It was no longer assumed that the ringing formula of the 'eagle of Meaux', Bishop Bossuet (d. 1704) – 'un roi, une foi, une loi' – bore any resemblance to the late eighteenth-century reality. During Louis XVI's reign, younger prelates thought more in terms of the Church as a Montesquian 'intermediary Order', still a buttress of the monarchy, but also its critic when the Crown appeared to be jeopardising the constitutional status quo. Ironically, it fulfilled such a role in opposition to a ministry led by a senior prelate, that of Loménie de Brienne, archbishop of Toulouse, in 1788. Clerical membership of bodies like the *parlements* or the Provincial Estates, as well as the General Assembly of the Clergy of France, provincial and diocesan synods in the 1770s and 1780s all offered a forum wherein a constitutional, libertarian rhetoric evolved capable of articulating national as well as sectional grievances and demands. The fading of Jansenism from the 1760s, its job accomplished with the defeat of the Jesuits, may have created the conditions in which the higher clergy could realign their Order with the *parlements* in the next decade as reformist politics merged into Revolution.

Conclusion

In France the Church–state relationship was looser than ever by 1790 and that reflected the situation elsewhere. Churchmen, like the laity, were more inclined to be critical of governments and their agents, less respectful of authority for its own sake, however sanctified by tradition. Enlightened absolutists had a reformed agenda which was no respecter of privileged corporations like the Church or of clerical preferences. On the other hand, generalising excessively about the clergy's attitudes is hazardous. As the largest organisation in eighteenth-century Europe, the Roman Catholic Church contained a cross-section of argumentative opinion at every level: the clergy carried over into discussion about statecraft the range of (often rancorous) views they had on matters of theology and belief. More conservative-minded men worried that government policies tended towards dispossession and had invaded the spiritual jurisdiction of the Church; others, of different temperament and conviction, found in the several national varieties of Jansenism on offer an outlet for reformist energies and recreating the Church according to a primitive model of Christianity.

In Protestant polities, state supremacy over the Churches had been a *fait accompli* since the Reformation, resulting in varying forms of Erastianism across Europe. The clergy were, in most Lutheran and Reformed German states, ready to follow precedent and trust that the good of the state was the priority for princes as it was for themselves. In return they expected some sort of protection from that state, although they increasingly hoped in vain. It was against the trend in Germany overall that as late as 1778 orthodox Lutherans successfully asked the duke of Brunswick to have the controversialist and playwright Gottfried Lessing submit all future works to the censor after he had published eleven diatribes against a senior Lutheran pastor, the *Anti-Goeze*. In the Church of England there was a sense that religious reform and concessions to dissenters would disrupt the equilibrium that had existed since the Revolution of 1688–9 by which Anglicans could too easily imagine that their state Church was a national one also.

On so many occasions between about 1750 and 1790 the established Churches in Europe had shown themselves unable to stop governments bent on policies deemed by hierarchies to be inimical to clergy interests: in Catholic states the trend had reactivated interest in the papacy as an additional protective force for 'national Churches' under pressure from governments (and often Church leaders) to make changes much less acceptable to middle- and lower-ranking priests; in Protestant Churches, a change of monarch (for example, Frederick William II's accession to the Prussian throne in 1786) or ministry was the best hope of obstructing alteration. But it must be stressed that religious reorganisation was usually intended by policy makers as a means of strengthening observance, and that the state itself was still regarded in principle as having an intrinsically Christian character. The Church–state relationship remained everywhere one of the foundation stones of public life, much more than an association of convenience, even if ministers like Turgot and the younger Pitt, with little personal interest in the Christian faith per se, tended to see it primarily in that light. Church–state ideologies and practices were capable of adaptation to changed circumstances with surprising flexibility in the late *ancien régime*. Most clergy had enough day-to-day practical problems to leave them without much time for the broader picture; equally, most could absorb moderate changes so long as there were few pastoral disadvantages.

It was the common experience of all parties that Church–state disagreements destabilised the state, though that awareness could not prevent such disagreements from occurring and introducing a tradition of public contestation whose effects weakened the legitimacy of *all* existing authorities once the Revolutionary wars swept across the continent in the 1790s. However high-minded the ideals impelling them, state policies in the Habsburg Empire and elsewhere sapped much of the institutional vigour of the Churches in the name of rationalisation and reform. Whether they wanted to or not, ministers often found themselves in alliance with an assortment of anticlericals and *philosophes* who battened on to any drive against the religious status quo. This configuration after 1750 introduced an inward defensive-mindedness into the Churches which went some way towards turning official attention away from vital missionary and evangelical activities. While Crown-sponsored reforms did little to diminish the inherent royalism of churchmen, the papacy, meanwhile, remained a target of convenience for an army of critics. Protestant leaders inherited a range of disparaging references on which they continued to draw while failing to notice that 'popery' had turned into 'Catholicism'; on the Catholic side, antipapalist critics during the century were pushing at an open door, and hostility to Rome made for comfortable posturing. Yet the papacy would turn out to have a capacity for survival in the period from 1790 to 1815 that most other princely regimes lacked.

Part 2

Revolution and its aftermath

5   Revolutions and the Churches:
the initial impact

Introduction

The Churches were an intrinsic part of the public sphere before 1789. Administrative structures were relatively fixed, conventions were widely respected. Dioceses and parishes criss-crossed the continent as a primary organisational unit; bishops, priests and ministers held national offices of responsibility; and the Churches possessed land-holdings on a scale that far exceeded any monarch, with tithe payments the norm in both Catholic and Protestant states. They stood to gain nothing from participating in the dismantling of what would soon become known as the 'old order', the *ancien régime*. It worked well enough to suit their interests, having an underestimated capacity for adaptability and mutation on the basis of alternative past precedents.

Apart from a minority of Utopian reformers in fringe denominations such as the Unitarians, the clergy were not natural revolutionaries. The events of the 1770s and 1780s showed them willing, however reluctantly, to give moderate reform schemes in Church and state a chance for, in the last analysis, the clergy were subjects no less than the laity and were required according to Gospel injunction to obey the lawfully constituted temporal powers. Monarchical government was, after all, divinely sanctioned in a fallen world. Reform offered opportunities to recognise further the vital infantry of the Churches, the lower clergy at work in innumerable parishes, and to reduce the inequalities between these men and the leaders of the hierarchy. Conservative churchmen could rarely discountenance reform schemes entirely, knowing of their appeal to those at the lower end of the hierarchy. Thus the first moderate stage of the French Revolution, from 1789 to 1791, was overwhelmingly popular with rank-and-file members of the First Estate. It was only after the Church was reorganised without reference to its members and Louis XVI was dethroned and executed that the Gallican Church emerged as a bastion of the counter-revolution. In France as elsewhere, where existing regimes were overthrown, clerical obligations of obedience were removed. The new republican order was not interested in restoring a purer Christian order; it was at best indifferent to the historic faith, and at worst viewed the clergy as its natural enemies and worked to extinguish their influence. For their part the clergy across Europe saw the revolutionaries as a fundamental threat to civilisation and, as dechristianisation followed the flag of French military success, enlisted every ally they could to preserve Christian practice and religious survival, looking especially to women within the family to defy the new authorities.

Anticipations of upheaval? The clergy and patriotism in the 1780s

There was no indication in the mid-1770s of the storms that would topple the Church in France less than a generation later. In the revised Catholic order following on the abolition of the Jesuits, the wealth and privileges of ecclesiastical establishments had survived largely intact and, in the Habsburg monarchy, would not be overthrown even by the Josephist assault of the 1780s. As has been seen, the established Churches had responded variously to royal reform programmes; in most countries, such as Spain, some of the clergy welcomed regalian or Jansenist reform, others hesitated, and most continued their round of worship and work. In Protestant states where royal supremacy had been a fact of life since the Reformation, recent changes were just the latest variants in a pattern over two centuries old. For members of the ordained ministry irrespective of denomination, parochial problems were too pressing to give them time to notice the high political contests going on off-stage. So despite enlightenment challenges and royal intrusiveness, the Christian life of Europe in the late eighteenth century was not strikingly different from how it had been 100 years earlier. The Churches were essentially stable institutions whose formidable privileges were mirrored in secular society and, if occasionally found onerous and irksome – as were tithe obligations – were nevertheless accepted as a legitimate foundation of society where custom and prescriptive right remained entrenched, part of the natural order of things.

Of course, Church reform was regularly discussed in the pre-revolutionary decades. Even in England, it was popular with elite laymen who took their faith seriously, like Sir Richard Hill, the independent country gentleman and Evangelical MP for Shropshire from 1780 to 1806, whose pamphlet *Skyrocket* (1782) advocated special taxes on the more lucrative offices of the Church, such as bishoprics, deanships and canonries. Hill was one of the few Methodists in the House of Commons, but, in loose alliance with young Evangelicals like William Wilberforce, was more interested in moral renewal than political reform. Interestingly, increasing the rights of the lower clergy (as opposed to their living standards) was not a subject that tended to preoccupy reforming governments anywhere. Similarly, where a Church retained its fiscal independence and contributed voluntarily to the national tax burden, as in France, how it levied its charge internally was seen as its own affair, and anomalies and inequalities were left for the hierarchies to sort out – or not. So while social and political divisions among the clergy remained striking on the eve of the French Revolution, they did not generate enough tension to cause governments to intervene, let alone provoke a revolutionary explosion.

Even in states where respect for authority was entrenched in the political culture, the later eighteenth century was still a time of increased influence for those who emphasised the rights of subjects (admittedly, usually confined to males holding property) rather than the respect due to rulers, and advocated consensual politics rather than absolutist power. Educated Europeans were fascinated by George Washington's military bid to secure independence for Britain's thirteen North American colonies; the Bourbon monarchies of France and Spain allied with him to achieve republican freedoms across the Atlantic (the United States was officially recognised in 1783), and the fashion for American-style liberty swept the old world through the 1780s. It generated and sustained a distinctive rhetoric of patriotism nourished by art, literature and colonial expansion that dominated much of European public life in the period from 1770 to 1790.

The Churches could not be immune from its force. Indeed, the clergy were as important as any other group in shaping this rhetoric, using it to make denominational claim and counter-claim as well as participating in the debate on invigorating ancient institutions. In England, 'patriotism' was associated particularly with the Whig opposition to Lord North's government (1770–82), and also with its bid to reduce the rebellious American colonies to obedience. Whereas the Anglican clergy (reinforced by incoming American loyalists with a taste for high church patriarchalism, like the Virginian Jonathan Boucher) for the most part lined up behind the ministry, dissenting ministers and congregations took the opposition side. Only in Yorkshire, the heartland of the Whig leader Lord Rockingham, were the established clergy ready to echo patriotic, libertarian rhetoric and play down its historic associations with a commonwealth, republican tradition that went back to the Civil Wars of the mid-seventeenth century. A landed parson, the Revd Christopher Wyvill, led the thoroughly respectable Yorkshire Association in the national fight for parliamentary and economical reform with the dean of York, John Fountaine, as one of his main allies. However, Rockingham's death in

1782, the unholy alliance of his successor Charles James Fox with Lord North in 1783 and the electoral triumph of the self-consciously virtuous Pitt the Younger in 1784 showed up the hollowness of patriot politics and marginalised the Yorkshire Association for a generation.

Patriot politicians placed the good of the state as the supreme good, making the first claim on any citizen, whether that led them to oppose or resist change. The question was often which state, and whose good? In Ireland, the minority of Protestants had for most of the century worn the mantle of patriots, defending their country against heavy-handed English domination, most recently organising themselves into Volunteer companies during the crisis brought on by Britain's involvement in the American War and winning legislative independence from Westminster in 1782. But where did Irish Roman Catholics fit into the patriotic picture? This was the issue that would not go away in the 1780s, as agrarian outrages and further campaigns against tithe payments caused some Anglican clergy, led by Bishop Richard Woodward of Cloyne, to declare the Church of Ireland in danger, and insist that Catholic demands for toleration and integration be resisted. Meanwhile, the Catholic hierarchy, ably led by Archbishops Butler and Troy, to the chagrin of hardline Protestants, distanced themselves from 'Whiteboy' agitation and outrages in the countryside and insisted to a sympathetic British government that their record of loyalty to the king put their patriotic credentials beyond doubt and entitled them to further concessions.

The religious overtones of patriotic discourse could not be ignored, as politicians worked on the emotions of the public, and tried to turn them into a force that could make or break government policies. For much of the century, fashionable society had deprecated 'enthusiasm' in religious life; the 'patriotism' of the 1780s seemed to some merely the transference of such unseemly emotion to political life where it was taken up by malcontents from the the the lower ranks of society. Archduke Albert wrote from Brussels in 1787 as joint governor of the Austrian Netherlands that 'the number of religious enthusiasts and those whose heads are heated with notions of patriotism is very great'.[1] Such a response could easily be generated by aggressive royal reformism, as in Hungary where Joseph II tried to enlist the Protestants as a weapon against 'patriot' prelates and nobles. His controversial tactics only led the Churches to join forces against an attack on their national identity.

Patriotism had a strong regional dimension, made an appeal to history for its validation, and involved the parish clergy as their pastoral concerns became entangled in political ones. These several aspects were all on

---

[1] Quoted in A. Beer, *Joseph II, Leopold II und Kaunitz: Ihn Briefwechsel* (Vienna, 1873), 485.

display in the Austrian Netherlands where Joseph II, frustrated by the resistance of other rulers to his scheme to exchange them for Bavaria, went ahead with a centralising reform programme, which, though holding out the Utopian promise of a pluralistic centralism, was perceived to ride roughshod over the provinces' time-honoured privileges, like the *Joyeuse Entrée* of Brabant. Already reeling from the impact of Joseph's Church policies, this provincial bastion of Catholic orthodoxy fought back from late 1786 onwards. Many of the major monasteries offered money and leadership to the malcontents while the ordinands recently moved into government-controlled seminaries also took up the 'national' cause. Within a few months a wave of patriotic indignation had swept Belgian society and compelled the Brussels government to abnegate all Joseph's reforms without consulting him. In the last three years of his reign, the emperor deployed the army against the rebels in the Netherlands with limited success. 'Patriots', including numerous clergy, would not be intimidated, and the struggle by the local Estates to protect historic charters eventually led to the creation of something entirely new: the United States of Belgium proclaimed on 7 January 1790 after Hendrick Van der Noot's volunteer patriot army entered Brussels in triumph. After Joseph's death, the emperor Leopold was obliged to cancel most of the ecclesiastical innovations in the Austrian Netherlands and agreed to close no further monastic houses. Across the frontier, in the United Provinces, patriotism defined itself as anti-Orange and anti-oligarch, looking to involve the lesser bourgeoisie in decision making for the first time in the Dutch Republic's history and bidding for greater religious toleration for the minority Churches. In political terms, this was a bid for innovation rather than restoration, comparable to the Genevan Revolution of 1782 but on a larger scale. Calvinist ministers helped articulate the populist demands of this cause, which could not prevail against the alliance of Prussia and Britain that secured the Dutch state for the *stadhouder* (the princely protector of the state and head of the Orange family), William V, in 1787.

Patriot politics in the 1780s were thus often an attempt to uphold and protect historic, local liberties (rather than liberty as an inalienable human right) from centralising forces for whom administrative convenience was always an admissible justification for change. Patriots tended to be restorers rather than innovators, with clerics involved in power struggles as much from pastoral concern as from personal ambition. These episodes were actually just the latest twist in a familiar historical pattern. They were played out in the urban centres of the Low Countries and Switzerland where, since the Reformation, presbyters had by convention aligned themselves with those struggling to extract wider participatory rights from the municipal oligarchs and princely families. More significantly still, these were, unusually, areas where republicanism was the norm in government and therefore patterns of deference were less rigid than in monarchies.

It must be stressed that most Protestant Churches were not caught up in Patriot politics even in Scandinavia where kingly power was consolidated in the 1770s. In Sweden and Denmark, the established Lutheran confessions by and large upheld royal authority even where they infringed local rights; admittedly, Swedish lower clergy had been among the critics of the religious reforms proposed by Gustavus III in the 1778–9 Riksdag, the first held under the 1772 Constitution, but thereafter they were less vocal. In Scotland, the Kirk was happy to see Henry Dundas exercise an oversight that by 1790 had no counterweight while, south of the border, the English parish clergy wanted to be left in peace to collect their rising tithe receipts and worried that the new prime minister might be too ready to grant concessions to dissenters. For a majority of Protestant clergy, certainly those belonging to established Churches, the politics of 'patriotism' before 1789 was a minority option with little to offer to most of them.

Recovery of clerical rights

Established Protestant clergy in Britain, Germany and Scandinavia – with some rare exceptions – projected liberty back into the national past when the yoke of 'popery' had been discarded, and were unhappy about its contemporary resonances which, it was feared, could damage the fabric of the confessional state. Like their Catholic counterparts, they confined themselves to upholding or restoring historic rights, not natural rights or the 'Rights of Man', let alone woman. Yet these self-interested defenders of ecclesiastical liberties, protecting their own livelihoods against encroachment, inspired by the past, set an example in spite of themselves to laymen across Europe campaigning against the excesses or abuses of royal power in the period from 1770 to 1790. In France, under Napoleon and after the Restoration, such a posture encouraged many to blame the Gallican clergy for encouraging a mood of political change that had ended in revolutionary cataclysm. The message seemed clear: flirting with reform encouraged institutional undoing and allowed anarchy to flourish. But 'reform' was not really a term churchmen of any denomination resorted to before 1789; 'reformation' was, as ever, their objective, and proposals for change were usually adopted or, more commonly, cautiously discountenanced, with an eye to increasing pastoral effectiveness and improving relations with the laity if only by reducing anticlericalism.

Whatever the outcome of 'patriotic' politics in The Hague, Geneva, Brussels and Antwerp, it would not challenge the reality in both episcopal and presbyterian systems that the wealthy or the well-born stood the best chance of advancement within the ordained ministry. It was a pattern calculated to stoke up resentments over the medium term, and to act as a destabilising force even at national level, possibly with revolutionary implications. Yet the persistence of deference in an hierarchical society was a formidable barrier to change. In England, overworked, underpaid curates took services for numerous non-resident clergy with few expectations that their efforts would be adequately recognised or remunerated. Yet they did not lobby Parliament or the bench of bishops to change working practices, and it was only fear of revolutionary contagion emanating from France that eventually prompted the slight improvements contained in the Curates' Act of 1796. Catholic Spain also had a clerical proletariat working away in some of few rural parishes fortunate enough to have a resident priest and, though there was habitual grumbling from some of them, there was an acceptance that this was the immemorial order of things. In Spain as elsewhere, reforming ministers and bishops were aware of their plight but, despite the excitement generated among students and academics in the Universities of Seville and Salamanca by the changes proposed at Pistoia, doing something to raise clerical living standards came well down their list of priorities.

This dilatoriness first had appreciable political repercussions in late *ancien régime* France, where the lower clergy were no longer prepared to conceal their disgruntlement at the gulf between their pastoral centrality and their material rewards, and organised to obtain financial redress and greater inclusion in the decision-making machinery of the Church. Significantly, the agitation included the beneficed clergy as well as their untenured assistants, the *vicaires*. The *portion congrue* had been marginally raised in 1768 and 1786, though nothing was done to correct the anomaly of the heaviest burden of clerical taxation (the *décimes*) falling disproportionately on those least capable of paying it. In some areas, such as Brittany, priests enjoyed a degree of comfortable material status that was compatible with a dedicated application to pastoral duties; in others, such as the Dauphiné in south-eastern France, three-quarters of the clergy were living on the *congrue*, and unsurprisingly they became a force for change under the leadership of Henri Reymond of Grenoble.

The leaders of the lower clergy found inspiration in the writings of Edmond Richer, an early seventeenth-century priest and Sorbonne theologian: he championed *curé* entitlements in his pro-Gallican tract, *De ecclesiastica et politica potestate* (1611). His latter-day followers, the Richerists, took their stand on the inherent dignity of the priestly office. It made them heirs to the seventy-two disciples as opposed to the bishops, the descendants of the Apostolic twelve. Though there was no necessary link between them, the culture of legal protest associated with Jansenism encouraged the Richerist revival of the later eighteenth century. Jansenist veterans skilled in canon law, such as Gabriel-Nicholas Maultrot, gave Richerism an enhanced intellectual credibility and helped turn it into another contemporary exercise in constitutionalism. The lower clergy were not looking to overthrow the hierarchal order of the Church but sought a more consensual, pastorally sensitive approach from the prelates, in line with the claim made by Reymond in his *Rights of the Curés* (1776) that 'they [the *curés*] *are* bishops each in his own parish'.[2] They sought a new constitutional settlement with fairer terms for all members of the First Estate. They believed that history was on their side, that a Richerist emphasis was squarely in line with the ways of the primitive Church; it was the counterpart in the 1780s to hopes that the pre-absolutist constitution in the state would be revived.

More progressive, politically attuned members of the episcopate, like Champion de Cicé at Bordeaux, were ready to be constructive. He negotiated a quid pro quo whereby in return for throwing his weight behind further increases in the *portion congrue*, his provincial synod in April 1788 would accept the edict granting limited toleration to non-Catholics, a dubious measure for many *curés*. For the most part, Church leaders were slow to react. They were unhappy at the various pamphlets circulating against 'ecclesiastical despotism', which resulted in one clerical author, the abbé Le Senne, receiving a *lettre de cachet* for his *Mémoire des curés* that appeared in 1780. Rather than produce viable reform proposals, the General Assembly called for government action. Unofficial, unauthorised meetings of *curés* were prohibited by the Crown in 1782, but the edict was only briefly and intermittently effective: Reymond and his colleagues would not be deterred either from emphasising their place of honour in the Church or urging priests to nurture a spirit of mutual solidarity. A belated rise in the *portion congrue* in 1786 was too little too late to halt the growing agitation or deprive the clergy of backing from that amorphous but increasingly important force in French public life,

---

[2] Quoted in Timothy Tackett, 'The Citizen-Priest: Politics and Ideology among the Parish Clergy of Eighteenth-century Dauphiné', *Studies in XVIIIth century Culture*, ed. Roseann Puntz, vol. 7 (Wisconsin, 1978), 307–38, at 313; *Priest and Parish in Eighteenth-century France* (Princeton, 1977), 312; *Religion, Revolution, and Regional Culture* (Princeton, 1986), 133–46, well summarises clergy collective active action from 1730 to 1786. Interestingly, in neither Brittany nor the Dauphiné had Jansenism made much headway. In the latter province Tackett has identified a 'veritable chasm' between the bishops (many of them major tithe owners themselves) and their parish clergy.

public opinion – one that politicians from different backgrounds were disinclined to ignore by this date.

The position on the eve of the French Revolution

The European crisis unleashed by the French Revolution from 1789 (intensified further after the outbreak of the Revolutionary war in April 1792) would place the Christian religion and Churches under pressures unparalleled since the Reformation. How well equipped were they for survival? In the 1780s, established Churches that clung to their privileges – as they all understandably did, since it underpinned their prestige – were vulnerable to pressures for change at several levels, from reforming governments, clergy and laity within their ranks keen to restore more primitive practices, and from religious minorities bent on securing enhanced civil and religious status for their adherents. Yet the eighteenth-century experience had already taught religious establishments how to survive in states prepared to do them few favours and with indifferent elites, and to act defensively to protect their own interests. Almost everywhere, the principle of a confessional Church remained intact and acceptable, albeit modified to accommodate minorities whose tenets and existence were adjudged compatible with the state's interests. Several historians have argued that the revolution followed on from the collapse of the old order in the state. But there is no equivalent sign of collapse discernable in the religious sphere and, during the period from 1790 to 1815, its capacity for survival and reinvention was all the greater.

Most national branches of the Roman Catholic Church had already undergone appreciable change in the course of the century, sometimes welcomed in the spirit of the Catholic Enlightenment, often resented when imposed by a heavy-handed state. Spain, Portugal, the Habsburg monarchy and most Italian states had all been areas where Tridentine reformation and royal diktat between them had shaken up Church structures appreciably since early in the century. It had been a painful process for clergy and laity alike and the mutual resentments it had fostered were still appreciable in the penultimate decade of the century. Change had brought into sharper focus the primary importance of the parish – and its priest – as the seed bed of good Christian practice. That combination of Tridentine missionary zeal and improved administrative practice at parochial level (seldom going together and usually coexisting uneasily), effectively in place *before* 1789, was of vital importance in explaining the Church's capacity to cope with the trials and tribulations to which it was subjected afterwards.

Anglican establishments had been rather slower to introduce institutional changes. The Church of England and its royal head tended to view alteration as a sign of weakness, though the consecration of the first bishops to Canada and the United States in the mid-1780s was a new token of adaptability at international level; at a parish level, the need for parliamentary authorisation made it painfully hard for the Church to cope with new population patterns. Anglicans had already made concessions to English dissenters – admitting their existence, for example – in the period between 1688 and 1750 and were loath to make more. For them the Revolution would be both a threat and an opportunity, since it helped rekindle Church of England loyalties where they had been flagging and vulnerable. Other Protestant communions in Prussia, Holland and Switzerland were more flexible. In all three cases orthodox theology had been significantly diluted and, in the latter two, pastoral energies were increasingly poured into local politics rather than supporting the faith handed down by the Reformation Fathers. They would be more inclined than not to welcome the early stages of revolution in France in a spirit of fraternity.

The French Revolution and the Church before the Civil Constitution of the Clergy, 1789–1790

However prepared for the sea change they would bring, it was events in France that moulded the life and witness of all confessions after 1790. The Gallican Church in Louis XVI's reign had, at various levels, been committed to reform politics without any intimations that this was a road that would lead to its own demise. But the reforms were to be those acceptable to the episcopal elite, the *prélats administratifs*, and would not entail any diminution of their hierarchical supremacy or significantly closer involvement of the parish clergy in Church government, either at national or local level. Where the *curés* were brought in from the cold, it was a concession from bishops trying to improve synodical apparatus and hold more conferences with their clergy, and not an entitlement. So whereas prelates became increasingly enamoured of the constitutionalism associated with Jacques Necker as a new model for the life of the French state, in the Church there was no move away from episcopal absolutism towards a more consultative model. *Curés* and *vicaires* would have to make do with the 'virtual representation' they had customarily enjoyed in command institutions like the General Assembly of the Clergy of France. Even among bishops of the calibre of Boisgelin, Brienne, Champion de Cicé or Louis de Conzié there was minimal public admission that the gap between the lower and higher clergy was becoming unacceptably wide and imperilling the Church's institutional coherence and vitality.

In 1787 and 1788 the French hierarchy was at the forefront of national events when the government finally admitted that the nation's dire fiscal problems would not admit of a solution without sanction from the political elite. In the first Assembly of Notables the opposition to Calonne was led openly by Brienne, archbishop of Toulouse, who, along with other colleagues, showed himself formidably well informed about France's problems and how to deal with them. Brienne eventually supplanted Calonne as first minister, only to lose the trust of the First Estate on a range of policies. The General Assembly of the Clergy meeting in mid-summer 1788 was unrelenting in its criticism of his plans and sealed the archbishop-minister's fate by offering him a most derisory sum as a *don gratuit*. In their remonstrances, the higher clergy declared themselves to be no less determined to protect the nation's liberties (of which their own were, naturally, not the least important part) than the *parlements* or the Provincial Estates. Yet from this point onwards in the French reform crisis, the political importance of the higher clergy waned fast, for 1788–9 saw not just the maturation of the Third Estate as the driving force in public life but the emergence and recognition of the lower clergy as their indispensable allies.

Public sympathy for boosting the political importance of the *curés* – the kinsmen and friends of the Third Estate – was in place by the time of the electoral agitation of the winter of 1788–9 on the eve of the Estates-General, and it was not ignored when Necker and his ministerial colleagues came to draw up the rules for the elections. Under the electoral regulation of 24 January 1789 the bishops and higher clergy had no places specifically set aside for them. Gauging the public mood astutely, Necker cast himself as the ally of the *curés*. The challenge to the hierarchy was unambiguous, as antinoble sentiments gathered momentum at a remarkable speed, and engulfed the Church along with the entire Second Estate. The rules meant that a prelate would have to stand for election just like anyone else, his vote would not count for any more than a beneficed clergyman and there was the added obstacle of electoral constituencies bearing no resemblance to diocesan boundaries. Even more marginalised and, in their own regard, humiliated were the chapters (one representative for every ten canons) and the religious communities (one representative each). In France before 1789, parish priests were by social definition not much involved in higher politics either nationally or regionally. That now changed at a stroke as the 'useful' lower clergy, citizens as well as subjects, exultant in their heightened sense of national identity, were given the chance to play a full part in the Estates-General. They took their place alongside the other new force in French politics, the Third Estate, guaranteed 50 per cent of the seats in the Estates-General. The Dauphiné *curés* caught the new mood brilliantly: 'The interest of the people and your own [the lower clergy's] are inseparable. If the people emerge from oppression, you will emerge from the humiliation into which the higher clergy have plunged you and you have endured for so long.'[3]

This is not to say that the clergy were unwilling to acknowledge the place of the bishop in the hierarchy; the issue was rather *how* he went about exercising that apostolic power. Prelates with a reputation for episcopal absolutism or absenteeism (or both) tended to fare badly in the elections to the Estates-General. Prestigious post holders such as Louis-Joseph de Montmorency-Laval, the king's almoner, were kept out of the representation, while prelates like the bishop of Mende who had packed the spectators' galleries with supporters found the clerical-electors unimpressed. The lower clergy concerted tactics wherever they could, often as part of a tactical campaign to exclude bishops and canons from representing them. *Curés* who were determined to exclude their bishop from election were hard to stop, as in the *sénéchaussée* of the Landes in the south-west where the bishops of Aire and Dax were kept out. Suspicions were so keen that one priest, Laborde of Ossages, was ostracised because he had been rash enough to eat at the palace. Patriotic higher clergy and those with some tactical flair were usually successful. Most of the *prélats administratifs* – Boisgelin, Champion de Cicé of Bordeaux, La Rochefoucauld of Rouen, Seignelay de Colbert de Castlehill of Rodez – were returned. Indeed, one of the most interesting features of the electoral contest involving the First Estate that spring of 1789 was the victory against the odds of one-third of the episcopate to make a final total of fifty-one places gained.

As an inherent part of the electoral arrangements, the three Estates produced *cahiers*, or lists of grievances and recommendations, for their deputies to take with them to Versailles. The nation at large, in the Third Estate, perhaps surfeited with the anticlericalism of so many *philosophe* texts, rejected merely negative criticism of the First Estate in favour of constructive suggestions for moderate institutional reform in Church and state. With the lower clergy in the driving seat, the *cahiers* of the First Estate reflected similar ideals. The clergy expressed a desire to share

---

[3] *Les Curés du Dauphiné à leurs confrères les Recteurs de Bretagne* (Paris, 1789?), 8.

equitably in the burden of taxation, though within a new constitutional framework with local Estates underpinning the Estates-General at the centre. For the Church itself, the *curés* thought in moderate Richerist terms. Thirty-four *cahiers* asked that all posts in the Church should be awarded on the basis of merit, while even more universal was the demand that pastoral experience be mandatory for anyone looking for promotion. The majority of *cahiers* wanted reforms in the regular Orders to continue and a reduction in the status of abbés and canons rather than their outright abolition. The bishops were reminded to put pastoral work before any other considerations and asked to reside in their dioceses. A fairer deal for the lower clergy was, of course, prominent in most *cahiers*, with an insistence that the *portion congrue* should be raised to a minimum of 1,500 *livres*. Significantly, nowhere was the abolition of tithe prescribed. Overall, the *cahiers* were, to a remarkable degree, rather conservative documents in the light of the events of the 1790s, and their lineal descent from the values of Tridentine Catholicism was patent. 1789 was, for the clergy, as much an opportunity for the nation's moral regeneration as its political revival. Thus all except thirty-six of the *cahiers* stipulated that there should be much more respect for the Sabbath among the whole population. Many, especially from areas with Protestant populations such as Toulouse and Saintes, were very cool about the working in practice of the 1787 Edict on Toleration. None sought an extension of the edict, or a non-consenual dismantling of the corporate privileges of the First Estate.

Once the Estates-General opened on 4 May 1789, the *cahiers* turned out to have limited relevance to the rapid pace of events in which the clergy played an underestimated role in precipitating the crisis in the Estates-General and creating revolutionary possibilities. The Third Estate leaders knew that the key to creating a truly national assembly was to have the powers of all three Orders verified in common rather than by Estate; to achieve that objective, they would need to win over a majority within the clergy. What followed was a rejection of absolutism in the Church, which paralleled that in the state. In June 1789 several *curés* finally broke ranks and went over to sit in the chamber of the Third Estate whose members had just, prompted by another frustrated politician-priest, the abbé Sieyes (sitting as a member of the Third Estate for Paris), declared themselves to be the National Assembly. Day by day throughout the second half of June other clergy, including several reformist bishops and higher clergy, followed their example to rapturous applause from the *Tiers* as the cause of national unity was thereby sealed. The heady atmosphere of patriotic fervour was inimitably caught by David in his preliminary sketch of the Tennis Court Oath (the original painting is missing), in which members of all three Orders, including the monk Dom Gerle, greet each other and take the oath not to separate until France received a constitution. This collapse of the internal unity of the First Estate in the Estates-General intensified the crisis of June–July 1789 and wrecked the hopes of all traditionalists for a meeting on the basis of orders. Then, with the fall of the Bastille, the recall of Necker to power and the king's visit to Paris, the Revolution was 'safe'. That could not be said of the Gallican Church, whose representatives now sat as part of an omnicompetent National Assembly and found that the erstwhile First Estate enjoyed no special immunities in the new constitutional but distinctly Erastian order.

In common with other 'privileged' institutions, the Gallican Church saw a massive reduction in its corporate wealth and independence between July 1789 and July 1790. Tithe and the *casuel* (clerical fees) were among the sacrifices on the night of 4 August. Their abandonment was, in an important sense, a free gift to landowners who had, for a long time, been obliged to keep rents lower than market prices to enable their tenants to pay the clergy. These losses were followed by the nationalisation and sale of Church lands in return for vague promises of state payment of costs and salaries. In casting around for a financial solution to the otherwise intractable problem of state indebtedness, the revolutionaries found Church property irresistible. In fact, this drastic confiscation was an over-reaction to crisis; there was no financial necessity to go so far and turn the Church into a sacrificial victim to the state's needs, but panic and patriotic enthusiasm were unstoppable.

The Church lost its material assets while its religious rivals gained: a much less restricted toleration was accorded to Protestants and, in December, to Sephardic Jews; in February 1790 members of the religious Orders were encouraged by a pension offer to renounce their vows and either take up parish ministry or head into secular life. Only those in teaching or charitable work were exempted. None of these changes destroyed the hope of the vast mass of lower clergy that all would turn out well. A tangible sign of good faith was the way many *curés* and, still more, higher clergy took up positions of responsibility in local government in 1789–90 as the old order imploded with no national structures yet in place to replace it. But the violence and intimidation of this period, epitomised in the 'October Days' of 1789 when the whole Assembly was compelled to follow the royal family and remove from Versailles to Paris, was profoundly unsettling. What place would there be for Gallicanism in the new France? Churchmen from a range of backgrounds used every parliamentary tactic to win the backing of like-minded lay politicians to have Catholicism declared the principal faith of the French in April 1790, and their narrow failure did not augur well for the moderate right.

The religious landscape of France was in meltdown. Observers in France and elsewhere noted the ease with which change was being accomplished, and there was a sense that its proponents were motivated more by anticlericalism than a zeal for primitive Christianity, and a determination to humiliate the Church in keeping with the prescriptions made a generation earlier by the leading *philosophes*. The vulnerability of religious institutions to change imposed on them had been repeatedly demonstrated since 1750, but what had happened in France struck contemporaries more forcefully than the Josephite changes of the 1780s in the Austrian Empire for three main reasons: its scale, its speed and, most of all, its origins in a completely new popular institution – the National Assembly. It gave a foretaste of the surprising ease with which transformations could be accomplished in the political culture of the 1790s. And there was much more to come.

The majority of deputies wanted to waste no time in rationalising and remodelling the Gallican Church so that in spirit and structure it became genuinely part of the new France. This work was to be ordered not by the clergy themselves – not even by the *curés* – but by the Assembly in the name of the nation, the ultimate source of sovereignty. When debate started in late May on what was called the Civil Constitution of the Clergy the clerical-deputies knew better than to challenge the Assembly's rights over the former First Estate. They were not in principle averse to reform, put forward several constructive amendments (which were almost all defeated), and hoped that moderate conduct would win the Church some kind of consultative rights over the proposal, perhaps in the form of a national council. When the legislation was approved on 12 July 1790 there was no hint of such concessions. Its radicalism was breathtaking. Among the most important provisions were changing diocesan boundaries to correspond with the new departmental ones, thereby reducing total episcopal numbers from 130 to 83, each bishop to be elected by taxpayers who could be non-Catholics; the abolition of cathedral chapters, with bishops henceforth to be counselled by a standing committee staffed mainly by twelve to sixteen episcopal vicars; parish priests were to be elected, salaried by the state according to a sliding scale of stipends for anyone who held ecclesiastical office. Officially, the concept of the priest in the hierarchy was now subordinate to the citizen-priest within the lay community. The title of the law was itself a neglected cause of discontent within the Church, for the use of the word 'civil' was telling. It implied that an assumption was made that the Church was unambiguously part of the civil order and that to talk of its *religious* constitution was either inadmissible or irrelevant.

Without doubt, the Assembly expected the Civil Constitution to be well received by the clergy, but the signs in the second half of 1790 were anything but favourable. After the king had reluctantly sanctioned the new law on 24 August, churchmen either ignored its provisions or protested against a reform that the Assembly deemed to be 'civil' but which thousands of priests found interfering in 'spirituals' in a way that compromised their office and its discharge. Had a national council been summoned at this point all might still have been settled without disruption. It did not happen and, in its absence, the failure of Pius VI to pronounce on the new dispensation or to give a lead one way or the other was noted on all sides. Meanwhile, most deputies were outraged at the Church's defiance of the Assembly's supreme sovereignty and were determined to reduce its membership to obedience in their primary role as office holders. Rather than delay any longer, a law was passed on 27 November requiring all the clergy to accept the Civil Constitution – or lose office and pension rights forthwith.

In early January 1791 a clear majority of the clergy in the National Assembly refused the oath to the Civil Constitution including all bishops but two, Talleyrand and Gobel (the latter being only a suffragan). Their stance set the Gallican Church on collision course with the revolutionaries in the legislature and in the provinces, and completed the destruction of the First Estate begun in June 1789. It also created an essentially artificial polarisation of Catholicism and the Revolution that would have occurred on nothing like the same scale had the deputies shown a degree of pragmatism about the practicalities of introducing the Civil Constitution. Instead, their determination to push through the law created a counter-revolutionary force in cassocks almost overnight and, even more importantly, alienated a large proportion of the population (including most women) who, if forced to choose between the Revolution and their Catholicism, would always opt for the latter. In their reforming zeal, deputies fatally underestimated the resolution and obduracy of the clergy, not to mention the massive attachment of the laity (in rural areas particularly) to their faith. They would not recognise that there could be compelling reasons for refusing the Civil Constitution, such as those invoked by the abbé Pierre Remaud, *curé* of Chavagnes-en-Pailliers, on 20 February 1791: the authority of the Gospel, the Fathers of the Church, the ecumenical councils and the bishops of France. In its way, Remaud's apologia was a classic summary of Gallicanism, no less valid than the version proclaimed by the supporters of the oath.

Every clergyman had to take the oath or leave his post, and by April it was clear that only a narrow majority of about 55 per cent were prepared to subscribe to the new order. For them there was promotion on a scale never seen before, with the leading protagonists for the Civil Constitution, many with Jansenist sympathies – Henri Grégoire, Joseph Gobel, Pontard and Lamourette prominent among them – taking up bishoprics vacated by the nonjuring or refractory clergy. For the latter, who predominated in the north-east, the west, and the south-west, destitution and exile lay ahead. With the Assembly omnicompetent, neither the king nor the papacy could protect them from this fate, and they had to rely as best they could on former parishioners for food, shelter and loyalty. There was, at least, some comfort in conscience to be gained from Pius VI's unequivocal condemnation of the Civil Constitution and the Revolution in general (10 March and 13 April 1791), and a minority of nonjuring clergy took advantage of the Assembly's short-lived dispensation by which they could say Mass for their people in specially licensed churches. This concession was cancelled in November, and by the time France went to war with Austria in April 1792 the laws against refractory clergy had been ratcheted up to include deportation. In this way, the nonjurors saw France go into schism, the historic liberties of the Gallican Church overthrown, its personnel divided and scattered, and its royal protector so much a prisoner that he was not allowed to visit Saint-Cloud to receive Easter communion (1791) from a nonjuror.

This was not, of course, the gloss put on events by the clergy who staffed the Constitutional Church inaugurated in 1791 and who, to a remarkable degree, were talented, exceptional men who had been kept from promotion by the social rigidities of the old First Estate. For them the reformed French Church was the fulfilment of Gallicanism (albeit in a somewhat Jansenist manner) rather than its abnegation. The majority had a strong Christian faith, but were keen to see Catholicism work in partnership with a progressive political cause rather than to obstruct it, and so give the lie to those earlier enlightenment writers who would have viewed any such creative synthesis as a contradiction in terms. Primitive Christianity would, it was hoped, return to France through the Constitutional clergy, united in their commitment to what one of their leaders, Pontard, bishop of the Dordogne, called in March 1791, 'Religion, *la patrie*, and the Constitution'. The way appeared open to construct a civic Catholicism renewing both Church and state in the process.

For the bulk of the subscribing parish clergy, this high calling was at odds with the reality of being intruded into parishes which so often had no wish for their services and were outraged at the discarding of their old priest. The new men were viewed as foreigners, outsiders in their midst, whose physical presence contaminated the church. Villagers banged home-made instruments outside their priest's front door to keep him awake at night, left dead animals on his doorstep, burnt him in effigy, and hid the keys to the church. Their ingenuity knew no end and was often planned and implemented by the women. At Caen in 1791 200 drunken women hurled stones at the altar of one celebrant and nearly killed him. So, overcoming the animosity of their parishioners was the first priority for the Constitutional *curés*. Pastoral commitment, slowly winning round the doubters, and a show of tolerance towards the nonjurors could, some-times, do the trick. With the hierarchy dedicated to having a priest in every parish, numbers were thinly spread and compounded the difficulties of securing followers. Necessity quickly caused the rules under the Civil Constitution stipulating five years' minimum experience before priests had their own benefice to be put into abeyance. Sometimes former members of the religious Orders were pushed into parishes, and non-elected clergy were nominated to benefices by bishops who could not afford to wait. In the diocese of the Calvados in Normandy, Bishop Fauchet's episcopal vicars had by 1792 left Caen to supplement inadequate numbers in the countryside.

Despite the setbacks in so many districts, in 1791–2 the Constitutional clergy never lost faith in the righteousness of the revolutionary cause. What undid them was the gradual disowning by the French state of its attachment to *any* Christian organisation, leaving the bishops and clergy stranded friendless between the left and right. This trend began under the Legislative Assembly *before* the inauguration of the Republic in the autumn of 1792. When invited to join in the Feast of Corpus Christi procession on 7 June 1792 by the *curé* of Saint-Germain-l'Auxerrois (in which Parisian parish it met), the Assembly decided that individual deputies were under no compulsion to go. The same month, every commune was ordered to erect an *autel de la patrie* (altar of the fatherland), a significant indicator that the Revolution was going to be its own religion. The abolition of the monarchy further increased the pressure on the 'patriotic' clergy. Most pursued their ministry as best they could in the winter of 1792–3, still using the same 'patriotic' language they had done throughout the Revolution, exhorting the faithful to fulfil their religious and political duties. At Bourg-des-Comptes in October 1792, Bishop Le Coz held a Mass attended by 'citizens as attached to the laws of their country as to those of their religion'.[4] The phrase thus discountenanced

---

[4] Quoted in N.-D. Chaline et al., *L'Eglise de France et la Révolution* (Paris, 1983), 50.

any sense that the two might be pulling apart as other developments indicated, for example entrusting the registration of births, marriages and deaths from September 1792 to the local municipalities, further demoting the status of the Constitutional *curé*.

Meanwhile most clerical-deputies in the Convention between September 1792 and June 1793 worked on in loose alliance with the Brissotins (the moderate pro-war grouping in the Convention) while remaining critical of their conduct on key issues such as the fate of Louis XVI. Their participation did not attract reciprocal favours from politicians, either at national or regional levels. Republicanism and Catholic Christianity were unable to coexist comfortably in the French experience of the 1790s and a drive to extirpate all manifestations of Christianity began in the autumn of 1792, one that widened the number of both Protestants and Catholics alike outside France who were forcibly made aware of the consequences stemming from the seismic dislocation of Gallicanism. Many across Europe subsequently found compelling the Burkean perspective that any contest with France must be a counter-revolutionary crusade in which the survival of civilisation itself was at stake.

Early reactions to religious change in France

That stark perspective compares strikingly with the situation during the constitutional monarchy (1789–92) when the rapid imposition of ecclesiastical reforms on the Church culminating in the Civil Constitution was not seen as exceptional, let alone a cause of war. The sects and minorities outside France that had initially welcomed the Revolution as furthering their cause were reluctant to admit that the model of cultural hegemony emerging by 1792 left no place for Christianity. If Pius VI had issued briefs against the Civil Constitution, he had been no less critical of the Josephist transformations in the empire a decade before, and they, too, were considered by informed opinion (including the numerous reformist-minded Catholics) as primarily intended to raise the status of the parochial clergy. In Spain, Portugal, some Italian states and the Habsburg lands, the Church had submitted to extensive Erastian amendment, and the Gallican Church, it might be said, was undergoing such a process on a scale commensurate with the wholesale remodelling of other institutions in France. If the end result turned it into a department of state then it would be in good company, comparable to Lutheran establishments in Denmark, Sweden and Prussia. It was only a minority who considered that the mechanics of reformation were weighted differently when changes were imposed not by an hereditary monarch but by a newly sovereign National Assembly whose members hardly bothered by 1791 to conceal their anticlericalism, their growing disdain for the black-cassocked deputies in their midst, the 'noirs' who would obstruct the general will of the nation as interpreted by themselves.

This positive though not uncritical interpretation of the events of 1789–92 in France sympathised more with the Bourbon monarchy's reduced status than with the Church's. The forcible return of the royal family from Versailles to Paris in October 1789, the refusal to permit Louis to leave the Tuileries for Saint-Cloud in April 1791 and the failure of the flight to Varennes in June compelled public notice and further confirmed the view of Burke's readership that the spectre of anarchy was stalking Europe. In England some Tory high churchmen, the Hutchinsonian William Jones of Nayland among them, were ringing the alarm bells early on seeing striking resemblances between France and Britain. He told Bishop Thomas Percy of Dromore (Ireland): 'Mr Burke's account of the literary cabal in France, applies very closely to the proceedings of our Disaffected Dissenters and Infidels in England. The Church and government in France have been ruined by their supineness; may better measures be adopted here.'[5] By supineness Jones meant not a failure to bring in reforms, but insufficient watchfulness against the Church's enemies, and he was terrified at the Church of England's vulnerability to energising critics like Thomas Paine. With each day the number of those sharing Jones' alarm increased as clerical *émigrés* fanned out across Europe from France and brought home to their hosts the realisation that the religious changes following the Civil Constitution had introduced schism and disruption into the Gallican Church from top to bottom. Against this background, those religious aspects of the Revolution that had originally encouraged loosely progressive opinion to think well of it tended to be forgotten. Nothing originally endeared itself to this constituency more than the extension of citizenship to Protestants and Jews under the Constitution of 1791.

Revolutionary benefits for Protestants and Jews

Fifteen Protestant deputies were elected to the Estates-General, including the pastor Rabaut Saint-Etienne, and Antoine-Pierre Barnave, both of whom achieved prominence in the National Assembly. Their people were the beneficiaries of the Declaration of the Rights of Man (August 1789), which established the general principle of religious liberty, and a decree of Christmas Eve 1789 ending every legal distinction between Protestants and Catholics. Patriots rejoiced, like this deputy from the

---

[5] 5 Jan. 1791, Bodleian Library, MS. Percy, c. 3, f. 47.

Morbihan: 'Today the nation itself recalls to its bosom those unfortunate children cast aside by fanaticism and intolerance... God alone has the right to judge men's conscience, and a simple error cannot be the basis for excluding someone from the constitution.'[6]

Propertied Protestants seized their new political opportunities quickly in 1790-1, stirring up tensions and old resentments as they did so. Toleration was not popular at the lower end of society; indeed, few issues were more calculated to generate violence, especially where members of the Reformed faith were numerous, like the city of Nîmes in south-east France, famous for its silk industry. Folk memories of the sixteenth-century French Religious Wars were rekindled as marginalised Catholics began to wonder if the Revolution was nothing but an elaborate Protestant plot. With the National Guard in Nîmes officered by prosperous Protestants, Catholics felt they had little choice but to organise in self-defence, and by the spring of 1790 they had their own pressure groups in Toulouse, Montauban, Uzès and Nîmes itself – and access to weapons. Local elections were the flashpoint for trouble first at Montauban in May (five killed, fifty wounded), then at Nîmes in June. In four days of street fighting starting on 13 June (the so-called *bagarre* or brawl), order collapsed completely, as many as 300 Catholics were slain while the Protestants (who kept control of the National Guard) lost only twenty. In practical terms, toleration could thus be extraordinarily divisive, with clear winners and losers, pushing the Catholics in the Gard *département* out of Nîmes and into the arms of the counter-revolutionaries. They could not accept the precipitant rise to local supremacy – on the back of the Revolution – of those who, until its eve, had possessed no legal existence. The bloody stand-off persisted into 1791 with murders and attacks on property spreading west and north of Nîmes, to Montauban, Alès and Uzès. Not surprisingly, Protestants had few problems about accepting the creation of the first Republic in 1792.

Jews in France had longer to wait to secure emancipation as, once again, the limited appeal of a policy of religious toleration was made clear. Reformers who thought in terms of Jewish integration within a unified political nation were in a minority; most gentiles who wanted change in the status quo preferred the guaranteeing of Jewish communal rights by the Estates-General, as several of the *cahiers* recommended. But then French Jews were a divided community with the Sephardim embarrassed by their more Hebraic, marginalised brethren, the Yiddish-speaking Ashkenazim of eastern France. The latter were, unlike the Sephardim of Bordeaux,

---

[6] Quoted in Timothy Tackett, *Becoming a Revolutionary: The Deputies of the French National Assembly and the Emergence of a Revolutionary Culture (1789–1790)* (Princeton, 1996), 262.

excluded from electoral activity, but it was apparent that they wished to preserve their community organisations, their rabbis and their syndics, much to the anger of the Third Estate in Alsace. In July–August 1789 anti-Semitic riots occured in seventy locations across that province, the counterpart to the 'Great Fear' in other regions. By then the Jewish deputies of Alsace and Lorraine, partly inspired by the *cahiers* submitted very late by the three groups of Jews in Paris – Portuguese, German and Comtadins – in the name of the majority of Ashkenazim had come out for full legal recognition in the new constitution, but not at any price: 'It is only to be better citizens that we ask for the conservation of our synagogue, our rabbis, and our syndics.'[7]

On 28 September the Assembly made the important symbolic declaration that the Jews were under the protection of the laws. But there was still no formal admission to citizenship, and the issue was not pursued vigorously for another three months when the abbé Grégoire, Robespierre, Custine and Adrien Duport made important philosemitic speeches backing Clermont-Tonnerre's motion of 23 December for their admittance into full citizenship. They were countered by deputies from the east, including the future director, Jean-François Reubell, deputy for Colmar, and La Fare, bishop of Nancy, who warned that concessions would spark off popular discontents that could get out of control. Maury, the unsubtle but effective defender of the clergy, was blunt in his refusal to concede citizenship. He reminded his colleagues how the Jews 'had passed seventeen centuries without ever mixing themselves in other nations'. They were not Frenchmen, but foreigners living in France, to be excluded from the nation.

For the moment, the Ashkenazim were a hopeless cause. It was therefore exclusively the Sephardim of the Bordelais and Avignon (a mere 4,000 people) who benefited from the first emancipation decree of 28 January 1790. It said much that in September 1790 the Ashkenazi Jews were specifically excluded from new laws admitting non-Catholics to judicial office and from the law of naturalisation. The Revolution had done nothing to change attitudes appreciably towards the Jews anywhere on the political spectrum, and it seemed there would be no real movement until the Ashkenazim showed a desire to give up their communal rights, the last vestiges of 'nationhood'. As Clermont-Tonnerre expressed it: 'It would be repugnant to have a society of non-citizens in a state, and a nation

---

[7] Quoted in Patrice Girard, *Les Juifs de France de 1789 à 1860. De l'Emancipation à l'inegalité* (Paris, 1976), 48; see also Arthur Hertzberg, *The French Enlightenment and the Jews*, (New York, 1968), 348–9, 354–9; Shanti Marie Singham, 'Between Cattle and Men', in Dale Van Kley (ed.), *The French Idea of Freedom: The Old Regime and the Declaration of Rights of 1789* (Stanford, 1994), 114–53, at 123–4.

within a nation.'[8] Just three days before the Assembly was dissolved, on 27 September 1791, he and his supporters at last won for all Jewish communities in France full equality as citizens. It was a splendid symbolic victory, but did it change very much? Popular suspicions about the legitimate place of the Jews in France had not been dispelled, while reformers remained fearful that they would put the brake on further reforms in the revolutionary state.

In the winter of 1791–2 most French Jews took the civic oath as their citizenship entitled them and required of them and, in doing so, they renounced all their 'privileges and exemptions'. No one was quite sure about exactly *what* they had renounced under the Emancipation Decree. Berr Isaac Berr, the lay leader of the Jewish community in Nancy, insisted that emancipation did not bring assimilation in its wake. Elsewhere in Alsace and Lorraine, many municipalities disagreed. In fact, many Ashkenazim also did not possess the amount of property required under the Constitution of 1791 for active citizenship and opted for their pre-revolutionary traditions, so opening up new divisions within their own communities. Jewish communal rights survived emancipation, alongside the Yiddish language, the debts of former Jewish communities – and popular anti-Semitism. The old prejudices may have been fuelled by the disinclination of Sephardim and Ashkenazim alike to become involved in republican politics; where they were active, the Jewish preference for federation (as in Bordeaux) aroused antipathy on the left

Elsewhere in Europe during the early 1790s, a guarded approach towards extending and deepening the toleration of Christian minorities prevailed, without extending this concession to non-Christian faiths. In that respect, the example of revolutionary France was not contagious; the Jewish emancipation decree was one of the finest fruits of the Revolution with no counterpart in other states. In the Habsburg domains the short reign of the emperor Leopold (1790–2) saw an attempt to heal the fissures opened up in this diverse polity over the previous decade, and for the moment the Edict of Toleration remained in force (hardly less could be expected from the former grand duke of Tuscany). For Leopold, France's religious policies were its own affair and he saw no need to intervene on behalf of his brother-in-law on that pretext. In Prussia, Frederick William II had already by the Declaration of Potsdam (9 July 1788) clarified the open-ended basis of his uncle's attitude to minorities from Jesuits to Jews.

---

[8] Quoted in Gary Kates, 'Jews into Frenchmen: Nationality and Representation in Revolutionary France', in Ferenc Fehér (ed.), *The French Revolution and the Birth of Modernity* (Berkeley, 1990), 103–16, at 113.

The new king felt that toleration had gone too far and had merely encouraged the growth of irreligion. Under the provisions of the declaration, Moravians, Mennonites and Jews were declared sects pernicious to the state and ordered not to hold public assemblies. This policy continued unchanged even after Prussia joined the war of the First Coalition against France in 1792. The impact of the Revolution on Germany did not then lead to an abrupt rediscovery of the value of the confessional state. Most governments had come to appreciate that there existed more accurate tests of loyalty than that offered by membership of an established Church.

The trend to religious inclusiveness in Britain and Ireland

Official recognition of minority religious allegiances increased apace in Britain from the 1770s. The death of the drink-soaked Young Pretender in 1788 gave Scottish Episcopalians the chance they sought to transfer their allegiance unequivocally to the Hanoverian dynasty. Prayers for George III were instituted almost before the Pretender was buried. Archbishop Moore of Canterbury was keen on toleration for Scottish Episcopalians, as he hoped they would have a pastoral effectiveness in Scotland which could benefit all Christians. It took some time for parliamentary misgivings to be satisfied (conservative opinion found it hard to envisage bishops whose jurisdiction was primarily spiritual), but with influential Anglicans like bishops Horsley and Horne lobbying the Pitt government and the Kirk raising no objections, the Scottish nonjurors received full toleration in 1792. One Scottish bishop insisted that their communion's voluntary adoption of the Thirty-nine Articles (still seen as excessively Calvinist by some nonjuring prelates) was a worthwhile sacrifice as 'a pledge of our appearing on their [English high churchmen] side' in the battle for orthodoxy 'against Arians, Unitarians, and all the enemies of Christ'.[9] By 1792 the tide of British loyalism – stimulated by Burke's writings against the Revolution – was flowing fast and Scottish Episcopalians were seen as useful recruits to that cause. So were Scottish Catholics, who were accorded their own Relief Act in 1793, the dawn of their 'Second Spring' as it has been called, with priests ministering in the expanding urban centres (Glasgow had its first appointment in 1792), at

---

[9] Bishop Abernethy Drummond of Edinburgh to Revd Jonathan Boucher, 4 February 1793, quoted in F. C. Mather, *High Church Prophet: Bishop Samuel Horsley (1733–1806) and the Caroline Tradition in the later Georgian Church* (Oxford, 1992), 134.

a remove from gentry control. Progressive Anglican opinion was still set on a relaxation in the subscription laws in the early 1790s, but found it hard to make way when their dissenting allies were coming under attack in the press. As one Norfolk paper reported:

> The friends to a Revisal of the Liturgy are combining with a certain class of Dissenters, under the name of the Unitarian Society, for the purpose of propagating Socinianism, by cheapening the books, and gratuitously distributing the pamphlets which recommend this heresy.[10]

Significantly, parliamentary attempts sponsored by the Foxite Whigs in 1792 to grant new freedoms to the Unitarians also came to nothing. It was in this heterodox quarter that the Revolution had been most ardently hailed, and the development of extremist politics in Paris had not dimmed the ardour of Priestley and his supporters.

English and Irish Roman Catholics were also offered new relief measures by the Pitt government. As fears of French extremism hardened, most of the Cabinet was determined not to alienate propertied opinion, whatever its religious complexion. Not so the Irish Lord-Lieutenant, Lord Westmorland (1790–5). He preferred to see matters from the angle of the rigid Protestants staffing the administration in Dublin Castle and, in the end, Pitt and Dundas felt that considerations of state security necessitated action to induce the majority of respectable Catholics from joining in an unholy alliance with the United Irishmen. One measure was pushed through the Dublin Parliament in 1792, another the next year with Pitt making it clear to the new chief secretary, Sylvester Douglas, that Protestant opposition to concessions was to be disregarded as self-serving and detrimental to British interests as a whole. Both Pitt and Dundas felt that 'the Catholics, being the majority of the inhabitants, must in justice and policy be admitted by degrees to a full participation of all the advantages now held exclusively by the Protestants . . . Mr Pitt thinks, truly, that such a monopoly is unjust and cannot long be maintained . . . '.[11] Thus the Revolution decisively affected British policy in religion, with toleration conceded as the price for loyalty and withheld when admiration for the French example made a group such as the Unitarians a security liability even before Britain and France went to war in 1793. Anglican sympathies went instead to the boatloads of clerical *émigrés* arriving daily from the continent.

---

[10] *Norfolk Chronicle*, no. 1051, 19 March 1791.
[11] *The Sylvester Douglas Diaries*, ed. F. Bickley (2 vols., London, 1928), vol. I, 34–6, quoted in Gerard O'Brien, *Anglo-Irish Politics in the Age of Grattan and Pitt* (Dublin, 1987), 164.

Clerical persecution and emigration

The *émigrés* were part of a clerical diaspora from France on an unprecedented scale, about 25,000 clergy in total or a quarter of the 'emigration', with important consequences for both the counter-revolution and inter-Church relations. Bishops and the higher clergy had mostly slipped across the borders during 1791, often in disguise with officials or national guards on their heels, as the authorities lost patience with their procrastination over taking the oath on the Civil Constitution. Nonjuring parish priests kept their ministry going well into 1792 despite the revolutionaries' identification of them as fifth columnists once war had broken out. As news from the Rhine frontier worsened, penalties were stepped up. On 26 August, declaring open season for 'priest hunts', the Assembly ordered nonjurors to quit the country within a fortnight on pains of deportation to Guiana if they were denounced by six citizens. Worse was to come when news of the reported fall of Verdun reached the capital on 2 September, and mobs took to the streets looking for 'traitors' and invaded the gaols. These were the notorious September Massacres that, as far as most European opinion was concerned, irretrievably tainted the Revolution and marked an inauspicious start to the Republic. Priests were high on the list of butchered victims. In three days (2–4 September), three prelates and approximately 230 priests died at the hands of anticlerical fanatics. In the Carmelite convent alone, 115 of 150 priests fell under 'the axe of vengeance', including the archbishop of Arles and the bishops of Saintes and Beauvais. There were comparable incidents of blood-letting in other centres of population, and incidents of sexual sadism against the female religious Orders that soon became public knowledge. This style of violence had been seen as early as April 1791 when a large band of men invaded Paris convents, some dressed as women, and the National Guard did nothing to stop them: 'they saw sacred virgins of all ages, timid young ones, sickly aged ones . . . stripped naked, beaten with switches, pursued in that dreadful state of nudity in all the corners of their houses and gardens, hunted down, beaten black and blue, covered with curses more cruel than death . . .'[12]

The Massacres marked the start of an anticlerical offensive – the deportation of nonjurors became automatic in March 1793 – that underlined the simmering hostility of the new regime to the refractories (and, incidentally, exposed a latent threat to the Constitutionalist clergy) and showed how much they had become the personification of the

---

[12] A. Cabanès and L. Nass, *La Névrose révolutionnaire* (2 vols., Paris, 1924), quoted in Madelyn Gutwirth, *The Twilight of the Goddesses: Women and Representation in the French Revolutionary Era* (New Brunswick, N.J., 1993), 313.

counter-revolution. Priests tended to head for the nearest frontier: Flanders clergy spilled over into the Austrian Netherlands; those from Alsace and Lorraine crossed into principalities east of the Rhine where Cardinal Rohan of Strasbourg was acting as muster-master general for the counter-revolution in that part of his bishopric beyond French jurisdiction; in the south and south-east, Spain, Savoy and Switzerland were easily reached. French clergy of all ages poured into the Swiss cantons during 1792. 'What a calamity', one aged priest in Constance told an English traveller by no means sympathetic to Catholicism, 'to be required to travel the world to find a bit of repose.'[13] Clergy from the Breton and Norman dioceses crossed to the Channel Islands and mainland England where most of their bishops had arrived a few months earlier. About 7,000 priests in total left France for the British Isles. By December 1792 there were over 3,000 in England and 3,500 in the Channel Islands, so numerous that one English traveller in Southampton wondered if 'the postillion had made a mistake and had carried us to a French town instead of an English one'.[14]

Seeking refuge in a Protestant kingdom like Britain was a policy born of a desperation for the refugees, but they needed shelter almost at any price and threw themselves on the mercy of Churches, government and public. Responsible behaviour was the key here; conduct that maintained the integrity of their religious practice and allowed for mutual protection and encouragement without upsetting the host population. The exiled clergy were fortunate in the diplomatic gifts of their leaders, men such as Jean-François De La Marche, bishop of St Pol-de-Léon before 1790, and the abbé Carron, whose emphasis on prayer and priestly good behaviour was designed to sustain the exiles without offending Protestant Britons. That their brethren were not always capable of attaining these exacting ideals did not, in the end, cause either influence or relief funds (meagre though they were) to dry up. La Marche headed a committee of episcopal exiles which attempted both to lead the lower clergy who had followed them across the Channel and maintain links with those at home, especially the vicar-generals trying covertly to run their old dioceses. It was an awkward, almost impossible, task, but the committee somehow managed to produce a coherent ecclesiological view of contemporary politics and the extent to which the clergy might try to accommodate themselves to a French polity without a presiding Bourbon monarchy.

[13] John Owen, *Travels in Different Parts of Europe in the Years 1791 and 1792* (2 vols., London, 1796), letter CXL, vol. II, 265, 11 May 1792.
[14] Quoted in Dominic Aidan Bellenger, *The French Exiled Clergy in the British Isles after 1789* (Bath, 1986), 3.

In Spain the exiles (about 6,000 by 1793) had less chance of organising, but their welcome was still overwhelming. Outside the monasteries where most were directed, prelates personally cared for scores of the dispossessed clergy. The impoverished bishop of Orense, in Galicia, put his meagre income aside to care for 320 French priests among whom his hospitality became legendary. Anglicans, too, responded generously to the exiles' presence. Even before the refractories' arrival, the British public was familiar with their sufferings through the speeches and writings of Edmund Burke and other early apologists for the counter-revolution. Elite anti-Catholicism in England had been ebbing away since the mid-century and the Church of England bishops saw its Gallican equivalents not as threatening papists but as the undeserving victims of a revolution without precedent. As Henry Courtenay, bishop of Bristol (1794–7), saw it: 'Many of them [the French clergy] have perished amid the Wreck of their country and their Religion, with a courage and resolution worthy of the Primitive martyrs.' The destruction of the 'throne and altar' alliance in France was similarly deplored by leading bishops like Samuel Horsley of Rochester, who joined the Committee for Emigration Relief formed under John Wilmot, MP. Every sort of charitable exertion was made on behalf of the exiles by bishops, chapters and the universities: Bishop Shute Barrington of Durham who, in principle, was as averse to pop-ery as any Anglican prelate, even housed some of the exiles at his palace at Auckland Castle. Parish clergy gave money and urged their congre-gations to be generous themselves. As Bishop Courtenay put it: 'While you suffer not your compassion to warp you from your watchfulness over the Protestant cause, let not on the other hand your humanity be dead-ened by groundless fears, and ill-founded suspicions.'[15] Over £41,000 had been collected by Anglicans by November 1793. Dissenters were less welcoming and, as a rule, even members of the established Church were, by the mid-1790s, apprehensive of increased interference by the exiles in English Church affairs, such as the attempts at proselytising by Catholic priests lodged in the Winchester area. A bill to counteract 'papal advance' was only halted in the Lords by Horsley's powerful opposition. First-hand familiarity with the foreign popish 'other' over time induced not only ecumenical sympathies in some quarters but a revival of some of the old tensions in others.

English Catholics, too, had their concerns over the Gallican presence. Its leaders, Lords Petre and Arundell of Wardour, Bishop Charles Walmesley and Bishop John Douglass (vicars apostolic of the Western and London Districts respectively) prominent among them, were initially

[15] *A Charge delivered to the Clergy of the Diocese of Bristol at the Primary Visitation of Henry, Lord Bishop of Bristol* (Bristol, 1796), 5, 6.

welcoming but pastoral letters concealed anxieties over clerical discipline. These men and others had been working hard to show English Protestants that the Catholics were loyal to the Crown and posed no internal threat, and they were worried in case the French clergy made a lot of noise and disrupted existing, improved Roman Catholic–Anglican relations. These cultural and political differences soon surfaced. English nuns arrived back from the continent in some numbers. In 1794 the English Carmelites, formerly at Antwerp, settled at Langhorn Manor, Cornwall, where in 1799 the first clothing of a nun in the western counties since the six-teenth century took place. In December 1792 Lord Petre told the foreign secretary, Lord Grenville, that the arrival of Benedictine nuns at Bodney, Norfolk, might make 'the whole body of Catholics' the 'objects of popular cry and odium' if they were allowed to flourish.[16] The position was only slightly eased that same month when the Vatican ruled that the English vicars apostolic had jurisdictional supremacy over all clergy, English and French.

Imposing uniformity was easier said than done, and there were con-stant petty problems involving social conduct, celebration of the Mass in private houses, and friction between Gallican and native Catholic clergy. For his part, Bishop La Marche was alert to the danger, deferred to English Catholic representations and tried, not always successfully, to re-strain the French priests from interfering in the ministry of their English counterparts or trying to poach their congregations. Chauvinist feelings on both sides also limited creative religious interaction, and it took many years for tentative exchanges to occur, as in the appointment of French priests as chaplains to prisoners-of-war or appreciation of each others' spiritual writings. As their historian argues, 'for all their numbers the French stirred little more than a passing ripple on the still waters of English Catholicism'.[17] If anything, Scotland was the scene of warmer relations between the native clergy and the French exiles, especially after the arrival of the heir presumptive to the throne, the comte d'Artois, at Holyrood House in 1796.

In Britain, as elsewhere, only to a limited extent did the fear of revolu-tion encourage the mutual co-operation of Roman Catholics and Protes-tants. After Corsica was seized by the British in 1794, George III was given a veto over Catholic episcopal appointments on the islands. There were precedents for this which played some part in reducing levels of dis-trust. In Quebec, for example, francophone Gallican clergy had come to terms surprisingly easily with a new British regime despite relations with France and Rome being curtailed. The Quebec Act encouraged good relations, as did interchangeable Gallican and Anglican approaches to

---

[16] Quoted in Bellenger, *The French Exiled Clergy*, 52.   [17] Ibid., 62.

Church/state relations. The first Anglican bishop on his arrival there in the mid-1790s described the Catholic Church as the only established one and his own merely a tolerated sect. It was more common for Catholic clergy to find that the experience of exile or conquest in the 1790s exposed them to cultural pressures from inside their own Church, ultramontanism for instance. Thus in the papal states the Vatican authorities undertook a re-eduction of the exiles in ultramontane ideas, and these unfortunates felt comparable pressures in Spain and Portugal.

Europeans were shocked at the ease with which a religious establishment like the Gallican Order could be toppled, and condemnations followed on from each other across the continent. The Orthodox Church denounced the revolutionary overthrow of established political hierarchies, and these criticisms were readily endorsed by the Ottoman authorities. Governments allied together against France from 1792–3 were nevertheless cautious about extending an open welcome to the religious refugees. If, on the one hand, they were keen to seal themselves off from Jacobin principles (in Spain local branches of the Inquisition had been confiscating incendiary French literature since 1789 with the chief minister Floridablanca's blessing), they were hesitant about accommodating unregulated those unfortunates whose profession and beliefs were inimical to the values of the new French Republic. The risk that the priest-*émigrés* could be a destabilising presence, even a security risk if they had been unwittingly contaminated by the Revolution, could not be dismissed. In Britain, Pitt's administration passed the Aliens Act (1792) to help establish the political *bona fides* of those fleeing Frenchmen; it was on the statute book before most of the nonjurors had crossed the Channel. The tactful Bishop La Marche soon established good working relations with several MPs and ministers close to the premier by impressing on episcopal colleagues that trying to influence British policy formation could be counter-productive. In fact, La Marche's caution in avowing counter-revolutionary principles eventually caused relations between him and Burke to cool appreciably. In Spain, the clergy were subject to the same stringent controls as lay *émigrés* and were required to take an oath not to discuss events in France. They had to live together in religious houses, away from Madrid and the provincial capitals; teaching and preaching were prohibited, though they could say Mass.

Loyalism and counter-revolution

There was, during the 1790s, an attempt by many European regimes resisting the French revolutionaries to renew the mutual identification of

Church and state, with immorality and libertinism presented as a sure sign of Jacobin political sympathies inimical to the welfare of both institutions. During that decade, the established Churches were on the front-line in defending the existing order from sedition, and state survival was assisted by drawing on confessional loyalties. Loyalist Anglicans thus welcomed such devices as the royal proclamation of 21 May 1792 intended to suppress 'all loose and licentious Prints, Books and Publications, dispersing Poison to the Minds of the Young and Unwary'. As an essential agency of social control, ministers of state and religion worked together to preserve their power bases and, with the dechristianisation experiments of 1792–4 in France as a terrible warning of what might happen, no opportunity was neglected of using scripture and the precepts found in it as one of the best preservatives of Church and state alike.

In Denmark, opposition to the Revolution was closely linked to anti-rationalist religious revivalism. Bishop Nicolaj Balle, bishop of Sjaelland, long a force in Lutheran cultural politics, took a personal initiative that directed public regard back to the catechism. In Copenhagen he began conducting well-attended biweekly reading sessions in 1793 and produced a devotional journal that attracted 30,000 subscribers. The Revolution commonly brought a new sense of the blessings of one's own order. Claus Pavels, a Copenhagen curate, praised the Danish government and all the benefits it conferred on the Danes, as opposed to those who lived under so-called 'popular' governments who were really pitiful slaves.

Governments and peoples who were aligned in opposition to France were aware by 1793–4 that a conflict of cultures was an inseparable component of revolutionary war. The fate of the Catholic Church – first the nonjurors evicted then the Constitutionalists discarded – was a warning that nothing less than the survival of Christian Europe was at issue, and it encouraged a heightened religious sensitivity at every level. With patriotism and Christianity freshly and more comfortably welded together as patriotism shed its radical connotations, politicians were keen to use the churches and their pulpits to inspire the whole population in the struggle. The clergy were encouraged to act as *de facto* antirevolutionary propagandists and recruiting agents as well as pastors. Innumerable sermons of this decade made clear the interchangeability of royalist and religious rhetoric, along the lines used by one Anglican loyalist, the Revd William Agutter, with his exhortation: 'Therefore, my beloved Brethren, whether as loyal Subjects to the best of Kings, or as Christian Soldiers to the King of Kings, be ye ready – be ye true to every engagement.'[18] Clergymen

---

[18] William Agutter, *The Faithful Soldier and True Christian* (Northampton, 1798), 2 Tim. vol. II.3.

such as Agutter were asked to stiffen the sinews of national resistance and fuel popular anti-Gallicanism, though not, of course, at the expense of the *émigré* priests. In Scotland, Dundas was relieved at the way ministers of the Kirk – directed by Dr George Hill, principal of St Mary's College, St Andrews – backed up the efforts of government to achieve social solidarity in the light of the threat from the continent. Ministers belonging to the Popular party were not, as during the American War, keen to flirt with the enemy, and their leader, the Revd John Erskine, was rewarded with a royal chaplaincy in 1793. As Dundas told Pitt: 'if I were to name what circumstance was of the most essential importance to the peace of the country, I would name the influence of the clergy over the people properly exercised'.[19]

Even in predominantly Catholic Ireland, Pitt's Cabinet was gratified at the impeccable loyalist sentiments expressed by the hierarchy, anxious not to jeopardise the pace of Catholic relief measures by rashly espousing French principles. The French Revolution accelerated the speed with which the Roman Catholic Church was moving towards peaceable integration into civil society in the British state for the first time since the Reformation, though that process in itself increased the political temperature with the revival of the Catholic Committee to lobby for relief and then its dissolution into warring factions in 1793; the new, prosperous Irish Catholic middle class was no longer to defer automatically to peers trusted by Dublin Castle, such as Lords Kenmare and Gormanstown. But could the bishops and clergy restrain their flocks from perceiving revolutionary action as a short-cut to emancipation? One group of pro-French sympathisers, the Defenders, saw themselves as the armed wing of the Catholic Committee by 1792, but it was the growth of the United Irishmen that was particularly viewed with alarm. 'The diabolical Jacobin spirit will ruin us all', bewailed James Caulfield, bishop of Ferns.[20] Rome, too, was urging obedience to government on John Troy, archbishop of Dublin, by 1792, and the following year there were meetings with officials over state endowments of education and payment of the clergy. The possibility of direct French intervention was at the back of everyone's mind in Ireland, and increased further the dominance of the Catholic question in the politics of this decade.

In Spain, more than one prelate had embraced the ideals of the Civil Constitution in 1791–2, and either corresponded with Grégoire or gathered in Madrid at the house of the condesa de Montijo, their great

[19] PRO, Chatham Papers, 30/8/157/1/144 quoted in Michael Fry, *The Dundas Despotism* (Edinburgh, 1992), 179 and 178–83.
[20] Quoted in Daire Keogh, *'The French Disease': The Catholic Church and Irish Radicalism, 1790–1800* (Dublin, 1993), 53.

patronness. The bishop of Barbastro, Agustín Abad y la Sierra, wrote publicly to many clergy on the French side of the Pyrenees (his diocese was near by), causing him to be denounced to the Inquisition in 1792 as a Jansenist. Luckily, his brother was named inquisitor-general before the end of the year and his case was dropped. The outbreak of war largely killed off this reformist flirtation, and between 1793 and 1795 the clergy produced a spate of sermons and pastoral letters justifying hostilities. Maledictions were hurled at revolutionary France and the 'filosofía criminal y falsa' that inspired it. Sermons could rant, or reason, or both. Fray Antonio Díez saw the genesis of the troubles in 'Neker, Protestante, Banquero', while the peripatetic Capuchin Fray, Diego de Cádiz, worked on the crowds across the country instructing them in Catholic preparations for conflict. Back came the interest in divine right monarchy as a counterblast to regicide. The *émigré* clergy themselves were pressed into the service of host states when it suited government purposes, as it did in Spain in 1793. Five pastoral letters from bishops in exile were published both in the periodical press and as separate pamphlets, while in Málaga a translation of a French priest's funeral oration for Louis XVI appeared. French victories on the field eventually acted as a disincentive to the efforts of the clergy in Spain. 'Even the whores ask you about Robespierre and Barère,' bemoaned a Madrid priest in 1795.[21] The bids to use religion as a barrier to the French 'poison' were by no means guaranteed success, especially where, despite the harsh new climate, currents of enlightenment sentiments lived on, alongside the anticlericalism they fostered.

In every state, the Churches in the 1790s rediscovered the virtues of monarchical regimes which, before the Revolution erupted, had been bent on reducing them to subordinate institutions. Equally, kings reckoned that returning to a religion-based justification for their power would lessen the chances of their suffering the fate of Louis XVI, not least because popular political allegiance was still denominated in confessional terms, its idioms marked by scriptural and liturgical overtones. A sovereign like George III had never doubted the good sense of a steadfast alliance of 'throne and altar'; the new Habsburg emperor, Francis II, rediscovered it to a degree that both his father (Leopold II) and his uncle (Joseph II) might have found eccentric. All but the most die-hard Protestants came to see the papacy as a useful partner in inspiring Europe to condemn the values of regicidal, republican France. In these unprecedented circumstances, as the armed struggle engulfed Europe in 1792–3,

---

[21] Quoted in Richard Herr, *The Eighteenth Century Revolution in Spain* (Princeton, 1958), 325.

there was no time for denominational oneupmanship, except against those minority Christians who still found something to approve in the French Revolution. As one popular pamphlet, first published in 1793 put it:

> Dissenter, – Churchman, – Catholic,
>   Whatever their persuasion,
> Good subjects are to me alike,
>   Of all denominations.[22]

The alliance between the *Aufklärung* and the Catholic princes also unravelled as the warning from France called into question the expediency of forwarding the Catholic Enlightenment any further. The doubts had predated 1789, and the Revolution confirmed the priorities of enlightenment as a dangerous irrelevance. The papal Bull *Auctorem fidei* in 1794 condemned Richerism, that vigorous step-child of Jansenism, and most of the work of the Pistoia synod (including vernacular worship and Erastianism in the form of the 1682 Gallican Articles), and it hardly caused a murmur, disinclined in practice though Catholic rulers might be to pay its injunctions more than lip-service.

Apart from France, the institutional power of religion retained a vigour that was again on display in the 1790s and gave the lie to any suggestion that indifference or unbelief had irretrievably sapped its strength in the course of the eighteenth century. The same trend could be found outside the established Churches where the extension and confirmation of religious toleration (however niggardly or reluctantly conceded) had allowed dissent to flourish with little or no hindrance. Influential minorities like the Methodists were not disposed to hazard their new-found national respectability by countenacing pro-revolutionary sympathisers in their ranks, even if the price was limited schism; in Ireland 'new light' Presbyterians worked towards an alliance with Catholic militants, but they could not bring a majority with them, who were easily persuaded to accept instead the augmented *regium donum* from the government. Patriotism and antirevolutionary feeling combined in the era down to the mid-1790s not to the extent that it could ever be taken for granted by governments, but at least they knew the hierarchies were squarely behind the war effort, a war for survival. Bewilderment determined loyalism as much as any other factor. It was not easy to grasp the enormity of what had befallen the French Church and civilised Europe. No wonder that abbé Augustin de Barruel argued for a grand underground conspiracy of

---

[22] J. Nott, *The Life and Adventures of Job Nott, Bucklemaker of Birmingham* (11th edn, Birmingham, 1798), 25, quoted in Robert Hole, *Pulpits, Politics and Public Order in England 1760–1832* (Cambridge, 1991), 107.

mystics, masons, *philosophes* and radical sectarians, driven by their mad systems, preparing an onslaught 'more numerous and more destructive than the inundation of the Vandals'.[23] Emotive language of this sort did not appear overstated to his many clerical readers already familiar with Burke's dark ruminations on the same theme.

Clerics preached ferociously against the Revolution, making the link explicitly between the national and antirevolutionary causes as in Germany. The Cistercian Fr Alois Specker in 1793 tried to rouse his countrymen to defend their homeland thus: 'Already the gallic cohorts have conquered a considerable part of our Germany. Already they are murdering and robbing our fellow brothers.'[24] Many in his Order were not unwilling to take up arms personally against the French revolutionary armies, lending credence to the charges of their enemies that they were but counter-revolutionaries in cassocks. The writings of several eminent historians – Maurice Hutt, W. G. Mitchell and Jacques Godechot among them – have shown the extent to which they were involved in planning and organising underground resistance to the French Republic. Royalist leaders like the Allier brothers in the Vivarais – they led an abortive attack on Mende in early 1793 – drew extensively on support from priests to make the clerico-royalist label an accurate description of their cause. In the Vendée revolt of 1793–5, troops in the 'Royal and Catholic Army' were given mass absolution before battle by the clergy who often fought alongside them. One of the most prominent was the abbé Bernier, *curé* of Saint-Laud d'Angers, an inspired organiser who tightened the structures of the resistance to the Republic, and later came over to Bonaparte. Priestly participation was endemic in the Vendée Revolt; similarly, local clergy were active in the defence of Catalonia against French invaders in 1794. The clergy paid a high price if they fell into the hands of their foes. Capture with sacred objects was most incriminating. One participant in the counter-revolutionary disturbances north of the Loire known as *chouannerie*, the priest Sainte-Pez, was arrested at Carfaintain in April 1794 when he was found to have a box of hosts, and a painting known to be a rallying sign for counter-revolutionaries. He went to the guillotine just three weeks later. In the Vendée, priests were pushed into the waters of the Loire weighed down with chain shot and nuns were executed in several villages, and yet these condign punishments could not stem the number of those willing to risk martyrdom. They included former bishops such as Hercé of Dol, shot on the beaches in 1795 after

---

[23] Abbé Augustin de Barruel, *Mémoires pour servir à l'histoire du jacobinisme* (4 vols., London, 1797), vol. I, iii.
[24] Quoted in Laurence Cole, 'Nation, Anti-Enlightenment, and Religious Revival in Austria: Tyrol in the 1790s', *HJ*, 43 (2000), 475–97, at 474.

the disastrous attempted landing of the *émigré* army at Quiberon Bay. This suffering was a far cry from the opulence of the pre-1789 First Estate and it played a considerable part in inspiring the laity in France to keep religious life and practice going, even without priestly ministrations. Elsewhere, it commanded admiration and played its part in confirming popular attachment to the Christianity which the revolutionaries either wanted to extirpate or refine beyond recognition.

6 The impact of the Revolution on religious life and practice, c. 1793–1802

Dechristianisation

Republican culture and practice in France during the Jacobin ascendancy of 1793–4 included a deliberate attempt to 'dechristianise' the state. A good republican, by Jacobin definition, could not be a good Christian; indeed, he could not be a Christian at all. The hopes held out in 1790–1 among the Constitutional clergy for a patriotic alliance between Gallicanism and the Revolution were thus, in only two years, put aside, as the state disowned the clergy and transferred their civic functions to officials, employing coercion to achieve its objective in cultural politics. Jacobins had overthrown the monarchy with relative ease; they would find the extirpation of Christian practice beyond their grasp. Nevertheless, it was the most inimical onslaught by any government against organised religion for nearly 1,500 years; it was at the heart of the sudden and very dramatic challenge in the 1790s to religious primacy in European culture. Though the Churches did not crack, the experience had profound consequences for Christian life and practice in France (and indeed beyond) for several generations. Europe had witnessed nothing like this destruction of religious buildings and murderous attacks on the clergy since the Thirty' Years War and the French Wars of Religion. And it had never seen a Christian state turn against that religion per se since the Dark Ages. That was certainly how the great powers fighting France in the Revolutionary war of 1793–1801 chose to present the situation to their troops and civilians. France was demonised because she had so flagrantly positioned herself outside a civilisation still essentially denoted by Christian monarchy.

There were two essential aspects to dechristianisation: a discrimination against Christianity that often took the form of intimidation and persecution, and the promulgation of alternative beliefs in French society. Laws against refractory clergy were already draconian by 1793, but they were newly applied to the Constitutional Church from that date. From Nevers, one of the main laboratories for dechristianisation,

L'antico duomo in Strasburgo divenuto tempio della nuova filosofia francese.

7. Strasbourg Cathedral transformed into a temple of Reason. A 'goddess' enthroned can be glimpsed in the background.

Collot d'Herbois and Laplanche were telling the Convention as early as April 1793 that the Constitutional priests were just as restless as the nonjurors. This assertion was, in part, due to Grégoire's followers (who had never been in principle opposed to the idea of a republic or believed that the revolutionary dialectic could be divorced from progressive Christianity) aligning themselves behind the Brissotins. When the latter were overthrown in the coup of 31 May–1 June 1793, members of the Constitutional clergy often joined in the Federalist revolt against Jacobin centralism and, even where they refrained, their opponents had no difficulty in presenting their conduct – and, by definition, all ordained ministers – as unpatriotic and as much a threat to the state as the Vendéen rebels or Condé's *émigré* army. In the winter of 1793–4, with Jacobin control over the provinces reasserted through the representatives on mission, the revolutionary armies and the clubs, individual clergy were expected to resign their orders of priesthood and get married. The alternative was imprisonment or, in some cases, death. Continuing to exercise a public ministry was not an option, for the revolutionary leaders of 1793–4 reasoned that Christian practice would perish once the ministers and clergy were removed. It was an explicable presumption but an erroneous one. Thus, whereas the dechristianisers practically eliminated the pastoral corps of the Huguenots of Languedoc (something even Louis XIV had failed to do after 1685), the determined members of the 'Church of the Desert' simply reverted to the covert practices of their forefathers.

Concurrently, churches of all denominations (plus synagogues) were shut and converted into granaries, arms dumps or municipal buildings where they were not demolished outright. Alternatively, they were transformed into 'Temples of Reason' and given over to celebrations or quasi-worship of a non-Christian kind, part of a series of festivals inaugurated to inculcate the populace in republican values by entertainment and spectacle as much as by edification. This was a chance for the revolutionaries to create their own 'sacred spaces' within an urban setting and fill them with the new patriotic symbols drawn from their own martyrology: Jean-Michel Lepeletier de Saint-Fargeau, Jean-Paul Marat and the child hero François-Joseph Bara killed in the Vendée, were all celebrated on such occasions as the Festival of the Martyrs of Liberty. When the Jacobins retook Lyon from the Federalists, the corpse of the Jacobin 'martyr' Joseph Chalier was exhibited for public veneration on 10 November, and his burial included parodic activities including the smashing of holy objects and a mock eucharistic celebration. These charivaris variously attracted the curious as much as the committed. Despite the displays, the novelty value and the alluring sight of local beauties transformed into 'goddesses', the cult of Reason in its variant forms (so much depended on the personal whim of the representative making the arrangements) had little to offer the average countryman who found his local saints – and superstitions – made more sense of a life of unrelenting toil dependent on the vagaries of the season. The absence of prayer or of any sense of an accessible supernatural presence comparable to Christ, his mother and the saints was a major departure from popular norms. The festivals devoted to Reason (and, by implication, unbelief) were little to the taste of Maximilien Robespierre, the dominant force in French politics between March and July 1794 and one who abhorred the atheism that he associated with the immoral politics of his enemies, 'false republicans' such as Georges-Jacques Danton, Camille Desmoulins and Jacques-René Hébert. Robespierre, a lifelong devotee of Rousseau, lost no time in introducing an official cult of the Supreme Being, one whose formularies preserved a semblance of divine mystery. Though a memorable service was held in Paris on Whit Sunday 1794 attended by all leading politicians, the new faith never had a chance to function as the confessional basis of the French Republic before Robespierre was overthrown in July 1794.

Dechristianisation and Jacobinism tended to go together outside France as part of those 'Jacobinical principles' that were such anathema to monarchists and churchmen. With the revolutionary armies fanning out into the Low Countries, the Rhineland and Italy during the mid-1790s, their foreign sympathisers often proclaimed their hostility to Christianity, its agents and symbols as a means of displaying their republican credentials even before French troops arrived: when a former monk called Biergans referred to 'Citizen Christ' in a speech at Düren in the Rhineland in 1795 French troops had to snatch him to safety from his incensed audience. The fall of Robespierre and the proscription of his supporters may have halted dechristianisation in France itself; it did nothing to counteract its export elsewhere through the most powerful agency in France – the army – which had always shown a genuine passion for dechristianisation's more destructive side. With charismatic generals and their troops operating semi-independently of the Directory between 1795 and 1799, ministers could have done little to stop this progress even if they had been minded to act. In the satellite states adjacent to France's frontiers, local republican elites were free to adopt vicious anticlerical policies, shutting down churches (including Protestant temples) and imprisoning or executing priests who tried to resist. The French were only too painfully aware that the confessional would not yield its secrets, and naturally this increased suspicion of clerical plotting.

Not surprisingly, the occupation of the Rhineland in the 1790s was unpopular, especially as dechristianisation came with it. The region already enjoyed sufficient toleration to make anything the occupying French army could offer of dubious value to Protestants who, in any case, had heard the stories of atrocities against Christian shrines and were deeply suspicious. Initially, most Lutherans rejected the new regime, most Calvinists supported it, while the Catholics were divided. Local circumstances and the confessional balance dictated responses, which by the mid-1790s were emphatically hostile. Catholics could see how the economic resources available to the Church had gone and they were suffering materially in consequence. The Revolution could work to the disadvantage of the poor: in Cologne the French had secularised church assets devoted to poor relief. There was wrangling over the Jacobins' efforts to regulate both Catholic and Protestant worship, priests defied anticlerical legislation and monks had to be manhandled out of their communities. Once dispossessed, the clergy seldom received any or all of the pension promised to them and came on to the streets looking for alms.

Though it it was only in regions permanently annexed to the Republic – Belgium, for example – that the full revolutionary religious settlement was imposed, the internal problems France had suffered as a result of her own tended to recur elsewhere. As was shown in Naples in 1799, where the Bourbons had been overthrown in favour of the Parthenopean Republic, such policies often led to a spiral of uncontainable violence and did nothing to win over moderate opinion, let alone the rural masses where there was no tradition of popular unbelief or an anticlericalism that merged into dechristianisation. When churches were looted and closed, and priests arrested as in the northern provinces of Spain in 1794, the French invaders' talk of friendship and liberation was shown up as hollow.

Dechristianisation outside France was too tainted by its links with pro-revolutionary politicians to have much hope of survival after their overthrow. In Napoleonic Europe, the prefectoral corps governing its far-flung boundaries in the emperor's name paid lip-service to the tradition, if only to ensure that any Catholic revival was contained. After 1814 it lived on underground in secret societies rather than in the population at large, though, as will be seen, it had done much to give anticlericalism an updated, populist virulence. In France itself, dechristianisation was a phenomenon that refused to emerge spontaneously. It was engineered, imposed and enjoyed by the revolutionaries: the sans-culottes, representatives on mission, and the citizen armies, the members of the clubs and the patriotic societies. Among these citizens the phenemenon caught the imagination very fast, compared by Forestier, one *conventionnel*, to a 'volcanic irruption' in its impact on younger, urban males from an artisan background. Individual representatives deliberately engineered a policy to their preference, irrespective of local wishes. In Tarbes (the Hautes-Pyrenées *département*) Monestier, a former *curé*, was bent on extirpating the faith he had formerly professed. As was later said of his activities in the Basque country: 'One day, at Orthez, he took a [figure of] Christ and trampled it underfoot; at Saint-Pé in the Pays Basque . . . one of his agents insisted that a [figure of] Christ be guillotined in front of the entire population.' Nearby, in Bayonne Cathedral, his colleague, the former Protestant, Pinet, celebrated a Year II Festival of Reason, preaching the desirability of eliminating all organised religion. 'How good it is', he told his audience, 'to celebrate this triumph in a place that has for so long been consecrated to deception.'[1]

Pinet was preaching to fellow zealots who comforted themselves that where the clubs led today the population at large would follow tomorrow. It was a delusion; the chances of achieving a dechristianised France (or, indeed, any other European state) when much of the nation had just emerged from a thorough-going process of *Christianisation* were tiny. The average Frenchman was not interested, and certainly not the average French woman. Some bourgeois with anticlerical tendencies were prepared to watch how the experiment progressed, like the sixty-nine-year-old Parisian Guittard de Floriban. He attended the Festival of Reason, considered the worship of the Supreme Being made up an agreeable festival, but welcomed the overthrow of the dechristianisers and was back at church services within a week of them recommencing. Variants in dechristianisation also militated against its success. Once the Jacobins fell (indeed even before Robespierre was executed) the central government persisted with the festivals, but without investing them with much serious religious content. Thus the much neglected second 'reign of Terror' from 1798–9 saw some vicious outbreaks of anticlericalism but little state-sponsored popular alternatives to Catholicism on offer.

The pre-1789 Church had found popular religiosity problematic and so, in their turn, did revolutionaries who, even using the considerable state resources available to them, were unable to persuade the masses to embrace the new republican creeds. A new calendar, street names and baptismal names were all passing fads, which failed to put down popular roots. Yet these cultural novelties should not mask the real importance of dechristianisation. Its impact lay not in inducing French citizens to adopt a non-Christian creed, but in showing the risks of professing attachment to the faith. The chaotic experiment of 1793–4 scared people into not practising as Christians, especially as the regime of 1795–9 was still essentially antipathetic under the guise of official neutrality and the severing

---

[1] Quoted in Alan Forrest, *The Revolution in Provincial France: Aquitaine 1789–1799* (Oxford, 1996), 222, 3.

of Church–state links. Mere conformists were thereafter less inclined to come to church. Dechristianisation also shattered the assumption that state and historic faith were mutually supportive. Henceforth, republicanism and Christian practice would be hard to align.

The continuing propagandist presentation of France after Robespierre as a Godless, Jacobin Republic actually concealed a complex and fascinating situation post-dechristianisation. The period 1795–1800 was one of unparalleled religious experimentation, a position made possible by officially permitting the free exercise of religion by the law of 3 *ventôse* Year III (21 February 1795): small groups were permitted to worship together, though the outward display of religious symbols remained banned, including clerical dress. The Directory was not particularly friendly to Catholicism, which it regarded, with some justification after the Parisian revolt of 13 *vendémiaire* (October 1795), as unrepentantly royalist. It tried to limit the influence of priests by requiring them to take oaths expressing loyalty to the Republic. It had minimal success. The regime's more committed supporters woke up to the electoral perils from the right in time to stage the coup of 18 *fructidor* (September 1797). Then ensued a fresh crackdown against the refractory clergy which disrupted the Church just as it was re-emerging above ground and served as an uncomfortable reminder of its precarious situation.

Some of the Directors half-heartedly patronised Theophilanthrophy, a benign deistic cult that held services with an ethical emphasis, often in premises shared with Christians. In numerical terms, its teachings were too abstract and rarefied to make it a rival to either the refractories or the Constitutionals. All groups were competing among themselves for adherents in the later 1790s as the pressure from the authorities was loosened. Grégoire's followers received no official endorsement from the Directory (which was vulnerable to military anticlericalism) and, deprived of this advantage, found it hard to prevent further inroads into numbers already weakened by apostasy. The Constitutional priests were fortunate in two senses, negative and positive. First, that the refractory clergy were prosecuted afresh by the state in 1797–8 just as they were becoming formidable and, secondly, the new organisational tidiness of their Church with the 'United Bishops' meeting regularly from late 1794 to concert policy, and a national council summoned in 1797. This was a creative, conciliar body. Yet it made only a limited impact on the public, still bewildered by the range of religious options on offer and unable to grasp the new reality in France that Church and state had been split apart and faith officially stood independently of the political order. Public uninterest or downright hostility was also apparent in the Dutch United Provinces after the French occupation of 1795 led to the separation of

Church and state. The minority Remonstrant party most benefited; they sponsored an effort to unite all Dutch Protestants in 1796 but it failed miserably. Meanwhile, the first Constitution of the new Batavian Republic (the *Staatsregeling* of 1798) had little to say about religious matters and anticlerical, pro-French republicans were briefly in the ascendant.

The Churches in a militarised Europe

With most states variously engaged for continuous periods in war on revolutionary France, both against its contaminating republican ideology and its territorial ambitions, the concept of the Church militant took on new levels of meaning. In all these countries, forces were being raised, particularly volunteer and militia regiments for home defence. All these extra contingents had to have colours and ensigns issued to them, and these flags were blessed by the clergy at official ceremonies that functioned as displays of solidarity locking Church and state together in a common struggle. These services had occured earlier in the century, but not on the scale or with the urgent symbolic weight attached to them in the 1790s. Significantly, regimental colours were laid up in cathedrals and parish churches upon disbandment. Front-line troops also received unprecedented levels of spiritual blessing and practical assistance from the clergy acting as chaplains in the forces, both on land and at sea. In previous eighteenth-century conflicts chaplains (where present at all) were attached personally to the entourage of the leading generals and staff officers; contact with the ranks was exceptional.

That tended to change during the wars of 1793–1802. As armies expanded, governments interested themselves much more in chaplaincy appointments rather than leaving this form of patronage in the hands of private individuals. In Prussia, a new importance was attached to ensuring that the front-line army was well supplied with (Pietist) chaplains; in Britain a chaplain-general to the army was appointed for the first time at the head of a new Army Chaplains Department (1796). In the Royal Navy, efforts were made to ensure that every seventy-four-gun man-of-war had a chaplain on board, messing with the officers in the wardroom, taking regular services and acting as a medical assistant when the ship was in action. There was no shortage of volunteers. As one correspondent told the archbishop of Canterbury in 1793, 'the young clergy, in general, [are] so eager to go as chaplains on board the ships';[2] when a battleship sailed without a chaplain (as still frequently happened) the Admiralty took more

---

[2] Lambeth Palace Library, Moore Papers, vol. 5, f. 54, Mrs Anne Romand to Archbishop Moore.

pains than in previous conflicts to insist that the captain every Sunday accompanied his reading of the Articles of War to the assembled ship's company with a short service from the Book of Common Prayer. It was not just Anglicans who were served; in 1794, the first known Catholic chaplain to a British regiment, Alexander McDonnell, was appointed to the Glengarry Fencibles. In a limited but important sense, armies and navies thus affirmed their Christian character, in stark contrast to the revolutionary forces of France, which assaulted rather than employed priests, and whose men died on the battlefield deprived of spiritual comforts.

Individual clergy often wanted to bear arms in person against the French. It was a demand that the hierarchy and the governments behind them understood but they were still reluctant to put priests in uniform except in the most dire emergency. That description well sums up Britain's plight in 1797–8 when Ireland was threatened by Hoche's 15,000-embarked army, there was mutiny in the fleet, a run on the Bank of England's gold reserves and a fear that an invasion of the south coast was imminent. Additional volunteer troops were desperately required, especially to watch the English Channel, and the archbishop of Canterbury, John Moore, came under much pressure from the younger clergy desperate not to shirk their patriotic duty and keen to swop their cassocks for a scarlet tunic. The issue was only finally resolved at a meeting of the archbishop with other episcopal colleagues at Lambeth Palace on 28 April 1798, when it was decided that Anglican clergy would not be authorised to accept commissions or enrol in any militia corps. Such aggression would have been to the taste of a senior Spanish prelate, the archbishop of Saragossa. He even suggested to Godoy, the new minister and favourite of Charles IV, the raising of an army of priests and monks to push back the French invaders of 1794. The government did not act officially on the offer, leaving it up to individual clergy to act as partisans if they wished. They usually did. The clergy's role in moulding public opinion during the war of February 1793–August 1795 confirmed the hatred and fear of the French for both seculars and religious. The archpriest of Cottanello near Rieti was one of the terrifying guerilla leaders of north central Italy. This was a country where the Catholic flag was adopted by many guerilla bands, like the 'Christian Army' formed by the peasant leader Branda with two Capuchin friars as his lieutenants, and a bodyguard of priests armed with pitchforks, mattocks, pistols and a crucifix.

The classic setting for priests carrying muskets as well as the sacrament was the Vendée in north-western France between 1793 and 1795. Universally recognised as leaders of their village communities, their deportation and internment predated the rebellion as part of a campaign by republicans against a highly 'clericalised' countryside. Those who escaped the net (in the area around Fontenay-le-Comte, it has been estimated that only 24 per cent of refractory priests remained in place) mostly went to war with their flocks and showed their competence, like the abbé Barbotin in the capture of Cholet. After the seizure of Chemillé, he became 'Almoner of the Catholic Army' and gave mass absolution before combat. Then there was the abbé Bernier, who in the summer of 1793 helped give a much firmer basis to the structure of the Vendéen military and civil organisation, in conjunction with a returned *émigré*, the marquis de Lescure, the 'saint of Poitou'. He was a member of the 'Conseil Supérieur', the high command of the rebels, along with the former Benedictine, Pierre Jagault, and the abbé Guyot de Folleville.

The ultimate failure of the rebellion resulted in 'patriots' singling out the clergy for arrest and punishment, whether they had been part of the 'Royal and Catholic Army' or not: dechristianisation played its part in enabling the bleu leadership to look on their royalist opponents as dehumanised. At Nantes clerics were notoriously among the principal victims of the *noyades*: priests joined laymen in boats where they were tied together and deliberately sunk on the river Loire; hundreds more were left to rot in prison or, as in the port of Rochefort, in old slaving ships hastily converted into floating dungeons. At Avrillé in Anjou, numerous priests joined the Daughters of Charity and over 2,000 layfolk were put to death by revolutionary troops between January and April 1794 because of their adherence to the Catholic order. In the incessant guerilla war mounted just to the north, the *chouan* irregulars expected the nonjuring clergy to offer spiritual comforts and military leadership, to act as chaplains and commanding officers concurrently. Muffled church bells summoned the insurgents to arms, while pilgrimages and religious processions acted as a front for banditry and antirepublican flying columns.

The religious complexities of this militarised Europe were nowhere better highlighted than in Ireland where the parish clergy fanned discontents on both sides of the question and deployed religious rhetoric for whichever cause they favoured. Sectarian divisions were appreciably exacerbated after 1795: hopes of unrestricted Catholic relief were dashed when Lord Fitzwilliam's viceroyalty was cut short by Pitt's Cabinet after he had served less than six months in office. In the race to win Catholics' allegiance going on between Westminster and the United Irishmen, the Fitzwilliam affair gave the supporters of Wolfe Tone (the inspirational Protestant lawyer and young man about Dublin so keen to have Presbyterians and papists make common cause) the advantage, for the new lord-lieutenant, Earl Camden, lacked the political weight to sideline the Protestant hardliners in the Dublin Parliament. With Pitt and Dundas having other priorities, Ascendancy forces in Dublin Castle, newly resorted to power, reasserted themselves. In 1795–8, the United Irishmen and the Defenders on one side, the Orange Order on the other, confronted each other with Catholic and Protestant clergy often becoming organisationally involved despite the disapproval of the Roman and Anglican hierarchies in Ireland. Both were desperate to attract favourable notice and patronage from Pitt's government, and that entailed showing an unbending anti-French line. The opening of Maynooth Royal College in 1795 for the training of Catholic clergy was acclaimed by Edmund Burke's friend and its first president, Thomas Hussey, as 'the salvation of Ireland from Jacobinism and anarchy.'[3] The scale of the new Catholic cathedrals in Waterford (1793) and Cork (1799) said much about Catholic self-confidence, and its leaders were loath to jeopardise it by endorsing insurrection against the beleaguered British state.

However, the bishops found it much harder to influence the militants at parochial level, especially in areas of acute confessional and political tension such as northern Leinster and southern Ulster. Whereas the government and Archbishop Troy of Dublin were primarily concerned with reconciling and empowering propertied Catholics, the republican, non-sectarian nationalism of the United Irishmen reached out to the unenfranchised and the landless. For all Wolfe Tone's passionate belief that the United Irishmen should reconcile disadvantaged Presbyterians and Catholics, the numerical preponderance of the latter outside Ulster gave superficial credence to critics' charges that the organisation was basically a mechanism for imposing Catholic supremacy by treasonable means, calling on French assistance. It eventually came too little, too late when the 1798 Rebellion was on the point of collapse.

One of the paradoxes of this bloody affair was to find Catholic clergy looking on the republican French as religious liberators, precisely the opposite light in which they were seen in virtually every other area of Europe. One of these was the Dutch United Provinces, annexed by France in 1795. Here the parish clergy were initially content to preach acceptance of the new order as a welcome liberation from discrimination by the dominant Protestant majority. In Poland, some of the Catholic clergy participated in armed resistance to the state's dismemberment by its most powerful neighbours, Russia particularly. One of those involved in Kósciuszko's rising (1795) was Fr Franciszek Dmochowski (1762–1808), once a Piarist schoolteacher, whose identification with the national cause and social improvement would lead him to Protestantism and marriage. But Polish priests fighting in the front-line for the Church and national

---

[3] Quoted in D. Keogh, *'The French Disease'* (Dublin, 1993), 34. See also ibid., 41–2 for services and sermons of 1797 expressing relief at French failure to land a large army in Bantry Bay.

liberty were much fewer than in Ireland. Much to the embarrassment of Catholic bishops, about seventy priests were ready to take part in the 1798 rebellion. Fr Thomas Clinch had been suspended as a drunkard by his bishop and took his place on a large white horse wearing his vestments under his outdoor clothes with a menacing scimitar hanging from his broad cross belt. Fr Philip Roche acted as one of the generals of the Wexford army; he was captured and executed after the decisive battle of Vinegar Hill and his corpse thrown into the river by government forces; Fr Michael Murphy of Boolavogue was killed in the last charge of the day at Arklow on 9 June; Fr John Murphy was executed afterwards at Tullow. Many Catholic priests travelled some distances to join with General Humbert's small invasion force landing in County Mayo, though their motivation was complex and varied according to the individual. As for Humbert's troops, veterans of the supremely anticlerical army of Italy, they were disgusted to find themselves fighting for a fervently Catholic population. Many United Irishmen would have indeed been happy to see the Stuart Pretender Cardinal Henry of York, the *de jure* 'Henry IX', restored in 1798 and, much to Wolfe Tone's amazement, some members of the Directory were seriously ready to entertain the proposal if it could have led to the erection of Ireland as another French satellite state.

Revolution, war and new twists to religious conflict

With the French revolutionary armies defining themselves by their anti-Christian militancy, it was not surprising that their opponents used Christianity and the defence of the historic faith as a recruiting device. When combined with protection of the homeland against the French 'barbarians', it had a formidable potency both for those who enlisted and those who resented the threat – either realised or potential – to their family, their village and their personal identity, given as much by the Church in its rites of passage as by the state. Elite politicians and senior members of the hierarchy in every state played on these fears as much from a sense of personal conviction as one of self-preservation. So where French commanders did order their forces to desist from attacks on church buildings and clergy, the effect was to diminish the appeal of irregular resistance to the Republic's conquering armies. This happened in the 'Pacification of the Vendée' following General Hoche's destruction of the *émigré* army at Quiberon Bay in 1795; similarly, General Bonaparte used magnanimity in victory towards the Catholic Church as a weapon in the political reconstruction of Italy in the wake of his army's irresistible progress south from the Alps in 1796–8. His nominal political masters at home, the Directors, might remain committed to a repressive anticlericalism but Bonaparte preferred to court the Church, to persuade the clergy that he and his troops were not by definition their enemies. 'It is my ambition', he told the French agent in Rome, 'to be the saviour and not the destroyer of the Holy See.'[4] Bonaparte cleverly used the ideals of the French Republic – liberty, equality, fraternity – as comparable to those of Christianity and, to some extent, it caught on among the clergy rather than their people. This did not inhibit him from permitting his forces to loot churches and send home treasures to help pay for the war – the seizure of treasure at the shrine of Loreto near Ancona (the holy house of Nazareth flown across the sea by angels) was the most blatant example.

Another problem for Bonaparte was that several of the new Italian satellite republics were staffed by committed local Jacobins who were fervently anticlerical on the original 1793–4 model. Their provocative policies undid much of the moderation Bonaparte was aiming at, as the churches were turned into Jacobin clubs, religious statues were pulled down, processions were banned and anticlerical literature poured from the presses. Prelates were intimidated into public declarations of support when they could not evade it (the future pope Pius VII, Chiaramonti of Imola needed no compulsion in submitting to the republican government of Milan), and provision was made for electing parish priests. On 8 May 1798 the Cisalpine Republic nationalised church property and dissolved the remaining monasteries. If these policies lacked the viciousness of Jacobin France, they were onerous enough to keep alive the association between republicanism and an anti-Christian stance. They caused an upsurge in guerilla activity in 1798–9 and more widespread disobedience in society at large as religious fervour intensified: many visions of the Virgin Mary and the saints were reported in the 1790s. When the procession of the Madonna at Imola in April 1798 was banned, a crowd invaded the cathedral, carried out the image and had their procession just the same, forcing the government to give way. At Orvieto a truculent Roman Jacobin who was believed to have behaved irreverently to relics was savaged by the crowds, and murdered in the piazza.

Religious allegiance was a prime factor in defining individual and collective identity in the turbulent Europe of the 1790s. But whatever Burke and his supporters hoped, it should not be thought that a common Christian front prevailed during that decade. Denominational differences would not so readily be marginalised, and established confessions found enemies to their status everywhere. In Scotland, the General Assembly of

---

[4] Napoleon to Cacault, *Correspondence de Napoleon I* (32 vols., Paris, 1858–69), vol. II, 78–9.

the Kirk in 1799 condemned itinerant preachers, evangelists and Sunday Schools in one breath, revealing Moderate anxieties that they were all cover for radical political networking. In England, even as the established Church preached godly solidarity in the face of the threat from the French infidels, the clergy were concerned at the rapid growth of dissenting chapels in the neighbourhood of London with their 'pretended Gospel Preachers' not susceptible to official control. Clergyman like John Haggitt, fellow of Clare College, Cambridge, and vicar of Madingley, were not complacent, blaming divines for preaching pagan morality to the exclusion of the peculiar doctrines of Christianity, especially justification by faith, so that 'this majority [of the clergy] neither preach, nor know, the gospel of Salvation.'[5] It was perhaps less the teaching ministry of the Church which was causing the slide than its pastoral limitations. Lord Buckingham expressed his concern to Bishop Pretyman of Lincoln (Pitt's old tutor and secretary) in 1800 about the weakness of the established Church in his county. He mentioned 'the very rapid increase of Methodism in this district, from the exertions of licensed and unlicensed teachers encouraged by the non-residence of Incumbents & Curates'.[6] New legislation and new exertions by bishops and archdeacons afforded some remedy without ending the increased tensions that often marked Anglican–dissenting relations at the turn of the nineteenth century.

But these were muted compared to the sectarian furies unleashed by the 1798 Rebellion in Ireland and its aftermath, in which about 30,000 died. Communal recollection of previous outbreaks of inter-confessional violence (particularly the 1641 Ulster massacres) intensified the bitterness to a degree which shocked observers. They had exaggerated the degree of rapprochement between Catholics and Presbyterians in the United Irishmen and overlooked the persistence of peasant violence since the 1760s. Denominationalism and the long historical memories that fuelled it could not be so easily put off by the average Irishman. Once fighting broke out in May 1798 many Protestants reacted to the sectarian violence inflicted on them with retaliation in kind, particularly members of the Orange Order. They included the Revd Roger Owen, rector of Camolin, who preached at 'pitchcappings', at which a cap full of boiling tar was poured over the heads of rebels. Owen was eventually 'pitchcapped' in his turn. Moderates like the Catholic bishop of Wexford felt powerless at events: 'The People could not be described . . .

---

[5] John Haggitt, *A Sermon preached at the Visitation of the Hon. and Rt. Reverend the Lord Bishop of Ely, at Cambridge, 12 June 1799* (London, 1800), 4, 20.
[6] 25 April 1800, BL Add. MS. 59003, ff. 31–4.

in reality the Devil was roaring among them...they would make it a religious War which would ruin them'.[7] However, the authors of some recent local studies, notably Kevin Whelan,[8] would very much like to believe that sectarianism was the product rather than the cause of the 1798 rebellion, and that in the first instance it was a political rising influenced by French principles and led by the United Irishmen.

At the time, the rebellion was deliberately presented by Protestant Ultras anxious to buttress the agencies of their Ascendancy as a popish conspiracy to return Ireland to Roman Catholic thraldom. The inflammatory, populist tome of Sir Richard Musgrave, linking the events of 1798 with earlier risings against Irish Protestants, persuaded its many readers. Its propaganist thrust gained the author a fame nothing in his career to date (he had been an Irish MP since 1778) had foreshadowed. Most of Pitt's Cabinet were not taken in. For them the lesson of the 1798 rebellion was that security considerations must be uppermost, and no amount of Protestant polemic would deflect Pitt and Dundas from imposing a parliamentary Union on Ireland, a settlement that included the parallel creation of the 'United Church of England & Ireland'. The ineffective Camden was replaced as Irish lord-lieutenant by the experienced imperial proconsul, Marquess Cornwallis; he took with him clear instructions to show leniency to Catholics with a view to including their final civil emancipation in the Union proposals. Thus Cornwallis visited Munster in 1799, where he tried hard to exhibit fairness to Roman Catholics and it paid off in terms of pro-Union addresses.

Despite the bloodcurdling bombast of Musgrave and his ilk, Irish Protestant opinion after the rebellion was no more of a monolith than it had ever been; educated Church of Ireland moderates were aware that their Catholic counterparts had stood apart from the rising and were as anti-French and pro-monarchist as they were themselves. Of course, rebellion had strengthened the conservative strands in Irish Protestantism, but these other voices could be heard and were heeded. Thus Burke's former follower, Lord Minto, set out a balanced, forceful and moderate view of Catholics in a speech of 1799 in the Westminster House of Lords that was published in Ireland and sold well. Good inter-faith relations somehow persisted in several parts of Ireland. Many Irish Protestants remained in favour of Catholic emancipation, as in County Wexford where Lord Ely, leader of the Whig interest, got on well with propertied Catholics.

---

[7] Quoted in J. C. D. Clark, 'The English Atlantic Empire, 1660–1800', in E. E. Rice (ed.), *Revolution and Counter-Revolution* (Oxford, 1991), 27–94, at 71.

[8] Kevin Whelan, *'The Tree of Liberty': Radicalism, Catholicism and the Construction of Irish Identity* (Cork, 1996).

Electoral considerations undoubtedly played their part, for Catholics could vote in parliamentary elections even though they could not yet stand as candidates themselves. In the event, Pitt's poor planning and George III's obdurate refusal to breach his coronation oath doomed the government's bid to include Catholic emancipation as part of the Act of Union, and the question would simmer uneasily for another three decades. Despite this omission and despite the 1798 rebellion, attitudes at the top had changed beyond recall: British elite politicians could no longer plausibly present Catholics as *ipso facto* potential traitors. Catholics could be patriots too when political ideology not religion defined loyalty, as Pitt argued in his resignation letter to George III of 31 January 1801. In line with this thinking, the Irish under-secretary, Edward Cooke, had brought a draft to London the previous summer of new Test Laws, one for Catholics and one for Anglicans. The draft would be discarded but the idea stood.

The Revolutionary War as a religious war?

The conflict beginning in 1792 was widely interpreted as a cultural struggle as much as a military one, with both sides drawing on competing ideologies to galvanise citizens and subjects in the struggle for supremacy. As seen above, a high proportion of clergy were happy to offer their services – and their faith – under the broad banner of counter-revolution. How far, then, can the Revolutionary war of 1792–1801 down to the Treaties of Lunéville and Amiens be regarded as, in a fundamental sense, a conflict between religion and irreligion? As far as the governments were concerned, to a strictly limited degree. In that respect, it was similar to previous conflicts ostensibly based on confessional acrimony – like the Thirty Years' War of the seventeenth century – where, as recent historians have repeatedly emphasised, the frenzied language of religious division barely concealed the *Realpolitik* of the several protagonists. Likewise, in the 1790s, strategic interests never ceased to be paramount at ministerial level, with states making peace when it suited their requirements rather than committing themselves open-endly to a crusade or holy war against revolutionary France. That was the language reserved for popular consumption. British ministers did nothing to deter journalists and clergy from presenting the war, as the Foxite lawyer Thomas Erskine put it, as one designed to 'save religion and its holy altars from prophanation'. He accepted that, despite being a sham (in Whig terms), it had worked: 'How it could succeed, for a moment, in an enlightened age, and with a nation of Christians, will probably be considered hereafter as one of the most remarkable events which has distinguished this age of wonders.'[9] This was only half the story at Cabinet level. Deep-rooted though their commitment to the restoration of the Bourbon monarchy and the extirpation of Jacobinism was, British Cabinet ministers like Grenville and William Windham knew that more pragmatic considerations of the British national interest were required by Pitt. Hence his willingness to defy Burke and send the *doyen* of the diplomatic corps, Lord Malmesbury, to negotiate a peace with the Directory at Lille in 1796–7. Francis II of Austria was likewise unwillingly to sign a blank cheque to protect the papacy against the French invader and play the role of 'the born Protector of the Church' that Pius VI required of him as Holy Roman Emperor in 1795. The emperor's foreign minister, Baron Thugut, was more concerned with the survival of the Habsburg Empire than with the successor of St Peter, and was brazenly willing to demand territory in the papal Legations as the price for protecting Rome. It made military sense, but it outraged the pontiff. Pitt's government also found itself acting as diplomatic ringmaster. International rivalries based on, for instance, the dismemberment of Poland were, in practice, a higher priority for Austria, Prussia and Russia, however much they professed abhorrence of the regicide French Republic. British diplomats did their best to keep allies, past and potential, up to the mark, but it took them four years to construct the Second Coalition (1799) after the collapse of the First. Clearly, there were definite limits for most regimes to keep fighting France once it was apparent, as it was by 1794–5, that over-throwing the Republic would take a sustained effort to accomplish. So countries changed sides much as they had done in previous European wars, Spain making peace with France under the Treaty of Basle in July 1795 then converting it into a defensive alliance under the San Ildefonso Treaty of August 1796. Thus the papal secretary of state, Cardinal Busca, may have wanted in December 1796 'to declare a war of religion against the French, who have turned against God, destroyed the Church in their country, maltreated and killed its ministers, and try by propaganda and arms to spread their errors',[10] but which Catholic power would take up his offer? Even Protestant Britain, on whom the pope and his advisers had by now come so much to depend, was bent on negotiating a settlement.

---

[9] Hon. Thomas Erskine, *A View of the Causes and Consequences of the Present War with France* (2nd edn, London, 1797), 55.

[10] Alan J. Reinerman, 'The Papacy, Austria and the Anti-French Struggle in Italy, 1792–1797', in Kinley Brauer and William E. Wright (eds.), *Austria in the Age of the French Revolution* (Washington, D.C., 1990), 47–68, at 61.

That said, ordinary men and women, living in an essentially rural continent, still defined themselves in the 1790s more in religious than in national terms, and the imposition of an irreligious, foreign culture was unacceptable. Elite politicians knew this as well as anyone. That was why they were happy to deploy the language of uncompromising Burkean enmity to Jacobinism when it suited their current political objectives, knowing that it would be echoed from thousands of pulpits and the cry taken up in the marketplace. Mobilising a people in the 1790s required politicians to have recourse to religious commonplaces and slogans. It was, quite literally, the only language that many people understood and, irrespective of how much or how little they grasped the finer points of their Christian faith and the economy of salvation it offered them, it defined their culture as nothing else yet did, and commonly provided the only infrastructure for whatever education or charitable relief might dignify their existence. As Bishop Samuel Horsley noted in his Charge to the clergy of the Rochester diocese in 1796, the great advantage of religion was that 'Popular opinion, with respect to the superiority of Christianity over every other Religion, is fortunately on the side of Truth.'[11] So given this fundamental dimension to the lives of the rural majority, patriotism necessarily had to be defined in quasi-religious terms or it would have aroused precious few to repel the invader from their homeland. Another senior bishop of the Church of England, Beilby Porteus, put the conservative case succinctly in a Charge delivered to the clergy of the London diocese in 1798–9: 'Those who are hostile to the British constitution are almost always hostile to the Christian revelation.'[12] The higher reaches of European society may have cooled in its Christian profession over the previous few decades (or, rather, have taken up new forms of spiritual expression), but the rural masses, as the experience of 1792– 1801 indicated, were still stubbornly attached to a pre-Enlightenment version of Christian culture, and it was one that proved remarkably resilient.

The revolt of the Vendée took on the character of a religious crusade. All the symbolism associated with it proclaimed as much with the universal wearing of the Sacred Heart and crosses, often combined with the royalist white cockade. The Sacred Heart, as a Vendéen curé exclaimed in 1793: 'is the livery and distinctive mark of Catholicism, just as the tricolour ribbon and medal of the federation are for adherents

---

[11] Samuel Horsley, *A Charge Delivered to the Clergy of the Diocese of Rochester* (London, 1796), 22.

[12] Beilby Porteus, *A Charge Delivered to the Clergy of the Diocese of London in the Years 1798 and 1799* (London, 1799), 15n.

of the new regime, like intruded priests and other constitutionalists'.[13]

By the spring of 1793 a 'Royal and Catholic Army' had taken shape, one
whose military culture was at the opposite pole to the republican forces
in the field against it. This one sang hymns and canticles as it marched,
and adopted the Marseillaise as an anthem but only with revised words
suitable for a Christian soldiery; they stopped frequently to pray, and
carried standards decorated with the image of the Blessed Virgin Mary.
Two chaplains in the centre of the army carried the holy sacrament and
communion vessels, closely guarded by 100 well-armed men when they
went into battle, for these were the energising emblems of a holy war
belonging to a force that came to think of itself in Old Testament terms
as the host of Israel. The deep religiosity of the Vendéen rebels gave them
confidence that death in the struggle would lead quickly to the rewards
of eternity. As one verse in the *Marseillaise des Blancs* put it:

> This death with which they menace us
> Will only be the end of our troubles.
> For when we see God face to face.
> His hand will bless our efforts.[14]

In the end, the Catholic and Royal Army was overwhelmed by superior,
better-equipped forces, a defeat that forced all the survivors to try to
explain this apparent token of divine disfavour. One priest ascribed God's
wrath towards the 'Whites' (as the counter-revolutionaries were known,
after the colour of their uniforms) for the frequent murder of republican
prisoners, betraying a ruthlessness far removed from the Gospel spirit.
Most survivors were too bewildered to go further into the matter and,
after the Quiberon Bay disaster, the crusading vigour drained away from
all but a minority who could not bring themselves to compromise with
the Directory.

A militant, populist Catholicism fuelled the revolt of the Vendée.
Elsewhere in Europe, it inspired ordinary people to arm and organise
themselves against a foreign invader and his acolytes bent on forcibly
rooting up a popular religious culture. The archbishop of Mainz was
genuinely popular to an extent he may not have appreciated until the
warm personal reception accorded him on his brief restoration in 1793.

---

[13] Quoted in F. Lebrun, *Histoire des Catholiques en France du XVIe siècle à nos jours* (Paris, 1980), 255.

[14] Quoted in Jean de Viguerie, 'La Vendée et les lumières: les origines intellectuelles de l'extermination', in Yves-Marie Bercé et al. (eds.), *La Vendée dans l'histoire* (Paris, 1994), 36–51, at 46.

Holy sites became recruiting posts for the counter-revolution, as the desire to make pilgrimages grew, often to places associated with reports of new apparitions and wonder-working miracles. The French authorities did not find it easy to halt these practices they correctly linked with sedition. At Herschwiesen in the Rhineland a force of French soldiers moved in to destroy a shrine and were stoned by a crowd of 4,000 which had gathered for ceremonies of exorcism and healing. At Alatri in the Roman Republic the population embroidered Our Lady of Victory on their flags and a priest in the town (July 1798) issued a call to holy war in the face of the Jacobin Republic: 'My fellow-citizens, if you do not assemble with all possible force to maintain the Catholic faith, we are lost. Remember that in past ages God gave victory to men who fought for their religion.'[15] These powerful feelings cemented a working alliance between loyalism and religion as nothing else could; it was emphatically on display in Naples in 1794 and again in 1799.

In the Austrian Netherlands, the Tyrol and Spain in this decade opposition to French invasion partly resembled a religious crusade for all those irregulars who participated. The Tyrolians imitated the Vendéens by dedicating their land in 1796 to the protection of the Sacred Heart of Jesus. It tended to be a ruthless, one-sided contest. Priest-led peasants who rose up in the Catholic mountain districts of Switzerland early in 1798 protesting at French annexation and the creation of the Helvetic Republic were massacred; the Belgian peasant uprising against the Jourdan law of conscription (September 1798) was bloodily suppressed and resulted in the mass proscription of the Belgian clergy (7,500 in all) who had earlier shown no desire to submit to the oath of 5 September 1797 imposed by the Directory requiring them to hate both monarchy and anarchy. Priests and peasants were not strategists or tacticians, but their inadequate organisation was partially compensated by a determination to protect their religion and their patrimony (such as it was) from violation. They were not always trounced by the regular troops sent against them. The *Sanfedisti*, the peasant army of the Holy Faith about 17,000 strong, led by Cardinal Ruffo, drove the French from southern Italy in 1799, and overthrew the satellite Parthenopean Republic in collaboration with Nelson's fleet. Ruffo shared the hardships of his troops – the *armata christiana* – and took every advantage of the rugged terrain. There could be an ugly, anti-Semitic side to this violence. In June 1799 anti-revolutionary peasant forces from Arezzo known as the *Viva Maria* plundered the ghetto in Siena and, after the garrison had surrendered,

---

[15] Quoted in O. Chadwick, *The Popes and European Revolution* (Oxford, 1981), 472.

took their revenge on the Jews who had benefited from the protection of the French army: thirteen were burnt alive on the toppled Tree of Liberty in the Piazza del Campo.

In as much as one can speak of an underlying common identity between movements such as the Vendéen rebels, the *Sanfedisti*, the United Irishmen and the Catalans, religion provided it. In Ireland, the insurgency and counter-insurgency of the late 1790s recalled the Vendée in its fury and the scale of the blood-letting, with Dublin Castle under Cornwallis and chief secretary Castlereagh finding it desperately hard to extinguish sectarian animosities in the countryside. In all these places, religion kept alive resentment of an alien political culture which threatened the faith witness of local commutities. The bonds between the parochial clergy and the rural laity could be exceptionally close. Priests were at the head of the village hierarchy and could not easily hazard a responsive leadership role, often submitting to a local preference for direct action irrespective of more cautious advice from the bishops. There is thus an indisputable sense in which at a popular level Catholicism and counter-revolution went together in the 1790s, and even Napoleon, in his concordatory settlements, had limited success in splitting them apart. Wherever the principles of the French Revolution took root, the Catholic Church was dispossessed of its social prominence, and it was only to be expected that its leaders would make common cause with the monarchs who had suffered a comparable loss. But, in the last analysis, religion was overwhelmingly the motor of the counter-revolution rather than royalism, a fact that that Louis XVIII and his advisers might find embarrassing but could not easily ignore in their calculations. Such was the scale and violence of this culture clash that elites and masses alike could only make sense of it in apocalyptic terms.

Revolution, counter-revolution and millennialism at the close of the eighteenth century

The watchmen of our religious establishment have a great charge upon their hands at this important time, when the *signs of the times* prove the hour of peril to be at no great distance.[16]

Despite, or perhaps because of, the Enlightenment the language, phraseology and content of the Bible maintained a cultural dominance across Europe into the 1790s. Even a non-Christian such as Voltaire, the accomplished enemy of the Church, was utterly steeped in scripture;

---

[16] *The London Review* (November 1796), 331.

his own – sceptical – interest in the prophetic books of the Old and New Testaments such as Isaiah, Daniel and Revelation continued a trend upheld by most intellectual giants of the immediate past, including his hero, Sir Isaac Newton. In a non-secular society like eighteenth-century Europe, the Bible was the automatic first recourse for men and women of every degree of literacy to make sense of their troubled times. Even revolutionary sympathisers saw what was going on in France in millennial terms, as a new dawn for humanity that would result in a degree of social harmony previously unknown. Precisely because of the promise it seemed to contain for the betterment of mankind, and themselves in particular, British Unitarian Christians did not lose faith in the Revolution despite its bloody excesses. For groups like them, a secular heaven-on-earth of progress was prognosticated by the forward movement of history towards social and political improvement; they could afford to overlook apparent setbacks at the hands of intolerant religious establishments.

Both revolutionary and counter-revolutionary discourses thus readily expressed themselves in millennial terms in which the prophetic and the political were often indistinguishable. Such a trend was not novel, but the scale of their expression during the 1790s was unprecedented. Most political crises in the course of the eighteenth century had a prophetic dimension to them. It was articulated in the revolt of the thirteen North American colonies against Britain when the hand of the Antichrist was commonly believed to be at work; more than one seditious American clergymen in 1775 had identified him as George III. A millennial strand was inseparable from popular religion in which the hope of a better future was readily extended to those on the social margins. Millenarian religion had an inclusive character that naturally appealed to the poor, the destitute and to women. More than one prophetess had joined Lord George Gordon in his antipopery crusade of 1780; another millenarian, Margaret Nicholson, had been released from Bedlam in 1785 only to try to assassinate George III the next year.

The French Revolution accordingly erupted into a world of gathering millennial excitement; the hopes for human progress articulated in the Enlightenment were, for most Europeans, only expressible using inspired, loosely scriptural language even when there was either an explicit denial or no implicit reference back to the Christian scheme of things. The *Illuminati* and growing number of Swedenborgians in London and other European capitals saw the events of the 1790s as confirmation of their divining of the future. Revolutionary apologists such as Tom Paine wanted to act as its midwives, as his incendiary, best-selling *The Rights of Man* made blatantly clear. Paine hailed the present time as an age of 'universal reformation' in which 'everything may be looked for'.[17]

It was precisely that uncertainty which so alarmed the states going to war with revolutionary France. Young people caught the feverish aspect of the decade and felt at home with its promise and uncertainty, while poets and pamphleteers had ready recourse to the millennial idiom. Samuel Taylor Coleridge wrote the prophetical poem 'Religious Musings' casting the French Revolution as the stormy apocalypse; he was a rational dissenter like Price, Priestley and Gilbert Wakefield and had, like them, consumed much energy in trying to unscramble the prophetical books of scripture and so make some sense of the present. Revolution and Revelation were intimately linked as handmaidens of what Coleridge hoped would be a 'blest future'. Most Romantic authors did not want this future to be atheistic. They looked, rather, for the recasting of religion along less worldly lines through a new Reformation, which would dispossess the Church and the clergy to achieve the religious renewal for which they longed. No one hoped more for the coming of the New Jerusalem than William Blake, with his theosophy set in a Swedenborgian background. His religiosity has not been easy to align with conventional Christianity for, as Blake wrote, 'To defend the Bible in this year 1798 would cost a man his life. The Beast & Whore rule without control.'[18] In other words, the Churches disseminated false scriptural teachings, which was itself a sign that the Antichrist had returned to hold the world in thrall. While Blake rejected the Church as presently constituted as beyond redemption, he nevertheless still looked to Christ as God, who would, in the fullness of time, accomplish a social transformation.

In England the Revolution evoked memories of the radicals of the mid-seventeenth century and the social levelling of the Anabaptists, especially as plebian converts believing themselves called on to speak out publicly also considered that their certainty of salvation absolved them from the usual moral constraints. Their number included the agrarian reformer, Thomas Spence, who habitually used scriptural language and became convinced that 'God was a very notorious Leveller.'[19] Politicians could not afford to ignore the trend. Pitt countered reformist prophetic pamphlets

---

[17] Thomas Paine, *The Rights of Man, being an answer to Mr Burke's attack on the French Revolution*, pt 1 (London, 1791), preface.

[18] Marginal comments in his copy of Bishop Walton's published critique of Tom Paine, quoted in David V. Erdman, *Blake, Prophet against Empire: A Poet's Interpretation of the History of his own Times* (Princeton, 1954), 276.

[19] Quoted in Iain McCalman, *Radical Underworld: Prophets, Revolutionaries and Pornographers in London, 1795–1840* (Oxford, 1988), 63.

by sponsoring a counter-prophetic line in tracts such as *A Prophecy of the French Revolution and the Downfall of Anti Christ*, which insisted on the providential benignity which had given Britain 'inestimable blessings' in Church and state.

Millenarian tendencies moved from spiritual to sacred and back again. When neither politicians nor higher clergy appeared capable of offering plausible guidance to the times, distracted ordinary people looked to anyone who came along offering reassurance or the promise of a better future. Many unscrupulous operators saw the commercial potential of this market. In the mid-1790s 'Prophecy men' travelled around Ulster and Connacht carrying with them new radical publications, broadly sympathetic to the Defenders and the United Irishmen but using a language and tone familiar to anyone conversant with the last book of the New Testament. In 1795 alone, three books of prophecies were published in Belfast, two in Strabane and one in Monaghan. All sold out quickly.

Women read and listened to the prophecies of this decade, and the number of prophetesses was high. The contrast of the opportunities offered to them in this field with the limited recognition accorded to their ministry in any of the mainstream Churches could hardly have been starker. In England, the most influential female prophet was Joanna Southcott, the 'Lamb's wife' (she confused her identity with the woman of Revelation, a biblical figure), who believed herself pregnant with the spiritual man, Shiloh. So did those thousands of others who hung on every word she uttered, and viewed the poor harvests of 1799 and 1800 as retribution for those who ignored her. She had her French equivalent. Pierre Pontard, Constitutional bishop of the Dordogne, had founded the *Journal prophétique* to report the prophecies of some Lyon millenarians to a wider audience, but it became the vehicle for his *protégé*, the Périgourdin prophetess Suzette Labrousse, who was alleged to have declared that the Civil Constitution was truly the work of God since she had prophesied it eleven years before. She also predicted the imminent resurrection of the first dauphin (d. 1789) and Mirabeau.

It was not just women and political radicals who scanned the scriptures in the 1790s; the clergy of most countries decked out their sermons with reference to the portents and signs of the times. Prophecy was a serious academic undertaking, and one that the clergy were unable to ignore since their congregations – high-ranking, middling sort or rural poor – all expected it of them. The unparalleled events of the Revolution ensured that its appeal stretched across the social hierarchy. Even Lord Malmesbury, the greatest British diplomat of his generation, copied out part of a religious discourse preached on Revelation chapter 16 in 1701 by Robert

Fleming, estimating its fulfilment in 1794. In the light of dechristianisation and the French advance into Italy, British theologians were obliged
to re-examine the habitual assumption that the papacy was to be associated with the beast in Revelation. That throne had appeared to be
tottering even before republican armies crossed the Alps. According to
one British observer in 1794, 'Many think that the papal power will expire
in him [Pius VI]; and observe, with apparent pleasure, that the niches in
St. Paul's church are now filled up, except one destined for the reception
of the portrait of Braschi.'[20]

The exile of Pius VI in 1798 and the fall of Rome sent preachers back
to their Bibles with alacrity, confident that the end of the century would
usher in the last days and the return of Christ in glory. Protestant apologists felt thoroughly vindicated and found it impossible to resist a note of
triumphalism that the historic enemy had been overthrown. Basil Wood,
a member of the Eclectic Society, invoked the memory of earlier victims of 'popery' in a sermon of 1798: 'How would it have gladdened the
dying moments of Ridley, Latimer, and Cranmer, and the noble army
of martyrs, who bled at the stake in this country, could they, when en-
circled with devouring flames, have looked forward to this auspicious
day!'[21] All sorts of possibilities appeared conceivable following Pius' humiliation: Louis Dutens, an Anglican priest and a Protestant from Tours,
hoped that the overthrow of the papacy could be the prelude to an ecumenical council which would reunite Christendom, but these views
in *Considérations théologiques sur les moyens de réunir les Eglises* (London,
1798) found almost no echoes among either Catholics or Protestants:
many of the latter equated the collapse of papal prestige with missionary opportunity. The majority of commentators still thought in terms of
toppling Antichrist from his throne, even a thoroughly orthodox high
churchman like Charles Daubeny, who believed the way was clear for
the re-establishment of primitive Christianity. Amid the fevered prog-
nostications, there could be discerned a wave of sympathy for the human
predicament of the holy father, sent off to die in exile in Valence. Claims
that the Antichrist should really be associated with Napoleon Bonaparte
rather than Pius VI rose appreciably. In France itself, in the face of exile
and dispossession of the country's Christian heritage, theologians tended
to see no hope for the Church through human resources alone. For the
Dominican, Bernard Lambert, the new age could not come fast enough.

---

[20] Robert Gray, M. A., *Letters during the course of a tour through Germany, Switzerland and Italy in the Years MDCCXCI, and MDCCXCII with Reflections on the Manners, Literature, and Religion of those Countries* (London, 1794), 375.

[21] Quoted in Andrew Robinson, 'Identifying the Beast: Samuel Horsley and the Problem of Papal AntiChrist', *JEH* 43 (1992), 592–607, at 601.

He decided that the Terror was the apostasy of the gentiles which prefigured the conversion of the Jews and the expansion of the universal Church. 'Let us hasten by our prayers and desires this happy revolution,' he exclaimed in a popular tract.[22] The ready resort to millennial language reflected the polarising effect of the Revolution on religion and politics alike. It was not an easy decade for religious moderates to express themselves in most European states.

The religious centre ground in the 1790s

As war swept the continent, the interest in religious reforms evinced by many states in the 1780s faded away. Politicians discouraged ecclesiological alteration, frowned on doctrinal debate, and mostly dropped such support as they had shown for moderate reformers and an independent-minded clergy; Jansenists in Spain and Italy, and latitudinarians in England, all found the flow of patronage dried up as the centre ground was squeezed. Thus the support of English Unitarians for the principles of the French Revolution was enough to damn their prospects of receiving a legal toleration. Former radical Anglican prelates like Watson of Llandaff now toed the line, publishing in 1793 a sermon on 'The Wisdom and Goodness of God in having made Rich and Poor', the appendix of which, highly critical of France for having abandoned constitutional monarchy in favour of a republic, attracted astringent notice from the young and pro-Jacobin William Wordsworth. Governments in the 1790s unhesitatingly exploited the Erastian inheritance of the Reformation Churches, whether they were episcopal or presbyterian in their traditions. Protestant Church leaders whose countries were at war with France were under pressure from above to rally their flocks in the loyalist cause and few failed to heed the call of patriotic duty. Interestingly, once peace returned, as in Prussia after 1795, then the spirit of religious reformation could be rekindled surprisingly quickly (see, chapter 7, below).

Since change had become associated with Jacobin politics, those who hankered after implementing schemes for Church or liturgical reform found that wartime was not the occasion to recommend them to the public. The young Habsburg emperor, Francis II, confirmed his late uncle Leopold's halt to ecclesiastical upheaval: he required the clergy to support the war effort with their words as well as their money and he could not afford to rekindle mistrust. Thus in 1802 he agreed to reopen some

---

[22] *Avertissement aux fidèles, sur les signes qui annoncent que tout se dispose pour le retour d'Israël, . . . etc.* (1793). See François Dupuigrenet Desroussilles, *Dieu en Son Royaume. La Bible dans le France d'autrefois XIIIe–XVIII siècles* (Paris, 1991), 140.

Hungarian monasteries suppressed some two decades earlier. There was, however, no attempt to unstitch the Josephite inheritance completely, for Francis still looked on priests as civil servants in cassocks, and state interference in Church affairs persisted. There was a perception that the quality of candidates for holy orders was declining, so the Habsburg state introduced reforms in theology teaching and the administration of seminaries rather than wait for the episcopate to take decisive action.

In France, the second half of the 1790s brought many clergy of the Constitutional Church out from hiding. Their leader, Bishop Henri Grégoire, had 6,000 unmarried priests left scattered across France, and many of these were marked down for assassination by Jacobins or nonjuring extremists. Indeed, a royalist death-squad murdered Audrein, the regicide Constitutional bishop of the Finistère, in November 1800. So Grégoire had an uphill task. His 'United Bishops', the governing body of the Constitutional Church, drew on the talents of men such as Le Coz, bishop of Rennes, the Catholic Girondin as he has been called, who never seems to have lost faith in the possibilities of the Enlightenment. His definition of the Church of Jesus Christ to his diocesan synod of 1799 has a wider application to the Constitutional Church as a whole, and showed how, under pressure of events as much as from conviction, it had moved from Catholicism towards *de facto* congregationalism: 'a religious society, in which citizens submissive to the laws of their government agree to offer to God worship both pure and sublime'.[23] Grégoire produced a periodical, the *Annales de la Religion*, as a means of connecting up his scattered clergy and people, and there was a renewed effort to find inspiration in the Jansenist roots of the Church. Slowly, in the late 1790s, a hierarchy of clerical assemblies was put in place to include both metropolitan and departmental synods, and a great deal of reliance was placed on a new intermediate authority – the archpriest, 'the eye of the bishop' – elected by a synod. The principle of election was still held dear by members of the Constitutional Church, but it was restricted to their own numbers rather than extended to the public as a whole. The national council of 1797 affirmed the principle of election for priests but departed from the Civil Constitution in declaring that all electors had to be adult male Catholics, the 'priesthood of the baptised'.

There was much stress on episcopal authority by the 'United Bishops'. The majority of Constitutional bishops already in office visited their dioceses with renewed zeal between 1796 and 1801, confirming, baptising and confessing, and the results were encouraging. The physical presence

---

[23] Quoted in N.-D. Chaline et al., *L'Eglise de France et la Révolution* (Paris, 1983), 54.

of the bishops also helped contain the presbyterian sympathies (part of the Richerist inheritance of the Constitutional Church) that remained dear to many parish priests throughout the period from 1795 to 1802. The 'United Bishops' were at their most creative in reshaping the worshipping life of their Church, including the translation of the liturgy into French. Not everyone was happy with it; more conservative members of the Church feared presciently it would give ammunition to their more numerous opponents in the refractory communion. Nevertheless, it was used in the Versailles diocese from 1799 and was grudgingly approved after extended debate by the second national council of 1801. Their meetings were a testimony to Grégoire's creativity within a broad Gallican framework and gave Church members some chance to participate in the decision-making process, even if the policy recommendations of the prelates were usually passed with few or no amendments.

The Constitutional Church leadership was ready in principle to work more closely with the refractories, though a formal agreement was never a possibility. Grégoire might in the *Annales de la Religion* urge reconciliation wherever possible, but the majority of his supporters were disinclined to go so far, or pay any attention to the peace feelers of the national council of 1797. The refractory party, feeling it had the numerical advantage, was not interested in launching any initiative designed to heal the schism. Neither would the Directory court Grégoire. It criticised both the expulsion of married clergy from their benefices, and the Constitutionalists' condemnation of obligatory observance of the *décadi*; it forbade local synods like the one convoked in Toulouse in June 1798 and, for good measure, banned publication of the *Annales* in 1798 as a vehicle for disseminating fanatical and retrograde ideas (although it somehow continued to appear). Recurrent internal squabbles and government indifference make Grégoire's achievement the more impressive. But there remained major limitations. His Church was weak in the countryside (there were numerous *départements* in which the Gregorien 'Church of France' was not represented), and it offered little to that vital constituency – women. As Olwen Hufton has pointed out, 'it was the determined boycott by women of the schismatic constitutional church between 1796 and 1801 which determined its ultimate demise'.[24]

Outside France, there were small but influential numbers of Catholics who were ready to accept that the republican regime in Paris was there to stay. For a time, in the mid-1790s, it seemed as if Pius VI himself might

---

[24] O. Hufton, 'The Reconstruction of a Church, 1796–1801', in G. Lewis and C. Lucas (eds.), *Beyond the Terror: Essays in French Regional and Social History, 1794–1815* (Cambridge, 1983), 21–52 at 23.

be moving towards that position. With Bonaparte's army of Italy poised to move against Rome, and well knowing how the Directory viewed the papacy as the symbol of resistance to French republican power, concessions were timely if a march on Rome was to be staved off. The papal brief *Pastoralis sollicitudo* (5 July 1796) proclaimed that subjects owed submission to established governments. It was an important breakthrough that was not to the taste of extremists on either side. Royalist refractories, aware of the pressure on Pius after the fall of Bologna to the army of Italy, claimed it was a forgery; die-hard republicans said the same. But clerical moderates in Italy took comfort from it. There, Jansenists among the parochial clergy had always been a minority, and the combination first of the dissemination of revolutionary principles, then of the French invasion of the peninsula made it hard for these moderates to maintain the faith. The revival of the Constitutional Church in 1795–6 came just in time to keep the flame alive for enlightened clergy sympathetic to Grégoire's politico-religious ideals and the Jansenist tradition, like Fr Eustachio Degola of Genoa, a friend of the disgraced Bishop Ricci and a talented journalist himself. Writing in the *Annali Ecclesiastici* (1797) he urged like-minded priest colleagues to take up manual labour to keep themselves from destitution and not allow hunger to make their pastoral work impossible.

Degola was one of several better-educated parish priests who persisted in seeing the Revolution as the opportunity to modernise the Church, eliminate anomalies and introduce greater social equality, earning themselves the name of 'Catholic democrats' in the process. Their message had a continuing appeal to the young ordinands entrusted to their care; at Milan the seminarians planted a Tree of Liberty in the quadrangle which was blessed by the dean following a patriotic speech while, in Genoa, many of the clergy encouraged the practice of taking new-born babies to the Tree of Liberty. At Taranto, Archbishop Giuseppe Capecelatro provocatively sported the republican cockade and began to sign himself 'Citizen Archbishop'. When the Austrians reoccupied Piedmont, about 3 per cent of the clergy were penalised as Jacobins for having taken an oath to the previous revolutionary regime. The newly installed revolutionary authorities did their best to encourage such 'patriotic' commitments. Jacobin administrators threw their weight against that majority of the hierarchy in Italy which would not adjust to the changed order, like the bishop of Comacchio in the Cisalpine republic who was refused entry to his diocese in mid-1797 as he had not been elected by the people. This political interference verging on intimidation was quickly condemned by the majority of other prelates who remained unreconciled to the presence of the French army in the peninsula and the Jacobin regimes that had been planted in their wake. For them, Bonaparte was a second Attila the Hun, ravaging Italy and despoiling Rome. This episcopal stance renewed the alliance between the Bishops and the country clergy, and brought home to progressive priests based in the towns the scale of their isolation. It was typical that when Florence was taken by royalist bands in mid-1799 they locked up all the Jansenists they could find as probable French sympathisers, prominent among them the retired Bishop Ricci himself. His disciple, Giovanni Andrea Serrao, bishop of Potenza in the kingdom of Naples (1782–99), who had acted as the civil commissioner of Potenza in the Parthenopean Republic, was singled out when Ruffo's *Sanfedisti* burst into the town in February 1799 and was murdered in his bed.

The overthrow of the papacy in February 1798 led to the creation of a Roman Republic which, unsurprisingly, attracted only minority support from the clergy, including the friars of San Lorenzo in Lucina who insisted in the pulpit that the coup was not contrary 'to our Roman Catholic religion, or to the discipleship of the gospel, or to the doctrines of the Catholic Church'.[25] Whether this was said from conviction or as a tactical ploy, the anticlerical conduct of the Roman Republic in 1798–9 placed moderate clergy in the city under unrelenting pressure. In July 1798 the Republic closed the College of Propaganda and, in early 1799, preaching was restricted by decree only to 'citizen-bishops' and parochial clergy. In all their policies, the republican politicians showed how much the French Jacobin Republic of 1792–4 was their model and how little concerned they were to make any concessions even to progressive priests. The bishop of Perugia told his clergy and people in December 1798 that true peace could only be found by obedience to the government in power, but this brave pragmatic gesture merely served to isolate him within the wider episcopate and was ignored by the Jacobin authorities. They preferred to impose an oath 'to hate monarchy, and anarchy, and to be faithful to the Republic and the Constitution', which further antagonised the clergy. Only the university of the Sapienza and most of the ex-Jesuit Roman College proved willing to submit, and they later recanted when Pius declared their conduct scandalous.

Despite all the events of the past decade culminating in the expulsion of the pope from his capital, there were Catholic clergy in most countries who would not give up their interest in reformist politics; they had to come to see that the interests of 'throne and altar' could be separated, indeed might have to be if the Church was to survive at all and minister to its flock. The example of Spain also suggests that counter-revolutionary

---

[25] Quoted in Chadwick, *The Popes and European Revolution*, 465.

forces could never take their cultural predominance for granted: the progressive ideals of the French Civil Constitution and the theological and philosophical books recommended at Pistoia had found favour at Spanish universities such as Seville and Salamanca and they had increased influence following Spain's withdrawal from the war, despite a royal order of 1794 closing down all chairs of natural law. There was a period of calm between 1796 and 1798, and Godoy's general policy provided for no return to the anti-revolutionary repression of Floridablanca of a few years earlier. Popular anticlericalism was growing and it was symptomatic that many French priests who had taken refuge in Spanish monasteries were falling into extreme poverty.

Godoy was sympathetic to moderate Jansenists and refused to permit the papal Bull *Auctorem fidei* from being published in Spain. The government kept open the mainstream of the Enlightenment through creative intellectuals like Gaspar Melchior Jovellanos, who became secretary of grace and justice in late 1797 with control of religious affairs. When Godoy retired in March 1798, the way was clear for a fight for control of the Spanish Church between Jansenists and ultramontanes. Grégoire in 1798, taking advantage of the Franco-Spanish alliance, wrote an open letter to the new inquisitor-general, Rámon de Arce, pleading for religious toleration in Spain against the practices of the Inquisition, but this was actually counter-productive. Jovellanos' fall on 24 August 1798 and his replacement by José Antonio Caballero, a leading ultramontane councillor, and Urquijo, the foreign secretary, more of a religious moderate, did not in itself quell the pamphlet war between ultramontanes and Jansenists for the ear of the king, with Grégoire (who could never stand idly by) and three other Constitutional bishops in February 1799 urging the Spanish episcopate to recover rights 'stolen' from them by Rome and the Inquisition. However, the king's consent to the publication of *Auctorem fidei* late in 1800 was decisive, and the Inquisition could at last pursue its enemies, above all Jovellanos. Meanwhile, in September 1798, royal decrees had ordered the sale of most real estate belonging to hospitals, poor houses, and other charitable religious institutions.

The clergy continued to read Voltaire and Rousseau despite everything. In 1799 there appeared the last of seven volumes of Hervás y Panduro's *Historia de la vida del hombre*, written by an ex-Jesuit living in Italy. He insisted that the Enlightenment could be reconciled with Catholicism, for the *philsosophes'* attacks on religion were irrelevant to their main hopes for transforming political and social institutions. It makes up the most interesting apology for change written by a Catholic priest in this decade and, while utterly untypical of Catholic opinion as a whole, it is a reminder that perhaps as much as 10 per cent of the clergy, regulars as well as seculars, would not give up their hopes for a better future in which a reformed Catholicism would be ready to align with any like-minded régime, be it monarchical or republican. That still left the vast majority of priests opposed to the revolutionary order and its values. When the Spanish government issued a decree in 1799 ordering that matrimonial dispensations should be granted by the bishops rather than by Rome, the hierarchy became apprehensive of schism and a majority of bishops for the first time in four decades began to question the received regalian wisdom and look to Rome as counterweight. It was a defining moment.

The role of the laity

With priests in France – and wherever else revolutionary influences were felt – largely proscribed, persecuted and penniless, they had no alternative but to leave day-to-day Catholic witness in the undirected hands of the laity on an unprecedented scale. Fortunately for the survival of the Church, these men and women proved more than capable of rising to the challenge. Surprisingly large numbers in France went on practising their faith in 1793–4. In the Vendée, where the priests had been driven out and the republican repression was vicious, followers of both the refractory *and* the constitutional clergy daringly undertook themselves what had until very recently been the exclusive concern of the priest. Laymen started burying the dead, marrying couples, and celebrating 'white masses' where the bread and wine were venerated rather than consecrated. Village 'notables' like the schoolmaster or sacristan wearing a surplice took services whether in a church that was officially closed, a private building or in the open air. These services were used in numerous *départements*, notably the Aisne, Marne, Yonne, Nièvre, Vienne, Ardennes and in Normandy, compelling evidence of a search for new expressions of faith and forms of religious sociability in dangerous times when the traditional parish structures had broken down. They were also found in French-occupied Belgium in 1798–9 where priests were deported for refusing to take an oath of loyalty in the aftermath of the rising known as the *Boerenkrijg*.

Once Robespierre was overthrown in France, caution was increasingly discarded, as the Catholic laity in many areas petitioned the authorities for use of church premises or the right to hold services, to oblige them to respect the limited right to toleration conceded by the law of 3 *Ventôse* Year III (21 February 1795). To petition was to resort to a weapon forged in the Revolution and it was an appropriate device to point out the right to religious freedom, including drawing attention to the Declaration of the Rights of Man. Petitions were made on behalf of both the refractory and the Constitutional clergy. What makes such evidence fascinating is how it shows ordinary Frenchmen moving away from the notion that the Church was compatible only with monarchy: 'Long live the Republic, long live the Constitution of the Year III', the villagers of Coulanges-la-Vineuse concluded their petition objecting to the closure of their church in 1798 as part of the left-wing clampdown in the aftermath of the coup of *fructidor*. The republican authorities were taken aback by the strength of public feeling on this single issue of religious freedom, its refusal to tolerate delay and bureaucratic procrastination. In the Seine-Inférieure, the *département* told the Convention as early as 28 March 1795 that 'the rural communes daily get into the churches to exercise their religion again' while, in the Limousin, there was a comparable public clamour to reopen the churches, and to have the bells ring out again despite the official ban – '*ces foutus messieurs* won't stop us from ringing them' – and when they succeeded, the crowds flocked again to the shrine of Saint-Victurnien to give thanks. This example from the Limousin was repeated on a nationwide basis.

In this agitation, so vital to securing the future of Christianity in France, the part played by women was crucial, filling the spaces left by the removal of the male ordained ministry. Well before the Jacobins had been overthrown, women had been brazenly defiant, as many representatives on mission found out at first hand. Even in the dechristianised Nièvre, women were remarkably undeterred from showing their vexation at the way officials wanted to obliterate their religion. Having marched into the district headquarters at Corbigny, they bluntly declared their intention of practising their religion again, and demanded the return of their church bells and uninhibited access to church buildings. Here as elsewhere women had taken the lead in resisting dechristianisation, ready to dig up Trees of Liberty (female images of Liberty were a favourite object of laceration or dismemberment) and replace the crucifixes taken away by the authorities. 'We are only women; they don't do anything to women,' those females accused of breaking the church doors at Toucy in 1795 insisted.[26] Women well knew how high the stakes were and recalled previous threats to their Catholicism. At Fons in the Quercy, during the Terror in early 1794, women encouraged each other in the face of pressure from Jean-Baptiste Bô (representative on mission) to eliminate Christian practice. They were terrified not that their children would become atheists, but that the one alternative would revive and ensnare them.

[26] Quoted in Sutherland, *France 1789–1815: Revolution and Counter-Revolution* (London, 1985), 216–17, where many other examples of popular resistance are given; quoted in S. Desan, *Reclaiming the Sacred: Lay Religion and Popular Politics in Revolutionary France* (Ithaca, 1990), 200, 204.

Once the grip of central government relaxed in 1795, there was no restraining them. In the Yonne and other *départements* women took the lead in reclaiming church keys and in forcing the reopening of churches (by rioting if necessary); they prevented refractory clergy from being arrested by the authorities, rescued them if they were apprehended, and insisted on their celebrating the Eucharist despite the risks. There were numerous instances of women ringing bells to summon other women to join them in prayers and hymns. Because they were less likely to be stopped, women were also entrusted with messages to concealed clerics about pressing pastoral matters such as the number of children to be baptised, who could be trusted to house the priest secretly, and the way to remote barns and granges where Mass could be said undisturbed. Whatever their reservations, it was difficult for priests to direct or control the faithful, and leadership roles could be readily reversed: at Blesle in the Haute-Loire in the Year V, two old and ailing refractories were rescued from house arrest and forced to hold a Mass for the villagers.

It was, above all, in their homes that women kept the faith alive, catechising their own children in the absence of a priest, reading from the Bible and telling the youngsters about the lives of the saints. Missionary refractory priests often left behind literature designed for just this purpose and it was heavily used by mothers: the faith of the archetypal parish priest of the nineteenth century, the *curé* d'Ars (born 1786), was nourished by his mother in these years when he discovered his priestly vocation in childhood. Women willingly risked their lives by hiding in their houses those sacred images and objects to which they had been devoted when they had stood in the parish church; it happened similarly in Belgium in 1797–8 when famous relics including the Holy Blood of Bruges were kept for safe-keeping at private addresses. An aristocratic woman still resident could play an important organisational and inspirational role, as did Marie-Thérèse de Lamourous, who stayed on in the village of Piau until obliged to leave in April 1794. By then there was a local network in place to continue her mission of organising clandestine worship and holding catechetical classes for the women and children. In France as in England and Italy, the popularity of the Christian cause among women strikingly crossed social barriers.

That was perhaps less the case in Ireland where Catholicism and revolutionary fervour were intertwined in a complex manner. The battle for the hearts and minds of Irish Roman Catholics was crucial in determining whether the nation would stay attached to the British Crown in the 1790s. The Church hierarchy preached loyalty to George III as best likely to guarantee constitutional benefits while firebrands in the United Irishmen and Defenders, plus a minority of parish priests, sedulously distributed their republican propaganda to a range of households and urged the laity to join the insurrection when it came. For this was a moment when, as Leonard McNally noted in 1795: 'Every man who can read or can hear and understand what is read to him begins in religion as in politics to think for themselves.'[27] The commitment of the United Irishmen to an enlightened, undogmatic Catholicism appealed to activists keen to elicit Presbyterian support in any rebellion, but it struck few chords among Irish countrywomen whose Tridentine-style allegiance was firm and of a recent date. This failure to connect has an underestimated importance in explaining the failure of the 1798 Rebellion. On the other hand, what the radicals had to say often had an electrifying immediacy absent from the loyalist side: its dialogues with the poor were too often dull or patronising. Conservatives like James Arbuckle were worried that too little was being done by the authorities, complaining to the great Ascendancy magnate, the 2nd Marquess of Downshire in September 1796:

Is it not a shame to government, to their Graces and my Lords, the Archbishops and Bishops of this land, that it was left to the munificence, public spirit and religious principle of a private citizen of Belfast to print and publish at his own expense 1,500 copies of Bishop Watson's *Apology for the Bible* in order to contend with the cheap editions of Payne's *Age of Reason* that are industriously circulated throughout the country?[28]

The distribution of tracts was a vital weapon in the conservative armoury in England too, with the elite persuaded that it was not safe to take popular loyalties for granted. To supplement the established clergy in their pulpits, there were pamphlets preaching the related virtues of Godliness and loyalty designed to be accessible to the rural poor, many of the most memorable written by women such as Hannah More (1745–1833) and Sarah Trimmer, and aimed at lower-class women in a family setting. They played their part in keeping the countryside quiet except in the subsistence crises and the worst winters (1794–5, 1800–1), but male urban readers were not so readily weaned from an interest in Tom Paine and Jacobinism by the loyalist pieties or 'Burke for beginners' contained in such tracts as More's *Village Politics, By Will Chip, A Country Carpenter* (1793), the prelude to her *Cheap Repository Tracts* (1795–8). The latter, nevertheless, enjoyed a circulation of 2 million copies, and this success story resulted in the creation in 1799 of the Religious Tract Society. In Scotland pamphlets were likewise directed to the lower classes, such as Alexander Dalrymple's *The Poor Man's Friend* (1793) and *Few Plain*

---

[27] To E. Cooke, 12 September 1795, National Archives of Ireland, Rebellion Papers, 620/10/121/27.
[28] PRO (NI), Downshire Papers, D607/D/180.

Questions to the Working People of Scotland (1792), and, for the middling sort, there were more religious periodicals than ever to choose from. The *Family Magazine* was launched in 1788, the *Evangelical Magazine* in 1793, and different denominations were bringing out their own titles.

In 1801 the *Orthodox Churchman's Magazine* was produced, the culmination of several years' hard effort by conservative Anglican high churchmen, including William Stevens and William Jones of Nayland, founding members of the 'Society for the Reformation of Principles', which had published a collection of tracts for the younger clergy entitled *The Scholar Armed against the Errors of the Times* (1795). There was no escaping the relentless press war against infidelity and its association with France in these years. Thus Trewman's *Exeter Flying Post* for 28 April 1796 carried an advertisement for Theodore Markham's illustrated *History of the Life of Christ*, which noted its relevance 'when the enemies of true Religion strive to level mankind with the Brute Creation', and this was thoroughly typical of the English provincial press. On the continent, the threat or reality of French invasion produced comparable polemic. The Spanish royal chaplain, Joaquín Lorenzo Villanueva, in his *Catecismo del estado segun los principos de la religion* (1793), updated Bossuet's divine right theory, and larded his attack on French philosophy with an insistence that religion alone makes subjects respect their king.

It was, in the last analysis, the failure of lay men and women to be impressed by the revolutionary alternatives to their own Christian religious culture which ensured that the dechristianising alternatives on offer from France failed to put down roots. On the contrary, the challenge from the new cultural order reawakened the religious vitality of Christianity. Clerical administration may have folded up, Church lands confiscated on a huge scale in continental Europe and the pope expelled from Rome, but the ordinary people of Europe, whether Protestant, Catholic or Orthodox, would not give up the practice of what was distinctively 'their' faith, 'their' religion. And no political grouping or even a state could ignore that underlying reality. Thus the huge groundswell of support for Catholicism in France in 1795–7 crippled the Directory's religious policy of trying to build up a popular following for its preferred official, republican cults, such as Theophilanthropy. Once again, Christianity showed itself a more powerful and attractive resource than the revolutionary creed. Of course, the clergy were grateful for the popular reaction in favour of the faith, but it did not come without a price: the laity had won an entitlement to be given a much greater share in the running of the Churches once 'normality' was restored at some far distant point. In particular, those lay members of the Protestant elite who had embraced Evangelicalism would have a national prominence in moral discussion which senior clergy would be hard put to equal. For a renewed and influential piety among British and German Protestants brought evangelicals right into the heart of the national establishments and, since they were usually fiercely antirevolutionary, their services were eagerly enlisted by the politicians.

Evangelicalism and the new moral emphasis of the 1790s

In Britain the great evangelical revival had its roots in the mid-century but it came of age in the revolutionary decade inside the Church of England, though evangelicals were still not yet to be found in the upper reaches of the hierarchy. It had an influence across every level of society, on men and women equally, and especially on those born in the 1750s or afterwards. Undergraduates were exposed to its teachings in both English universities, as Evangelicals were well established at St Edmund Hall, Oxford, and Magdalene College, Cambridge, by the 1790s. Many at the latter came from households and schools in Yorkshire, and they dominated the small undergraduate intake. These young men lived lives in which sin was taken seriously and their dress, behaviour, and spiritual and academic record were monitored by the Elland Society, a religious group associated with the college since the 1770s. The flame was further fanned by preachers such as Charles Simeon (1759–1836), fellow of King's and perpetual curate of Holy Trinity church, Cambridge, a man convinced of the depravity of human nature, urging his hearers to repent and accept redemption through the inward working of God's grace. The message had an immediacy and an appeal that was catching, with Simeon 'not penetrating like dew, but coming down like "hailstones and coals of fire"' according to one who heard him.[29] He held informal meetings every Friday evening, divided his followers into separate religious societies, and exerted a tremendous influence on the next generation of Evangelical Anglicans. Neither Simeon nor his message posed a threat to establishment: unlike the rational dissenters, few Evangelicals had an interest in radical politics, though they found the war an agonising matter in conscience. On the one hand, they deplored Jacobins and dechristianisers, on the other their country was in alliance with Catholic powers to restore popery in France. So when William Wilberforce in 1795 supported a motion for peace with France it had a particuarly unsettling effect on public opinion. Evangelicals were ruthless towards those who dared to deviate from the path of orthodoxy in the faith. The vice-chancellor of Cambridge in the early 1790s was the first professor of natural philosophy

---

[29] John Stoughton, *Religion in England* (2 vols., London, 1884), vol. I, 124, quoted in Peter Searby, *A History of the University of Cambridge*, Vol. III, *1750–1870* (Cambridge, 1997), 329.

in the university, the leading loyalist and Evangelical, Isaac Milner (1750–1820), who filled his college (Queens') with fellows who shared his religious tastes. This friend of Wilberforce used all his influence in the university to secure the expulsion of William Frend, the Unitarian fellow of Jesus College, an action that embodied the determination of Anglican Evangelicals to tolerate no deviation from a strict line of credal orthodoxy and loyalty to the existing constitution.

Many Methodist leaders sought precisely the same combination, but struggled to impose their authority on the 'Connexion' (as Methodists denoted their semi-detached relationship to the Church of England) after John Wesley's death in 1791 left it with no obvious successor to him. His legacy was an organisation of 72,500 members in 114 circuits with 289 itinerant preachers and about 470 preaching houses. But would this inheritance remain intact? Mainstream Methodism largely drew apart from the established Church during the 1790s, and the ensuing contest for control of the movement showed a degree of ideological diversity that concerned the authorities. Wesley's lieutenants, such as Thomas Coke, were sticklers for orthodoxy and loyalism, but were under pressure from a dynamic minority who wanted to hold their own communion services in their own chapels and were suspicious of the repressive statutes rushed through Parliament from 1792. Wesley's followers were breaking up into distinct groups: 'Church Methodists' and 'Methodist Dissenters'. Worries about the loyalty of the latter grouping persisted, and the number of those found to be members of the pro-revolutionary London Corresponding Society appeared to bear them out. Matters came to a head in late 1795 when the Methodist leadership was under sustained government pressure for pledges of political loyalty or running the risk of penal legislation.

Church and state needed to be sure that the Methodist people were no threat to the status quo, and the Conference could delay a purge of dissidents no longer. Prompted by Coke, radicals under Alexander Kilham (1762–98) were thrown out in 1797 and founded their own breakaway Methodist New Connexion, strong in Yorkshire, Lancashire and parts of the north Midlands. None of this suggests that Elie Halévy's famous thesis – that Methodism saved England from revolution in the 1790s – bears close scrutiny.[30] Indeed, the government and the bishops found Methodists an unsettling presence, riven by internal instability, lacking a secure leadership, and more likely to be stirring up anti-establishment sentiments than reinforcing the agencies of authority. Despite the internal wranglings, Methodist numbers continued to grow at an exceptional rate, perhaps by as much as 22 per cent in 1794–5, years of rising food

---

[30] Elie Halévy, *England in 1815*, vol. I, *A History of the English People in the Nineteenth Century* (London, 1961).

prices. Yet this still amounted to only about 1 per cent of the population at the turn of the nineteenth century, hardly an unstoppable force. Where they were strong, it was important for clergy, landowners and magistrates to know that the 'Connexion' was loyal; where Methodists were few, they had had no more than nuisance value.

Though their theologies were almost identical, political suspicions complicated and sometimes poisoned relations between Methodists and Evangelicals in this period. Much of the distrust centred on Sunday Schools. Some Anglicans had never been happy with them, with clergy in cities as far apart as Coventry and Chester forestalling efforts to get them started. Sunday Schools were still largely cross-denominational, and doubts about the political sympathies of the Methodists in the 1790s in turn nourished all the old fears that these could be nurseries of political subversion. Churchmen worried that that Wesleyans were using them to win over converts or that Paineite sympathisers had gained a foothold. Writers in the prestigious loyalist periodical, the *Anti-Jacobin*, alleged that Sunday Schools were frequently the channels for the diffusion of malign religious and political principles. Concerns over the non-Anglican Sunday Schools, which expanded massively between 1795 and 1800, were particularly marked; the leading high churchman, Charles Daubeney, canon of Salisbury, even criticised Hannah More for her foundation of Sunday Schools in the Somerset village of Blagdon for being 'schismatical in tendency'. Most prelates doubted the religious impulse behind their foundation. Critics such as Bishop Samuel Horsley of Rochester feared that much of the impetus came from Jacobins otherwise confined underground by the provisions of the Seditious Meetings and Treasonable Practices Acts of 1795.

But wartime anxieties could not stop expansion, and perhaps the majority of beneficed clergy, who felt they knew their parish, were well pleased with the pastoral benefits of Sunday Schools where they exercised personal control. One Norfolk rector and former Cambridge don, who had taken pains for 'near twenty years with a neglected & abandoned people', had 100 youngsters at Sunday School and was convinced that these would play their part in the 'protection of the Church'. He tried to help his former pupils into trade after they had left.[31] For the most part, Evangelicals remained persuaded that Sunday Schools were an excellent means of winning the ordinary populace to Christ and reducing the appeal of dissipation and radical disaffection among young people. Protestants of every hue shared this instinct, and though cross-denominational co-operation declined in the 1790s, it was still powerful enough to ensure

---

[31] Revd Baker to W. W. Bulwer, 23 June 1790, Norfolk Record Office, Bulwer of Heydon collection, BUL 4/118/9.

that a central society for the movement, the Sunday School Society, founded in 1803 by William Fox, a Baptist deacon, included both Anglicans and dissenters on its board. It had a precedent in the London Missionary Society of 1795 (one of several founded in that decade), which attracted support from Anglicans, Methodists and Congregationalists.

It is typical of the evangelical impulse that women were to the fore in these schemes. In the Bath and Wells diocese, the redoubtable Hannah More had established Sunday schools in as many as ten parishes by 1796, with 1,600–1,700 pupils on the registers. Leading members of the movement were in no doubt about the importance of women in preserving society and furthering the Gospel cause. Thus, for Wilberforce, women were 'the medium of our intercourse with the heavenly world, the faithful repositories of religious principles for the benefit both of the present and of the rising generation'.[32] Women like More and Trimmer were implacable in their mission to reform English society with tracts and Sunday Schools, but their indefatigable evangelical energies found additional outlets. They were committed to the campaign gathering momentum among Evangelicals for the abolition of the slave trade.

Moral earnestness was in vogue in late eighteenth-century Britain, part of a determination from the king downwards to sweep away the licentiousness that was commonly alleged to be active at every level of society. Moral reform became a substitute for political reform in Britain in the 1790s, with Evangelicals having this much in common with Robespierre, that both looked to moral regeneration as the prerequisite to the emergence of a new society. It was a dominant issue for Evangelicals coming to prominence in British public life with ready access to Parliament and the press as a means of influencing wider opinion. The Evangelical revival in Protestantism was as much an enemy to the excesses of popular culture as Tridentine Catholicism had been. Its message was uncompromising: damnation awaited rich and poor alike if they neglected salvation and their soul's welfare by a fondness for worldly gratifications. Methodism came down hard against its followers having anything to do with wakes: as early as 1784, the Leeds Conference had resolved that none of the membership should attend any wake or feast, but rather preach and plead against them when opportunity offered. Ten or fifteen years on, few Methodists would have lightly ignored that injunction.

No group in society was exempt from this new emphasis on self-control and the upholding of family values, and the king and queen were

---

[32] *Practical View of the Prevailing Religious System of Professed Christians* (13th edn, London, 1818), 367.

frequently acclaimed as setting just the right standard of abstemiousness for dark and difficult times. The French Revolution gave the issue of moral reformation (especially in sexual matters) in the British press and debating societies a new urgency: the higher orders had to set a better example to the lower classes of society if they wished to avoid the fate of their French counterparts. Britons would have to resist the plot to sap their country's martial strength by the Directory, warned Bishop Shute Barrington of Durham (a prelate broadly sympathetic to the Evangelicals), who, 'finding that they were not able to subdue us by their arms, appeared as if they were determined to gain their ends by destroying our morals'.[33] Attention focused on the lax morality which Evangelical critics detected as prevalent among the British upper classes, and this was the impulse behind the Bill brought in by the retired diplomat Lord Auckland and Bishop Horsley of Rochester in 1800 which would have made adultery a criminal offence. The Bill failed, but the discussion went on.

Individual members of the nobility did their best to adjust to the new critical spirit. Indeed, Paul Langford has claimed that politicians and noblemen were exposed to a new public prurience in George III's reign, and that towards the end of the eighteenth century more peers took an active part in public affairs as the result of religious revival among a portion of them. All groups lobbied hard for a much stricter observance of the Sabbath as a register of godly health, and even princesses were not exempt from Evangelical strictures. George III's sister-in-law, HRH the duchess of Gloucester, produced a memorandum for herself in 1798 to see if she was anything more than a nominal Christian by Wilberforce's standards, and confessed herself uneasy about the Evangelical drive to enforce the sanctity of Sundays, noting that 'I was taught from my Infancy to respect the Sabbath-day; but I was not taught to look upon it as a day of "lamentation & woe".'[34] The clergy tried to lead the way towards a new spirit of sharing in common hardships. With wheat scarce in the winter of 1795–6, both Houses of Parliament pledged to reduce their own consumption by one-third. The archbishop of York recommended the gesture to his clergy, their parishioners and neighbours 'in their several districts', and his pastoral exhortation was to be read after the second lesson at the morning service.

These signs of the religious vitality of English Protestantism had their counterparts on the continent where the excesses of the Revolution had

---

[33] *The Times*, 3 March 1798.
[34] Quoted in *The Harcourt Papers*, ed. Edward William Harcourt (14 vols., Oxford, 1800–1905) vol. VI, 306–7.

persuaded many across the social compass that progress would be best accomplished by religious conversion rather than any reliance on mankind's natural moral sense. These evangelical impulses had actually started in Germany among Lutherans and the Reformed and in Lutheran Scandinavia a decade or so before the French Revolution. They would persist well into the next century. This recalling of Christian identity was intensified in the face of the French values exported by their troops pushing east across the Rhine during the 1790s. It took several forms. In eastern Jutland and western Norway there was a popular awakening with Pietist and Moravian overtones in the 1790s. Mysticism remained attractive to the elite, with its yearnings forcefully expressed among the circle and correspondents of Princess Amalie Gallitzin (1748-1816) at Westphalian Münster. Many pious noble landowners helped organise services with lay preachers where all prayed, sang hymns and read scripture. The emphasis on access to the scriptures was a marked feature of evangelical revival in Lutheran and Reformed circles. Thus the 'Christianity Society' (1780) of Basel set up a Tract Society (1802) to publicise its mission of propagating a cheap Gospel text with emissaries and correspondents prominent in Nuremburg and Stuttgart. Such work prepared the way for that wider awakening which would be apparent after 1800. In the Catholic world, too, revival would occur, fanned by the laity and, against expectation, directed by the papacy to a degree unknown in the eighteenth century.

Papal revival and recognition, 1798–1802

The Treaty of Tolentino (February 1797) established the Cispadane republic largely on the basis of land belonging to the papacy; the provinces of Avignon, the Venaissin and the legations of Bologna, Ferrara and Ravenna were ceded by the Vatican, which also agreed to pay France a fine of 30 million *livres*. For his part, Bonaparte gave his word that the troops under his command would not harm the Catholic religion in the legations. The papacy was grateful that the occupying power had done no worse, the secretary of state, Cardinal Busca, grateful that, notwithstanding the hard conditions, the Catholic religion remained intact. Indeed, between March and September 1797 Franco-papal relations prospered, with Pius going so far as to drop hints about negotiating a concordatory settlement between Paris and Rome. This relative harmony did not survive the coup of *fructidor*, when the Directory took a pronounced anticlerical turn. It used the excuse of a fracas in Rome resulting in the death of a French general to have Bonaparte's successor, the more compliant General Berthier, act on secret instructions from Paris and occupy the city in February 1798. A Roman Republic was proclaimed forthwith, but, embarrassingly, Pius VI would not quit the city. Reluctantly, the French authorities had him bundled into a carriage and sent off to house-arrest at an Augustinian convent in Siena, and then to Florence. He died, still the captive of the French government as 'citizen Braschi, exercising the profession of pontiff', at Valence in the Dauphiné on 29 August 1799.

The Directors were confident Pius VI would be the last successor to St Peter and that, with the head removed, other senior churchmen would simply abandon an unequal struggle and retire into private life. According to this scenario, despite the irredeemably superstitious masses, the supreme leadership of the Church was doomed to extinction. Jacobins across Europe, enjoying what would prove to be their last taste of power before Bonaparte took control, relished the moment. As one journalist put it, 'The death of Pius VI has just put the seal on the glory of modern philosophy.'[35] The whole public culture underpinned by the papacy was dismantled in the Roman Republic during the winter of 1798–9. Down came the papal arms from public buildings, in came the republican calendar and new place names so that, for instance, the Castel San Angelo became the 'Castle of Genius'. There was a bid to inculcate a republican patriotism by having military spectacles in the streets, discouraging attendance at communion, and prohibiting the wearing of clerical habits in the streets. Catholic worship was permitted, but under severe constraints. Thus the new Republic ordered all members of the chapter of St Peter's to call themselves 'Citizen Canon' and 'Citizen Dean'. It banned monastic vows, closed monasteries and convents, and suppressed the confraternities.

Three months after Pius's death on French soil, the coup of 18 *brumaire* (November 1799) overthrew the Directory and brought Napoleon Bonaparte to power as first consul. Contemptuous of the artificial cults encouraged by the Directory, Bonaparte was no dogmatic anticlerical and accepted that Christianity had not withered away as many of his colleagues had predicted. That being so, if tolerating Catholicism on his terms would win his precarious new order the loyalties of the French clergy and laity in a way no previous revolutionary regime had done then he was willing to try it. Edicts of 28–30 December 1799 (7–9 *Nivôse*) at once showed his conciliatory aims by removing any state obstacles to Sunday observance, replacing the oath of hatred for monarchy by one simply requiring loyalty to the constitution, and releasing priests still incarcerated on the islands of Ré and Oléron. Still more remarkably, Pius VI

---

[35] *Le Clairvoyant* [a Grenoble publication], quoted in J. Godel, *Histoire religieuse du département de l'Isère, la reconstruction concordataire* (Grenoble, 1968), 35.

was buried with full pontifical honours in December 1799. In response, French refractory priests remained cautious about abandoning their allegiance to Louis XVIII. Prelates meeting in Bavaria in February 1800 signalled their disapproval of the oath of loyalty, and circulated news of their decision, which was, eventually, endorsed by three archbishops and eleven bishops. By contrast, the laity were delighted at the way the Consulate had abruptly terminated the second 'reign of Terror', and allowed exiles to come back.

The realpolitik of the Consulate reflected the diminution of French international power in 1799–1800. The allies put together a Second Coalition in 1799 which, for a moment, looked like destroying the Bonapartist state at its inception. The satellite states in Italy and elsewhere, lacking an external protector, were overthrown and Austrian power in the peninsula was again a force to be reckoned with. The papacy was the immediate beneficiary. The emperor Francis was ready to act as the protector of the Holy See and oversee a protracted conclave on recently acquired Austrian territory (Venice) to elect a successor to Pius VI; Bonaparte may not have wished for the Catholic Church to recover its head, but the initiative lay in Habsburg hands in 1800 until the battle of Marengo on 14 June restored French power and pride. By then, there was a new pope, Cardinal Luigi Barnabà Chiaramonti, bishop of Imola, fifty-eight years old, a Benedictine monk who had publicly declared in a Christmas sermon in 1797 that democracy and equality were reconcilable with Christianity. The conclave witnessed heated private discussions between the cardinals on the fundamental question of how far the new pope should come to terms with the legacy of the French Revolution. Was conflict or compromise to be the preferred option? Chiaramonti's election as Pius VII suggested that compromise had won. He was certainly not the preferred choice of the Habsburgs, as their refusal to permit his coronation to take place at St Mark's, Venice, and his return to Rome as soon as was practicable (July 1800), testified. But Bonaparte saw his opportunity and, a few days after Marengo, addressed an assembly of clergy in Milan and expressed his hope of having 'the happiness of removing every obstacle which might hinder complete reconciliation between France and the head of the Church'.[36] He also began to put out feelers towards a new religious settlement for France in partnership with Pius VII. Then, in September 1800, Pius sent Cardinals Spina and Caselli to Paris.

It was a characteristically daring move by Napoleon, an admission that the worldwide Catholic Church, however damaged by the Revolution

---

[36] Quoted in F. Markham, *Napoleon* (London, 1963), 79; see also M. Hutt, *Napoleon: Great Lives Observed* (New Jersey, 1972), 28.

and its repercussions, was simply too powerful to be ignored. 'Skilful conquerors have not got entangled with priests. They can both contain them and use them,' he told his brother Lucien in April 1801. Interestingly, the First Consul thought not just in terms of a straightforward religious toleration on the basis of *Ventôse* 1795; he would resurrect the Church–state alliance, blow fresh life into Gallicanism but this time as an ally of the Bonapartes not the Bourbons. And this new Gallicanism would be sanctified by the pope himself, for Bonaparte had no intention of directly involving either refractory or Constitutional clergy in his secret negotiations. As the consul foresaw, for Pius an end to the schism in France that would also enhance papal authority was eminently desirable. Pius was well served in the final stage of discussions by one of the most formidable diplomatic talents of his generation, Cardinal Ercole Consalvi, the secretary of state, whose shrewd realism complemented his master's spiritual vision and leadership. Discussions lasted eight months and threatened to collapse on several occasions before the Concordat was finally signed on 15 July 1801, with France exploiting papal vulnerability after Austria made peace with Bonaparte by the Treaty of Lunéville in February 1801.

Pius had the worse bargain but he could congratulate himself on achieving international recognition from the strongest power in Europe only two to three years since the papacy's nadir. That recognition had come at a high price: first, the breaking of the bonds between the Bourbon monarchy and the French Church and the rebuilding of the alliance of 'throne and altar' on Bonapartist foundations; secondly, the refusal of an important section of the refractory Church to accept either the terms of the Concordat or the way in which they were required to receive it from papal hands. There was no return to the confessional state: Catholicism was acknowledged as 'the religion of the majority of the French' with the legal right to existence of Protestants and Jews protected. The land the Church had owned before 1789 would not be transferred back (article 13 of the Concordat). There was nothing for Richerists in all this. The electoral provisions of the Civil Constitution were abandoned along with the pretensions of the priesthood to independent power. Bishops would be chosen by the First Consul, invested with spiritual authority by the pope, and obliged to take a declaration of loyalty to the government; parish priests would be exclusively nominated by the episcopate and subject also to the new oath. Bishops and clergy alike would be paid out of the public purse.

Many nonjuring bishops found utterly unacceptable the stipulation that they should surrender their offices to Pius VII who would then 'appoint' a new episcopate for France, drawn from Grégoire's followers as well as the refractories. The alternative would be loss of office. As the bishop of Lombez saw it, the pope was acting *ultra vires*: 'The Pope is head of the Church, but he does not dominate it. He is the successor of the Prince of the Apostles, but he does not make up all the apostolic college.'[37] Of ninety-three surviving refractory prelates, fifty-five eventually obeyed; the remainder were deprived by the pope, though their jurisdiction continued to be recognised by a large body of the faithful. Thus was initiated the minor schism of the *Petite Eglise*, especially strong in parts of the west, Poitou and the Lyonnais. The Constitutional leadership had no such misgivings. Meeting in their second national council in Paris, on 14 July 1801, delegates proclaimed the duty of obedience to the established power in France and its laws. The government was delighted: Fouché even showed Grégoire an advance draft text of the Concordat, and invited some of his colleagues to an official dinner at the Tuileries after the the national council ended. In April 1802 seven Constitutional bishops were nominated. Confronted with the threat of even more such candidates, Pius' representative swallowed his pride and instituted them without officially giving up the papacy's reservations about those who had declined to retract their 'errors'.

Bonaparte insisted on still more concessions from the Vatican in the form of the seventy-seven Organic Articles added unilaterally to the Concordat immediately before its promulgation in April 1802. The Articles curtailed the powers of clergy to act independently of the state from the publication of papal Bulls and the convocation of national councils down to the creation of new parishes. Hierarchical duties were spelt out explicitly. Bishops could not leave their dioceses or re-establish chapters without first obtaining permission from the government; four-fifths of the parish clergy would have no security of tenure, with all except those in the chief towns of a canton removable at will. Dioceses would correspond exactly with the *départements*, a stipulation accepted a decade previously by the Constitutional clergy. Pius refused to recognise the Organic Articles, but they became law all the same. Under the Concordat and separate Organic Articles of April 1802, the 480,000 Calvinists and 200,000 Lutherans in France received an unprecedented degree of official recognition. There was provision for the formation of consistories (intended to ensure dominance by the social elite), and salaried pastors from 1804. But Protestant synods could only gather with the express permission of the government. Disaffection from this quarter was no more to be permitted than from Roman Catholics.

---

[37] Quoted in A. Mathiez, *Contributions à l'histoire religieuse de la Révolution française* (Paris, 1907), 268. See also J.-E.-B. Drochon, *La Petite Eglise, essai historique sur l'église anticoncordataire* (Paris, 1894), 32–3.

The new settlement was sealed on Easter Sunday 1802 at Notre Dame Cathedral when the First Consul and other senior members of the regime attended a solemn Mass to confirm the new order of Church–state relations. A few days previously, the Law on Cults of 18 *germinal*, Year 10 (8 April 1802) had been passed through the legislature. The Churches had been restored and at a stroke the enemies of France could no longer present the war, when it resumed in 1803, as any form of a religious crusade. Christians of all persuasions were free to worship unhindered, albeit on the consul's terms. Napoleon would show over the next thirteen years that religious opposition would not be tolerated any more than any other form of dissent in this highly efficient autocracy. That tendency was immediately on display when that enduring organ of Jansenist reformism, the periodical *Nouvelles Ecclésiastiques*, was shut down in 1803. From the beginning, the Church–state alliance was more unequal than any previously seen in France and did little to wean the clergy away from their royalism, whatever the official formularies. Meanwhile, the extent to which spiritual as well as Church life would recover in France after 1802 as well as elsewhere in Europe remained to be established.

7   Religion in Napoleonic Europe, 1802–1815

Introduction: a crisis of public faith?

Most commentators thought the new century was starting with the mainstream Churches unable to take their continuing importance – or even their survival – for granted. On the surface, it might appear that the Protestant communions could take advantage of the traumas suffered by Roman Catholicism, but closer inspection suggested otherwise. As the continuator of the great eighteenth-century historian, J. L. von Mosheim, chancellor of Göttingen University (a latitudinarian in the Erasmian tradition), noted with primary reference to Germany and England (though not excluding Catholic Europe from his judgment):

> Religion is outwardly professed, rather than inwardly cultivated. Where zeal is visible, it is chiefly among sectaries that we perceive it; and among them it is sometimes carried to excess, and frequently accompanied with ignorance. On the other hand, too many of the clergy, in the ranks of the establishment, appear to be unimpressed with a due sense of the importance of religion, and consider divinity merely as a liberal profession, the source of honor and emolument.[1]

Getting that vital constituency – middle-class, urban Europeans – into the churches Sunday by Sunday was stretching the resources of most confessions, especially the established faiths, in an era when the whole pattern of dynastic settlement was in upheaval and the values of the new secular order were at best neutral over the truth and utility of the Christian faith. It was not just in the France of the Consulate (1799–1804) that the sabbatarian habit was ceasing to be (in Durkheim's phrase) 'external and coercive'. A Prussian court rescript of 1802 noted that habitual Sunday observance at public prayers was a declining practice: baptism and confirmation were the only services drawing in significant numbers in the towns. By that date there were many signs of the estrangement of the German Protestant elite from an identifiable faith, with a Berlin

---

[1] J. L. Mosheim, D.D., *An Ecclesiastical History Ancient and Modern, from the Birth of Christianity to the Beginning of the Eighteenth Century,* trans. Archibald Maclaine, D.D. (6 vols., London, 1811), vol. VI, 349 [Charles Coote, LL.D., was the author of vol. VI].

newspaper predicting the extinction of Christianity in Germany over the next twenty years. If bourgeois attendance and religious profession was more stable in England, the unprecedented growth in population and the commercialisation of agriculture and industry still put pressure on the late Georgian Church which it was ill equipped to bear. In 1799 a commission in the Lincoln diocese reported that only one-third of the people were coming to churches in the 100 parishes looked at (some of them were Methodists); communicants made up just one-sixth of the adult population.

Regional variations in England remained appreciable. In Europe as a whole, rural areas were better able to keep observance going – local officials and military movements permitting. Piety had deep roots in the mass of the rural population, a point that should be borne in mind when assessing recent claims – on the basis of wills and last testaments – that it plummeted in Upper Austria between 1780 and 1820. If the point is conceded, it is strikingly at odds with other Habsburg provinces such as the Tyrol, and the independent electorate of Bavaria. A parish report in the Munich diocese in 1797 had suggested that scarcely 10 people in 1,000 missed Sunday Mass attendance. Here, Tridentine Christianity was alive and well, while in Spain it was still being successfully extended. Thus the stipulation that everyone should make an annual confession was judged to have been finally achieved in the Spanish Church, as in the diocese of Pamplona in 1801. With the good health of Christianity in the towns and cities far from assured, the maintenance of a high level of instructed, rural religious practice assumed a new level of importance, which depended crucially on political stability of a sort that had not been seen in the 1790s. Would Napoleon Bonaparte be willing and able to deliver it?

The Napoleonic religious settlement for Europe

The Concordat and the inauguration of the empire in 1804 appeared to open the way to the start of a healing process for Catholics as well as Protestants and Jews in France. The enactments of 1801–2 constituted a far-reaching attempt to realign religion and revolution in a publicly acceptable manner that would best ensure the perpetuation of the Bonapartist regime. Napoleon saw that he could never construct a broad level of support for his authority on the basis of the revolutionary cults patronised in the 1790s by republicans, and still fitfully kept going into the new century by a few enthusiasts. The worship of Reason and the Supreme Being, along with the practice of Theophilanthropy, had offered gleams of religiosity to *Idéologues* and deists who admired men such as the comte de Volney, men who were beginning the study of the human origins of religious practice. They either rejected Christianity or associated it with reactionary politics, but these substitute religions were too abstract, too faddish, to take hold of popular affections. The people of France had rejected them, and Napoleon went back to the Churches.

He appreciated the damage that the spread of French-style republicanism across much of western Europe had inflicted on Church structures, and the political sense of reversing it – up to a point. This insight was not easy to translate into policy: the papacy may have undergone a minor revival at the behest of the emperor; every other constituent part of the Church had to overcome the cultural unease of working in tandem with Bonapartist institutions, both in France and wherever else French imperial hegemony extended over the years from 1802 to 1815. The emperor and most of his officials would do Christians no favours. Catholicism had a decorative exterior which conferred dignity on the new regime and a tradition of obedience which Napoleon believed could be made to work in his favour. If it worked against him, the emperor was willing to move against the clergy more ruthlessly than Joseph II had ever done a generation before.

What he would find harder to achieve was the extirpation of the rural population's deep-rooted religious allegiance and identity. As the previous chapter showed, it had become used to taking the initiative when deprived of clergy, services and church buildings; most were not diehard monarchists, so Napoleon risked the loyalties of a sizable proportion of his own people when the empire fell out with the papacy and he brought in a much more restrictive Concordat than the 1801 model, that of Fontainbleau, dating from early 1813. This was to repeat the policy error of the Directory which Napoleon had initially corrected at the start of the Consulate. Beyond France's already extended natural frontiers, Christianity would prove the principal inspiration of those ordinary men and women for whom the arrival of French troops inevitably brought with it religious repression and a vicious anticlericalism, all part of an alien, imperialist culture. If Napoleonic hegemony was eventually swept away, it was because religion so satisfied hearts and minds that it was a key component of patriotic inspiration, including the German 'War of Liberation' of 1813–14. It was not just the unlettered laity of Europe who treasured their religious heritage and practices; the turbulence and instability of over a decade's fighting and state insecurity frequently led disaffected revolutionaries, libertines and the heirs of the *philosophes* to reclaim their Christian identity and, in so doing, give the faith an exciting, prestigious edge it had not known for upwards of a century. For many of them, the future lay in rediscovering a medieval past where Christianity and monarchy became mutual supporters once more. It compensated for the damaging loss of status the Catholic Church continued to endure on the European continent, as in the attempts to replicate a French-style Concordat elsewhere. Other monarchical states could not resist preying on the Church in the new order.

Encouraged by securing the Concordat in France, Napoleon Bonaparte adopted it as a model of compact uniformity for other dependencies. The device appeared nicely calculated to end the recurrent instability seen in secular state–papal relations for most of the previous century and, while endorsing papal headship over the Church, set in stone the presumption that the Church was a subordinate institution in a Europe Napoleon intended to dominate. The presumption would be underlined by a land resettlement, which Napoleon calculated would prove too tempting for Catholic monarchs to resist. In other words, concordatory dispensations would both rationalise Church structures along the lines of the Civil Constitution of the Clergy and act as a means of winning the Consulate princely endorsement without resorting to arms.

The Peace of Lunéville opened the way for wholesale ecclesiastical reordering following on from the settlement between the consul and the pope. Having first introduced the Concordat of 1801 into the new, greater French *départements* of the Rhineland and Piedmont, most of 1803–4 was spent trying to secure a Concordat for the Italian Republic (a Napoleonic satellite state). The terms eventually secured were more favourable to the Church than in France, with clergy exempted from conscription and the endowment of all bishoprics and seminaries. Purchasers of Church land were, however, to remain undisturbed and the government's right to choose bishops was extended. Pius VII was satisfied with the terms of this Concordat, much less so with the way it was supplemented by tight state regulation in a Josephist spirit by Count Melzi d'Eril in Milan, a Voltairean anticlerical at heart and a prominent leader in the revived Cisalpine republic, whose enthusiasm even Napoleon adjudged excessive. There was much wrangling about its implementation, so that it was only applied to northern Italy by a Napoleonic decree of May 1805. Pius took a measure of comfort from its provisions, stabilising the Catholic order in much of the peninsula when, in central Europe, the Church was confronted with the crumbling of a range of institutions from the empire downwards.

Christianity and the end of the Holy Roman Empire

Recent scholarship has emphasised the extent to which the empire remained viable as a polity until almost the eve of its extinction. The imperial constitution may have been anachronistic, but its existence was instrumental in preserving the religious equilibrium established by the

Treaty of Westphalia (1648). As late as 1785, Joseph II's attempts to unscramble the territorial status quo had led to several (mainly Protestant)
princes uniting uneasily behind Frederick II of Prussia in the *Fürstenbund*
to thwart his plans. The prince-bishoprics were anomalous as state units,
and yet that did not stop their ecclesiastical rulers from implementing
policies that were as enlightened as any pursued by their secular equivalents. It appeared as safe a way as any of preserving themselves from
the encroachment of land-hungry neighbouring states anxious to consolidate their territories. The prince-bishoprics and, therefore, the historic
German constitution, survived until the outbreak of the Revolutionary
wars in 1792 and the spread of French armies to the Rhine frontier by
1797, bringing with it the destruction of major sees, including Cologne,
Trier, Mainz and Liège, as independent governing units. The principle of secularisation of the ecclesiastical states having been agreed after
the Treaty of Rastatt in March 1798, the major German powers did little to save them. They were too busy facing up to difficult negotiations
with the Directory over territorial realignments following the expansion
of France. Under the Treaty of Lunéville (1801) it was agreed that if
France was to occupy the prince-bishoprics on the left bank of the Rhine,
then the German princes could have those on the right bank. The Diet
of Regensburg the same year accepted the scheme of ecclesiastical disendowment with expressions of regret but few meaningful demurrals.
One prince-bishop was left, Karl von Dalberg (b. 1744), clerical states-
man, admirer of Febronius, friend of Napoleon. He was moved from
Mainz to Regensburg and became the primate of all Germany and last
archchancellor of the empire.

At this juncture, Pius VII, keen to act in the spirit of the new Concordat
with Bonaparte, agreed to the creation of new dioceses on the west bank of
the Rhine to replace the dismantled ecclesiastical principalities. Frederick
William III and Francis II, however, did not wait for a Reich committee
to confirm the abolition of all the electorates on 25 February 1803 (bar
a reconstituted Mainz with its main city moved to Regensburg) before
they occupied Hildesheim and Münster on the one hand, and Salzburg
and Passau on the other. The German princes (most of whom were promoted to kingly status in 1805–6) were eagerly dismantling the imperial
constitution, and a papal brief of February 1803 threatening with excommunication Catholics who participated in secularisation was not enough
to stop the process, especially with Protestants in control of the two most
important councils of the Diet in 1803. This interdict had much less of
an impact than Francis II's proclamation of the *Hauptschluss* as law on
27 April. Article 63 of the 1803 settlement expressly guaranteed Church
property other than from the former independent ecclesiastical states,

religious Orders and religious charitable institutions which had already passed under civil jurisdiction. After 1803 all southern and western states simply affirmed their right to appropriate Church property and there was no attempt either at paying compensation or obtaining popular consent. Prebends and chapter officers from the Catholic nobility suddenly found their comfortable existence turned upside down. There was, occasionally, resistance, as in the kingdom of Württemberg when officials took over lands owned by the Grand Master of the Teutonic Order, and troops had to be called out to quell demonstrations.

Deposed prince-bishops were usually treated with politeness and as much personal consideration as the circumstances permitted, and resistance seldom extended beyond non-co-operation. The subjects of the ecclesiastical rulers were not usually prepared to put their lives at risk by a show of physical force; Catholic apologists considered that the Church in Germany would benefit from modernisation and updated boundaries, while the papacy, learning to live with secularisation, calculated that the new bishops would be much more responsive to Pius VII than ever their illustrious predecessors had been to successive popes. There was some uneasiness where German Catholics found themselves under Protestant rule. Sensing the delicacy of the situation, the kings of Prussia and Württemberg promulgated edicts of toleration intended to reassure their new Catholic subjects. But this could only be done within a legal framework far removed from the conventions that had held sway for so long under the Westphalian regime. From this point, the different communions jostled to gain converts and Catholics soon sensed that, whatever the letter of the law, they might end up as second-class citizens. Meanwhile, those of their co-religionists who had exchanged a prince-bishop for a Josephist monarch like the king of Bavaria found that the popular religious practices uneasily tolerated throughout the last decades of the eighteenth century fell foul of the new regime. In a resurgence of pre-1789-style reform Catholicism, pilgrimages, feast days and local cults were once again under scrutiny and confessional unity imperilled.

Secularisation and the dismantling of the 1648 Treaty of Westphalia with its principle of *cuis regio, eius religio* carried over from the 1555 Treaty of Augsburg completely altered the confessional balance of power within the Reich. Only Austria and Bavaria were left as states where a Catholic majority was ruled over by a Catholic dynasty. The Protestant states were the major beneficiaries while the *Reichskirche* lost not only the autonomous ecclesiastical states but the episcopal and monastic lands within them.

There is, then, an important sense in which the unstitching of the Westphalia settlement confirmed for the Protestant Churches in central

Europe the confessional ascendancy they had been progressively achieving since the 1760s. The principle of secularisation had been a feature of the Treaty of Basle (1795) between France and Prussia, an indicator of the extent to which Churches whose Erastianism was part of their historical inheritance, could live more easily than their Catholic counterparts with the rulers of a militarised Europe and their commitment to wholesale change. The new balance did not lead to any displays of religious triumphalism in polities where Protestants had either a new Protestant head of state or were more numerous than Catholics. Protestants in the new states of Berg and Westphalia knew how much they owed to Bonapartist policies and they acknowledged them quietly, as did their co-religionists inside France's newly expanded eastern frontier on the Rhine. Where Protestants formed part of a religious minority, such as the former subjects of the prince-bishops in Germany, they took full advantage of the assurance of toleration. The concession should not be overstated: even in those states toleration was becoming the norm rapidly by the 1780s. Events outside Germany mirrored these developments. In the new Batavian Republic, non-Calvinist Protestants, Catholics and Jews all enjoyed much higher degrees of civic freedom than under the Orange family and its hardline Calvinist allies. The creation of the kingdom of Holland in 1806 encouraged more of them to come forward and serve the new dispensation.

The pro-French Max-Joseph of Bavaria (acceded as elector 1799, king from 1806) and his chief minister, Maximillian von Montgelas, were among the biggest winners under the reorganisation of 1803, absorbing ecclesiastical states including Bamberg, Freising, Augsburg and Passau, the 900,000 individuals living within them, and all the accompanying lands. Montgelas (b. 1759) was the model of an enlightened bureaucrat in this era, courtly and efficient at the same time, devoted to the new Bavarian kingdom's well-being and unconcerned at its having no obvious ecclesiastical legitimacy (that was to be found in the constitution of May 1808).

It only remained to put the seal on these changes by declaring the empire at an end. Napoleon speeded the process when he declared himself emperor of the French on 18 May 1804, and Francis II responded on 10 August when he decreed that the imperial title was hereditary within Austria and thereby began the process of distancing himself from any official involvement beyond Habsburg frontiers. For just two more years this arrangement continued until, in the aftermath of his crushing victories at Ulm and Austerlitz, Napoleon, seeing himself as the new Charlemagne, set up the Confederation of the Rhine and, with Germany now under Bonapartist rather than Habsburg sway, insisted that Francis acknowledge as much by resigning the imperial title. With talk that there could be a Protestant emperor for Germany circulating, Francis duly did so on 6 August 1806, laying down his crown after an official proclamation. The Holy Roman Emperor was now *de jure* as well as *de facto* the emperor of Austria. It was a richly symbolic moment in the long history of a Christian Europe, though its practical implications were nominal.

Church and state in France, 1802–1814

The official return of Christianity in France brought much comfort to Catholics and non-Catholics alike. As one Oxford professor opined in 1806: 'all the freaks and fancies of a vain philosophy have been openly condemned and renounced, and the Religion of Christ, restored with no small triumph'.[2] The problems facing the Gallican hierarchy as they settled down to business again following the promulgation of the Concordat were immense if not insuperable. First and foremost, they had to establish a working relationship with the Bonapartist government through the departmental prefects and the bureaucrats in the new Ministry for Religious Affairs in Paris. This required considerable sensitivity on both sides. The Ministry was headed by Jean-Etienne-Marie Portalis (1745–1807), a moderate who had fled abroad at *fructidor* 1797 and only returned after *brumaire* 1799. He was a practising Catholic who successfully walked the tightrope of enforcing imperial religious policy while maintaining the confidence of the episcopate. Napoleon's authoritarian temperament made it natural for him to assume that the Concordat and the Organic Articles had reduced bishops and clergy to a primary status as servants of his state; Portalis, in practice, tempered that assumption. His removal from the scene by death in itself precipitated many of the Church–state ruptures of the late empire. Some bishops, too, were ready to be co-operative and work with the Bonapartists, for example Duvoisin, bishop of Nantes, and Napoleon's uncle, Cardinal Joseph Fesch, archbishop of Lyon and primate of the Gauls. Clerical support for the regime could bear important fruit. At Vannes in Brittany, the *curés* acted as intermediaries between the *département* and the rural masses, greatly facilitating the work of the prefect. It appears to have been a relationship seldom reproduced elsewhere.

The bishops and clergy had to operate a Church that many talented colleagues rejected as an insult to true Gallicanism to be exclusively found,

---

[2] Edward Nares, *A Sermon Preached at the Primary Visitation of the Most Rev. the Lord Archbishop of Canterbury, holden at Ashford, in Kent, 13 June 1806* (Canterbury, 1806), 19–20.

they protested, in the *Petite Église*; what it lacked in numbers, it made up
for in purity. Instead, the *concordataire* bishops had a few former Constitutional bishops as equals alongside them in the post-1802 dispensation,
creating a Church unity in name only. The bitterness of 1790–1801 was
still too recent to produce a collegial spirit and prelates first consecrated
before 1790 were no less ill at ease with imperial followers such as Fesch
or Cambaccérès. The bishops had, nevertheless, been handed extensive
powers over the lower clergy in the Concordat; this was a Church as far
removed from presbyterianism as it was possible to be. This considerable
patronage was usually operated against former Constitutional clergy even
when they were known to be popular locally. Priests from the rival allegiances found it hard to tolerate each other after 1802 and the divisions
opened up by this failure of the attempt at clerical cohabitation should not
be lightly dismissed as a factor in alienating individuals from the Church.
There were also not enough priests to put in parishes: only 36,000 secular
priests in 1814 compared to 60,000 in 1789. So trying to reinstate the pre-
revolutionary ratios between priests and parishioners was a quite unrealistic objective. Regional variations were pronounced, with *départements*
like Aveyron, Ardèche, Lozère, where resistance to dechristianisation had
been strongest, having far fewer shortages than those where the opposite
had been the case. In that, they corresponded to the geographical realities
of religious life in France overall. What clergy there were tended to be
older, with 42 per cent of active priests aged sixty or over in 1814. Younger
men were conspicuous by their absence. It was not just a question of
money. The lower clergy had received minimal consultative rights, their
subordinate status had been confirmed by the Napoleonic settlement and
it would not be reversed. In effect, the Revolution had brought them next
to nothing, and the ideal of citizen-priests that had been so influential in
the 1780s was dead and buried less than a generation later. Instead, there
were the first glimmers of a revival in monastic work. The crypto-Jesuit
Pères de la Foi led by Louis Barat were pioneering missionaries in cities
such as Amiens, Lyon, Poitiers and Bordeaux until they were suppressed
by the emperor in 1807, two years before *all* missionary activities fell under his ban. By that date Napoleon had reverted to a militant distrust of
Catholicism and the 1801 Concordat was fast becoming a dead-letter.

Franco-papal relations, 1804–1815

Cardinal Fesch, French ambassador to the Holy See, was keen that Pius
VII should come to Paris to crown his nephew as emperor of the French in
person. But there were others in the Vatican who were less happy at their

master acting as 'imperial chaplain' and endorsing a regime which was legitimate only in that it reflected French military power on the continent. Against majority advice in the *curia*, Consalvi threw his decisive influence behind the scheme, and Pius duly departed across the Alps, presiding at the rites in Notre Dame Cathedral on 2 December 1804. He gained little for his troubles from either imperialists or high monarchists – there were no concessions on the key issues of divorce, having Catholicism declared the religion of the French state, or receiving back the lost papal provinces in the Legations and the Avignonat – though he lingered in Paris for the first three months of 1805. Pius gained rather than lost prestige from his visit, to outward appearance the highpoint of Franco-papal relations. Worse was to come, as the emperor insisted on the papacy's institutional subordination to his hegemonic schemes and Pius refused to comply. The high price he paid for this recalcitrance was offset in another by becoming, for the clergy of Bonapartist France, far more of a friend to their interests than the emperor.

Pius believed that he had more than met Napoleon half-way and looked for concessions from the emperor towards the papacy; but the victor of Austerlitz and Jena was no more ready to extend them to the holy father than any other ruler. There were minor altercations over Pius' failure to annul Jerome Bonaparte's marriage or move against Lucien Bonaparte, exiled to Rome for his embarrassing republican preferences; these were as nothing compared to the pope's determination to retain his freedom of political manoeuvre and not be absorbed into the greater French states-system. An exasperated Napoleon ordered troops into the papal states in November 1805 for a brief occupation to show what might happen *permanently*, and sent another force to occupy the ports without Pius' consent a few months afterwards. In 1806–7, French demands mounted appreciably: British and Russian subjects must be expelled from the papal states as part of the policies by which Napoleon ratcheted up the pressure on his remaining enemies. Pius agreed to this, cancelled his resistance to the Italian Concordat, consented to have one drawn up for Germany, had Consalvi resign as Secretary of State (17 June 1806) and yet dug his heels in over joining the alliance against Britain or creating sufficient French cardinals to give them a third of the electoral college. The price he paid for his stubbornness was the occupation of the papal states by a French army in November 1807, with General Miollis' troops moving into Rome on 2 February 1808. Pius VII became a prisoner and most of the cardinals were expelled. For a year the battle of wills between the troops and the clergy continued until the emperor lost patience, annexed the papal states to the empire on 17 May 1809 as the departments of Tiber and Trasimène and turned Rome into an 'imperial free city'. Pius replied by issuing on 10 June the Bull *Quam memorandum*, which declared excommunicate all who took part in this illegal occupation. It could not save him from arrest on 6 July 1809 and ignominious removal from Rome over the Alps to Valence and thence to Savona in Liguria. There the supreme pontiff remained under house arrest, stubbornly and persistently refusing to treat with the imperial government or accept the large income Napoleon offered as an incentive. He lived quietly, praying, reading, making do with only one servant, and never losing hope that he would be vindicated. In the background, his servants in the ramshackle papal bureaucracy implemented a very effective policy of passive resistance in the face of imperial occupation.

For two years, Pius invested none of the prelates named to dioceses by Napoleon until, as a gesture of good will, he made a verbal agreement in September 1811 for metropolitans to invest them on his behalf. Napoleon regarded this as a moment to increase the pressure on Pius rather than reduce it. He was transferred to the palace of Fontainbleau south of Paris in mid-1812, where on 25 January 1813 he was bullied into signing a new Concordat ('of Fontainbleau') in which concessions were extracted for the government of the Gallican Church that passed beyond those mutually agreed in 1801–2. Pius retracted his signature in March 1813, and Napoleon, by this date on the defensive militarily, sent him back to Savona (January 1814) and released him (March 1814). The pope returned to Rome almost at once leaving again for Genoa – and safety – during the Hundred Days when Napoleon returned briefly to resume his imperial power before final defeat at Waterloo.

Napoleon's determination to break the will of the pope might appear disproportionate, even counter-productive. It certainly reflects the absolutist power available to the emperor by 1810 that made the idea of resistance to his wishes in any quarter intolerable; it also displayed the hard core of anticlericalism within the Bonapartist state that it sometimes suited the emperor to emphasise. Of course, by his intractable policy towards the pope he was hazarding what remained of the good will of French Catholics towards his regime (the garlands, hymns and illuminated streets when Pius arrived in Valence told their own story) and the number of unyielding Gallicans in the French Concordatory Church was too few to make their condoning of his actions of any significance. Just as with the thorny issue of conscription, he would not lose face by changing policy. Pius was more patient and, in his own way, no less stubborn. His quiet endurance conferred on him a spiritual influence which the regime was powerless to counter and, in the medium term, it was the emperor who lost prestige and Pius who gained it.

Church and state in Napoleonic Europe

Outside France, the working alliance between state and Church remained as close as ever, though the one-sided nature of the relationship was confirmed. Napoleon's intimidation of the higher clergy in France had parallels in most other polities. Wherever one looks, politicians and administrators did not hesitate to interfere in Church affairs should policy – in wartime usually connected with state survival – warrant it. The wholesale rearrangements of German ecclesiastical territories and titles in the early 1800s are the clearest instance of this trend, but it can be seen in a host of minor ways, such as pressure on bishops to reorder parish boundaries, close 'redundant' churches or give lower clergy improved pay without calling on governments for the extra sums required. These initiatives, such as the transfer in 1807 by Eugène de Beauharnis of the cathedral of Venice from Saint Peter's to St Mark's, could be undertaken promptly, much more so than in the late *ancien régime* medley of competing jurisdictions where delay was endemic and historic anomalies accepted as part of the scheme of things. Catholic and Protestant Churches were similarly affected by this confirmation of Erastianism in the first decade of the new century: princes and ministers wanted the theological hallowing of the continuing struggle against French hegemony in Europe and offered almost nothing in return to protect confessional privileges, property or status, beyond the unspoken assumption that churchmen would not find quite as much disruption as their equivalents were experiencing in France.

France had closed her monasteries between 1790 and 1792, and most German Catholic states followed suit a decade later, raising ready money from land sales and property without making the ideological fuss that republicans had done in the first phases of the Revolution. Dissolution of the regular Orders throughout the Holy Roman Empire was under way between 1803 and 1806, and proceeded rapidly after 1806 when all legal restraints were removed. For rulers in Austria and Bavaria, it was a resumption of Josephist practice, the precedents were in place, and war had inured populations to confiscation and disruption in a manner not felt in the 1780s. So the state's commissioners arrived and in the name of the king arranged the details of closures and pensions; more importantly, they supervised the inventory and seizure of monastic property and treasures, with many of the latter irretrievably lost or stolen in the processes of confiscation. The massive land loss the French Church had suffered in 1790 (confirmed in 1801) was thus extended to the rest of Catholic Europe. Rulers would no longer have to contend with an ecclesiastical order that used land ownership as the basis of its power.

Patronage rights passed from monasteries to princes, who used this extended influence to ensure that benefices were awarded to clergy of proven loyalty. There was an element of constructiveness in all this: in the kingdom of Württemberg, the government opened the seminary at Ellwangen in 1812 and a Catholic university with five chairs of divinity. The essential point is that this was a decision made by the state on behalf of a Church whose independent institutional life was precarious and whose resources and endowments had mostly passed out of its hands. The importance of the regular Orders in supplementing the work of the parish priests was conveniently ignored and missionary efforts suffered in consequence. Monks became parish priests or schoolmasters, abbey churches were handed over to the parish for their use, as were most collegiate churches. Nuns were usually allowed to stay together, though their numbers in Germany both decreased and aged, with few novices permitted.

There as elsewhere in Catholic Europe the parish and diocese were confirmed as the supreme units in the Church, not because this suited the hierarchy as under the Tridentine decrees two-and-a-half centuries earlier, but because the state willed this arrangement as the best agency of control for its purposes. The parish clergy were as valuable to the life of any state in the 1800s as they had been in the 1760s, their role as state officials now additionally expedient – not to say enticing, as so many of them had lost their tithes. This was even more the case with bishops. Here Napoleon's protracted wrangling with Pius VII proved costly since, with dioceses often vacant as a result of the impasse, administration faltered and pastoral life suffered without episcopal oversight, as in southern Italy. Murat's royal government, installed in Naples two years after the French had driven out the Bourbons and his brother-in-law Joseph Bonaparte had left for Spain, was ruthlessly interventionist in religious affairs, using priests as conscription agents and instituting civil registers of birth and death, but also restoring some cathedral property and reopening some seminaries. The king, Joachim Napoleon as he styled himself, was thus not without good will towards the Church (he had plans for clerical pensions) and wanted to work with his priests. The problem was that his good intentions were vitiated by the emperor's breach with Rome which necessarily affected Naples, and bishops could not be appointed or translated. By 1815, nearly 100 of the 131 sees in the kingdom were vacant.

Only in Russia and Britain was there evidence of continuity in Church–state relations, at least outwardly. The accession of a new tsar, Alexander I, in 1801 led to numerous solemn services at which the sanction of the Orthodox Church for the young emperor was given amid an atmosphere of general rejoicing and a sense of new purpose in the life of the state. Alexander soon showed that he had a respect for the Russian Church and its spiritual traditions that neither his father, Paul I, nor Catherine the Great, his grandmother, had possessed. In England, scholars are divided about the health of the established Church. Only a minority would probably endorse W. R. Ward's view that 'As a working establishment, the Church of England collapsed even quicker than that of France'[3] in the Napoleonic era except in agreeing that local variations in its work were appreciable. Its loyalist rhetoric of the 1790s was redeployed against France once hostilities resumed in 1802, but it lacked the crusading zest and originality of earlier years and could not quite conceal a sense of vulnerability that reform on a scale unseen since the Reformation would somehow come in, whether piecemeal or imposed by the state.

With rural poverty growing and urban radicalism weakening town congregations when dissent did not do so, the Church of England's dependency on the state was growing. The Anglican clergy as a whole had no answer from within their ranks, apart from legislative restrictions, to the unstoppable growth of undenominational itinerant preaching. Richard Mant, rector of All Saints, Southampton, saw in itinerancy a return to the disorder of the Commonwealth period of the 1650s when the Church of England and its hierarchy had been abolished. It had been widely adopted by Independents and Baptists from about 1780 and did much to raise their numbers. In 1811 the former premier and leading layman, Viscount Sidmouth, failed to have a Bill licensing itinerancy complete its parliamentary stages. The days when loyalty to the British state could be persuasively defined in confessional terms had passed. The British government would not endorse Anglican policy preferences if they offended the religious susceptibilities – and the loyalist instincts – of most Protestant dissenters, especially those Methodists who feared Sidmouth's Bill would have an unwanted impact on their established arrangements for preaching.

In Ireland, whereas episcopalian Protestants felt comforted by their amalgamation under the Act of Union into an Anglican organisation encompassing both Canterbury and Armagh, the Irish Catholic hierarchy had to come to terms with the disappointment that Union had not been accompanied by emancipation. That did not lead them to break off links with Dublin Castle. They recognised the power of the militarised British state in Ireland and that though, so long as George III lived, emancipation would not come, when he died, good behaviour might finally secure

---

[3] W. R. Ward, 'Revival and Class Conflict in Early Nineteenth-century Britain', in his *Faith and Faction* (London, 1993), 285–98, at 287.

their dearest wish. That said, they maintained a respectable distance from the Castle, and the bishops became increasingly popular with the lower clergy after 1808 when they rejected all thought of clerical pensions and a royal veto on appointments. Meanwhile, the imprisonment of Pius VII (1809–14) and the impossibility of gaining access to him meant that six Irish sees could not be filled. It also made Pius look to Britain in a way which made Catholic relief less likely. It was yet another reminder of clerical dependency on the dominant states-system, one which, at the highest levels, transcended the denominational divide.

The Evangelical revival continues

If there was an unstoppable popular dynamic to early nineteenth-century Catholicism it was eclipsed in intensity by the continued spread of evangelical religion across most parts of the Protestant world with the British Isles as its heartland. As one minister of the Church of Scotland noted in 1802: 'Never, perhaps, was the Bible more diffused through every corner of the land: never were abler apologies written in its defence; and never were such zealous attempts made for its propagation in the world, as in the age in which we live.'[4] Popular Protestantism – unashamedly Trinitarian in its colouring – was on the march inside the existing denominations, but outside it the obstacles to its growth and expression became inhibiting. This was a movement in tune with lay instincts and not readily susceptible to clerical steering. In Cornwall, early nineteenth-century Methodism was marked by convulsions and willing acceptance of supernatural forces that many in Conference found unsettling, trying as they were to strengthen the disciplinary hand of ministers without alienating the voluntarist assistance of lay preachers and class leaders, many of them still women. The fact was that Wesleyan Methodism in the 1800s found revivalism awkward to handle, and confrontation between Conference and the evangelical leaders was a regular occurence. Jabez Bunting, the man who had emerged as effective successor to John Wesley as leader of the Connexion, was willing to confront and drive out dissentients within his ranks. In the first decade of the new century, revivalism and radicalism still tended to run together and Bunting would not tolerate the conjunction. Robert Southey articulated concerns in 1803 about the potentially subversive chracter of Methodism when he defined it as an Ecclesiastical Corresponding Society. Bunting was embarrassingly aware that this conclusion might be drawn and insisted throughout his early career that sin and democracy were interrelated.

[4] Revd James Steven, *The Unrivalled Felicity of the British Empire. A Sermon Preached at the Salters' Hall, November 7, 1802* (London, 1802), 22.

Only in Ireland did Wesleyan Methodism suffer little from internal dis-sensions, and its leaders managed to double membership between 1791 and 1815 to 29,000. The Connexion's fissiparous tendencies in England had been highlighted by the Kilhamite secession of the mid-1790s, and that was not the end of it. There was another break away from the main-stream in 1808 when Methodists in Cheshire and Staffordshire held a series of outdoor meetings which produced the same convulsions and hysteria that had marked the original wave of Methodism in the 1740s. These Methodists took seriously the visions its adherents experienced and condoned the use of exorcism to 'cast out Satan' at prayer meetings. Their chief organiser, Hugh Bourne, was expelled by Conference when he refused to abandon these camp meetings (Conference came out against them in 1807) and, by 1811, his followers had coalesced with other radi-cals to form the Primitive Methodists, a body that attracted many from lower down the social ladder than the Wesleyans. Primitive Methodist influence was strongly felt in some parts of the north of England and the West Midlands, but the new grouping was incapable of making a wider impact on the nation and numbered only 25,000 in 1821.

That may have been partly due to the other Evangelical attrac-tions on offer to the British public. The great expansion of nonconfor-mity in Wales began in the 1800s while, in Scotland, there was a revival beginning in Perth in 1799 that would make the Highlands and the crofters in particular a stronghold of the Free Kirk. More significantly over the medium term, the minister of the Scottish parish of Kilmany, Thomas Chalmers (1780–1847), underwent a personal conversion which led to the spreading of evangelical waves throughout the established Scottish Church within only a short space of time. In both England and Wales, Independent and New Connexion Baptist ministers (those who had re-jected the Unitarianism of its parent body) were increasingly itinerant. It all made up part of an exciting revivalist culture that included camp meet-ings, the public delivery of testimonies and conversion experiences. Here was a chance for ordinary men and women to assert their right to atten-tion, to resist clericalising agendas, to get away from the humdrum activi-ties of a rapidly industrialising and dislocating everyday world in search of something much more exciting. The raw emotionalism of the Protestant revival won over scores of thousands to a form of religion the Anglican establishment was structurally inhibited from replicating. Its particular attraction to the wives or daughters of artisans – millers, weavers, printers, skilled men who feared that mechanisation would downgrade and demean them – was very evident. These were people who knew their Bibles and encouraged others to use them for, however valued conversion was as an outward sign of grace, it was inspired by and led back to scripture, not to a retreat into religious subjectivism. Indeed much of the revival looked to a tolerant form of Calvinism for inspiration, one not inconsistent with preaching the Gospel to all. This was explicitly the case in Anglican Evangelical circles and, by the 1810s, was causing enough episcopal disquiet to constrain Evangelicals to debate with their critics rather than devote their energies exclusively to winning souls for Christ.

As the wisest spirits in the Church of England appreciated, the Evangelical revival posed no significant threat to the British establishment or to the national task of winning the long war against France. Its values were annually gaining ground within elite society. Beilby Porteus, the veteran bishop of London (d. 1808), delighted Wilberforce and his friends in Parliament by endorsing the Evangelicals' position on key issues such as the slave trade, Sabbath observance and elite immorality. If his age and formative influences made it awkward to describe the bishop in technical terms as an 'Evangelical', that was certainly possible with Spencer Perceval, premier from 1809 until his assassination in the Commons lobby in May 1812.

It was becoming safe, even desirable, to recognise that loyalism was by no means exclusively identifiable with Anglicanism. It could cause gloom among those with unrealistic expectations of the British state's privileging of the Church of England. According to one archdeacon in 1813: 'Things seem to be going on well abroad, but here all is in a fair way of being given up to Catholics, dissenters, & every thing but the Church. What possession this demon of laxity & indifference seems to have taken of the nation. When it will all end it is vain to conjecture.'[5] Other contemporaries saw this rectification of confessional imbalances as justifiable, if only from the necessities of wartime survival, and these more generous perceptions of loyalism helped doom Sidmouth's Bill against itinerant preaching; they also kept up pressures to repeal statutes discriminating against dissenters, such as the Five Mile and Conventicle Acts of the 1660s. There was appreciable Anglican Evangelical liaison with nonconformists in such bodies as the non-denominational London Missionary Society, and the abolition of the slave trade in the British Empire in 1807 was, to a considerable extent, a victory for Evangelicals and orthodox dissenters working harmoniously together on the basis of shared biblically inspired values. The influence of Quakers, Methodists, even Unitarians (who finally received legal recognition under an Act of 1813) had a profound impact on progressive public policy in most areas of British life, including education and social welfare as well as slavery.

---

[5] R. Nares to Bishop George Gleig, the Scottish Episcopal Primus, [May 1813], NLS, Gleig Papers, ff. 91–2.

Such values were becoming unstoppable within much of the Protestant world as the spiritual pleasures of orthodox Christianity – confirmed by conversion experience as the inward working of God's grace – were discovered afresh in the Napoleonic era. In Lutheran Scandinavia, the individual catalyst for change was Hans Nielsen Hauge (1771–1824), a farmer's son dissatisfied with what he viewed as a worldly generation of Norwegian bishops and clergy. Hauge was a compelling popular preacher and adept at schooling his assistant preachers in his puritanical evangelicalism, one that had no respect for the powers in Church and state if they were adjudged to be infringing Gospel ordonnances. Beginning his travelling ministry in Norway in 1796, he also visited Denmark regularly and had a formidable impact in rural areas where land reform was transforming the basis of society. He was at regular intervals between 1806 and 1811 hauled before the Danish courts for contravening the 1799 press law, but it did little to impede the effectiveness of his itinerant ministry. The Swedish Church was influenced by great pastors such as Henric Schartau (1757–1825), a power at the University of Lund and a major influence on a generation of ordinands, with his stress on Pietism and upholding tradition within the community. There was much discontent with the Prayer Book of 1810 and the Catechism of 1811 among evangelically minded Lutherans who would subsequently break away and form the 'New Readers' in the middle of the century.

Eighteenth-century Switzerland had tended towards a more rational and undogmatic form of Protestantism than anything seen since the Reformation. The ordained ministry retained an affection for this faith of their fathers. So much was apparent from the Genevan catechism of 1814, which referred to Jesus Christ not within specifically Trinitarian terms but by the lesser Pauline phrase as the first-born of all creation, suggesting honour rather than worship. This rational restraint was at odds with the more fervent religious devotions finding favour with the laity. Necker's daughter, Germaine de Staël, helped further interest in German mysticism through her influential *De l'Allemagne*, and her advocacy was complemented by first-hand contemporary testimonies. The celebrated Russian mystic Baroness Krudener had visited the Pays de Vaud in 1809, and established contacts with the Moravian Brethren. Both Lausanne and Geneva became centres of religious reawakening in a way not seen since the Reformation.

As in the sixteenth century, it was the Swiss–Scots interaction that proved fruitful, although by contrast with the 1550s, Scotsmen were coming to these cities to instruct and inspire rather than to be taught themselves. The important figures here were Alexander Vinet, known as the Protestant Pascal, and the Scottish layman Thomas Erskine of

Linlathen. Less fervent and Calvinist than Robert Haldane at Geneva, Erskine tore away the formality of the Vaudois Church. Haldane held his own Bible classes to reacquaint theological students with scripture and pull them back from a set of religious observances he feared rested excessively on good sense and good manners. He became central to the *Réveil* or evangelical reawakening in the city after the recovery of independence from France in 1813. The example of the ministers was not lost on the laity, who formed the *Société Evangélique* to force the evangelical pace. Recruiting members from the elite, the *Société* pioneered Sunday Schools, founded a school for girls, and interested itself in missionary work. European religious vitality was thus being renewed as part of a wider pattern of cultural change in which the beauties of mystery and the mystic were being rediscovered.

Christianity and Romanticism in early nineteenth-century culture

The history of modern scepticism is the key to all the monstrous phenomena of the modern age.[6]

As is well known, the period between about 1795 and 1815 brought a remarkable creative outpouring across Europe, which is customarily classified as the beginning of the Romantic era. This book is not primarily concerned with the cultural renaissance in itself, rather with its impact on institutional religion and the extent to which the mainstream Churches and their congregations benefited or suffered in the process. In other words, what, if any, are the links between Christianity and Romantic culture?

So much of this new spirit in Germany came from a mingling of Pietism and enlightenment concerns. Pietism's validation of emotional and mystical experience was antipathetic to rationalism and, in combination with its emphasis on self-questioning, helped pave the way for Romanticism. The importance of figures such as the church official, preacher, publisher and writer Johann Ludwig Ewald (1748–1822) is coming to be appreciated as an explanation of how periodicals, sermons and school reforms were, if anything, more important than they had been in the 1750–1800 era in spreading new perceptions of religious faith. Ewald, an admirer of Rousseau, wanted the catechism to be directed from doctrinal statements and moralistic teachings towards encouraging young people to follow closely the example of Christ's earthly life. Old

---

[6] Novalis, *Christianity, or Europe*, quoted in Hans Reiss, *The Political Thought of the German Romantics* (Oxford, 1955), 134.

doctrines such as predestination and the Chalcedonian formula could be reinterpreted if they no longer contributed to faith.

There can be little doubt that, for some of the generation born in the 1770s, the incessant warfare and state conflicts that preoccupied the major European powers for most of their lifetime acted as a spur to imitate Goethe and retreat within oneself and find calmness there and there only. It is no coincidence that young Germans determined to rediscover the world afresh benefited from the peaceful and creative decade of 1795–1805 in Prussia, a relief from the pressures of wartime denied their British equivalents. Hopes had been so high for general change in the 1790s, but the arrival of Napoleon Bonaparte rather than the New Jerusalem had a souring effect on many intellectuals as well as clerics. Disappointment translated millennial expectations into poetry of transcendent vision, as M. H. Abrams in *Natural Supernaturalism* and Harold Bloom's *Visionary Company* have persuasively argued. Instead, the Utopian dream gained renewed fervour from the ideal of Christendom as an imaginative alternative to the reality of revolution and war, especially among young intellectuals disillusioned with the course of events. Novalis (1772–1801) (a.k.a. Georg Friedrich Philipp von Hardenberg), a well-connected Thuringian baron rather than the death-obsessed youth of nineteenth-century myth, led the way in his poem 'Christianity or Europe' of 1799, with its invocation of those 'beautiful and glittering times when Europe was a Christian country'.[7]

Yet much of this visionary aspect had nothing to do with Christ, his Mother or the saints, and it tended to run outside Christian channels altogether. The sense of the transcendent within this culture battled against the solipsistic and the escapist. Romanticism's emphasis on man as an autonomous agent, generating his own selfhood, worked against Christian influence, with its implication that the study of oneself was more urgent than the worship of God; its imaginative looseness was uninhibited, seldom willing to be constrained by either social or intellectual convention. There was a sense of loss in Romantic culture which would not be satisfied with Christian reassurances of salvation. Homesick for the abiding and eternal young Romantic intellectuals might be, but they would not easily be bought off with assurances of heaven.

The cultural leaders of the 1790s and 1800s were interested in religion as an expression of the poetic rather than the dogmatic. Since Kant had first published and emphasised the importance of the sublime, intellectuals could keep hold of a certain religious pathos while eschewing specific articles of belief. Coleridge, moving from his original radical

---

[7] See G. H. Holt (ed.), *The Triumph of Art for the Public* (Washington, D.C., 1980), 179–97.

unitarianism, became insistent that religion is not science. Subjectivity was not disdained as part of a disengagement with natural theology as conventionally taught. Nowhere were these trends more obvious than in Germany, whose leading protagonists are well known. In his short life, Novalis produced some hugely influential writings, including the Romanticised hymn book *Geistliche Lieder* (Spiritual Songs) and the 'sermon' on the French Revolution *Die Christenheit oder Europa* (Christendom or Europe), the latter less a work of theology than a poetic essay, and by no means orthodox. With Novalis, as for so many intellectuals of his generation, Christian spirituality fed into and helped bring Romantic sensibility to maturity; he longed for a new, individualistic Romantic religion (well expressed in his poetic novel *Heinrich von Ofterdingen*) that was was only indirectly bound to Christianity and, far from condemning the Revolution, in which he saw some positive values. He had nothing to with Pietist circles largely hostile to the Revolution and was an inspiration to a new generation of converts to Catholicism.

This revival (for want of a better word) therefore tended to take place outside the established Churches, and rarely reinforced Christian dogmatics, contenting itself with the free expression of spiritual impulses within what was only loosely a Christian framework. It tended towards pantheism rather than revelation, the recognition of God in the universe, with mankind destined to lose itself in the infinite rather than face the divine judgment seat. The extent to which the intellectual revival in religion had an impact on the lay public (especially in rural areas) and influenced the parish clergy in the discharge of their duties remains to be charted. Caution is required. Though Germans had access to a new metaphysics, it was one operating essentially independently of Christianity. Nevertheless, in a German context, the links of some of the leading thinkers of their day with the Lutheran Church should not be minimised. Thus Fichte at Jena and Schelling and Hegel at Tübingen (the latter's first essay was a 'Life of Jesus') all started their careers as theological students, leading Nietzsche to dub them later as 'concealed theologians'. Their insatiable interest in the phenomenology of religion – and Christianity in particular – was continuously apparent. To take two examples: Fichte's *Guide to the Blessed Life* (1806) brought him to a kind of Christian Platonism under the inspiration of St John's Gospel; Schelling's *Philosophy and Religion* (1804) argued that faith and knowledge are one, with the reunion of God and man as the aim of both. Hegel is the odd man out in this respect. By the late 1790s Hegel had moved away from identifiable Christianity in favour of a cohesive *volksreligion*, rational yet appealing to the common people; a few years later, his religious concerns had given way to philosophical ones, to find fruit in his great *The Phenomenology of the Spirit* (1806).

It was left to Friedrich Schleiermacher (1768–1834) to attempt some sort of reconciliation between Protestantism and post-Kantian German culture, and to remind his fellow countrymen that the arts and philosophy were no adequate substitute for theology. Schleiermacher came from a Pietist background, a pastor who had undergone a crisis of faith before serving as chaplain at the Charité hospital in Berlin (1796–1802), a 'Moravian of a higher order' as he called himself, reaching out in the first instance to those whom he called 'the cultivated despisers of religion'. His lectures on religion (*Reden über die Religion*) were first published in 1799. In conjunction with his later *The Christian Faith* (*Christliche Glaube*) (1821–2) they have with ample justice been called 'probably the most original re-exploration of the Protestant theological position since the Reformation'.[8]

These publications were a far cry from Luther's return to an authoritative and therefore consolatory view of scripture. Schleiermacher insisted that a shared doctrinal standard mattered much less than a striving for the infinite, and he produced a subjectivism that would wrench Protestantism away from doctrine towards a mixture of Romanticism and Pietism based on the individual, in which the redemptive force of Christianity was measured by experience and history. The Church, for Schleiermacher, was a fellowship (*gemeinschaft*) created by men's voluntary actions, and he deployed a pantheistic concept of nature which had echoes of Goethe. His courting of heresy through an appeal to the emotion and the subjective intuition of the individual at the expense of dogma apparently offered little comfort to the Church, yet Schleiermacher's pastoral ministry in Berlin combined with the dynamism and originality of his theology gave his fellow Lutherans a creative inspiration they were not inclined to disown in haste: his teachings would be translated after the Wars of Liberation into Pietism and orthodoxy. The rejection of the rational was viewed by his generation not as obscurantism but as an essential first step on the road to truth, for people wanted desperately to find again a personal God rather than a chilly and distant Creator.

Contemporary Catholic thinkers who wanted to link the Romantic sublime more overtly to Christian teachings were often denied an institutional base, since the secularisation of Church lands weakened many of the Church's most active intellectual centres, including those seminaries, universities and monasteries where the Catholic Enlightenment had taken root. The rush to secularise within the Habsburg Empire that was affirmed in 1803 thus both materially deprived the Church and had the

---

[8] Quoted in Bernard M. G. Reardon, *Religion in the Age of Romanticism* (Cambridge, 1985), 31.

effect of pushing it to the intellectual margins for the first time in over a millennium. One exception was Munich (mainly after 1815), another was Lucerne in German Switzerland, whose most outstanding product was Joseph Heinrich Alois Gügler (1782–1827), who went back to a typological tradition and injected it with new life. In *The Sacred Art* (*Die heilige Kunst*) (1814–18) and *The Cyphers of the Sphinx* (*Die Ziffern der Sphinx*) (1819) he portrayed both Old and New Testaments as a richly symbolic vision of human history in its God-orientated rhythmic development that would, in the fullness of time, bring together all creatures in harmony under God.

An independent thinker, like Karl Wilhelm Friedrich von Schlegel (1772–1829), son-in-law of Moses Mendelssohn and a Catholic convert, found in the poetic that positive representation of the totality of being which was only indirectly present in philosophy, and the highest expression of that poetic reason is to be encountered in biblical revelation, as he pointed out in *Geschichte der alten und neuen Literatur* (1815). For men like Schlegel it was because they valued mystery and enchantment that faith once more became an attractive proposition, and they turned backwards to Christian medievalism as part of a search for stability in the present. As a young man Schlegel could hardly contain his spiritual ambition, telling Novalis in 1798 that he wanted to write a new Bible, and follow where Muhammad and Luther had trod.

In their positive reassessment of Christianity, thinkers like Schelling might lambast the *Aufklärung* as a negative expression of philosophy, but they tended to read the Enlightenment as possessed of a harmony that was far from the case. The late Enlightenment contained within itself the trends which the next two generations would affirm and extend: Rousseau had popularised the cult of sensibility, Herder had awoken his countrymen to the cultural validity conferred in the first instance by history rather than philosophy, while Robert Lowth had indicated the treasury of the Old Testament considered as poetry rather than Hebraic chronicle. Moreover, most of the Churches had by the start of the nineteenth century learnt to live with a non-dogmatic interest in the faith. In Scotland, the culture of sensibility dovetailed in with the popularity of evangelicalism and the continued philosophical stress on 'common sense'. The popular novelist Susan Ferrier proclaimed the importance of religious sensibility in best-selling fiction like *Marriage*, her first novel of 1818. There were other points of convergence: cultivation of the human spirit was not too far from the classic emphasis of religious conversion, and there was a respect for religion implicit in the culture of the 1800s that was far removed from the inimical French dechristianisers of the previous decade. Few now denied the cultural significance of Christianity and its power in the lives of men and women, whether expressed inside or outside the established communions. Yet if the Romantic insistence on enlightenment through personal struggle (and often torment) had more than a passing resemblance to Christian notions of life as pilgrimage, the clergy could never have agreed with Novalis that 'Eternity, with all its worlds, all past and future, is either within us or nowhere.'[9]

The survival of popular Catholic religion, 1802–1815

Never was there a period in which the Laity evinced a stronger desire and resolution not to abandon the principles in which they were educated.[10]

The states of Napoleonic Europe, their revenues and lands swollen by ecclesiastical confiscations, may have found it quite straightforward to reconfigure Church organisation. It was much less simple to mould the laity, especially the Catholic laity. The Revolution and the Napoleonic era brought a limited recovery of interest in Christianity among the genteel which, on the one hand, articulated a yearning for comfort amid the disruptions of the age and, on the other, amounted to a fresh interest in the possibilities of spirituality reacting against late-enlightenment materialist currents. The world-weariness that engulfed the early nineteenth-century intellectual Chateaubriand, led many – as it did him ('I wept, and I believed') – back to embrace the historic faith. He talked in 1802 about people hurrying to the house of God as they might to physicians in time of plague. Chateaubriand's famous book of the same year, the *Génie du Christianisme*, uses an artistic appeal to the senses to register the truth of Christianity; God's purpose is disclosed in sculpture, literature, agriculture and Gothic cathedrals. Though Chateaubriand was articulating emigration ideology, the second edition was dedicated to Napoleon as one 'whom Providence has marked from afar for the accomplishment of his prodigious plans'. It uncompromisingly justified the place of the Church in French society, castigated Voltaire's malign influence and warned that when 'men lose the idea of God, they rush headlong into all sorts of crime in spite of laws and punishments'. Chateaubriand expected the emperor to take his point. The book appeared six days after the promulgation of the Concordat on 8 April 1802. Chateaubriand was not alone among the European elite in finding a new faith for the new century. The Spanish author Pablo Olavide, having escaped from the Inquisition, had lived outside Paris since 1780 and spent time in prison during the Revolution,

---

[9] Quoted in ibid., 8.   [10] Nares, *A Sermon*, 22.

produced anonymously *El Evangelio en triunfo, ó historia desenganado*, the letters of a 'false philosopher' who is won back to religion by the letters of a good padre and then converts his friends. It had gone into eight editions by 1803, and was the Spanish best-seller around the turn of the century.

Yet the flight back to religion within the landowning European elite at the beginning of the nineteenth century should not be exaggerated. The majority of this group, less intellectually alert than Chateaubriand, had never doubted either their Christian faith (its consolatory power is hard to underestimate) or its social utility. The Protestants among them in Britain and Germany had been open to evangelical influences for two to three decades before the *Génie* appeared. Christian convictions did not prevent noblemen in Italy and southern Germany from going along with the latest ecclesiastical reform schemes drafted by Bonapartist officials, commonly *Jansénisant* in outlook despite the hard lessons learnt a generation or two earlier in the Habsburg monarchy of how difficult they could be to implement.

So one sees, remarkably, the power and persistence of Jansenism in a non-theological form with Napoleonic hegemony in Europe acting as a most effective facilitator. Rulers placed Church policy into the hands of ministers whose agendas differed little from those familiar to Peter-Leopold of Tuscany and advocated in the Synod of Pistoia. Thus, in Württemberg, the Church committee set up to oversee change was from 1807 in the hands of Benedikt Werkmeister, an ex-Benedictine and Catholic reformer. He was keen on a range of Jansenist-style reforms plus a vernacular liturgy. Personnel continuities were marked. In the kingdom of Italy, Giovanni Bovara returned to direct the ministry of religious affairs, having held comparable office in Lombardy under Maria Theresa and in the Italian Republic created by First Consul Bonaparte. It was, for such men, a second offensive, a fresh chance to take advantage of the confused state of Catholic Europe and win the day. From a clerical angle, the problems were compounded by old Jansenists who were being assisted by younger officials to whom administrative efficiency was the supreme good and Napoleonic business methods an inspiration. Lawyers, policemen and administrators trying to stamp on any sign of religious recrudescence often had republican or masonic backgrounds, or both.

In their anxiety to impose concordatory-style Catholicism on the countryside, they imagined they had reduced the bishops and priests to obedience and now they would reduce the laity to order. Encouragement came from the highest level. In 1811 Napoleon called a national council of the French Church. Number 49 of its policy document called 'Views on the Organisation of Catholic Worship' declared it the duty of the Church 'to lend a hand in the eradication of superstitious practices, those shameful leftovers of medieval barbarism', by which was meant popular religion in most rural areas of the country. But, in the process of trying to complete the overthrow of a familiar culture grounded on religious identity and practice, Napoleon's supporters completed the alienation of the rural Catholic masses from the new European order and guaranteed the failure of Bonapartism to achieve a popular following beyond the French frontier. For, as Michael Broers has insisted, 'the reforms of the Concordat ran counter to the deepest values of the common popular culture of Catholic Europe'.[11]

To be an ally of the emperor came to be seen as being by definition anticlerical and, usually, anti-Christian. Resistance in the countryside to the new edicts and orders on religion tended to be passive and obstructionist; understandably so when the civil servants could call out troops should there be insurgency or rioting. It was no less effective for that, hamstringing the Napoleonic drive for efficiency beyond the towns. Officials and reformist clergy alike approved of the prohibition of pilgrimages, failing to see their uses as a time-honoured rite of communal solidarity as well as a day off work for husbands and fathers. In the kingdoms of Italy and Naples especially, the parish priest would respect the letter of the law and play the good civil servant the state expected him to be by reading out banning notices from the pulpit, knowing that a large percentage of his people would ignore them. He would very likely join them and risk death or imprisonment by celebrating Mass and joining in the carnival in defiance of the civil and military authorities. It was not just saints' days but the services associated with Holy Week that pitted the regime against the parish. Most officials requested reduced numbers of services rather than banning street processions and vigils. They had a sufficient respect for opinion on the streets and in the fields not to bring malcontents out into open rebellion, particularly after the empire began slowly to founder in 1811–14. Thus, in Italy, laws imposed by Paris on divorce were ignored and, in Naples, the anticlerical minister of justice, Francesco Ricciardi, dared not circulate those articles of the Code Napoléon (Napoleon's systematised legal reforms) that allowed for the civil marriage of priests. A reconciliation between the Catholic Church in French-occupied Belgium and Napoleonic officialdom was never achieved. The priests were predominantly counter-revolutionary, ultramontane and proud of the way they had endured persecution. No agreement about a concordat was reached and they persisted in their principled recalcitrance, despite being able to ordain even fewer new clergy than was the case in France.

[11] Michael Broers, *Europe under Napoleon 1799–1815* (London, 1996), 113.

The demolition of Church power was nowhere more forcefully embodied than in the way troops were deployed to close down nunneries, monasteries and wayside shrines. The wholesale abolition of convents across Catholic Europe and the failure to arrange satisfactory pension arrangements for former regular clergy was particularly resented by the laity. They had been ready enough, as their parents and grandparents before them, to enjoy a joke about monastic lifestyles and cloistered self-indulgence, but such banter was articulated within a familiar social order in the countryside, one whose endurance seemed axiomatic. Then within two decades it was gone, and in a strange inversion, a gentle, almost hereditary anticlericalism was transformed into a vituperative denigration of the new, secular order that had inflicted this upheaval and sent them much more rapacious landlords than the abbots and priors had ever been.

Generations of country men and women had found the monasteries and convents of central Europe a place of refuge and relief, a last resort in times of dearth, and for women of all backgrounds taking the veil had offered a rich community experience which, for spinsters particularly, was not easily found in the outside world. France itself was something of an exception. Female religious Orders such as the Ursulines and the Visitandines were provisionally re-established with government connivance in 1807, and the Daughters of Charity had also just about survived. The formidable Sophie Barat had even managed to establish the *Dames de la Foi in* 1800; by 1815 she had established convents in six French towns. For the most part, nuns found no sympathy from the majority of Napoleonic officials charged with enforcing these decrees. They were expected to go back to their families without fuss. No matter that their people were often dead or, when still alive, had no wish to reincorporate them into the family circle. So thousands of female ex-religious drifted into the towns and could be found begging on the streets between 1805 and 1815 or, in extreme cases, taking up prostitution.

Whatever the decrees said, it could be hard to pull the sisterhoods apart. They were too used to each other's company to make a clean break with the disciplined intimacy that had been their main adult experience. The institutions shut down, the conventual life went on with so many clandestine groups reassembling that the state had to intervene to forbid living in groups of more than four. These further enactments did not guarantee success. Thus larger female communities were receiving unofficial aid in Bologna and much of the kingdom of Italy as late as 1810. In Italy and southern Germany, noblemen and women were once again appreciative of the monastic Orders offered relief by employing former monks and friars as tutors and private chaplains, as well as attending

Masses on suppressed saints' days. Officials did their best to deflect blame for not moving against such practices fast enough, but, as one local prefect told his superiors in Milan: 'their [the monks'] seclusion was voluntary, their practice of retreat came from a sense of conversion . . . For these reasons they have received the not indifferent generosity of the townspeople, and have been given a house where twenty of them live.'[12]

Officials miscalculated the capacity of the laity to hang on to popular religious observances which had, if anything, grown more necessary for them as a result of wartime events. Moreover, much of Catholic Europe had grown accustomed to doing without the services of a priest (or one whose politics were unacceptable to them); confirmations could be few and far between in remote parishes where there was no bishop. Lay cults and observances of preference, however officially classifiable as 'superstitious', filled the vacuum and had helped keep them loyal to Catholic practice in the darkest days. Devotion to the Sacred Heart and the Stations of the Cross intensified and was encouraged by the Church; the Stations were popularised throughout Italy following the missions of Fr Luigi Mozzi, an ex-Jesuit, into the diocese of Treviso in 1801–2.

One of the casualties of wholesale Church reorganisation in the 1800s were the confraternities. Where they did not disappear, they were decisively downgraded, and obliged to focus their devotions not on their own chapel but the parish church. The French authorities in Italy were bombarded with petitions to keep the chapels open, but they were disregarded. These closures in fact gave some satisfaction to both bishops and parish priests, whose own jurisdiction was thereby consolidated. Thus, in Italy, the *Santissimo*, the brotherhood of eucharistic devotion, survived, but stripped of its endowments and able to hold Masses only during daylight hours, and then with a policeman present: state officials would not risk such bodies using religion as a cover to disguise their plans to destabilise the Napoleonic polity, however remote the possibility. The confraternities suffered a diminution in their socially prestigious membership, but the urge among laymen to demonstrate their piety and combine it with office-holding was not easily stifled. In northern Italy, the *fabbricieri*, officers of the fabric, comparable to churchwardens, were a power to be reckoned with throughout the Napoleonic era, and there are numerous recorded instances of clashes with the priest over expenditure, church fittings and fixtures.

On the whole, the observant laity and parish clergy tended to co-operate when officials turned up the pressure. Their resistance tactics could not prevent the loss of many local festivals, public processions and holidays in

[12] Ibid., 112.

the face of the regime's determination to enforce the ban. Bishops were often forced into nominally sanctioning changes they privately deplored. They were under intense pressure in the Napoleonic states-system to spearhead the fight against 'superstition', or give up office to someone who might go faster and further if he had Jansenist sympathies. Because the Church was being stripped of powers and duties in areas involving social policy – including hospitals, charity and education – excessive recalcitrance at episcopal level could be counter-productive. In southern Italy, the *luoghi pii laicali*, funds for the expenses of buildings and worship, were confiscated and administered as secular charity by the municipality. This necessarily weakened the ties between clergy and laity, for the indigent would knock first at the town hall rather than the presbytery. Understandably, the Church wanted to staunch the flow of duties to the secular state. Nevertheless, there can be no doubt that bishops across Europe signed edicts presented to them by officials and then, like the parish clergy in their turn, turned a blind eye to popular disobedience. In the last analysis, the hierarchy knew who had the Church's best interests at heart, who would risk their lives in its cause. While the Napoleonic era may have seen the Catholic Church on the defensive as an institution and pushed to the sidelines, it drew strength from the commitment of the laity to its survival as offering a way of life they preferred to the alternatives on offer from the imperial state and its satellites. Nowhere was that point more vividly underscored – in blood – than in Spain.

'The Spanish ulcer'

Popular Catholicism formed the bedrock of opposition to Napoleonic imperialism and the efficient enlightenment values by which it operated. The unique capacity of the Catholic faith in rural areas to act as an anti-revolutionary recruiting agency had been amply demonstrated in the 1790s during the Vendéen Wars. Significantly, Napoleon had taken no personal part in the counter-insurgency campaign adopted against those rebels. Had he done so, it is possible he might have been more cautious in invading Spain and expecting the general population to accept easily the replacement of the Bourbons by the Bonapartes plus control of the Church and the clergy to a degree that surpassed anything attempted by either Charles III or IV. On the other hand, he knew that rural resistance could and had been successfully stamped out where it had occurred previously (including the Vendée); what he could not have foreseen was the scale of national resistance on this occasion. The emperor called the Spanish rising 'an insurrection of monks' (Fouché on 31 December 1808 opined that the Spanish monks were the most dangerous enemies France then faced). The verdict was accurate in that it recognised the leadership of the clergy, misleading in its implication that what would become for Napoleon his 'Spanish ulcer' did not involve most of the Spanish population in a war of resistance which showed what a potent cocktail patriotism and Christianity could be.

The Spanish regular and parish clergy had repeatedly shown themselves to be obstructionist towards their own domestic reformers, but they displayed a new sort of ferocity towards the subjugation, both personal and institutional, imposed by the French occupying forces. Their arrival was the more resented coming, as it did, so soon after the abdication of Charles IV and the accession of his son Ferdinand VII following the Tumult of Aranjuez (17–19 March 1808), an event popular with most clergy. It turned their gaze away from the generous terms offered by Napoleon under the Constitution of Bayonne of early 1808, brought in after the abdication of the Bourbons. The Constitution was intended to assure the Spanish governing class – and the prelates in particular – that no religion other than Catholicism would be tolerated, and that the regular Orders would not be dispossessed. Despite the Bayonne provisions, the higher clergy were cautious, knowing how repressively the French had behaved to every other Catholic power in Europe from the papacy downwards; it was also not easy for them to overlook majority feelings in the provinces where co-operation was readily viewed as collaboration. For the bishops to excommunicate the insurgents or otherwise fail to condone their activities would be to compromise their own right to influence events.

What really vitiated French gestures of good will was the replacement of the Bourbons by the Bonapartes as Spain's ruling dynasty. French efforts to install Joseph Bonaparte as king encountered popular and bloody resistance not just in Madrid, but in Badajoz, Cartagena, Cadiz, Valencia, the Asturias and Andalusia, where local people overthrew and often murdered those governors and *corregidores* who would not proclaim Prince Ferdinand as regent and death to the French. This bloody response and counter-response coupled with the British landing in Portugal in August 1808 soon ended Napoleon's inclination to be generous to the Spaniards, and he put himself at the head of an army to restore French control in Madrid and the central and southern provinces. Having identified the clergy as the leaders of resistance to French control, two-thirds of Spanish monasteries were dissolved by Napoleon in late 1808, then all were closed down in August the following year by King Joseph (acting at Napoleon's behest), who desperately needed all the material assets of his bankrupt kingdom. The Inquisition was also disbanded at the same time. The enactments simply hardened resistance among Spanish churchmen whose insistence that the defence of monarchy and Catholicism were commensurate appeared vindicated, for this was a sacred war against a person whom one priest contemptuously referred to as 'the thief of Europe, the Attila of the present century, the enemy of God and of his Holy Church'.[13] The prosaic truth that the Spanish religious communities were under threat by 1806 from the Bourbon monarchy (it had proposed an edict to secularise their goods) was soon forgotten as friaries and nunneries gained new friends as patriotic emblems of resistance to the unwanted outsider.

It was the scale of resistance to Napoleonic power that made this rising exceptional, with the crusading spirit summoned up as the only appropriate response at a time of national emergency. As the leaders of village communities, the clergy could not stand by when churches were ransacked, shrines desecrated and colleagues assaulted. Their message to their flock was the straightforward one of repentance and resistance. Thus the Napoleonic intervention of 1808 was presented by many Spanish clergy as a visitation for the sins of Godoy and his allies. The resemblances of the delinquent Spaniards to the Old Testament Jews appeared blatant. One priest told his congregation: 'The Lord hath punished you for your sins. Oh Spain, do you not think that you are as deserving as Judea of punishment? Have you not provoked the just wrath of the Lord with your sins and crimes?'[14] But from pulpits and marketplaces they also urged their people to take up arms and often fought in person, as did Fr Merino, priest of Villoviado in the province of Burgos, who made all the roads in the area unsafe for French detachments and killed prisoners in retaliation for French atrocities. Many bishops gave up governing their diocese for commanding an army or a local junta. Examples abound. Bishop Menéndez of Santander was made regent of Cantabria before he was defeated and forced out of the country; Bishop Martínez Jiménez of Astorga was made head of the junta for armament and defence until his diocese was subjugated; the aged bishop of Coria issued two pastoral letters urging young people to take up arms against the foreign invader and was murdered by a French detachment coming from the nearby town of Ciudad Rodrigo. His was the only episcopal death during the Peninsula War, but scores of lower clergy died, often in vicious and degrading circumstances that served to kindle the desire for revenge and kept the cycle of violence going, one so well known to posterity from Goya's haunting artistic depictions.

[13] Quoted in William J. Callahan, *Church, Politics and Society in Spain, 1750–1874* (Harvard, 1984), 89.
[14] Quoted in W. J. Callahan, 'Spain', in W. J. Callahan and D. Higgs (eds.), *Church and Society in Catholic Europe in the Eighteenth Century* (Cambridge, 1997), 34–50 at 50.

The regulars were to the forefront of this resistance, serving as members of local juntas, supporting Spanish troops in the defences of Zaragoza and Gerona in 1800–9 and turning religious houses into recruiting stations. There was extensive destruction of holy places (including the pilgrimage shrine of Our Lady of Vega, patroness of Salamanca) in the vicious hill fighting, and guerilla bands could readily turn on each other in preference to the French forces in a dispute over territory. Only gradually did liaison between Spanish irregulars and Wellington's army become stabilised between 1809 and 1813. The duke himself always recognised the vital power of the clergy in Spain, and did his best to use them as intermediaries, notwithstanding the massive cultural chasm between these unlikely allies. British officers included several Hanoverians like Commissary Schaumann, who came from a country one priest in 1808 depicted as 'inhabited chiefly by heathens and heretics who worship Luther; that is why God has given them long winters and barren soil – a miserable land!'[15]

As elsewhere in Europe, a minority of clergy were pleased to be offered the chance of French-style freedoms, some – the *afrancesados*, the Frenchified – even welcomed the foreigners as modernisers. Jansenist sympathisers were prominent. The party (or *pistoyense* as Jovellanos dubbed it) at Salamanca University had survived a government-backed drive against it after *Auctorem fidei* had been introduced into Spain in 1801. The most significant *afrancesado* was Juan Antonio Llorente (1756– 1823), previously secretary general of the Inquisition, who under Joseph was charged with the task of imposing a French-style Concordat on the Spanish Church. Joseph was in principle ready to uphold Catholicism as the national religion; his problem was that only a tiny minority of Spanish Catholics had any interest in his preferences or pronouncements. The rest aimed to drive him out. The majority of the bishops were in exile, either because they would not tolerate the policies of the French or had been expelled. For those who remained, passive resistance was the order of the day, even for the least militant in the hierarchy. By 1813 most Spanish dioceses had no bishop and, though Joseph managed to obtrude six new prelates into various sees, their authority over clergy and laity was nominal.

Gradually the various juntas opposing Bonapartist power in Spain learnt to co-operate through a *Junta Central*, and a Cortes was convened in Cadiz in September 1810. There were clerical deputies (97 priests among the 308 deputies, though the regular clergy were entirely excluded), but the reformers among them were not representative of the wider Church.

---

[15] Quoted in Christopher Hibbert, *Corunna* (London, 1961), 51–2.

Following vicious debates over ecclesiastical reform, which brought conservative and radical divergences out into the open, the Cortes produced a liberal constitution that bore little resemblance to the ideals inspiring priest and people fighting the French. Most controversially, it closed down the Inquisition and restricted the number of religious houses that could be reopened once the French had gone. Although the cardinal primate, Luis de Borbón, Godoy's brother-in-law and archbishop of Toledo, accepted the revolutionary decision to vest sovereignty in the nation rather than the king and, by swearing the oath publicly, won round all but one of his episcopal colleagues to do likewise (it helped that the constitution affirmed the Catholic nature of the realm and designated four ecclesiastics to sit on the Council of State), several senior clergy refused to co-operate with the implementation of some of its decrees. The bishop of Santander threatened to expel anyone who read the decree on the Inquisition, while the archbishop of Santiago left his diocese rather than accept the abolition of the *Voto de Santiago*, a general tax supporting himself, the chapter and the city's hospital.

During 1812–13, as Wellington's advance north gathered pace, the Cortes of Cadiz and its decrees became less important as they became more anticlerical, and Ferdinand's return to Spain on 22 March 1814 ended, for the time being, the influence of the moderate reformers. For most this had always been a dynastic war against Jacobinism and not a struggle for constitutional reform. Local juntas, desperate for clerical participation in their councils knowing the power of the priest and prelates over their people, refused to endorse most of the Cadiz proposals. The Church emerged from these desperate years debilitated and still divided: both Bonapartists and loyalists had extracted large amounts of money and valuables from the clergy; monasteries were converted to secular use or allowed to rot, and the dispersal of their residents ended the traditional system of alms relief just when ordinary Spaniards had most need of it with yellow fever sweeping across Andalusia and the Mediterranean littoral, causing the deaths of scores of clergy. Thus in 1814, the Spanish Church was exhausted from years of struggle within itself and with the French. Ferdinand would need remarkable skills of leadership to rekindle a sense of mission in it, though without the regalian character of his grandfather's time.

Spanish clergy were not alone in concerting resistance to the outsider. At the battle of Bergisel on 13 August 1809, 15,000 Tyrolean peasants defeated regular troops with a Capuchin priest – Fr Joachim Haspinger – commanding the left flank. This Tyrolean revolt was at every point a combination of religious revival and reassertion against 'French' values. There are also interesting comparisons between the role of the Spanish clergy in inspiring and directing resistance to Napoleonic imperialism at home and their counterparts in one of the Bourbon monarchy's principal overseas territories: Mexico. There, too, clerical energies were poured into an insurrection against external authority with the anticolonial revolt of the creoles starting in 1808. It was part of a defence of clerical power, autonomy, income and prestige against policies such as the amortisation of Church property imposed by secularising ministers in the service of the regime. In Mexico as in Spain, the Catholic Church was long-established and popular, and many priests were very willing to sanction their largely Indian parishioners taking up arms. But unlike Spain this revolt was directed against the Bourbon monarchy rather than a foreign interloper, and the clergy gave the Mexican rebels a ready-made leadership cadre whose existence sapped the legitimacy of the colonial power. The Spanish and Mexican clergy were both crucial in forming a body of opinion that over time would achieve their policy objectives, and the Spanish example in particular furnished a model for other Europeans who rejected Bonapartist hegemony.

Religion and the overthrow of Napoleonic Europe, 1812–1815

Historians once had much to say about nascent national consciousness as a factor in explaining the ability of the allies to defeat Napoleon after what remained of the *Grande Armée* limped home from Moscow in 1812. In contemporary scholarship, however, by comparison with diplomatic hard-headedness, international finance and the material exhaustion of French manpower resources, national inspiration is accorded a reduced and qualified role to play in the years from 1812 to 1815. But what about the possibility that religion was, as was usual in European society, the real stuff of popular politics, the principal incentive (family apart) for any man to take up arms in defence of hearth and home? The role of national Churches in channelling opposition to French domination of the continent must be considered.

This book has consistently stressed the motivating force of religion in the French Revolutionary and Napoleonic wars, so it should be no surprise to see it having a decisive if not a determining force in the Bonapartist endgame of 1812–15. Also, to discuss manifestations of patriotic and national feeling in any European polity in the early nineteenth century without reference to their basic grounding in popular religious sentiments is implausible. Christianity had survived Napoleonic resentments and remodellings: the Churches would not be cowed and so long as they held out against repression and official disdain the clergy could inspire their listeners with the vision of the status quo ante, of a world at peace living under the pre-Bonaparte authorities in Church and state – an alluring prospect for any ordinary individual who had managed to survive thus far. Short of planting officials in churches, there was not much the prefectoral corps could do to inhibit unrestrained preaching: it was always on the pulpit staircase that effective policing broke down. Finding a cleric and choir willing to be coerced into singing a Te Deum in a city like Rome (deprived of its bishop, Pius VII, from 1808 to 1814) on an imperial birthday or military victory became harder than ever for the Napoleonic authorities.

In tsarist Russia, there were no more reliable upholders of royal power – defined as coeval and in mystic union with the motherland – than the clergy, who were obviously delighted at Alexander I's growing interest in the mystical spirit of Christianity which, along with Freemasonry and Pietism, was spreading widely throughout Russia in the early nineteenth century. The opening of the massive new basilica of Kazan Cathedral in St Petersburg, deliberately imitative of the classical grandeur of St Peter's, Rome, in autumn 1811, prompted a solemn ceremony confirming Church–state bonds on the tenth anniversary of the tsar's consecration. All the royal family followed the metropolitan in procession behind the sacred ikon of the Virgin from out of the central portal and around the great square. There could no higher priority than confronting and overcoming any threat to this divine ordering of things. During the dark weeks of October 1812, Alexander I found comfort from reading the Old Testament prophets and gaining a new dimension to his sense of the mystic: 'I simply devoured the Bible', he wrote later, 'finding that its words poured an unknown peace into my heart and quenched the thirst of my soul. Our Lord, in his infinite kindness, inspired me in order to permit me to understand what I was reading.'[16] In 1813 he went on to the offensive with his army, his patriotism and mysticism co-mingling, his reading of the eleventh chapter of Daniel convincing him that the all-powerful king of the south was about to be cast down by the king of the north. Some Russian patriots were hard put to distinguish between Pius VII and Napoleon as first-choice candidates for the Antichrist, and found the centuries-old rivalry between Orthodoxy and Catholicism gave an additional edge to events: many Muscovite clergy looked on Poland as the spearhead of schismatic Rome directed against Holy Russia, and the presence of 100,000 Polish soldiers in Napoleon's invading army of 1812 did nothing to diminish this perception.

[16] Quoted in Alan Palmer, *Alexander I: Tsar of Peace and War* (London, 1974), 253.

Resistance did not mean merely offering Masses for the defeat of the French or hymning Te Deums on the retreat from Moscow. In most parishes on the route of the French invader in 1812, the priest played the same proactive role in encouraging resistance as his Spanish equivalent, and many were executed for their pains: battle-hardened members of the *Grande Armée* knew that their opponents had no more accomplished recruiting sergeant than the average cleric. Some went further. In August 1812 a band of guerillas led by Fr Sakharov claimed to have killed and captured over 200 French troops. Religion as a motor of national revival transcended denominational differences. In Austria after 1809 and Prussia from a year or two afterwards, one finds hymns readily adopted to a patriotic purpose. If hymns kindled religious devotion, their use could by extension benefit the state, for these were tunes that most of the adult population would know.

The laity did not need much encouraging to link patriotism and Christianity, for the early 1810s continued and intensified a religious revival in the higher social circles, especially in Prussia, the spring after the 'spiritual winter' of the Enlightenment as traditional Protestant historians dubbed it. The supernaturalist school of theology led by Franz Volkmar Reinhard (1753–1812), chief court preacher to the elector of Saxony after 1792, was fast disseminating its influence across northern Germany, one that the remarkable events of this era only encouraged. This rediscovery of faith was an emotionally charged phenomenon not easily confined within confessional boundaries, possessed of an intensity making it almost a second Pietist Awakening. But, despite the debt to the Pietist life of the Moravian Brethren, it was more than a revival. The French Revolution, then defeat at Jena and occupation gave Prussian reconstruction a transcendental significance. It embodied a determination to celebrate Christian values defined as contrary to those implicit in enlightenment and revolution and, it was claimed, upheld by the archenemy of the War of Liberation – Napoleonic France. At Kalisch (on the borders of Prussia with the Grand Duchy of Warsaw) the tsar concluded a convention with Frederick William III with a final clause that captured the mood of religious fervour: 'Let all Germany join us in our mission of liberation. The hour has come for obligations to be observed with that religious faith, that sacred inviolability which holds together the power and permanence of nations.'[17] The French polity was at once a material threat to the Hohenzollern state and a spiritual menace, and its dismantling became the overriding objective for those numerous Prussian noblemen and women whose Christian faith had suddenly become the defining aspect of

---

[17] Quoted in ibid., 261.

their lives. They would have totally endorsed Schleiermacher's preaching of January 1808 that to abandon the nation to a foreigner was a violation of the divine order of the universe.

Religious revival there may have been, but the Prussian state remained loath to relinquish its Erastian preferences. In October 1810 the government under Karl von Hardenberg nationalised the land belonging to both Protestant and Catholic Churches and took final control of all ecclesiastical institutions. It was a key part of the state's attempts to get to grips with the financial problems that were inhibiting Prussia from rebuilding itself as a major power after Jena. The monarchy was also wary about allowing preachers full scope to stir up unfettered anti-Napoleonic feeling until as late as 1813, when there were those calling on the people to take an active part in public affairs rather than simplify glorify the ruler. In fact, Prussian Protestantism was still firmly wedded to the king: Frederick William III withdrew from public life in 1810 after his wife's sudden death rather than commit himself to any idea of a patriotic crusade, and the nation stood loyally by him in February 1812 when Prussia signed a new agreement with Napoleon. It took a further twelve months and the French retreat from Moscow for Frederick William to join Alexander in a war for the liberation of Europe. In the last analysis, level-headed considerations based on the good of the monarchy determined Prussian policy making in Berlin much as they did in every other European capital. Only when a decision had been made to go to war with France could religious revival and anti-Gallicanism be encouraged uninhibitedly.

Conclusion

The Churches had been placed under unprecedented pressures during the Napoleonic Empire. Boundaries had been altered at every level from the imperial and the national to the parochial, the religious Orders were dissolved on a scale not witnessed since the Reformation, and all states – whether under imperial sway or not – insisted on obedience and adaptation from the clergy that had not always been forthcoming. But securing their allegiance was a prize worth striving to win, since that combination of religion and patriotism was virtually unstoppable, as Napoleon found to his cost. The end of the Holy Roman Empire necessarily closed down the ecclesiastical territories within it and bishoprics whose foundation dated back to the origins of Christian Europe. This was an epoch-making change in religious history that coincided with the territorial consolidation of Catholic Austria and Bavaria: innovative legal and institutional means were required to deal with the various confessions in the new German states, especially those which had absorbed the former ecclesiastical authorities. Members of the Catholic hierarchy who controlled sees transferred to the thirty Protestant states within the German Confederation found themselves abruptly shorn of political influence. Once the shock had passed, circumstances offered little choice but to look directly to Rome and ultramontanism. The way in which the latter would develop in the nineteenth century was by no means clear in 1805-15: the papacy was brazenly intimidated by Napoleon, and Pius VII became his prisoner on French soil. However, the holy father's exemplary – and politic – patience and refusal to be browbeaten was enough in itself to compel admiration and make those once suspicious of papal claims to sovereignty more willing to think again.

Equally importantly for the future of European Christianity, the Churches could draw on the absorption and retention by the laity of the sound and extensive teaching of the faith undertaken between 1600 and 1780. It had flourished in adversity and there was little that the enlightened servants of Bonapartism could do to counter it. So confronted by these hostile, suspicious or just indifferent politicians, the clergy fell back on their popularity with the ordinary laity, and showed themselves ready to make concessions to popular religious feelings that pandered to 'enthusiasm' and 'superstition'. Yet this was a surefire way to religious renewal, and confessional leaders were in no position to neglect the mainsprings of revival from whichever direction they sprang. Anything which helped bring people back to public worship served this purpose, for many families had reacted to the confusion brought about by war and political change by not going to church at all, and they would be reluctant returnees thereafter. On the other hand, it is easy to overlook pressures making for a renewed interest in the Christian mysteries at home and in church: the calamitous times, the death of loved ones on and off the battlefields, the example of martyrs for their faith over the last two decades. Those that came back – or never went away in the first place – included a high proportion of wives and mothers who were ready to take direct action to protect *their* parish priest and *their* church. Both the hierarchy and officialdom – for different reasons – found women who well knew that the moral leverage they possessed was awkward to deal with. But, with a high percentage of European males bearing arms, at least they made up a dependable congregational body.

Enlightenment ideals persisted despite the squeeze of state repression and popular dislike; clergy of differing opinions within a confession slowly made working accommodations with colleagues with different views (as in France where the old wrangling between Constitutionals and nonjurors was not easily forgotten) and, sometimes, even inter-denominational relationships were eased. A yearning for a united Christian order can be found in the writings of Novalis, Walter Scott and others, with Catholic revival fuelled by the way recent events had confirmed its political conservatism. It would, however, take more than Bonapartist hegemony on the continent to nullify longstanding Catholic–Protestant intolerance. The feeling persisted in some British quarters that, in the words of a clergyman celebrating Trafalgar: 'French power has likewise been raised up as a scourge to purge the iniquities of surrounding countries, the inhabitants of which have . . . so shamefully departed from the faith and practice of the Gospel of Christ.'[18]

While such sentiments of complacency or, to put a more charitable gloss on them, relief, were heard from many pulpits in most states, they impinged little on the day-to-day work of the ordained ministry who laboured hard in war-torn times. Clerics accepted that adversity was putting their ministry to the test, not just in terms of their reduced numbers and the growth of lay indifference but in the massive loss of infrastructure on the continent: everything from chalices and vestments to furniture and church buildings. Their example was quietly inspirational. Immediately before 1815, there were the first signs of a recovery in the number of Catholic ordinands in France. With ordinands exempt from conscription under the Italian Concordat, the numbers of those attending the surviving seminaries slowly rose. Meanwhile, in Britain and Germany, the influence of Evangelicalism and Pietism was filtering into the established Churches and well beyond, as the irresistible rise in missionary societies during this decade disclosed. Once Napoleon was sent into exile for the second and last time in mid-1815, the Churches could not only congratulate themselves on having survived his rule, but also having nurtured a deeper form of Christian commitment, which, with encouragement from the post-Vienna settlement order, might yet yield a rich harvest. The last chapter explores the extent to which those hopes were justified.

[18] Revd John Eyton, *A Sermon Preached on the Occasion of the Late Naval Victory, in the Parish Church of Wellington, Salop, 10 Nov. 1805* (Wellington and Ironbridge, 1806), 20.

8   Religious revival after 1815?

The religious climate of 1815–1830

The final overthrow of Napoleonic France at Waterloo in June 1815 and the drafting of a new European settlement at the Vienna Congress did not in themselves usher in an awakening of faith across the continent. As the previous chapter showed, that process (whether going on within Church structures or outside them) was already in place, often prompted by and in response to the limited sympathies for religious expression of the French emperor, his satellite allies and their formidable military and bureaucratic forces. What assisted revival in the 1815–30 period was that virtually every polity from Britain to Russia and from Sweden to Naples was concerned to foster (and supervise) the growth of belief and practice rather than restrict it, seeing in the Churches the most important forces for stabilising the foundations of the Restoration order. Of course, this was in one sense merely the latest manifestation of those Church–state alliances which were a perennial part of European society; and yet a generation of revolution and warfare had shattered the continuities of centuries, toppled thrones (including, for a time, that of St Peter) and exposed the vulnerability of all institutions to *force majeure*. In the wake of the Vienna settlement, it became a policy imperative no government could ignore – least of all, those kings restored to ancestral thrones and territories – to sacralise as best they could a monarchical order of things, which meant ensuring that the Churches were more effective in acting as guardians against disaffection than they had been before 1790. The crowned heads of 1815–30 were inclined to overlook the fact that in the first instance it had been their fathers and grandfathers whose drive to impose Church reforms had undermined political stability.

A world without Napoleonic hegemony was accordingly a world in which Christian religious culture was permitted scope for growth. According to many, such as the leading apostle of counter-revolutionary values, Joseph de Maistre, in his *Soirées de Saint-Pétersbourg* (1821), Europe had to be nothing less than re-christianised around the twin polarities of continuity and tradition. As he expressed it in a work of 1819: 'without Christianity, [there is] no general liberty; and without the Pope, no true Christianity ... Sects and the spirit of individualism are multiplying in a frightening manner. Wills must be either purified or enslaved.'[1] Apologists for the religious right were not alone in expressing themselves in these terms. The more pragmatic monarchists also wanted to reclaim the unsurpassed heritage of Christian Europe, to emphasise that their own time must be in tune with the rhythms of that bequest while having decided misgivings about the continuities of the 1810s and 1820s with the 1770s and 1780s. It was not just revolutionary and imperial Europe that had squandered its Christian inheritance, but the latter decades of *ancien régime* (right and left both found that sort of terminology acceptable) with its irresponsible indulgence of the *philosophes*, whose deism and atheism had sapped the historical European order of its vitality. Humanity's fallen nature had ensured the worst would follow, as it duly did.

Continuity was problematic for Catholic intellectuals in countries such as France and Spain where the return of the Bourbon kings could not disguise the ruptures that had occurred in national life from the Napoleonic interlude. Official documents might proclaim 1815 the twentieth year of Louis XVIII's reign, but the post-1815 order could not be made to resemble the pre-1789 one with the stroke of a pen. Besides, there were ambivalences and embarrassments about the role of both Church and state in Louis XVI's reign that limited cultural reconnection between the eighteenth-century monarchy and the restored one. Just as Louis XVIII made no attempt to undo the Napoleonic bureaucratic order in favour of the competing and confusing jurisdictional arrangements of pre-revolutionary France, so the Gallican Church of 1815 bore only a passing resemblance to its 1789 predecessor. Some of the senior bishops and clergy of the Restoration Church were sacerdotal survivors from the 1780s, but land, monastic establishments, diocesan and parish boundaries, buildings and infrastructure of every kind had been altered, abolished or sold off over two-and-a-half decades. During Louis's *de facto* reign (1814/15–24) further changes occured in the French Church,[2] but they were engineered by a monarchical state to facilitate the primary missionary purpose of the Gallican Church, a purpose so powerful that it had formed an alliance of convenience in 1801–2 with Bonaparte and discarded the Bourbons.

A wish to re-establish continuities with the Christian past manifested itself in more Churches than just the Gallican. In a Europe whose

---

[1] Quoted in *The Works of Joseph de Maistre*, trans. J. Lively (London, 1965), 146–7.
[2] See below, pp. 326, 327, 329.

inhabitants yearned for stability, there was a renewal of interest in medieval Christianity, its liturgies, buildings and personalities, which was encouraged by the massive popularity of Sir Walter Scott's novels (they were translated into most European languages) as well as a range of other best-selling celebrations of chivalry and devotional life in a medieval golden age, such as the Catholic convert Kenelm Digby's *The Broad-stone of Honour* (1826). This did not, before 1830, amount to a full-blown Gothic revival, but the signs were there, with most church building being undertaken in that idiom. It sat well with the vogue for authentically antiquarian Gothic secular architecture that saw baronial splendour as uniquely compatible with the heraldic pomp and display exhibited so conspicuously by princes and peers all over Europe in the 1820s. Elaborate titles and a new and genuine interest in the religious Orders were not just the outward signs of a contrived medievalism and an escape from the continuing birth pangs of modernity: they suggested that the landed elites would not so easily hazard their status by flirting with progressive causes as their fathers had done and was indicative of the quiet confidence of Catholics that a resurgence of the faith might, after all, be accomplished.

It was an appropriate moment to bring back those servants of the faith who might be as effective against lingering Jacobinism as they had been against sixteenth-century Protestantism: and so the Jesuits were universally restored on 7 August 1814 by the Bull *Sollicitudo omnium ecclesiarum*. There was a cadre of some 600 ready to start work again and they began immediately, arousing surprisingly little concern in Protestant kingdoms. It was another sign that enlightenment currents were ebbing in favour of a rediscovery of history and missionary purpose; another was Pius VII's re-establishment in 1817 of the Sacred Congregation of Propaganda, and his condemnation (September 1821, confirmed and extended by Leo XII) of the indifferentism allegedly encouraged by the Enlightenment and Freemasonry. Restoration thinkers wanted mystery back in their religion, and the continuing dynamism of Romantic culture was able to provide it.

In painting, it can be found inimitably in the work of the Dresden artist Caspar David Friedrich (1774–1840), one of the purest of European Romantics, whose painterly evocation of the mystery of the forest's stillness haunted the imaginations of his contemporaries. His canvases were suffused with a sense of loss and melancholy that penetrated profoundly to the uneasy heart of Restoration culture; more satisfyingly than the obsessive search for a mythic Gothic past that could not quite stifle the sense that revolutionary rupture could all happen again. Friedrich's work had pantheistic implications – he once remarked of his painting 'Swans in the Rushes', c. 1819–20, 'The divine is everywhere, even in a grain of sand; there I represented it in the reeds'[3] – but the habitual and often incongruous presence of the Crucifixion in an empty landscape permitted an alternative Christian interpretation. Other German painters sought to recapture a sense of art placed in the service of the Church. Many such became followers and colleagues of the painters Overbeck, Pforr and Cornelius, members of the quasi-religious brotherhood of St Luke (founded in 1809), a group mockingly known as the Nazarenes for their explicit religious commitment. In 1819 no fewer than nineteen German painters attached to the group were Catholics. They tried to revive medieval-style workshop practices, and specialised in fresco paint-ing, decorating the Casa Massimo in Rome (1819) and several Munich churches. In all these cases, this was art in the service of the faith rather than the 'sacralisation' of cultural objects as religious substitutes. It would be some time yet before that tendency would be witnessed on any scale in nineteenth-century Europe.

If a Friedrich canvas could be read as a search for a purer realm of being, the presence of Christ on the Cross so often found there also evoked the sense in which the religious impulse of 1815–30 sought ex-pression in atonement for the death and destruction that had afflicted life for the previous quarter of a century. It attracted interest at the highest levels, as in Louis XVIII's decision to have a church built in Paris on the site where the bodies of his brother, sister-in-law, other members of the French royal family and innumerable victims of the Terror in 1793–4 had been dumped; just outside the capital, the great shrine of Saint-Denis, desecrated during the Revolution, was rebuilt, the scattered royal re-mains it had formerly contained decently reinterred, and new monuments erected to the martyred king and queen. It was a token of reparation that could also be found outside the sphere of high art in acts of devotion and pilgrimages sponsored and supervised by the Catholic clergy. There were renewed efforts to encourage Parisians to visit Mont Valérian, the holy hill west of Paris at Suresnes; its chapels had been ransacked in the Revolution, and in 1811 the Order of the Legion of Honour turned the last church on the site into a state orphanage. After the Restoration, Mont Valérian became a place of public expiation with a fervent cult of the Cross preached by the restored religious Orders in their own version of the Sermon on the Mount.

The missionaries returned to their work in France with the Jesuits tak-ing the lead in the cities. The cult of the Sacred Heart flourished, with

---

[3] Quoted in Joseph Leo Koerner, *Caspar David Friedrich and the Subject of Landscape* (London, 1990), 16.

many dioceses dedicating themselves to it. Louis, however, knew that to give in to the reiterated requests coming from the ultras to dedicate the whole nation to the cult made little political sense. Instead he discreetly limited himself to donating the altar in 1823 to Sophie Barat's convent of the Sacred Heart at the Hôtel Biron in Paris. In France, the Reformed Churches forged ahead with comparable initiatives in the 1820s sponsored by organisations such as the 'Society of Christian Morality'.

Elite spirituality discovered in Orthodox Christianity another source of inspiration in the 1815–30 period. The arrival in western Europe of Alexander I during the last months of Napoleon's rule stimulated interest in Russian religion, especially since the charismatic figure of the tsar was drawn towards mystic expressions of the faith. For Alexander, the architect of the 'Holy Alliance', was insistent that European order could only be securely established on religious foundations, and Orthodoxy for him thus possessed mutually coalescing spiritual and political elements. His western allies, while less than persuaded and ready to indulge him, were still willing to be impressed by the tangible holiness to be found in the Orthodox faith, and appreciated its centuries-old continuities. This sympathy for Orthodoxy was only reluctantly extended into active support for Serbs and Greeks trying to free their lands from Ottoman control; George Canning (British foreign secretary, 1822–7) and Metternich (Austrian chancellor, 1809–48), were both bent on upholding Ottoman territorial integrity and were wary of Russian ambitions in the area on the ostensible grounds of its various treaty rights to protect Orthodox Christianity. Public opinion was less constrained.

Much has been made of the appeal of Greek pagan culture in eliciting western support for their revolt against Turkish overlordship in the 1820s, but it was at least as much the perception of beleaguered Orthodox Greeks which whipped up public sympathies and persuaded Philhellene volunteers to head to the Peloponnese. Bishop Germanos of Old Patras had effectively turned the conflict into a religious war when he raised a banner emblazoned with the Cross on the monastery of Ayía Lavra on 25 March 1821, and he became the most important leader of the revolution in the Peloponnese. Many priest-participants even thought of themselves as 'Romioi', citizens of that New Rome that had been the eastern empire ruled from Constantinople. Incidents like the hanging of the patriarch Gregorios and the massacre of thousands on the island of Chios were fully reported in the west and caused consternation as much among Protestant as Catholic readers. The war pointed up the divisions within Orthodoxy between the Greeks and those living closer to the centre of Ottoman authority; the patriarchate in Constantinople preferred not to endorse rebellion rather than hazard its precarious position under Ottoman protection. The murder of Gregorios elicited anathemas, which Greek prelates disregarded. Instead they chose to see the patriarchate as vacant and omitted any mention of the current holders of that office from the liturgy.

The clash between Christian and Muslim betokened the degree to which interfaith intolerance remained endemic. For another religious minority – the Jews – the return of peace in 1815 did not bring significant benefits. They had improved their status during the Napoleonic era, especially in Germany. In 1813 Bavaria had granted Jews state citizenship with some important controls on their activites. The 1812 Edict of Toleration in Prussia applied to Jews, subject to reservations about numbers. In the enlarged Prussia of 1815 40 per cent of them lived in newly acquired Posen, making up 6.5 per cent of the population, and their freedom of movement was restricted. This compared favourably with Jews under Russian control, where no fewer than 650 restrictive laws applied in the Pale of Settlement. Civic equality was not easily achieved where social distrust was longstanding, as was the case in the Germany of the *Vormärz* era when emancipation was openly criticised. Meanwhile, Rome put Jews back into the ghetto and in November 1826 Leo XII prevented them from owning real property in Italy.

Protestant religiosity

If there were many signs of Catholic revival after Waterloo, the Protestant Churches were no less remarkable for showing every sign of religious vitality, thereby continuing the momentum that most denominations had exhibited for upwards of half a century. The 'awakening' in Germany had begun before the Napoleonic Wars ended, and was in full flood for twenty years afterwards. The revival movement (*Erweckungsbewegung*) was the last dynamic mass religious movement of German history, and it put liberal theologians on the defensive. Johan August Tittmann (1773–1831) produced his *Supernaturalism, Rationalism and Atheism* in 1816. An astute thinker based at Leipzig, he argued that the last two descriptive nouns in his title were effectively in the same category. Schleiermacher remained a commanding figure into the 1820s. Although he emphasised feeling and was antirationalist, his orthodoxy was still in doubt to the revivalists. In Prussia the Silesian noble Baron Hans Ernst von Kottwitz (1757–1843), the 'patriarch of the revival in Berlin', was an important patron of the young clergy opposed to Schleiermacher. Revival crossed the usual social barriers with little difficulty, a tendency well seen in the *Maikäferei*, or the May bugs, a group of young army officers, officials and literati that met regularly in Berlin from 1816. Starting off as a socialising discussion group, religious issues soon predominated. Like earlier moments of growth in Pietism, these latest ones tended to occur outside the aegis of the state Churches; militant Pietists of the 1810s combined the cultivation of the spirit with a persuasion that the ecclesiastical establishment had been poisoned by rationalism. This perception was popular among the Pomeranian nobility and led to police observation, though not to curbing of their meetings for prayers and praise. These conventicles had landlords and day labourers all praying together as 'true believers', one aristocrat (Heinrich von Bulow) reported, having spent a day discussing the Bible and Luther's writings with his gardener. This cliquishness predictably led to Jacobin accusations from pastors and officials unsympathetic to their beliefs, but these Pietists really offered no threat to the state since they upheld conservative views, and did not allow religious expression to subvert paternalist assumptions of social control in either town or countryside. Their stock rose in in the 1820s when Crown Prince Frederick William became their protector.

There could be no disguising the dynamism of Protestantism within Prussia nor the tensions the same phenomenon generated elsewhere, in Ireland for instance. The late 1810s and 1820s witnessed the 'Second Reformation' in that country, a final bid by Protestant evangelists to convert Catholics by means of educational projects, tract distribution, open-air Gospel meetings and landlord outreach, which could offer inducements in the form of rent reduction or improved accommodation. It was a sign that the Evangelicals were a power to be reckoned with inside the Church of Ireland with the Hon. Power le Poer Trench, archbishop of Tuam from 1819–39, and 'converted' in 1816, leading the assault against popery. The archbishop said in 1827: 'We are proselytisers. We plead guilty to this terrific and unpardonable charge . . . Am I to be told that for fear of offending an unscriptural church I am to join in league with its priesthood . . . to withold the Book of God from his condemned and perishing creatures?'[4] For all the fine words, the Protestant surge in Ireland during the 1820s made few converts; the Catholic hierarchy and Daniel O'Connell's Catholic Association between them ensured that Romanists had a redoutable defensive network in place at the parochial level. The 'Second Reformation' is important, however, as evidence of a militant edge to popular Protestantism and the absence of a common front between Presbyterians and Anglicans, with the former fettered until 1828 by the civil disabilities imposed by the Test and Corporations Act and the latter in no hurry to unshackle them. Relations between landlords and popular Orangeism were never easy; they may have agreed

---

[4] Archbishop le Poer Trench, quotation from his speech to the Hibernian Bible Society in 1827. Joseph D'Arcy Sirr, *A Memoir of the Honourable and Most Reverend Power Le Poer Trench, Last Archbishop of Tuam* (Dublin, 1845), 486.

in principle on the necessity of evangelising the papist peasantry but not on much more. That it tended to be voluntary Evangelical societies that led the charge against Catholicism rather than the institutional resources of the United Churches of England and Ireland says a great deal. Indeed, by 1830 accommodation between the Church of Ireland and its Presbyterian sister Churches had hardly advanced from where it had been in the aftermath of the 1798 rebellion. The 1820s were also characterised by controversy within the Presbyterian Church over the presence of Arian ministers in its ranks, a dispute not exactly calculated to reassure the Church of Ireland hierachy. Conversely, the high church revival within Irish Anglicanism fostered by prelates including John Jebb, Bishop of Limerick, running concurrently with the 'Second Reformation' did little to assuage Presbyterian distrust. As David Hempton has argued, what made for reconciliation in the longer term was the 'unprecedented religious mobilisation of the Irish protestant laity'[5] in the 'Second Reformation', with evangelists bypassing the usual agencies of social and religious control in Protestant Ireland.

English dissent, too, enjoyed simultaneous denominational growth and contraction. Presbyterians and Quakers were sunk in unedifying internal disputes that Independents and Baptists did not permit to stunt their outreach. Independents were reinvigorated by a generation of inspiring evangelists, the London Missionary Society acting as the handmaiden of greater organisational cohesion until a Congregational union was formed in 1831; Baptists were divided by Fullerists (moderate Calvinists) and hyper-Calvinists, the latter viewing the true Church as an elect remnant of the faithful and consequently having no time for associational life, foreign missions or Sunday Schools. Methodists, too, had their divisions. Revivalism went on in the major English cities at least to Peterloo (the Manchester 'Massacre' of 1819) and in Cornwall, that separate world beyond the Tamar river, for much longer. Two thousand men and women from all social backgrounds were converted at Redruth in 1814 over a ten-day period, their example so affecting 'that bystanders wd. be stuck in a moment, & fall to the ground, & roar for the disquietude of their souls'.[6] However, the main Wesleyan Connexion, under the leadership of Jabez Bunting (1779–1858) in the 1820s, was moving towards a

---

[5] David Hempton, *Religion and Political Culture in Britain and Ireland: From the Glorious Revolution to the Decline of Empire* (Cambridge, 1996), 102–3. On the 'Second Reformation', see Desmond Bowen, *The Protestant Crusade in Ireland, 1800–70* (Dublin, 1978); David Hempton and Myrtle Hill, *Methodism and Politics in British Society 1750–1850* (London, 1984).

[6] Quoted in W. R. Ward, *Religion and Society in England 1790–1830* (London, 1972), 83. See also D. Luker, 'Revivalism in Theory and Practice: The Case of Cornish Methodism', *JEH* 37 (1986), 603–19.

more rigid connexion, a more disciplined growth within formalised eccle-siological structures in which spontaneous religious expression was not encouraged and catechetical instruction was, as in the Sunday Schools. Here, itinerancy was coming to an end in favour of permanent premises and assured, usually respectable congregations. The Primitives benefited numerically from those Methodists with no appetite for this form of min-istry, but Bunting would not be deflected. Other formalising changes were introduced: the title 'Reverend' came into general use for preachers on the Missionary Committee after 1818. Two years later, Bunting as Con-ference president proposed a laying on of hands for preachers admitted annually into their office. That Bunting accomplished his objectives of disciplining the Wesleyan Connexion testified to the desire of so many in the circuits (particularly the upwardly mobile who put in the funding) for a less evangelical, peripatetic ministry towards structures at once more permanent and authoritarian.

Role of the papacy in theory and practice

Having survived decades of persistent alteration to the Church extending to outright dispossession and persecution, it was hardly surprising that Catholics across Europe came to regard the papacy as the one dependable defender of their faith. They felt vulnerable to further change as a result of the altered map of Europe following the Vienna Congress. Thus Catholics in the former *Reichskirchlich* lands and the Rhineland and Westphalia (newly part of Prussia) in 1815 adopted neo-ultramontane positions to guard against any recrudescence of Febronianism, or development of Protestant or masonic hegemony. Such a stance found appreciable theoretical endorsement. Ultra theorists such as de Maistre, looking out bleakly on the fallen world around him, were in no doubt that true 'restoration' would come, as he put it in *Du Pape* (1819), when human-ity recognised that only the spiritual sovereignty of Rome could protect it from the consequences of sinfulness. This was to echo the mature Fichte, for whom the Revolution was part of an era of 'absolute sin', in which man had grown indifferent to spiritual ideals.

It was not just ardent monarchists who saw in the person of Pius VII and his successors the primary agency of order. The French poet and social reformer, F. R. de Lamennais (1782–1854), broke with legitimism in his *De la Religion considérée dans ses rapports avec l'ordre politique et civile* (1829), arguing instead that Catholicism must be based on the capacity of popes to overawe kings and emperors, not the other way round; by this means a progressive world order could be founded which made min-imal concessions to secular forces in society. But Lamennais' call for an alliance of pope and people found few friends in Rome: in 1832 Gregory XVI condemned the liberal theory of the Church's relation with civil society in the encyclical *Mirari vos*. This hard line reassured members of the hierarchy who had experienced the original French Revolution at first hand and had grumbled that the papacy was too inclined to compromise. The cardinal-bishop of Montefiascone was convinced that such temporising indicated that masonic influence had even infiltrated the Vatican.

Gregory ascended the papal throne in 1830 and found he was the fortunate legatee of three gifted predecessors. Pius VII's principled resistance to French intimidation made it hard for the Vienna powers to deny him the return of virtually all the papacy's possessions, barring Avignon and the Venaissin. Pius did what he could to be accepted as an equal in the great power diplomacy during the heyday of the Congress system which coincided with his own pontificate, and his construction of the Braschi Palace underlined the fact that the dynastic ambitions of the popes had not expired with the eighteenth century. Yet this pontiff was always ready to adapt current ideas for his own purposes. Thus he governed the Papal States from 1816 according to the liberal Bonapartist model while preserving the pre-revolutionary institutions, an arrangement which pleased few and led to a further growth in the number of Cardinal Consalvi's enemies. Pius' main concern was to restore the apparatus of Catholicism across Europe with all speed, easing the way by co-operating with right-wing monarchists in France and Spain but accepting that the best interests of the Church were served by signing concordats with non-Catholic powers, like Orthodox Russia (1818) and Protestant Prussia (1822). The latter was an important act of statesmanship. Prussia now had a population that was two-thirds Catholic and Pius thought it appropriate to gamble on granting Frederick William III the right to veto the episcopal choices of Catholic chapters in the hope that this concession would speed the work of Church recovery in western Germany. He was right.

Pius VII's replacement was Annibale Semattei della Genga (1760–1829), a former nuncio to Louis XVIII, who took the title Leo XII. He owed his adoption by the college of cardinals to the votes of the *zelanti*, conservatives who wanted to see the influence of the long-serving secretary of state, Consalvi, terminated. Indeed, the new pope made putting a conservative into that great office his first priority after his coronation. It was the harbinger of a more right-wing regime than anything experienced under Pius VII, for Leo had few doubts at his accession that the theory of the Christian state demanded absolutism: back to the papal states came the feudal aristocracy and ecclesiastical courts of the

pre-revolutionary pattern, their efforts supplemented by spies and zealous priests monitoring private lives; the Jesuits became far more powerful
than they had been in the previous reign, and the Index and Holy Office
were both reinforced. Though more narrowly clerical in outlook than his
predecessor, Leo was neither unimaginative nor unbending. Much to the
surprise of some of his initial backers, he accepted the existence of newly
independent republics in Latin America as a *fait accompli*, negotiated
concordats with Protestant Hanover (1824) and the United Netherlands
(1827), and promoted the emancipation of Roman Catholics in Britain
and Ireland. Above all, the energies of this mild pontiff were poured into
galvanising the Church into rediscovering its missionary purpose and,
though it did nothing to enhance his popularity, he derived immense satisfaction from declaring 1825 to be a Jubilee Year and personally serving
twelve pilgrims a day at his own palace. Pilgrims poured into Rome on
a scale not seen for half a century. The total was still a disappointing
94,000, most of them Italians, headed by Francis I, king of Naples, and
500 followers. This could not compare with either the scale or the social
range of 1775 (let alone earlier Jubilee Years), when the bourgeoisie and
noble grandees had come to the city in their scores of thousands.

Leo was succeeded by Pius VIII who reigned from March 1829 to
November 1830 and had to respond on behalf of the Church to the
widespread outbreak of revolutions in Europe. He was not by preference
much of a politician, having the same primary concern for pastoral and
doctrinal matters as Leo XII. Moderate hopes in the conclave that he
would act sensitively were gratified by his improvements to the administration of the papal states and his pragmatic reaction to revolution where
his first concern was much less the protection of legitimism than safeguarding Catholic Church order. Pius was willing to be guided – up to
a point – by his pro-Austrian secretary of state, Cardinal Albani. He
condemned the Polish insurgency of 1830 and declared the alliance of
Catholics and Liberals against William I of the Netherlands as 'monstrous'. But in France the holy father rejected Albani's plea to declare
against the 1830 July Revolution overthrowing the Bourbon Charles X.

His main criterion was always how the new Orléanist monarchy would
behave towards the Church, and when King Louis-Philippe announced
that he would abide by the 1801 Concordat Pius was prepared to respond
appropriately: on the one hand he awarded Louis-Philippe the traditional
title of 'Most Christian Majesty'; on the other, he refused admission to
the papal states of some pro-Bourbon clergy fleeing France. There were
thus none of the tergiversations of 1791–2 over the Civil Constitution;
instead, it was Pius VII's model of conduct in 1800–2 towards Bonaparte

which illuminated his namesake's conduct in the crisis of 1830. It made supremely clear how contingent the alliance of throne and altar had become, how unattached to legitimism the papacy was in practice. The primary concern for the papacy was which crowned head which would cause least disruption to the continuing recovery of the Catholic Church after the profound trauma of revolutionary and Bonapartist dislocation.

Church, state and the changing patterns of confessionalism

Church–state bonding was reaffirmed after the 1815 settlement and the cessation of assaults on the essentially Christian character of European culture. Overt hostility may have ceased, but monarchs and ministers were determined to restate the *de facto* supremacy of the state in a relationship defined on their terms. The Restoration monarchies were not constrained by the competing and confusing jurisdictional networks of pre-1789 Europe; centralising monarchy had come of age during the Napoleonic era, and it remained after 1815. Ministers wanted their own way with Church leaders, Protestant, Catholic, Orthodox and Anglican, much as they had done before 1789, though they gave their ecclesiastical counterparts scope for manoeuvre since all parties recognised that dissensions among the leaders of Church and state had given revolutionaries of the late eighteenth century an opening that they had been quick to exploit.

Led by Russia, some of the powers went as far as articulating this ideal in inter-power protocols, drawing up the Holy Alliance of Christian nations in September 1815, an instrument signed by Austria and Prussia, but not by either the Holy See or the British, Lord Castlereagh, the foreign secretary, dismissing it as a 'piece of sublime mysticism and nonsense'. Alexander I was personally committed to Christian values; that much was clear, but he also intended the Holy Alliance to be a vehicle to protect the continent from the principles of liberalism and nationalism embodied in France since 1789. Thus, as part of a new search for international security, the Alliance notoriously reserved the right to interfere in the affairs of sovereign states in the defence of monarchical absolutism which would usually, by extension, involve protecting the Church.

Politicians appreciated that Catholics had little choice but to accept their protection on their terms. The Catholic Church in most areas of Europe had been an active or covert counter-revolutionary force and, the objective of restoration achieved, it had accumulated enough enemies on the left among Jacobins, republicans and radicals to uncouple appreciably from the progressive causes it had flirted with before 1790 and, to some extent, with Grégoire and the Spanish Jansenists, over the next two decades. With the hierarchy's scope for independent manoeuvre thus circumscribed, the politicians could drive a hard bargain in limiting religious policy making judged inappropriate to a regime's best interests, usually any manifestations of ultramontanism. Pius VII set the example of diplomatic watchfulness required to show the powers that the Church's compliancy could not be taken for granted. Thus, notoriously, the Catholic Church did not join the Holy Alliance of 1815 on the ostensible basis that it would mean subscribing to a manifesto also signed by schismatics and heretics, namely Britain and Prussia.

This get-out clause paved the way for Secretary of State Consalvi to be courted rather than coerced by the powers for the remainder of Pius' pontificate. Though the concordats with Bavaria in 1817 and Naples in 1818 showed the limited capacity of Rome to reclaim powers of patronage in national Churches, the pope was a patient and experienced diplomat who insisted on the conditionality of the papacy's endorsement of policy making by Catholic states. It was a lesson not lost on his successors. Leo XII showed himself determined to risk Spanish ire by recognising from 1827 onwards that Bourbon power in the New World had succumbed to the military skills of Simon Bolívar; in filling South American sees himself, the pope was standing up for the principle seen in action on and off since the turn of the century that the pastoral work of the Church would always have priority over its commitment to the principles of legitimist politics. Such papal pragmatism was not calculated to induce lay politicians to increase the hierarchy's sphere of political influence.

Echoes of the Josephist tensions of the 1780s were often heard in the relations of the Catholic Church leadership in the Austrian Empire with that leading architect of the post-war international system, Chancellor Clemens von Metternich. The latter was in many ways a product of a recognisable imperial tradition; he wanted Vienna to have the last word in Church affairs throughout the emperor Francis I's domains and to control contacts with Rome. Metternich had no intention of reversing the reduced material status of the Church following the secularisation of 1803 onwards; the Church must be content with the crumbs it had left and get on with its mission. Despite the efforts of the influential Redemptorist, Clement Maria Hofbauer (1751–1820), and others in Vienna to limit state controls over the Church in education and marriage these remained in force as a token of Josephism, enduring restraints on any manifestation of ecclesiastical autonomy. For all this, Metternich never doubted that the Catholic Church was an indispensable defence against anarchy and an ally against the secret societies he saw as plotting the overthrow of the Vienna settlement. Accordingly, he regarded progressive priests suspiciously, and campaigned against Bernard Bolzano and his followers in Bohemia.

But Catholic revival did not much suit Metternich either, at least before the revolutions of 1830 made him reconsider his religious policies. When the revival reached the Habsburg lands, it was not identifiable with the official Austrian position, and he distrusted the international group in Vienna arguing for a reassertion of clerical values. Apart from Fr Hofbauer, it numbered prominent Catholics (mainly converts) from Germany, the Schlegels, Adam Müller, Zacharias Werner – plus other outsiders including the Hungarian magnate, Ferenc Széchényi, and immigrants such as Carl Ernst Jarcke and Georg Phillips from Prussia, and Friedrich Emanuel von Hurter-Amman from Switzerland. These men cherished ideals which were at once cosmopolitan and ultramontane, enlightened but not of the Enlightenment. They were deeply critical of the immobility of the *Vormärz* regime in the Austrian lands, and their presence and good relations with many of the bishops and clergy meant that Metternich and his colleagues found the Catholic Church rather less an agency for stability between 1815 and 1830 than they had hoped. In the Rhineland, Bishop Colmar of Mainz and his supporters used the journal *Der Katholik* (founded in 1821) to articulate their resentment at the Church being pushed to the margins by the state and became some of the most important proponents of ultramontanism in western Germany.

Such Catholics found it hard to come to terms with constitutional arrangements that guaranteed religious liberty, such as the eight articles pertaining in the new kingdom of the Netherlands after 1814. Maurice de Broglie (1766–1821), bishop of Ghent, insisted that only the Roman Catholic Church as the religion of the state was in a position to uphold genuine religious freedom, but he was sentenced to exile from his see in 1817 by the Brussels courts for this obstructionism. This did not end the agitation in the Church, relations with the Vatican remained awkward, sees remained unfilled, and a concordat eventually signed in 1827 had not been implemented when revolution erupted in Belgium in 1830.

Even France was, after 1814–15, much less of a Catholic confessional state than ardent monarchists in the circle of the Bourbon heir presumptive, the comte d'Artois, would have preferred. The charter of 1814 gave Protestants and, to some extent, Jews guaranteed rights of public worship and participation in the life of the kingdom. In other areas of religious policy, the Bonapartist settlement of 1801–2 was similarly not dismantled; Louis XVIII's ministers could rely on clerical celebration at discarding the hated Fontainbleau Concordat to obscure the fact that there would be no juridical restoration of the First Estate, no return of its lands and legal immunities, to parallel the restoration of the monarchy. For two years, negotiations between the Tuileries and the Vatican went on about a revamped concordat more favourable to the Church. The end-product, the Concordat of 1817, was actually that of 1801 with a monarchist rather than an imperial seal, Louis XVIII having quietly abandoned a contentious scheme for one more favourable to the Holy See. Supporters of the moderate Decazes regime of 1816–20 shrewdly reckoned that whereas they could take Catholic support for granted, it was essential to appease the beneficiaries of Bonapartism by limiting concessions to the religious right. Sufficient that the Church could resume its mission work without state interference on the proviso that the hierarchy would stay out of politics.

Such a strategy made for an uneasy relationship with loyal monarchists and the papacy alike: the king was criticised by Leo XII in June 1824 for breaching the 1817 agreement and tolerating laws inspired by the Revolution. By that date, a reaction against moderation was already in full flow under the successive conservative ministries of Richelieu and Villèle, precipitated by the assassination of Artois' only son, the duc de Berry, in 1820, and the growing crisis in Spain. At the heart of the ultra programme was a central role for the Church, a colourful re-creation of an imagined high medieval past in which France would be rechristianised through a prayerful and privileged Church and the Gospel light taken once again to North Africa where the French army was busy trying to conquer territory in Algeria. What the ultras saw as the real Restoration was inaugurated by the exotically Gothic coronation of Charles X at Reims where the holy oil of Clovis, believed lost during the Terror, was miraculously and opportunely recovered. It set the tone for the hectic six-year reign (1824–30) of an old man in a hurry, who viewed his historic title of 'his most Christian Majesty' with an unimaginative literalism: he refused to consider the possibility that Christianity could find any other authentic political expression than in legitimism.

This uncompromising counter-revolutionary agenda thus moved to the centre of public life. It made for a last flourishing of Catholic confessionalism in France – the parish clergy recovered much of their power in the village schools, there were new laws on sacrilege – but its Gallican character was dubious, given the prominence of the Jesuits in the mission field and in education, and the ultramontane leanings of the king. Nevertheless, clergy aspirations to restoring France and themselves to an imagined pre-1789 order of things were for a time unbounded. It was an unrealistic dream; the laity were beyond their control, and society could not be rechristianised on the scale they envisaged. The more cautious members of the hierarchy – and their numbers are not to be underestimated, for the splits within the secular right had their equivalents within the Church – were aware that the legacies of the revolutionary and Bonapartist eras could not be wished away quite as easily as many in the king's entourage imagined; the Church's identification with clericalism and legitimism was hindering its pastoral effectiveness among the many opposed to Polignac's reactionary policies in 1829–30. Though the July Revolution of 1830 came as an unwelcome shock to most bishops and priests, the minority wedded to legitimism at any price was far smaller than in the Revolution of 1789. Louis-Philippe's obvious unwillingness to dismantle the concordatory arrangements nearly thirty years old facilitated his grudging endorsement by the hierarchy. It also showed the extent to which, by comparison with 1790, the priests and politicians caught up in revolutionary events were ready to talk with each other and, where necessary, compromise.

That was much less the case south of the Pyrenees. In Spain, the Church was more uncompromisingly associated with the absolutism of the extreme right than anywhere else in Europe and was ready to present this as the patriotic cause. Once restored to the ancestral throne, Ferdinand VII inaugurated several years of uncompromising reaction and put aside the 1812 Constitution, reckoning correctly that such an approach would be smiled on by the great powers. Just as Pius VII brought back the Jesuits, so King Ferdinand revived the Inquisition – only latterly abolished by the Cortes of Cadiz – as a sign of how much he repudiated the recent past. He developed a tight working relationship with conservative ecclesiastics between 1814 and 1820, purging the cathedrals of canons who were sympathetic to the work of the Cortes of Cadiz. All went swimmingly until Ferdinand had a constitution forced on him by the military coup of 1820 (the Inquisition was abolished afresh at the same time) and was effectively a prisoner in Madrid by 1822 when authority was vested in a five-man Regency Council. Though this body included two senior clergy, they were not representative of the Spanish Church at large. The sale of monastic property to the highest bidder was the last provocation and, once again, regular clergy buckled on swords over their cassocks to take up arms against Catalonian liberals. There was also much disquiet within the Holy Alliance when the Congress of Verona convened in 1822 and it led to a successful, though controversial, French invasion to restore the Bourbon status quo ante the following year. Thereafter, from 1823 to 1833, Ferdinand had sense enough to work with political moderates in a way that contrasted strikingly with Charles X's behaviour in Paris. The Catholic hierarchy swallowed the concessions to liberalism and grudgingly went along with this adaptation while retaining its underlying loyalty to the die-hards on the far right of politics. This identification of interests over the long term was less than pastorally sensitive and hazarded the Church's material wealth when civil war erupted again after Ferdinand's death in 1833 ushered in a disputed succession. Interestingly, a survey held in the Toledo diocese in 1825 showed that perhaps one-third of the parish clergy were less attached to the supremacy of 'throne and altar' than their hierarchical leaders.

In Protestant England, the established Church similarly associated itself with the long Tory administration of the 2nd earl of Liverpool (1815–27) on the assumption that it was the likeliest way to preserve its confessional privileges from dissenting and Catholic claims to more extensive participation in the life of the nation. It had been the clergy who, more than any other group, had encouraged the public into putting aside personal and sectional interest to regard the war as their first duty, a religious duty, and they intended to call in the debt from the state once Napoleon had been safely consigned to exile on St Helena. The Liverpool Cabinet, for its part, expected the clergy's continued services in preaching loyalty and good order during the tense years of social and economic dislocation in England from 1815 to 1820; the fall-back position of linking religious duty with preserving a vulnerable social order was taken up once again as the British state came under sustained pressure from its own subjects.

Evangelical weight within the establishment was increasing year on year, but still more influential with ministers was the high church Hackney Phalanx and its dedication to propagating and protecting Anglican religious practices. Under such pressure, it was not surprising that the government lost no time in underwriting a major programme of church building in the years after Waterloo. The Church Building Act of 1818 provided £1 million to construct churches in new centres of population administered by a Church Building Commission; this important agency had its voluntary counterpart in the Society for Promoting the Building and Enlargement of Churches and Chapels (1818) to co-ordinate donations from members of the public and offer assistance to parishes that did not qualify for help by the parliamentary grant. Within a year of its foundation the Society had received 110 applications for help, and 35 grants had been made. The state made a further grant of £500,000 under the 1818 legislation in 1824. Methodism, firmly under Jabez Bunting's control, also preached restraint and respect for the British constitution, lining up behind Liverpool and Castlereagh even after Peterloo. Bunting insisted that his superintendent ministers must drive out any democrats from their congregations. Some lay preachers in

Manchester – and that was not an isolated case – equated the Methodist constitution with the unreformed parliamentary franchise; others that the Conference was even lending the government money! These urban radicals severed their links with the Connexion during the 1820s.

The return of greater prosperity in that decade did not in itself ease the position of the Church of England. It could take some comfort from the fact that the new monarch, George IV (1820–30), was no less committed at his accession than his father to shoring up the Test and Corporation Acts; on the other hand, the number of MPs voting to repeal this legislation when the motion to do so came before the Commons was rising steadily, and the perceptible growth of dissenters' numbers since the 1790s made it embarrassing for Anglican apologists to be too strident in arguing against change. The issue, however, became absorbed into the more compelling one of whether to grant Roman Catholics political rights at the same juncture, a position the Pitt government had adopted in 1801 at the time of the Act of Union and had thereafter remained on or just under the surface of British political debate. Canningite willingness to countenance 'emancipation' forced the Liverpool Cabinet to maintain an uneasy public silence on the question, and the opposition Whigs had been committed to confessional realignment since Fox's time. This conjunction compelled the supporters of what was newly called the 'Protestant Constitution' in the 1820s to organise and mobilise public opinion against the threat to the constitutional inheritance (as they depicted it) of 1688, in which Church and state in England were mutually supportive. The king's brothers, the dukes of York and Cumberland, gave their blessing to the creation of Brunswick Clubs throughout the kingdom as centres for anti-Catholic agitation, the one populist vent that might deter the politicians from 'betraying' the Williamite inheritance.

There seems little doubt that, judging by the number of petitions sent to the House of Commons, the Protestant agitators had English public opinion behind them. Even in the early nineteenth century, there was nothing like the cry of 'No Popery!' to incite the average Englishmen to making his feelings vociferously known. The problem for the Brunswick Clubbers was that Catholic emancipation was seen at Westminster less as an English problem than an Irish one and, in the interests of the newly created United Kingdom, English interests would for once have to yield to John Bull's other kingdom after O'Connell's Catholic Association was formed and its founder was successfully returned at the County Clare by-election of 1828. By that date, Liverpool was dead, new political alliances had been formed at Westminster between Canning's followers and Whigs looking to the grandee Lord Lansdowne for a lead, and the administration of the duke of Wellington and Robert Peel was the last obstacle facing the proponents of emancipation. In the interests of public order in Ireland, Wellington defied the majority of his party supporters and most Catholic disabilities were removed in 1829 just as those of Protestant dissenters had gone in the spring of 1828.

The Anglican hierarchy had campaigned hard for its confessional privileges in England and Wales to be maintained, in so doing exaggerating the extent of change which would be foisted on it. It was the symbolic importance of what had been done that most stunned the leadership as it, like the Gallican Church in 1830 faced with a new monarchical order, had to come to terms not just with additional rights for dissenters and Catholics, but the advent of a new regime (Lord Grey's Whig government in 1830 took office in the same year as a new king, William IV) ready to legislate for additional changes to Church powers and property. Most Anglicans were still keen to believe in the sanctity of the alliance of 'throne and altar', and looked on political reformers as a menace to Church and state alike. As one anonymous English parson wrote in 1821: 'They are here as in France, enemies to religion, for as no government can continue without having this as its basis, by destroying the one they insure the downfall of the other.'[7] The painful reality was that the bishops could take nothing for granted about unconditional state support after 1828–32, a lesson their French counterparts had taken most of the 1790s and longer to absorb.

The Orthodox Church in Russia came as close as any other denomination to working within a Christian monarchical framework under Alexander I between 1815 and 1825, guided by Prince Alexei Golitsyn, procurator of the Holy Synod since 1802 and, from 1816, minister of spiritual affairs and education. But the hierarchy was perplexed about the tsar's eclectic willingness to learn from non-Orthodox and non-Slavic versions of Christianity. Alexander was constantly alert to the further intensification of his faith from this direction as, for instance, from the mission of the Yorkshire Quaker, Daniel Wheeler, to St Petersburg in 1817. Golitsyn's sympathies for such sects led to intense battles for the tsar's attention in the early 1820s, with the young monk, the Archimandrite Photius, gaining the kind of influence Rasputin would later have in Russian high society, and helping to engineer Golitsyn's downfall. In consequence, the last years of Alexander's life were free of any but strict Orthodox religious influences and other Christian traditions were no longer patronised.

In Prussia, the Hohenzollern monarchy treated the Protestant Church as a department of state. New consistories were set up in 1815, staffed

---

[7] [A Country Clergyman], *The Signs and the Duties of the Times* (London, 1821), 15.

with clergymen and lay officials, and functioning as part of the central administrative apparatus with powers to initiate disciplinary action against the clergy and order their dismissal. Changes to confessional arrangements and practice were immense. It occurred quite suddenly, on 27 September 1817, when Frederick William III united the two Protestant Churches in Prussia under the *Unionsurkunde*. It made for, as has recently been shown, an aggressive and systematic confessional statism unprecedented in Prussian history, a new turn rather than a restoration. What made it different from other Church unions occurring elsewhere in Germany – in the Palatinate, Rhein-Hessen, Baden-Waldeck and elsewhere – was that it was imposed by the monarch without any attempt at obtaining consent. Likewise, the new unified liturgy of 1821, or 'New Agenda' (*Agendenstreit*), as it was known, cobbled together by the king himself, and the source of additional tension inside and outside the newly united state Church.

This unsurpassed exercise in Caesaro-papism, a 'reconfessionalisation', did not go uncontested by otherwise loyal subjects who were outraged that the king had inflicted his masterplan on the Lutheran Church in the 300th anniversary year of Martin Luther's nailing of his anti-Roman theses to the cathedral door at Wittenberg. Those leading the renewal of orthodoxy within Lutheranism were particularly stunned, like Claus Harms (1778–1855) of Kiel, who published ninety-five theses of his own at Kiel's main church in which he castigated theological rationalism as 'antichrist' and 'Gog & Magog'. Many congregations fought to remain outside the Church Union, often with aristocratic backing. The 'Old Lutherans' of Silesia wanted to remain a self-regulating confession despite a Cabinet order of 1825 ending public confusion over the union and pressurising the 2,439 congregations still outside it to join in. The Prussian aristocracy, entrenched in the revived local Estates, were not sympathetic to what Frederick William had engineered, and religious policy became a focus of aristocratic resentment after 1815. The king's reforming zeal made him appear a Jacobin to his critics, both those gathering in the Estates or assembling in secret prayer conventicles. Meanwhile, on the streets of Berlin, as on those of Paris, London and Madrid, the challenge confronting the Churches was less confessional organisation and liturgy than ministering to the urban masses to ensure that they were not lost to the Christian inheritance.

Religion and urbanisation in post-Napoleonic Europe

The population explosion of the early nineteenth century exacerbated the difficulties confronting the urban ministry of the Churches for upwards of fifty years: shifting settlement patterns, rival forms of male sociability, sectarianism, popular anticlericalism and hostile local politicians prominent among them. Nothing less than a multifronted missionary initiative was required if some lost ground was to be recaptured, a test of initiative the clergy actually passed quite well between 1815 and 1830. It was a considerable success story in the light of the revolutionary experience, one which would limit the further damage inflicted by the growth of socialism and secularism much later in the century. Evangelical work in the parishes was actually well under way in England before the end of the Napoleonic Wars; comparable re-energising began in earnest elsewhere with the return of peace, the encouragement rather than the obstructionism of governments, the fresh institutional poise of the Churches and the widely held perception that the Christian religion was an essential bulwark against the instability and upheaval ascribed to the French Revolution and its consequences.

The return of 'normality' to Britain in 1815 ushered in a five-year period of exceptional stress because, in a young population, a majority of adults had come to maturity knowing nothing other than war and the distinctive social tensions arising from a combination of continental blockade and industrialisation. Parliament had enacted a series of *laissez-faire* statutes between 1809 and 1814 that had precipitated a decline in status for craftsmen; the celebrated Luddite agitation in parts of the north Midlands, Lancashire and Yorkshire made ministers aware of just how pronounced social cleavages had become in parts of the country undergoing rapid urbanisation, and the rioting, marching and agitation that accompanied the economic depression of 1815–20 reinforced the picture. Protestant dissent (at least until the 'Peterloo Massacre' of 1819) was, in the popular mind, more closely associated with the plight of the dispossessed and the impoverished than the Church of England. Whether fair or not, it was undeniable that clergy incomes had risen steeply since 1790 while the poor were getting poorer, but prosperity was not always the handmaiden of complacency.

Recent scholarship reveals the extent to which the 'unreformed' Church of England from 1810 to 1830 was capable of undertaking energetic urban pastoral initiatives without first prompting from either bishops or politicians. As Mark Smith has shown,[8] in the Oldham and Saddleworth districts of east Lancashire, church building (part of the Commissioners' programme mentioned above), frequent preaching and home visits helped keep the bulk of the laity loyal. Some of these northern parishes covered

---

[8] Mark Smith, *Religion in Industrial Society, Oldham and Saddleworth 1740–1865* (Oxford, 1994).

large townships with medieval boundaries that were anachronistic in the light of population changes. They would function more rationally after it became easier to subdivide them following the Church legislation of the 1830s. Administrative rearrangement counted for less than pastoral competence. In many circumstances, the Church of England *was* institutionally flexible enough to respond to the movement and growth of populations. Antique structures could be much less of a problem than those recently inaugurated. A comparison with the Catholic Rhineland is instructive here. The three dioceses of the new province of the Lower Rhine under the archbishop of Cologne – Trier, Münster and Paderborn – all covered large and disparate areas with growing populations. Arguably, pastoral effectiveness was meagre by comparison with the parishes of industrialising Lancashire, falling within the awkward and over-extended boundaries of the Chester diocese.

Anglican clergy had no recourse to the pilgrimages and festivals that were once again taking to the streets of Catholic Europe, an important means of stimulating popular religiosity, even if these occasions always threatened to evade clerical control. Genuflexion was not the ingrained response of most people in the crowds after 1815 when the procession passed. Indifference or contempt might prompt jeering, as might anti-clerical conviction, for the towns of France in particular were awash with discharged Napoleonic veterans, easy recruits for radical agitators and the opponents of reviving Church influence in public life. These were often joined by law or medical students, not from high spirits alone but from a Voltairean conviction that such events were deplorably superstitious. Despite the risk of disruption, parish festivals in an urban setting were a vital aspect of post-war Catholic witness. Goethe, who saw the festival of St Rochus celebrated with gusto at Bingen in the Rhineland, claimed that revolutionary rule had not diminished the religious instinct.

Prussian officials continued the efforts of the last two electors of Cologne and the revolutionary and Napoleonic governments to limit the duration of pilgrimages to just one overnight break. Pilgrims inside western Germany between 1816 and 1824 were usually female, usually unmarried, and few of the men had either bourgeois or elite backgrounds. A high proportion of the artisanate tended to attend – with clerical approval. For them, at least it was a day off work. For the Catholic bourgeoisie, it was less their indifference to public profession of the faith – though, admittedly, many had lost the habit that came easily to their grandparents – than their reluctance to associate with a vulgarised religiosity that brought them into contact with their social inferiors. Piety, where it was practised at all within middle-class families, was becoming

home-based for French Catholics as it was for German Protestants. The Churches found winning back professional men – lawyers,
doctors, judges, *rentiers* – in most countries difficult to achieve; often there
was indifference where there was not outright hostility. The collapse or
remodelling of the confraternities, both numerically and in terms of prestige, exacerbated this trend, for the *grande bourgeoisie* were unhappy
at having to mingle in communal parochial festivals. Where confraternities did survive (and the Austrian government officially permitted
their revival in 1817), they were smaller in number, had a socially less
distinguished membership, and could not tempt urban middle-class
males in the way they had, by and large, managed to do before the early
1790s.

Processions could be a means of claiming contested sacred spaces in
town centres and suburbs; increased chances of a confrontation could
really bring the crowds out, ignite popular religious passions, and perhaps
involve some of those who otherwise might head for the political clubs
and the taverns. All these trends were well seen in the southern French
city of Nîmes, where Catholics after the Restoration were in denial about
accepting that Protestants had full civil status. Corpus Christi feast days
were particular ordeals for Protestants who lived on the processional
route; they had to lock themselves and their families into their houses
and hope the day would pass off with no more than taunts and petty vandalism from the Catholics outside. Mission priests were regular annual
visitors, preaching a mixture of hell-fire, damnation and royalism, the sort
lampooned by the novelist Stendhal in *Lamiel*. The outdoor processions
and services of penitence on these occasions could arouse near hysteria.
During the 1826 mission, Nîmes Protestants were obliged to stay indoors
every evening when the churches emptied. This self-imposed segregation
was a token of how sour inter-denominational relations could be: with
Catholics dominant on the town council, Protestants hardly dared use
the municipal hospital from fear of being poisoned.

Because of the longstanding confessional tensions, the Nîmes bourgeoisie on both sides of the divide were likely to be active in the life of
their local churches to a degree not always replicated in comparable urban
settings. But even among those who stayed away from church on most
Sundays, there is little evidence of any overt atheism. That phenomenon
was too tainted by its Jacobin associations to be socially acceptable among
the respectable and the propertied, those who had often added former
Church properties and land to their rent rolls and therefore had a vested
interest in confining the scope of the clergy. So in parts of Spain, France,
Italy and the Austrian Empire, one finds anticlericalism persisting among

the 'middling sort', ever apprehensive that the Catholic parochial clergy were bent on extending social control over their wives, daughters and employees and using sacramental means – the confessional is the obvious example – to maintain their dominance.

This was an attitude with deep eighteenth-century roots that the Napoleonic experience had not eliminated. The bourgeois male preference for ethics without dogmatics was particularly marked in France, often sitting alongside a lukewarm response to Louis XVIII and a positive disdain for Charles X; it was probably linked to the surviving, 'unchurched' juring priests (Grégoire himself was active in public life for most of the Restoration era), who could not forget their Rousseau and the effort to put theory into practice during the 1790s. The present state of research makes it hard to explain male absenteeism with any degree of assurance. Material self-interest was never far away, the lurking fears that Charles X and his Jesuit allies would try to dismantle the Bonapartist land settlement left intact under the Charter of 1814. Journalists played on these fears to undermine support for the regime among the urban bourgeoisie in the late 1820s. The interest of the middling sort in upholding their local church could be similarly damaged in Protestant polities by excessive clerical zeal to protect their own interests. Such was the case in the Durham diocese in the wake of the Ambrose Williams case. As the *Durham Chronicle* reported on 18 August 1821:

... churches look like deserted sepulchres, rather than temples of the living God; [He] that raises up conventicles in every corner ... that deprives them of all pastoral influence and respect ... Sensible of the decline of their spiritual and moral influence they cling to their temporal [power] and lose their officiousness in political matters, even the semblance of the characters of ministers of religion.

The fall-out from such a *cause célèbre* would poison clergy–laity relations in more than one parish for upward of a generation.

While their husbands may have stayed at home or gone to meet each other at their masonic lodge, bourgeois women remained staunch in their religious commitment between 1815 and 1830. They were definitely not among the laity lost to religion. In one sense, that simply marked a continuation of a trend in female religiosity that was a constant feature of the time span of this book; in another, it was becoming more conspicuous, given the gradual falling away of a male middle-class presence in urban congregations in most European countries (with the possible exception of Britain). The Church offered a pattern of sociability which suited most women, an unrivalled venue for gossip and neighbourliness. For those struggling to bring up a large family and supplement their husband's wages by piece-work, it also offered the only hope of education for their children, whether in Sunday or day schools, while priests and ministers might be more sympathetic to their individuality than their own spouse, a point that contributed not a little to domestic tension. There were signs of the Churches wanting to reduce the scope available for women under-taking initiatives not susceptible to clerical – and male – control. Thus one again finds traditional gender roles constraining Methodist women by the early nineteenth century. The mainstream confessions had, ad-mittedly, seldom been comfortable with this intrusion of women into leadership, but the disruptions of 1790–1815 had often prevented clergy having any choice in it. The return of peace and sympathetic regimes permitted moves against such practices. It does not seem to have done anything to reduce the female presence at services of every sort. Men were reasserting control even if they were numerically inferior in atten-dance. But one should be cautious about overstating this tendency, and it is most plausible to talk of a *gradual* feminisation of religion in the early nineteenth century, one more apparent in the Catholic Church than in the Protestant confessions.

Feminine commitment to the Church gave popular Catholicism the appearance of strength that the various cults and observances reinforced. Overall, there was not much difference between the lowest classes in their religious observances comparing 1780 with 1825. Superstition was still endemic in the countryside and would be for the rest of the century. But the clergy were more ready to respect the limitations of what they could achieve in improving popular morality, and take some comfort in bringing more than ever before to respectable cults like the Sacred Heart. This devotion thrived after the Napoleonic Wars, alongside 'superstitious' usages like that at the shrine of Begona in the Basque provinces where clergy from the church portico sprinkled the sky with holy water at the start of a thunderstorm. The practice was acceptable to urban workers, skilled and unskilled, as a form of local patriotism, but approval was sel-dom converted by them into regular, personal Christian practice. The 1790–1815 period had created additional political and military forms of sociability among ordinary urban males aged six to sixty that proved an effective counterpoise to the influence of the clergy. Conscription, peasant boys uprooted from countryside to towns – one Italian bishop described his boys as 'wrested from the Church's bosom and herded into barracks' – and unemployment all worked against religious influences. It was hard to get them into church services, and many had never been to Sunday Schools which, in any case, had declined rapidly during the Napoleonic era in much of continental Europe. Attendance at those schools or at catechism classes was hard to impose on the younger generation. Even the regular confession of schoolboys was not easy to revive. In Rouen it led to a school mutiny and closure until an agreement on practice could be reached. In England there was a sense of a dangerous underworld of infidels and demagogues taking radical heterodoxy on the march again; it led to the trial of Richard Carlile for blasphemous libel in 1819. That said, millenarian overtones remained endemic in radical language and radical Spenceans actually took out dissenting ministers' licences (posing as Unitarians) to open 'chapels' which operated as debating clubs. In the course of the 1820s, interest moved to deist religious worship rather than radical subversion, with preachers reading excerpts from texts such as Volney's *Ruins of Empire* and Shelley's *Queen Mab*.

Catholic populism in Italy and Ireland

It should not be assumed that the Churches were invariably on the side of the Restored monarchies of post-1815 Europe or in principle opposed to the identification of many laity with the cause of the nation. Of course, this identification was not problematic when statehood and nationhood were closely aligned. Thus Protestantism and patriotism went together in many confessional states, as in Prussia or two of the three component states of the United Kingdom. The problem came where the post-1815 states too forcefully distanced themselves from any sense of national identity or denied it altogether. National sentiments and Christianity could be closely linked, despite the obstacles posed by the frequently anticlerical and republican agendas of the nationalists. In Madrid, one of the liberal clubs may have argued in 1820 that they were 'the true Christians' and the opponents of 'the enemies of Jesus Christ', but such an assurance was unpersuasive in Spain and elsewhere. Only when liberalism was either not present or subdued was there room for an alliance of sorts. Thus unreconstructed Catholicism was as important in the Belgian crisis of 1830 as it had been in that of 1787–90. But it was particularly in Italy and, above all, in Ireland, that Catholicism and nationalism were ready to make an accommodation.

In Italy there was an existing tradition of a minority of clergy ready to back Jansenist and/or Bonapartist reform programmes of the sort that had been current since the 1780s. That minority – and its descendants – had not gone away in the years after 1815, and they accepted the return of the kingdom of the Two Sicilies, the papal states and some of the small duchies with an ill grace. A handful joined the revolutionary sects; those who resisted their appeal themselves looked sympathetically on those in their flocks who could not. There was another incentive for Italian lower clergy to move into the nationalist camp: the large-scale Austrian presence in the Veneto and elsewhere in the north-east, a kingdom of Lombardy-Venetia that rested on the diktat of the Vienna Congress and a Habsburg army for its justification rather than any attempt at popular consent. This post-1815 arrangement, a key part of Metternich's 'system', had none of the benign reformism that had characterised the Grand Duchy of Tuscany before 1790 and was the antithesis of any principle of national self-determination. Lombardy-Venetia made few concessions to the Church. A Napoleonic-style concordatory system was in operation, so gaining from its overthrow was a possibility.

Austrian military power was too strong to divert clergy from their primary pastoral endeavours in these years; however, some priests participated in the revolutions in Naples in 1820 and in Piedmont in 1821, protesting against corrupt government and a raw deal for the Church rather than any principle of Italian nationhood. In the 1820 Revolution, Fr Luigi Minchini led 7,000 *carbonari* into Naples, with both secular and regular clergy among them. It was a grand gesture that failed, though not badly enough to prevent further priest recruits to the *carbonari* for a variety of reasons, including resentment of their bishop as the agent of an interfering central government ready to discountenance awarding benefices on the basis of family preferences ('receptive churches'). Among those arrested after the abortive Neapolitan coup of 1828 were several clergy, who had permitted other conspirators to meet regularly in a canon's house or the sacristy of a church. The penalty for membership was at the minimum unfrocking – provided the authorities could find a prelate prepared to undertake it.

What distinguished Ireland from Italy was the willingness of the episcopate to endorse the national cause as represented by the Catholic Association, founded early in 1823. Initially this Association was primarily concerned with Catholic rights rather than the repeal of the Act of Union; O'Connell succeeded brilliantly in identifying Irish Catholicism with Irish nationalism and they remained inextricably linked after emancipation was achieved in 1829. Hibernian patriotism had brought radical Catholics and Protestants together in the 1790s; in the 1820s most Protestants were by definition excluded from the campaign as a Protestant Irish patriotism was turned into a contradiction in terms. O'Connell insisted in his July 1826 letter to the Catholics of Ireland that 'the Catholic people of Ireland are a nation', called on the masses to join his Catholic Association and ratcheted up electoral pressure on the British government, but he was not really working for his members' interests, as became clear when the franchise in Ireland was restricted under the terms of the 1832 Reform Act. He depended on the support of the clergy as organising agents at parish level, keeping the rural populace committed and taking their monthly penny subscription from them (the hierarchy sanctioned this 'rent' in 1824), ensuring that his Association was a genuine national movement, almost a national confederacy. O'Connell had some vociferous allies among the Irish bishops, none more so than James Doyle, bishop of Kildare and Leighlin, 'the Pope of Ireland' as the Whig wit and cleric Sydney Smith dubbed him. More than 8,000 copies of his *A Vindication of the Civil and Religious Principles of the Irish Catholics* were published in 1823, in effect the manifesto of the Catholic Association. Despite occasional disagreements with O'Connell, Bishop Doyle kept his colleagues on the bench behind the Association. No wonder that O'Connell wrote in June 1828, 'The approbation of Doctor Doyle will bring in our cause the united voice of Ireland – I trust it will be the vox populi – vox dei.'[9] Doyle was acting as *de facto* spokesman for an Irish Catholic episcopate which was both more visible and collectively effective than at any time since the Reformation. Elsewhere, the apparatus and personnel of the Churches could be less impressive at making the impact they sought in public life.

Church adminstration and the challenges of the new era

The Churches were acutely aware of the challenges confronting them after 1815, and equally conscious of the limitations in what they could achieve quickly after the dislocations of revolution and war. Clergy numbers had fallen drastically since 1790, bishoprics stood empty, Church lands and property had been secularised, many of the finest minds would no longer entertain thoughts of taking holy orders, and they could not presume on the unqualified support of the middling sort for their ministry. In Prussia's new western provinces, where the arrangements of centuries had been undone, the Catholic Church was in chaos. With dioceses and parishes often unfilled for years on end, and priests few in number, the laity were left to the uninhibited expression of popular religious values.

War and secularisation of Church lands had acted as midwife to the kind of streamlined Church men like Ricci, Grégoire and Watson had envisaged, one where the pastoral rather than either the political or the philosophical was privileged. The Churches preserved what they could of their own (historic) structures while trying to be endlessly adaptable when confronted by such seismic external changes as the creation of new territorial units in Germany, Italy and elsewhere. Even in England

---

[9] Quoted in Wendy Hinde, *Catholic Emancipation: A Shake to Men's Minds* (Oxford, 1992), 69–70.

where the established Church had been a bulwark of resistance to Napoleon, there was no room for complacency after 1815 and, to be fair to Archbishop Manners-Sutton of Canterbury, the other prelates and interested laymen, there was little sign of it. Statutory attempts to improve the curate's lot and insist on clergy residence had been made before 1815. Despite the rabid attacks in radical literature such as, notoriously, the Unitarian John Wade's *Black Book* (1820–3) with its exposure of sinecures in Church and state, it was less a question of Anglicans resisting reform, than deciding on the extent of it and how it would be imposed.

In leadership terms, it would be hard to overstate the importance of the episcopate in creating the right conditions for recovery. Money could be a huge obstacle to success. In Spain, where the Church was resurgent between 1814 and 1820, it proved impossible to halt a slide in the income of the kingdom's bishoprics from 52 million *reales* in 1802 to 34 million by 1820, brought on by the effects of war, confiscation and agricultural depression. Episcopal incomes were thus on average well below what they had been half a century before. Such a fall still left Spanish prelates with a considerable income, and might even have engendered a desire to sample – relatively speaking – 'apostolic poverty' and thereby set an example that would impress liberal critics of the Church as well as insiders. Instead, it impelled Spanish prelates to concentrate on making good the shortfall rather than writing it off. Pastoral efforts were directed towards anathematising liberalism and shoring up religious truths by Inquisition-like agencies. Thus 'Juntas of Faith' or episcopal inquisitions in Valencia, Tarragona and Orihuela were set up without Madrid's approval in 1824 to 'encourage' liberals to return to the faith. They were shut down by 1827 as a result of royal intervention.

One answer to reduced land holdings and the revenues they generated was to consolidate the numbers of bishoprics. Such a policy commended itself even to a conservative regime like the Bourbon kingdom of Naples: it gradually curtailed the number of dioceses from 131 to 81 between 1818 and 1834. It was still difficult enough for the remaining bishops to resume control of their episcopal lands or raise the 3,000 ducats a year stipulated as the minimum income by the Concordat of 1818. 'I've made numberless efforts', complained one prelate, 'I've toured the three provinces where the property is and seen the officials in charge of it. I've written and rewritten numberless letters, and I have been at my wits' end to know what else I can do to get possession or even to discover what I own.'[10] When prelates turned their minds away from revenue raising, they

---

[10] Quoted in O. Chadwick, *The Popes and European Revolution* (Oxford, 1981), 579.

discovered that the destruction of powerful corporations and feudal rights in Italy since the mid-1790s made decisive episcopal leadership a real possibility. Meanwhile, pastoral work could not wait, as some areas of the kingdom had not had a confirmation tour since the 1780s. In Ireland a young bishop, James Doyle (only thirty-three when appointed to Kildare and Leighlin in 1819), helped to complete the work of Tridentine reform that had been going on for almost a century. In the 1820s he brought in rural deaneries, annual synods and frequent theological conferences and retreats, opening a diocesan college at Carlow to which he invited the Sulpicians in 1824. Though he insisted on the highest standards, clerical discipline and morale were both greatly raised. Here was a model of Catholic leadership not easily surpassed on the continent.

In France, distinguished survivors of the pre-1789 Gallican episcopate such as Antoine Eustache d'Osmond (1754–1823) and A.-J.-C. Clermont-Tonnerre (1749–1830), as bishop of Nancy and archbishop of Toulouse respectively, provided continuity and stable leadership for the Restoration regime. What they lacked in pre-1790 revenues they made up for in pastoral impact and inspiration to younger members of the episcopal corps, those who had known only deprivation and hardship rather than what the ex-bishop Talleyrand had memorably called the 'douceur de vivre' for the French elite before the Revolution. The signing of the 1817 Concordat with the papacy acted as an inducement to several leading Gallicans who could not accede to its Napoleonic predecessors to come in from the cold and thereby enhance the ranks of the last years of the alliance of 'throne and altar' in France.

Anglican prelates barely suffered in comparison with their Gallican counterparts. The discovery of Percy Jocelyn, bishop of Clogher, closeted with a guardsman in the back room of a London alehouse in August 1822 gave anticlerical authors a rare case of immorality to engross them. Sympathetic to the outlook of the Hackney Phalanx, Liverpool and Wellington took care to name to Church of England bishoprics men of learning and pastoral competence rather than putting the claims of their relations and Church politicians first. As Liverpool's biographer, Norman Gash, wrote: 'scholarship, impeccable moral respectability and conscientious performance of pastoral duties' typified Liverpool's appointees, with the preferment of those with evangelical views like Henry Ryder, George Murray and John Kaye setting a precedent.[11] Once in their dioceses, there was a greater emphasis on residence than in the eighteenth century, with many bishops including John Fisher of Salisbury and George Burgess of

---

[11] Norman Gash, *The Life and Political Career of Robert Banks Jenkinson, Second Earl of Liverpool 1770–1828* (London, 1984), 202.

St David's reactivating diocesan administration through installing energetic archdeacons and rural deans, thus beginning the work of creating an enhanced sense of the diocese as a pastoral mechanism in its own right. Liverpool was adamant that bishops taking the least prosperous sees like Bristol, Gloucester, Oxford and Peterborough could not expect to hold cathedral dignities to supplement episcopal incomes at the lower end of the scale. Thus in 1815 he insisted that the Hon. Edward Legge would have to sacrifice the deanery of Windsor if he was going to become bishop of Oxford, and Legge eventually did so. A decade later, it had become normal procedure. Such a determination to reward genuine worth had, arguably, been an habitual feature of patronage in the eighteenth-century Church, but it was more emphatic after Waterloo, even, it has been claimed, 'a strand in the growing meritocratic web created by an industrial society'.[12]

Most English cathedral chapters were set well away from the growing industrial centres and were not characterised by the social diversity of their canons. Serious challenges to their existence did not exist, though revelations in radical literature about the scale of their land ownership (often distorted) were calculated to antagonise the nation when it was struggling with the post-war economic downturn. The threat of limited state disendowment grew in the 1820s as the possibility of a Whig administration increased, especially after Liverpool's death in 1827. Anglican higher clergy did not dismiss in principle the possibility of eliminating some of the more glaring discrepancies in income between dioceses, possibly merging some of the poorer ones (like Bristol and Gloucester), as had happened several times in Ireland. An example was set at Durham by Bishop William Van Mildert. He voluntarily gave up large amounts of episcopal property and endowed a university with the proceeds, one that was intended to function as an intellectual bastion of northern Anglicanism against the challenge from Whiggery and dissent. What bishops, deans and canons in the Church of England could not accept were government schemes imposed on them, the sort that had so damaged the material resources of the continental Churches since 1790.

In England, at least chapters and canons still existed, whereas in France the higher clergy as a distinctive cadre within the Gallican Church were a shadow of their former selves. Neither the 1801 nor the 1817 Concordats had been kind to them; they had been identified by both bishops and administrators as obstacles to the smooth exercise of power within the Church; in an underfunded Church, the practicality of restoring their land

---

[12] William Gibson, 'The Tories and Church Patronage: 1812–30', *JEH* 41 (1990), 266–74, at 274.

holdings was hard to contemplate, and there was no provision for state money. Where there was still a diocese to which they could be attached, cathedral chapters mostly struggled on in France, but were marginal to the life of the Church overall. It was much the same in Italy. Where cathedral chapters did survive, as in southern Italy, with diminished endowments, few could afford to make new appointments. The canons grew old away from the eyes of most other clergy, a poignant reminder of more prosperous times in the Church order. And yet this corporate diminution was not as pronounced as the canons of collegiate churches not attached to cathedrals. Most of those had been disbanded or disendowed well before 1815 and neither bishops nor Restoration governments were keen to see them installed again. Unfairly or not, they were deemed an obstacle to pastoral progress.

So were the monastic Orders. Monasticism – on a limited scale – had continued during the Napoleonic era only in Spain, Austria and Russian Poland, and in exile in Britain, although former monks and nuns often remained in smaller, unofficial cells, living out a disciplined life as best they could. With the abolition of mortmain a feature of virtually every concordat, governments could afford to be more relaxed about monasticism than they had been before the Revolution. Where conventual life recommenced after 1815, communities were free of that state meddling and remodelling which had been such a feature of pre-1789 ecclesiastical life in Catholic Europe. It was thus left to the clergy themselves to make a decision at local level, in the knowledge that where monastic lands had been acquired by lay owners on the open market, there was no question of either restitution or compensation. It could be hard going. The Vatican trumpeted the success stories such as the reopening of the Grande Chartreuse in 1816, but there was no attempt to force former monks living on pensions back into the cloister. There were many casualties: some twenty old mainly minor Orders never returned. In Spain, the Minims of Andalusia were so constrained by agricultural depression in the 1820s that they refused to accept novices who could not afford to pay for food and lodging. Generally, few monasteries could offer serious charitable relief to the needy. On the whole, it was easier to revive teaching or nursing Orders rather than the contemplatives. The pressure was on the latter to justify their existence, so that monks became heavily involved in parish life, something many had experienced before 1815, and enclosed female Orders were given papal permission to teach in Spanish schools in 1817. Smaller Orders, often diocesan and parochial, sprang up with pastoral aims, renewing the pre-revolutionary zeal found in female communities. There were 14,226 nuns in France in 1815 and that number rose appreciably down to 1830.

Paradoxically, the willingness of so many men and women (the latter particularly) to embrace those difficulties contributed to the rehabilitation of the monastic ideal in Restoration Europe, one that was also assisted by cultural interest in forms of medievalism generally. Anticlericals found it harder to interest the lay public in the old salacious stories of life in the cloister. But most former religious did not return, unwilling to give up their new lives as secular priests or as schoolteachers. The clergy in Venice in 1821 numbered 700, with about 150 ex-religious among them. One religious Order did spring back to something like its former status in 1814: the Jesuits. Their return focused anticlerical sentiment, although they attempted to give it the lie by concentrating on mission work, often working alongside members of the female religious Orders. There were tensions within the Jesuits between those ageing survivors in the Order pre-1773 and the younger, more vigorous men who were anxious to begin the work of reconstruction. After coming close to schism in the election of a new general in 1820, the Society became more coherent in the 1820s and benefited from Leo XII's restoration of their old exemptions in 1826.

The real hope for Church renewal lay as ever with the parish clergy and the crucial problem (with the exception of the Church of England, where the reverse applied) was that there were simply not enough of them. France was something of an exception. Ordinations doubled from 1,185 in 1816 to 2,357 in 1830 as clerical confidence – partly from its new prominence in public life under Charles X – increased. Most of those entering the priesthood tended to be both peasants and ultramontanes. With the disruption of academic facilities and the collapse of many universities during the Napoleonic Wars, there was a tendency for confessions to rely on their own institutions for clerical training. This would in time encourage the growth of a professional ministry, but that was not how it looked during the Restoration era. The Russian ministry of education under Golitsyn continued the practice of requiring diocesan bishops to send seminarians on to the universities; that was not mandatory in Catholic polities. Seminaries were nowhere overcrowded between 1815 and 1830, while those who entered them from the social elite tended to be noticeably fewer; taking holy orders was increasingly unlikely to guarantee anyone an exceptional income or learned leisure. It could be a vicious circle. In Italy, seminaries lacked teaching staff because priests were in short supply, and it was harder than ever to persuade young men to come forward for ordination. In the diocese of Treviso after the Restoration an average of twenty-two priests died annually but an average of six entered the ministry. Clerical instructors had few incentives to volunteer their services when the prospect was essentially bureaucratic interference, uncompetitive staff salaries, and a shortage of educational materials. There were plenty of books from disbanded monasteries on the market, but seminaries could seldom afford the prices.

Oxford and Cambridge knew different pressures. There had been successive attempts over several decades to offer lectures in divinity (Edward Bentham at Oxford and John Hey at Cambridge had been pioneers) that intending ordinands would find useful, and with them had come competitive honours examinations. These trends intensified during the Regency and George IV's reign (1811–30). They did not in themselves broaden the social base of Anglicanism. It remained unusual for anyone born outside the landed and professional elite to enter the higher reaches of the Church of England between 1815 and 1830 (though arguably slightly more so than in the 1770s/1780s), and those taking orders after receiving a degree were aware that competition for a lucrative benefice was stronger than ever, that the profession was overcrowded with too many priests chasing too few jobs. Curates were at last better paid, which was just as well as many of them would never have their own parish.

Those who did enjoyed comfortable incomes and excellent housing. British agriculture had prospered during the long wars against France, and the vicar's glebe as part of it. But the post-war reduction in prices and the value of land coupled with incipient mechanisation in the countryside had impoverished many families in the southern and Midland counties, as William Cobbett's *Rural Rides* famously recorded. Though aware of the pastoral tensions it was likely to generate, Anglican incumbents still insisted on their tithe payments and, when coupled with the presence of many of them acting as justices of the peace, the result was the intensification of anticlericalism in the countryside. The clergy in Surrey, Hampshire and Wiltshire often had to arm themselves for protection in the late 1820s as the 'Captain Swing' riots led to a wave of cattle maiming and rick burning. The picture varied from parish to parish and from diocese to diocese, but it is the combination of social pressures facing incumbents just as the confessional state came apart following the repeal of the Test and Corporation Acts and the granting of Catholic relief in 1828–9 that indicates the level of pressure for change within historic Anglican structures.

Whereas Anglican clerics were desperate to hold on to their assets, the clergy elsewhere in Europe found that much of theirs were either dispersed or dilapidated. In most parts of Italy communities could barely afford to keep their parish churches roofed against the elements, and everywhere the signs of vandalism, iconoclasm and wartime destruction were still visible. Filling the churches with statues, stained glass and the quality of fittings and fixtures that had distinguished Europe's Catholic churches before the Revolution was a material impossibility. Not surprisingly, priests preferred to put pastoral concerns first. While they had little need to worry about the confraternities as rivals for the attention of their flocks, outside interference was growing.

In 1819 the Naples government reformed the receptive churches and subjected the appointment of the parish priest to the *concursus*, with the bishop as well as the corporation choosing their pastor. Residence was stipulated and the plan drew much criticism from the clergy and their families who had benefited from the former scheme, often going back over several generations. The shortage of clerical numbers gave the bishops and secular ministers the excuse they wanted to return to pre-revolutionary rationalisation of the Churches. The priority accorded to increased flexibility made parochial reorganisation essential. Even the holy father participated: in Rome the papacy reduced the city's eighty-one parishes to a more sensible forty-four. In France the concordatory system of having only one parish per canton (about 3,000 in total) was abandoned, much to the pleasure of most Catholics, and the creation of new dioceses from 1822 also helped the Church adapt faster to changing patterns of population and settlement. On the whole, financial prospects were worse than they had been since the seventeenth century for the average priest. Only in Spain did the average incumbent have an easier time of it. The old problems of the 1760s remained to plague the Spanish Church in 1820s, with a significant proportion of beneficed clergy doing no pastoral work and having a low clerical profile in poor rural districts. The Spanish Church suffered acute financial problems despite basking in royal approval, for Ferdinand had no compunction about racking the Church's revenues to supply the treasury. Sixty per cent of the archdiocese of Santiago's revenues were appropriated by the Crown between 1814 and 1820. Agricultural and commercial depression went on after 1814 and the value of the tithe suffered proportionately. Collection agents could risk their lives trying too hard to enforce demands, and parish clergy could do little about it. By contrast, in France, clerical incomes were not spectacular but attractive enough for the growing number of ordinands from unprivileged rural backgrounds. Then came the Revolutions of 1830 to throw such recovery as there had been into doubt.

Conclusion: the position in 1830

Whatever Indian summer of 'throne and altar' the Churches had enjoyed since 1815 came to an abrupt end when Europe was convulsed by revolution in 1830–1 on a scale not seen since the 1790s. Even the

English and Irish Churches had to confront the statutory break-up of the confessional arrangements that had endured since the late seventeenth century, and the Church of England was compelled to admit defeat in its efforts to restrict dissenting competition. Russia, Prussia and Austria finally ended the charade of the Holy Alliance in 1830 (there having been no further meetings of the powers after Verona in 1822); whatever dim possibility there had been of Maistrian-style theocracy was now revealed as pure fantasy. These were disappointing times for those who had survived Napoleon and yearned to have a stable order in Church and state based on popular good will without the concessions to reformers of the 1770s and 1780s. So it was predictable that the papacy in the person of Gregory XVI deplored the way the events of 1830 confirmed the conjunction of liberalism and indifferentism, thereby adopting the perspective of his immediate predecessors. In his only encyclical – *Traditi humiliati nostrae* of May 1829 – Pius VIII had blamed the failing power of religion and the breakdown of the social and political order on indifferentism in matters of faith, the activities of the Protestant Bible Societies, attacks on the sanctity of marriage and Church dogmas, and secret societies. There was, according to this eclectic diagnosis of the ills of the era, little in the modern world calculated to strengthen the beliefs of the faithful.

The results when the relationship between Church and state uncoupled could be quite spectacular and very different. In England the state was, in the last analysis, willing to detach itself from the privileged confessional bonding with Anglicanism and thereby obtain some protection from the radical challenge, whereas in France the alliance of throne and altar collapsed in 1830 with the Gallican Church opting to rescue itself from the wreckage of the Bourbon polity. Superficially, it might seem that revolution and religion were again aligned against each other, but the early 1830s would not be a repeat performance of the early 1790s. O'Connell's agitation in Ireland had shown that Catholicism and constitutionalism could be combined and, in France certainly, expediency pushed the Church towards exploring the possibilities of civic Catholicism under Louis-Philippe. This stumbling initiative took shape at parochial level where many churchmen had learnt the lesson of the 1790s and distanced themselves from the fate of dynasties: pastoral dedication must never again take second place to political involvement.

In the heat of the moment, it could be hard for some to contain themselves. Thus in 1830 the bishop of Nîmes refused to pray for the new 'king of the French', Louis-Philippe (formerly the duc d'Orléans), during services; other clergy in his diocese preached brazenly against the government from their pulpits, while thousands of Catholics involved in teaching and administering poor relief refused to take the oath of allegiance.

These struggles dragged on into the autumn of 1830, then slowly faded as monarchical ultras in the Church sensed that the departure of the Bourbons would not easily be reversed. The Spanish Church could not disentangle itself from its branch of the Bourbons with such facility and paid a high price for it. Anticlericalism had increased fast in Spain in the 1820s as a result of the political struggle. The poverty of the Spanish Church entailed both less prestige and less respect from its inability to play its traditional social role. Thus it could not cater for the poor as once had been the case. During the serious economic crisis of 1834 in Madrid, Barcelona and other cities, monasteries were torched and some religious murdered in the outbreaks of anticlerical violence.

The revolutionary events of 1830 did not in themselves stall revival, or lessen the medieval nostalgia of so many cultured Europeans. The Holy Alliance may have faltered but Friedrich Schlegel (d. 1829), a bitter enemy of Hegel, sustained a sense of imperial and Catholic mission to the end of his life. 'The religious hope of a true and complete regeneration of the age, by a Christian system of government, and a Christian system of science' forms the conclusion to his *The Philosophy of History*, first published in 1829. Such enthusiasm for an imagined Gothic past could certainly be escapist, a distraction from the ruptures of the post-Napoleonic order, but it could also function as a pastoral inspiration which nourished some of the best clergy taking up high office in the 1820s and 1830s. Others, no less talented, simply got on with the task of serving their parishes and keeping congregations motivated, as Protestants had so often been, by biblical teaching, or the inward working of grace.

If fault-lines in the revival were patent by 1830, the diversity of that revival should not be underestimated, nor should the ability of the Churches to use the gifts of clergy and laity alike to its advantage. The post-war revival had never been much more than fitful, mainly a rural phenomenon, which declining numbers of ordinands in some Catholic states made hard to sustain until the 1840s. If, by the fourth decade of the nineteenth century, it was back to hard times again for the Churches, the established ones particularly, that was scarcely an unfamiliar predicament for most confessions. And yet adversity had earlier encouraged Christian creativity and adaptability, and it would do so again.

Glossary

Antichrist	figure whose evil attributes are diametrically opposed to those of Jesus Christ. His appearance at the end-time (see Apocalypse) will indicate that the end of the world and the return of Christ in glory are imminent
Apocalypse	those signs and portents heralding the final time of the earth before Christ's Second Coming and often associated with the Revelation of John in the New Testament and canonical prophetic writings such as the Book of Daniel in the Old Testament
Arianism	a heterodox form of the Christian faith denying the equal status of Christ within the triune Godhead
body toll	an additional tax imposed on Jews in some parts of Europe
communion	an organised Christian denomination or group of believers
conciliarism	Roman Catholic emphasis on the final authority of (international) Church councils in policy making as opposed to the pope
concordat	negotiated treaty between the papacy and lay state establishing and apportioning mutual rights and powers over a (national) Catholic Church
curia	the papal court and government
confessional	area in a Roman Catholic church in which a priest hears a penitent's confession of sin and grants sacramental absolution

decalogue	the Ten Commandments given by God to Moses and the People of Israel in the Book of Exodus
deism	a non-dogmatic, non-Christian form of religious belief in a Supreme Being
diocese	a bishop's sphere of jurisdiction
episcopalian	government of the Church by bishops
Erastianism	doctrine which emphasises the subordination of the Church to the state
eschatology	the doctrine of the four last things – death, judgment, heaven and hell – and the end of the old earthly order immediately preceding Christ's return to earth in judgment
ex voto	gift made by a pilgrim or visitor to a holy place in the hope of receiving spiritual benefits in return
Gallicanism	attachment to the national liberties and privileges of the Catholic Church in France, classically articulated in the Declaration of 1682
heterodoxy	the opposite of orthodoxy; heretical beliefs departing from the Nicene Creed, usually involving the denial of Christ's divinity
high church	the opposite of low church, those members of the Church of England who emphasised its sacerdotal character, continuities with the pre-Reformation era, and its exclusive rights and privileges within the state
indifferentism	spirit of indifference professed in religious matters
infidelity	the conspicuous or concealed rejection of the main tenets of the Christian religion
Jansenism	Catholic party originating in seventeenth-century France and condemned by the papal Bull *Unigenitus* in 1713. Its anti-Jesuit stance was

widely adopted within France and popular in the Paris *parlement*. In the second half of the century Jansenist emphasis on conciliarism became an important strand of anti-absolutist politics within secular states. Jansenism outside France used still more loosely to describe Erastian, regalian policies of church reform often part of the Catholic Enlightenment

Kirk	habitual shorthand reference to the established Church of Scotland
latitudinarian	member of the Church of England anxious to minimise dogmatic and ecclesiological differences with other Protestant communions; a style of churchmanship particularly influential between 1690 and 1760
mortmain	lands held inalienably by the Church (amortised) and as such not subject to taxation
pantheism	a diffusive religious perception based on a sense that the divinity is to be found and experienced in nature
Porte	name given by other European states to the Ottoman sultanate and seat of central power at Constantinople
Precisionism	a narrowly defined doctrinal version of Protestantism popular in some parts of Germany, Scandinavia and Britain restricting salvation to a small minority of practising Christians
rational dissenters	undogmatic English Protestants, usually Arians, sometimes Socinians, who rejected most credal definitions of the Christian faith as unscriptural and considered that reason was at all times the key to understanding a sense of divine purpose for the world and for the individual
Reformed Churches	Protestant communities historically based on a Calvinist, Presbyterian tradition, though often interpreted radically by the eighteenth century

regalism	Catholic churches looking in the first instance to the monarchy for support. The term has a particular application to Spain
Richerism	an early seventeenth-century ecclesiological position which revived after 1750 in the Gallican Church emphasising the rights and status of the parish clergy
Rota	the highest papal court in Rome, open to appeals in specified areas of civil and criminal law from other states in Catholic Europe
secularisation	the confiscation and disendowment of the Catholic Church within the German Empire after 1803
Socinian	a non-Trinitarian form of Christianity, which denies the divinity of Jesus Christ, his atonement and the doctrine of original sin
Unitarians	the term used to describe Socinians by the 1790s

Bibliographical suggestions

The following list is designed to do no more than get the Anglophone reader started in approaching relatively recent publications in this rich field. Most of the texts suggested below contain their own comprehensive bibliographical apparatus.

1 CHURCH STRUCTURES AND MINISTRY

Eamon Duffy, *Saints and Sinners: A History of the Popes* (New Haven, 1997) covers the whole spectrum of eighteenth-century pontiffs magisterially and entertainingly, while Owen Chadwick, *The Popes and European Revolution* (Oxford, 1981) actually deals with most of the eighteenth century and looks well beyond Italy. E. E. Y. Hales, *Revolution and Papacy, 1769–1846* (London, 1960) retains its value. For Orthodoxy, Charles A. Freeze, *Catholics and Sultans: The Church and the Ottoman Empire 1453–1923* (Cambridge, 1983), makes a sound starting point. The Catholic background is admirably supplied by a previous volume in this series, R. Po-Chia Hsia, *The World of Catholic Renewal 1540–1770* (Cambridge, 1998) and Louis Châtellier's *The Europe of the Devout: The Catholic Reformation and the Formation of a New Society*, trans. Jean Birrell (Cambridge, 1997). The essays in W. J. Callahan and D. Higgs (eds.), *Church and Society in Catholic Europe in the Eighteenth Century* (Cambridge, 1979) cover a lot of ground at the price of unevenness. Adrian Hastings, *The Construction of Nationhood: Ethnicity, Religion and Nationalism* (Cambridge, 1997), Mary Anne Perkins, *Nation and Word, 1770–1850: Religious and Metaphysical Language in European National Consciousness* (Aldershot, 1999) and D. A. Bell, *The National and the Sacred: The Origins of Nationalism in Eighteenth-century France* (Cambridge, Mass., 2001) have all recently reminded historians how much the Churches have helped in the formation of national identity. National histories of the Churches vary appreciably. For France there are now two panoramic volumes as monumental as they are enjoyable: John McManners, *Church and Society in Eighteenth-century France* (2 vols., Oxford, 1998). Derek Beales, *Joseph II*, vol. I, *In the Shadow of Maria Theresa, 1741–1780* (Cambridge, 1987), and P. G. M. Dickson, 'Joseph II's Reshaping of the Austrian Church', *HJ* 36 (1993), 89–114, are alike indispensable. On Germany there is the superbly wide-ranging Nicholas Hope, *German and Scandanavian Protestantism 1700–1918* (Oxford, 1995). For Spain the relevant sections of J. Lynch, *Bourbon Spain, 1700–1808* (1989) are thoroughly reliable and can be read alongside Richard Herr, *The Eighteenth-century Revolution in Spain* (Princeton, 1958). For the Italian states, after Chadwick one can consult *Rome in the Age of Enlightenment: The Post-Tridentine syndrome and the Ancien Régime* by H. Gross (Cambridge, 1990); Sir Harold Acton, *The Bourbons of Naples 1734–1825* (London, 1956) retains its classic status. For Poland, the most recent text is Jerzy Kloczowski, *A History of Polish Christianity* (Cambridge, 2000), translated by Malgorzata Sady, first published in Paris in 1987. Its scholarly merits are offset by its 'official' Church line. Henry Marczali, *Hungary in the Eighteenth Century* (Cambridge, 1910) remains surprisingly useful for the Anglophone reader, especially when read in the light of B. K. Kiraly, *Hungary in the late Eighteenth Century* (1969). The essays in John Walsh, Colin Haydon and Stephen Taylor (eds.), *The Church of England c. 1689–1833: From Toleration to Tractarianism* (Cambridge, 1993) give some idea of the current dynamism of this subject area, and could be supplemented by J. C. D. Clark, *English Society 1660–1832: Religion, Ideology and Politics during the Ancien régime* (Cambridge, 2000). For the Scottish 'Moderate' party, Ian D. L. Clark, 'From Protest to Reaction: The Moderate Regime in the Church of Scotland, 1752–1805', in N. T. Phillipson and Rosalind Mitchison (eds.), *Scotland in the Age of Improvement* (Edinburgh, 1970), 200–24; J. Dwyer, 'The Heavenly City of the Eighteenth-century Moderate Divines', in J. Dwyer and A. Murdoch (eds.), *New Perspectives on the Politics and Culture of Early Modern Scotland* (Edinburgh, 1982), 291–318 is also important. For their opponents, John R. McIntosh, *Church and Theology in Enlightenment Scotland: The Popular Party, 1740–1800* (East Linton, 1998) should be used cautiously. On the 'Tridentine surge' in Ireland see Kevin Whelan, 'The regional impact of Irish Catholicism 1700–1850', in W. Smyth and K. Whelan (eds.), *Common Ground: Essays on the Historical Geography of Ireland* (Cork, 1988), 253–77. This may be supplemented by L. M. Cullen, 'Catholic Social Classes under the Penal Laws', in Thomas Power and Kevin Whelan (eds.), *Endurance and Emergence: Catholics in Eighteenth-century Ireland* (Dublin, 1990), 57–84. C. D. A. Leighton, *Catholicism in a Protestant Kingdom: A Study of the Irish Ancien Régime* (Dublin, 1994) is full of insights as is P. J. Corish, *The Catholic Community in the Seventeenth and Eighteenth Centuries* (Dublin, 1981). Charles Issawi, *Cross-cultural Encounters and Conflicts* (Oxford, 1998) deals lucidly with western perceptions of the Orient. The uneasy relationship with Islam is treated in Barbara Jelavich, *A History of the Balkans*, vol. I, *Eighteenth and Nineteenth Centuries* (Cambridge, 1983); P. F. Sugar, *Southeastern Europe under Ottoman rule, 1354–1804* (1983); J. McCarthy, *The Ottoman Turks: An Introductory History to 1923* (Harlow, 1996), and W. H. McNeill, *Europe's Steppe Frontier, 1500–1800* (Chicago, 1964). Minou Reeves, *Muhammad in Europe* (Reading, 2000), considers the slowly changing perceptions of the Prophet in Europe, and both updates and supplements Norman Daniels, *Islam and the West: The Making of an Image* (Edinburgh, 1960) and David Pailin, *Attitudes to other Religions* (Manchester, 1984). There is relatively little in print on the religious Orders in continental Europe. D. Mitchell, *The Jesuits* (London, 1980) remains a reliable general guide to that order. A.-E. N. Tachiaos, *The Revival of Byzantine Mysticism among Slavs and Romanians in the Eighteenth Century: Texts Relating to the Life and Activity of Paisy Velichkovsky* (Thessalonica, 1986) details the slow revival in Orthodox monasticism. Jo Ann Jay McNamara, *Sisters in Arms: Catholic Nuns through Two Millennia* (Harvard, 1996) is a sound introduction to the subject., and Colin Jones, *The Charitable Imperative: Hospitals and Nursing in Ancien Régime and Revolutionary France* (London, 1989), has much of value on the work of the *congréganistes* in nursing. On the parish clergy, the most reliable modern introduction must be B. Julia, 'The Priest', in M. Vovelle (ed.), *Enlightenment Portraits*, trans. L. G. Cochrane (Chicago, 1997), 356–92. G. L. Freeze, *The Russian Levites: Parish Clergy in the Eighteenth Century* (Cambridge, Mass., 1971) holds the field for non-Russian readers on this topic. Coverage of religion and the arts in the eighteenth century is extremely scanty. Readers are best advised to start with M. Craske, *Art in Europe, 1700–1830* (Oxford, 1997), and then consult studies of particular artists such as W. L. Barcham, *The Religious Paintings of Giambattista Tiepolo: Piety and Tradition in Eighteenth-century Venice* (Oxford, 1989). Music fares rather better. See Neal Zaslaw (ed.), *Man and Music: The Classical Era. From the 1740s to the End of the 18th Century* (Englewood Cliffs, N.J., 1989), 126–65, essays in D. Wyn Jones (ed.), *Music in Eighteenth-century Austria* (Cambridge, 1996), Malcolm Boyd and Juan José Carreras (eds.), *Music in Spain during the Eighteenth Century* (Cambridge, 1998), and J. R. Watson, *The English Hymn: A Critical and Historical Study* (Oxford, 1997).

2 BELIEFS, SOCIETY, AND WORSHIP: THE EXPRESSION OF CHRISTIANITY IN EUROPE, C. 1750–1790

Books on John Wesley are legion, but Henry Rack, *Reasonable Enthusiast. John Wesley and the Rise of Methodism* (London, 1989), remains so far unmatched as a biography. W. R. Ward in *The Protestant Evangelical Awakening* (Cambridge, 1992) covers both the German and the British dimensions and much more besides. For the opportunities Methodism presented to women there is Earl Kent Brown, *Women of Mr Wesley's Methodism* (Studies in women and religion 11) (New York, 1983). Judith Jago, *Aspects of the Georgian Church: Visitation Studies of the Diocese of York, 1761–1776* (Madison, N.J., 1997) confirms that the state of the Church of England in one large diocese had withstood the Methodist challenge quite successfully. For the uneasy relationship between popular religion and Tridentine Catholicism there is Jean Delumeau's classic, *Catholicism between Luther and Voltaire*, trans. J. Moiser (London, 1977). Many of the conceptual and methodological problems associated with the study of popular culture are examined in Marc Venard, 'Popular Religion in the Eighteenth Century', in W. J. Callahan and D. Higgs, *Church and Society in Catholic Europe in the Eighteenth Century* (Cambridge, 1979), 138–54; M. P. Carroll, *Madonnas that Maim: Popular Catholicism in Italy Since the Fifteenth Century* (Baltimore, 1992); Bob Scribner, 'Is a History of Popular Culture Possible?', *History of European Ideas* 10 (1989), 175–91; Tim Harris (ed.), *Popular Culture in England, c. 1500–1850* (Basingstoke, 1994), 1–27. Judith Devlin, *The Superstitious Mind: French Peasants and the Supernatural in the Nineteenth Century* (New Haven, 1987), is the best guide for a slightly later period. For England, Robert W. Malcolmson, *Popular Recreations in English Society 1700–1850* (Cambridge, 1973) and Bob Bushaway, *By Rite: Custom, Ceremony and*

Community in England 1700–1880 (Brighton, 1982). O. Davies, 'Methodism, the Clergy and the Popular Belief in Witchcraft and Magic', *History* 82 (1997), 252–65, is seminal. Clarke Garrett, *Spirit Possession and Popular Religion: From the Camisards to the Shakers* (Baltimore, 1987), has much of value. For a look at two areas where moral standards were supposed to be slipping, Leah Leneman and Rosalind Mitchison, *Sin in the City: Sexuality and Social Control in Urban Scotland 1660–1780* (Edinburgh, 1998), and Linda Kirk, "Going Soft": Genevan Decadence in the Eighteenth Century', in John B. Roney and Martin I. Klauber (eds.), *The Identity of Geneva. The Christian Commonwealth, 1564–1864* (Westport, Conn., 1998), 143–54. Female religiosity is the main topic of Edwin Welch, *Spiritual Pilgrim: A Reassessment of the Life and Times of the Countess of Huntingdon* (Cardiff, 1995). The latter is recent but should be used with caution. For other British eighteenth-century examples see Thomas Gibbons, D.D., *Memoirs of Eminently Pious Women* (2 vols., London, 1804). David Vaisey (ed.), *The Diary of Thomas Turner, 1754–1765* (Oxford, 1984) tells us much about the attitude to faith of the upwardly mobile in mid-century England. Diaries are covered in an important article by Christina Sjöblad, 'From Family Notes to Diary: The Development of a Genre', in 'Forum: Sweden in the Eighteenth century', *Eighteenth-century Studies*, 31 (1998), 491–521. On religious publishing there is Thomas R. Preston, 'Biblical Criticism, Literature, and the Eighteenth-century Reader', in I. Rivers (ed.), *Books and their Readers in Eighteenth-century England* (Leicester, 1982), 97–126.

3 INTELLECTUAL CHALLENGES AND THE RELIGIOUS RESPONSE

Ole Peter Grell and Roy Porter (eds.), *Toleration in Enlightenment Europe* (Cambridge, 2000) covers most European countries reliably in its subject area. It can be supplemented for central Europe by J. Whaley, 'Pouvoir Sauver les Apparences: The Theory and Practice of Tolerance in Eighteenth-century Germany', *BSECS Journal* 13 (1990), 1–16. For an English text on the Catholic Enlightenment in Germany see L. Swidler, *Aufklärung Catholicism, 1780–1850* (Missoula, 1978), which focuses mainly on liturgy and the Church. For Italy in particular Franco Venturi, *Italy and the Enlightenment: Studies in a Cosmopolitan Century*, ed. S. Woolf (London, 1972) and 'Church Reform in Enlightenment Italy: The Sixties of the Eighteenth Century', *Journal of Modern History* 48 (1976), 215–32. For France, R. R. Palmer, *Catholics and Unbelievers in Eighteenth-century France* (Princeton, 1949) still does yeoman service, and also worth consulting is G. Bremner, 'Jansenism and the Enlightenment', in *Enlightenment and Dissent* 3 (1984), 3–14. A. O. Dyson, 'Theological Legacies of the Enlightenment: England and Germany', in S. W. Sykes (ed.), *England and Germany. Studies in Theological Diplomacy* (Frankfurt, 1982), 45–62, is a comparative exercise. B. W. Young's *Religion and Enlightenment in Eighteenth-century England: Theological Debate from Locke to Burke* (Oxford, 1998), is lucid and unapologetic about the importance of the clergy in the 'English' Enlightenment. R. L. Nichols, 'Orthodoxy and Russia's Enlightenment, 1762–1825', in R. L. Nichols and T. G. Stavrou (eds.), *Russian Orthodoxy under the Old Regime*

(Minneapolis, 1978) offers the non-Russian reader an indispensable perspective. G. P. Henderson, *The Revival of Greek Thought, 1620–1830* (Edinburgh, 1971) shows the impact of enlightenment thinking in south-eastern Europe. Responses to a particular calamity are covered in Thomas Downing Kendrick, *The Lisbon Earthquake* (London, 1956). The Counter-Enlightenment, it has been argued, should not be seen as a distinct movement but as a reaction proceeding dialectically from within the Enlightenment itself. Jonathan B. Knudsen, *Justus Möser and the German Enlightenment* (Cambridge, 1986); cf. Isaiah Berlin, 'The Counter-Enlightenment', in *Against the Current: Essays in the History of Ideas* (Oxford, 1989), 1–24. Darrin M. McMahon, 'The Counter-Enlightenment and the Low-Life of Literature in Pre-Revolutionary France', *Past & Present* 159 (1998), 77–112, is a brilliant reworking of some of Robert Darnton's original considerations on 'Grub Street' authors. Thomas O'Connor, *An Irish Theologian in Enlightenment France: Luke Joseph Hooke, 1714–96* (Dublin, 1995) is a model study of a neglected cosmopolitan Catholic thinker. For another, Alfred J. Bingham, 'The Abbé Bergier: An Eighteenth-century Catholic Apologist', *MLR* 54 (1959), 349. For Voltaire's disagreements with atheistic minded *philosophes* see John Pappas, *Voltaire and D'Alembert* (Bloomington, 1962). On the key figure of Rousseau, Ronald Grimsley, *Rousseau and the Religious Quest* (Oxford, 1968) is in a high class. For progressive French clerics go to Robert Darnton's *The Kiss of Lamourette: Reflections in Cultural History* (London, 1990). Their Anglican equivalents are looked at in John Gascoigne, 'Anglican Latitudinarianism and Political Radicalism in the late Eighteenth Century', *History* 71 (1986), 22–38. For Prussia, Günter Birtsch, 'The Christian as Subject: The Worldly Mind of Prussian Protestant Theologians in the Late Enlightenment Period', in E. Hellmuth (ed.), *The Transformation of Political Culture. England and Germany in the Late Eighteenth Century* (Oxford, 1990), 309–26, is illuminating. For universities G. M. Addy, *The Enlightenment in the University of Salamanca* (1966); C. E. McClelland, *State, Society, and University in Germany, 1700–1914* (Cambridge, 1980); L. W. B. Brockliss, *French Higher Education in the Seventeenth and Eighteenth Centuries: A Cultural History* (Oxford, 1987); S. Lindroth, *A History of Uppsala University, 1477–1977* (Stockholm, 1977). Hans Frei, *The Eclipse of Biblical Narrative* (New Haven, 1977), is definitive on that subject. On Lessing, H. Chadwick, *Lessing's Theological Writing* (Berkeley, Calif., 1956); on Kant, James Collins, *God in Modern Philosophy* (London, 1960). E. Cassirer, *Philosophy, and Kant's Life and Thought* (New Haven, 1981) is strong on the Enlightenment context. On one important mystic, Signe Toksvig, *Emanuel Swedenborg: scientist and mystic* (New Haven, 1948).

4 CHURCH AND STATE

For the Church of England's relationship to the state there are two important articles by Stephen Taylor, 'William Warburton and the Alliance of Church and State', *JEH* 43 (1992), 271–86, and 'Whigs, Bishops and America: The Politics of Church Reform in Mid-eighteenth-century England', *Historical Journal* 36 (1993), 331–56. That Church's distinctive episcopal character is highlighted in Peter M. Doll, 'Anglican High Churchmanship and the Establishment of the

First Colonial Episcopate in the Church of England: Nova Scotia, 1787', *JEH* 43 (1992), 35–59. For the essential French background, Dale K. Van Kley, *The Damiens Affair and the Unraveling of the Ancien Régime, 1750–1770* (New Haven, 1984); J. Swann, *Politics and the Parlement of Paris under Louis XV, 1754–1774* (Cambridge, 1995); John Rogister, *Louis XV and the Parlement of Paris* (Cambridge, 1995). On coronations and their importance in the French polity, see John McManners, 'Authority in Church and State: Reflections on the Coronation of Louis XVI', in G. R. Evans (ed.), *Christian Authority. Essays in Honour of Henry Chadwick* (Oxford, 1988), 278–95. Spain is well covered in William J. Callahan, *Church, Politics and Society in Spain, 1750–1874* (Cambridge, Mass., 1984) and the Habsburg empire definitively in Derek Beales, *Joseph II*, vol. I (Cambridge, 1987); W. W. Davis, 'The Origins of Religious Josephism', *East Central Europe* 1 (1974) should also be consulted. On Ricci there is S. J. Miller, 'The Limits of Political Jansenism in Tuscany: Scipione de'Ricci to Peter Leopold, 1780–1791', *Catholic Historical Review* 89 (1994), 762–7, and C. A. Bolton, *Church Reform in Eighteenth-century Italy* (The Hague, 1969). Russia is examined in G. L. Freeze, 'Handmaiden of the State? The Church in Imperial Russia reconsidered', *JEH* 36 (1985), 82–102. One of the smaller German states is expertly treated in T. C. W. Blanning, *Reform and Revolution in Mainz 1743–1803* (Cambridge, 1974).

5 REVOLUTIONS AND THE CHURCHES: THE INITIAL IMPACT

On 'revolutions' outside France, S. Schama, *Patriots and Liberators: Revolution in the Netherlands 1780–1813* (London, 1977) covers the situation authoritatively for the Dutch United Provinces. For the Austrian Netherlands, J. L. Polasky, *Revolution in Brussels, 1787–1793* (Brussels, 1987). W. W. Davis, *Joseph II: An Imperial Reformer for the Austrian Netherlands* (The Hague, 1974) is copious and may be displaced on publication of Derek Beales' second volume on Joseph II. Investigations into the way religion shaped the French Revolution must start with Dale K. Van Kley, *The Religious Origins of the French Revolution: From Calvin to the Civil Constitution, 1560–1791*, (New Haven, 1996). For France, the writings of Timothy Tackett are central. Apart from his *Religion, Revolution, and Regional Culture* (Princeton, 1986), see his 'The Citizen Priest: Politics and Ideology among the Parish Clergy of eighteenth century Dauphiné', *Studies in XVIIIth century Culture*, ed. Roseann Puntz, vol. 7 (Wisconsin, 1978), 307–38. See also the perceptive and elegant John McManners, *The French Revolution and the Church* (London, 1969). Most recently Nigel Aston, *Religion and Revolution in France, 1780–1804* (Basingstoke, 2000). Nigel Aston, 'Survival Against the Odds? The French Bishops Elected to the Estates-General, 1789', *Historical Journal* 32 (1989), 607–26, makes a modest attempt at revisionism. A general article on the *cahiers* that incidentally deals with religious issues is George V. Taylor, 'Revolutionary and Non-revolutionary Content in the Cahiers of 1789: An Interim Report', *FHS* 7 (1971–2), 479–502. The background to the religious legislation of the National Assembly is considered *inter alia* in Timothy Tackett, *Becoming a Revolutionary: the Deputies of the French National Assembly and the Emergence of a Revolutionary Culture (1789–1790)* (Princeton, 1996). There is no up-to-date book covering the French Constitutional Church, but H. Dupre, *Two Brothers in the French Revolution: Robert and Thomas Lindet* (Hamden, Conn., 1967) has one of that Church's leading bishops as one of its co-subjects. On the diaspora of French exiled clergy Dominic Aidan Bellenger is definitive in *The French Exiled Clergy in the British Isles after 1789* (Bath, 1986). On Catholic–Protestant tensions there are several articles by James N. Hood including 'Revival and Mutation of Old Rivalries in Revolutionary France', *Past & Present* 82 (1979), 82–115. There is much scholarly writing on French Jewry and the Revolution, including Shanti Marie Singham, 'Between Cattle and Men', in Dale Van Kley (ed.), *The French Idea of Freedom: The Old Regime and the Declaration of Rights of 1789* (Stanford, 1994), 114–53, and Gary Kates, 'Jews into Frenchmen: Nationality and Representation in Revolutionary France', in Ferenc Fehér (ed.), *The French Revolution and the Birth of Modernity* (Berkeley, 1990), 103–16. See generally E. Benbassa, *The Jews of France* (Princeton, 2000). On the key role of women in religious disputes there is Ruth Graham, 'Women versus Clergy, Women pro Clergy', in Samia I. Spencer (ed.), *French Women and the Age of Enlightenment* (Bloomington, Ind., 1984), 128–40. 53. Jacques Godechot, *The Counter-Revolution. Doctrine and Action 1789–1804*, trans. Salvator Attanasio (Princeton, 1971), has classic status on its subject, although is somewhat dated and inclined to make less of the religious dimension than most current scholarship, which is distilled in J. Roberts, *The Counter-Revolution in France 1787–1830* (Basingstoke, 1990). For the general background to religion and loyalism in Britain, Robert Hole, *Pulpits, Politics and Public Order in England 1760–1832* (Cambridge, 1991), and David Hempton, *Religion and Political Culture in Britain and Ireland: From the Glorious Revolution to the Decline of Empire* (Cambridge, 1996). The best single study of the leading Anglican high churchman of the 1790s is F. C. Mather, *High Church Prophet: Bishop Samuel Horsley (1733–1806) and the Caroline Tradition in the later Georgian Church* (Oxford, 1992). For Austria there are chapters in C. A. Macartney, *The Habsburg Empire, 1790–1918* (London, 1968), and Germany, K. Epstein, *The Genesis of German Conservatism* (Princeton, 1966). T. J. A. Le Goff and D. M. G. Sutherland, 'Religion and Rural Revolt in the French Revolution: An Overview', in János M. Bak and Gerhard Benecke (eds.), *Religion and Rural Revolt* (Manchester, 1984), 69–79, consider the place of religion in the origins of the conflict in the west of France. For the Vendée itself, Claude Petifrère, 'The Origins of the Civil War in the Vendée', *French History* 2 (1988), 187–207; D. S. Sutherland and Harvey Mitchell, 'Resistance to the Revolution in Western France', *Past & Present* 63 (1974), 94–131 is an authoritative article. The essays in E. E. Rice, *Revolution and Counter-Revolution* (Oxford, 1991) make a convenient starting point for the European impact of the French Revolution.

6 THE IMPACT OF THE REVOLUTION ON RELIGIOUS LIFE AND PRACTICE, C. 1793–1802

Michel Vovelle, *The Revolution against the Church: From Reason to the Supreme Being*, trans. Alan José (Oxford, 1991) is an accessible introduction to the topic.

Suzanne Desan's 'Redefining Revolutionary Liberty: The Rhetoric of Religious Revival during the French Revolution', *JMH* 60 (1988), 1–27, and O. Hufton, 'The Reconstruction of a Church, 1796–1801', in G. Lewis and C. Lucas (eds.), *Beyond the Terror: Essays in French Regional and Social History, 1794–1815* (Cambridge, 1983), 21–52, have already gained the status of classic texts, while Ralph Gibson, *A Social History of French Catholicism 1789–1914* (London, 1989), covers far more than the revolutionary decade. In British terms, Emma Vincent, *The Responses of Scottish Churchmen to the French Revolution, 1789–1802 Scottish Historical Review*, 73 (1994), 191–215, is the latest word on its subject and, more generally, her *A War of Ideas. British Attitudes to the Wars against Revolutionary France 1792–1802* (Aldershot, 1998) and William Stafford, 'Religion and the Doctrine of Nationalism in England at the Time of the French Revolution and Napoleonic Wars', *Studies in Church History* 18 (1982), 386–8. On clergy afloat, consult W. E. Smith, *The Navy and its Chaplains in the Days of Sail* (Toronto, 1968) and Gordon Taylor, *The Sea Chaplains* (Oxford, 1978). For the momentous changes in the Habsburg empire see Kinley Brauer and William E. Wright (eds.), *Austria in the Age of the French Revolution* (Minneapolis, 1990). For western Germany, T. C. W. Blanning, *The French Revolution in Germany: Occupation and Resistance in the Rhineland, 1792–1802* (Oxford, 1983) is indispensable. On popular risings in Italy against the French, see, most recently, Laurence Cole, 'Nation, Anti-Enlightenment, and Religious revival in Austria: Tyrol in the 1790s', *HJ* 43 (2000), 475–97, an excellent essay showing the significance of religion in powering resistance to revolutionary ideology and French invasion, as well as J. A. Davis, '1799: the "Santafede" and the Crisis of the Ancien Régime in Southern Italy', in J. A. Davis and P. Ginsbourg (eds.), *Society and Politics in the Age of the Risorgimento* (Cambridge, 1991), 1–25. There has been a surge of publication on Ireland in the 1790s to coincide with the bicentenary of the 1798 rebellion. Two essays in the collection edited by Hugh Gough and David Dickson, *Ireland and the French Revolution* (Dublin, 1990), Eamon O'Flaherty, 'Irish Catholics and the French Revolution', 52–67, and Jim Smyth, 'Popular Politicization, Defenderism and the Catholic Question', 109–16, deal concisely with some of the main religious issues. Daire Keogh, *The French Disease* (Dublin, 1993) is an another comprehensive guide to the tergiversations of Irish politics in the revolutionary decade and the attempts by the Irish Catholic hierarchy to prevent their people from Jacobin 'contamination'. Patrick Comerford, 'Church of Ireland Clergy and the 1798 Rising' and Kevin Whelan, 'The Wexford Priests in 1798', in Liam Swords (ed.), *Protestant, Catholic and Dissenter: The Clergy and 1798* (Dublin, 1997), 219–52 and 165–85, consider the extent of their success. The millenarian aspects of the decade feature in, inter alia, James Hopkins, *A Woman to Deliver her People: Joanna Southcott and English Millenarianism in an Era of Revolution* (Austin, Tex., 1982); Clarke Garrett, *Respectable Folly: Millenarians and the French Revolution in France and England* (Baltimore, 1975), W. H. Oliver, *Prophets and Millennialists: The Uses of Biblical Prophecy in England from the 1790s to the 1840s* (Auckland, 1978), and Andrew Robinson, 'Identifying the Beast: Samuel Horsley and the Problem of Papal Antichrist', *JEH* 43 (1992), 592–607. See most recently David S. Katz and Richard H. Popkin, *Messianic Revolution: Radical Religious Policies to the End of the Second Millennium* (Harmondsworth, 1999); Eugen Weber, *Apocalypses: Prophecies, Cults and Millennial Beliefs through the Ages* (London, 1999). For the ways in which religion shaped political and literary expression in Britain the following recent studies can be recommended: Robert M. Ryan, *The Romantic Reformation: Religious Politics in English Literature 1789–1824* (Cambridge, 1998); E. P. Thompson, *Witness Against the Beast: William Blake and the Moral Law* (Cambridge, 1993); J. Mee, *Dangerous Enthusiasm: William Blake and the Culture of Radicalism in the 1790s* (Oxford, 1992). For aspects of rapidly changing patterns of morality in Britain under evangelical pressure, see W. B. Whitaker, *The Eighteenth-century English Sunday: A Study of Sunday Observance from 1677 to 1837* (London, 1940); Donna T. Andrew, '"Adultery-à-la-Mode"; Privilege, the Law and Attitudes to Adultery 1770–1809', *History* 82 (1997), 5–23, and Muriel Jaeger, *Before Victoria: Changing Standards and Behaviour 1787–1837* (Harmondsworth, 1967). Robert Hole, 'Tracts and Sermons as Media of Debate on the French Revolution, 1789–1798', in Mark A. Philp (ed.), *The French Revolution and British Popular Politics* (Cambridge, 1991), 1–17 provides a fine introduction to its subject.

7 RELIGION IN NAPOLEONIC EUROPE, 1802–1815

E. E. Y. Hales, *Napoleon and the Pope* (London, 1962) charts the stormy relationship between Bonaparte and Pius VII, while H. H. Walsh, *The Concordat of 1801* (New York, 1967) remains a handy summary of this defining document. See also W. Roberts, 'Napoleon, the Concordat of 1801 and its Consequences', in F. J. Cappa (ed.), *Controversial Concordats: The Vatican's Relations with Napoleon, Mussolini and Hitler* (Washington, 1999), 34–80. John Martin Robinson, *Cardinal Consalvi 1757–1824* (London, 1987) covers the career of the pope's right-hand man for so much of his pontificate. Michael Broers, '"The War against God": Napoleon, Pope Pius VII and the People of Italy, 1800–1814', *The Historian* 69 (2001), 16–21, is a succinct summary of affairs from the foremost authority on Napoleonic Italy. For Britain, W. R. Ward, 'Revival and Class Conflict in Early Nineteenth-century Britain', in his *Faith and Faction* (London, 1993), 285–98, has much of value. D. Lovegrove, *Established Church, Sectarian People: Itinerancy and the Transformation of English Dissent 1780–1830* (Cambridge, 1988) also discloses the extent of the challenge to the established Church. For Ireland, Vincent J. McNally, *Reform, Revolution and Reaction: Archbishop John Thomas Troy and the Catholic Church in Ireland, 1787–1817* (Lanham, Md., 1995) is far more than a one-man biography. For later Pietism there is H. Lehmann, 'Pietism and Nationalism: The Relationship between Protestant Revivalism and National Renewal in Nineteenth-century Germany', *Church History* 51 (1982), 39–53; Christopher M. Clark, 'The Politics of Revival: Pietists, Aristocrats, and the State Church in Early-nineteenth-century Prussia', in Larry Eugene Jones and James Retallack (eds.), *Between Reform, Reaction, and Resistance: Studies in the History of German Conservatism from 1789 to 1945* (Oxford, 1993), 31–60. Bernard M. G. Reardon, *Religion in the Age of Romanticism* (Cambridge, 1985) is a reliable introduction to the intellectual background to religious upheaval, as is Thomas Franklin O'Meara, O.P., *Romantic Idealism and Roman Catholicism: Schelling and the Theologians* (Notre Dame, 1982). For Novalis, a start can be made with William Arctander O'Brien, *Novalis: Signs of Revolution* (Durham, N.C., 1995); for Hegel, Laurence Dickey, *Hegel: Religion, Economics, and the*

Politics of Spirit, 1770–1807 (Cambridge, 1987). On Protestant reawakening there is Andrew L. Drummond, *The Kirk and the Continent* (Edinburgh, 1956). Swedish Protestant history can be followed in Hope, *German and Scandinavian Protestantism* (above) and also H. M. Waddams, *The Swedish Church* (London, 1946).

8 RELIGIOUS REVIVAL AFTER 1815?

On Caspar David Friedrich, see C. J. Bailey, 'Religious Symbolism in Caspar David Friedrich', *Bulletin of the John Rylands Library* 71 (1989), 5–20; C. J. Bailey and John Leighton, *Caspar David Friedrich: Winter Landscape* (London, 1990). See also Joseph Leo Koerner, *Caspar David Friedrich and the Subject of Landscape* (London, 1990). For the argument that the 'modern' was emerging in the religious sphere as well as in others in 1815–30, see P. Johnson, *The Birth of the Modern* (London, 1991); P. W. Schroeder, *The Transformation of European Politics 1763–1848* (Oxford, 1994); E. D. Brose, *The Politics of Technological Change in Prussia: Out of the Shadow of Antiquity 1809–1848* (Princeton, N.J., 1993). See also Hugh McLeod, *Religion and the People of Western Europe 1789–1970* (Oxford, 1981), and the wide-ranging essays in David Laven and Lucy Riall (eds.), *Napoleon's Legacy: Problems of Government in Restoration Europe* (Oxford, 2000), and Rainer Liedtke and S. Wendehorst (eds.), *The Emancipation of Catholics, Jews and Protestants: Minorities and the Nation State in Nineteenth-century Europe* (Manchester, 1999). On the close links between Catholicism and legitimism in Restoration France there is Brian Fitzpatrick, *Catholic Royalism in the Department of the Gard 1814–1852* (Cambridge, 1983). G. Cubitt, *The Jesuit Myth: Conspiracy Theory and Politics in Nineteenth-century France* (Oxford, 1993) begins with the restoration of the Bourbons and the Jesuits in France in 1814, while Martyn Lyons, 'Fires of Expiation; Book-burnings and Catholic Missions in Restoration France', *French History* 10 (1996), 240–66, provides more fascinating background materials. For an essay that challenges the new orthodoxy about the feminisation of Catholicism in the nineteenth century, see James F. McMillan, 'Religion and Gender in Modern France. Some Reflections', in Frank Tallett and Nicholas Atkin (eds.), *Religion, Society and Politics in France since 1789* (London, 1991), 55–66. He develops the theme further in his *France and Women 1789–1914: Gender, Society and Politics* (London, 2000). On the 'Second Reformation' in Ireland, see Desmond Bowen, *The Protestant Crusade in Ireland, 1800–70* (Dublin, 1978) and David Hempton and Myrtle Hill, *Methodism and Politics in British Society 1750–1850* (London, 1984) for that and much else. F. O'Ferrall, *Catholic Emancipation: Daniel O'Connell and the Birth of Irish Democracy 1820–1830* (Dublin, 1985); S. J. Connolly, *Priest and People in Pre-Famine Ireland 1780–1845* (Dublin, 1982); S. J. Connolly, *Religion and Society in Nineteenth-century Ireland* (Dundalk, 1985) make up a trio of fine books. Wendy Hinde, *Catholic Emancipation: A Shake to Men's Minds* (Oxford, 1992) is a straightforward introduction to that important subject as it affected British high politics. Michael A. Mullett, *Catholics in Britain and Ireland, 1558–1828* (Basingstoke, 1998), is helpful here as in previous eras. William Gibson, 'The Tories and Church Patronage: 1812–30', *JEH* 41 (1990), 266–74, argues for the care attached by Lord Liverpool's government in making senior church appointments. See also Elizabeth Varley, *The Last of the Prince Bishops: Bishop Van Mildert and the later High Church Movement in the Church of England* (Cambridge, 1992). Mark Smith, *Religion in Industrial Society: Oldham and Saddleworth 1740–1865* (Oxford, 1994), is a fine cameo portrait showing the resilience of Anglicanism against an industrial setting. Cf. W. R. Ward, *Religion and Society in England 1790–1830* (London, 1972), full of pungent but ever efficient scholarship on nonconformity and much more. James C. Deming, *Religion and Identity in Modern France: The Modernization of the Protestant Community in Languedoc, 1815–1848* (Lanham, Md., 1999) is a fine study of early nineteenth-century French Protestantism. On religious (re)attachment among the Prussian nobility, Robert M. Berdahl, *The Politics of the Prussian Nobility: The Development of a Conservative Ideology 1770–1848* (Princeton, 1988) is very useful, as are Christopher Clark, 'Confessional Policy and the Limits of State Action: Frederick William III and the Prussian Church Union 1817–40', *HJ* 39 (1996), 985–1004; Christopher Clark, 'The Politics of Revival: Pietists, Aristocrats and the State Church in Early Nineteenth-century Prussia', in L. E. Jones and J. N. Retallack (eds.), *Between Reform, Reaction and Resistance: Studies in the History of German Conservatism from 1789 to 1945* (Oxford, 1993), 31–60, and Robert M. Bigler, *The Politics of the Protestant Church Elite in Prussia, 1815–1848* (Berkeley, 1972). For German Catholics there is J. Sperber, *Popular Catholicism in Germany in Nineteenth-century Germany* (Princeton, 1984) and for the Austrian Empire see generally Alan J. Reinerman, *Austria and the Papacy in the Age of Metternich* (2 vols., Washington, D.C. 1979 and 1989). D. Saunders, *Russia in the Age of Reaction and Reform, 1801–1883* (London, 1992) is a first-rate guide to the spiritual currents of Alexander I's reign. E. A. Kossmann, *The Low Countries 1780–1940* (Oxford, 1978) has much of value on religious life in the kingdom of the Netherlands between 1815 and 1830. Religious aspects of the Greek War of Independence are authoritatively covered in Charles A. Frazee, *The Orthodox Church and Independent Greece 1821–1852* (Cambridge, 1969), Douglas Dakin, *The Greek Struggle for Independence* (1974), and Richard Clogg (ed.), *The Movement for Greek Independence 1770–1821* (Basingstoke, 1976).

Index

NEW APPROACHES TO EUROPEAN HISTORY